Floating Voice

Drygland
113 Bond St
St. John's, NL
A1C 1T6

For Kim and Wayne
with Best wishes
Stan Drygland
St. John's, Newfoundland
2004

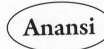

Anansi

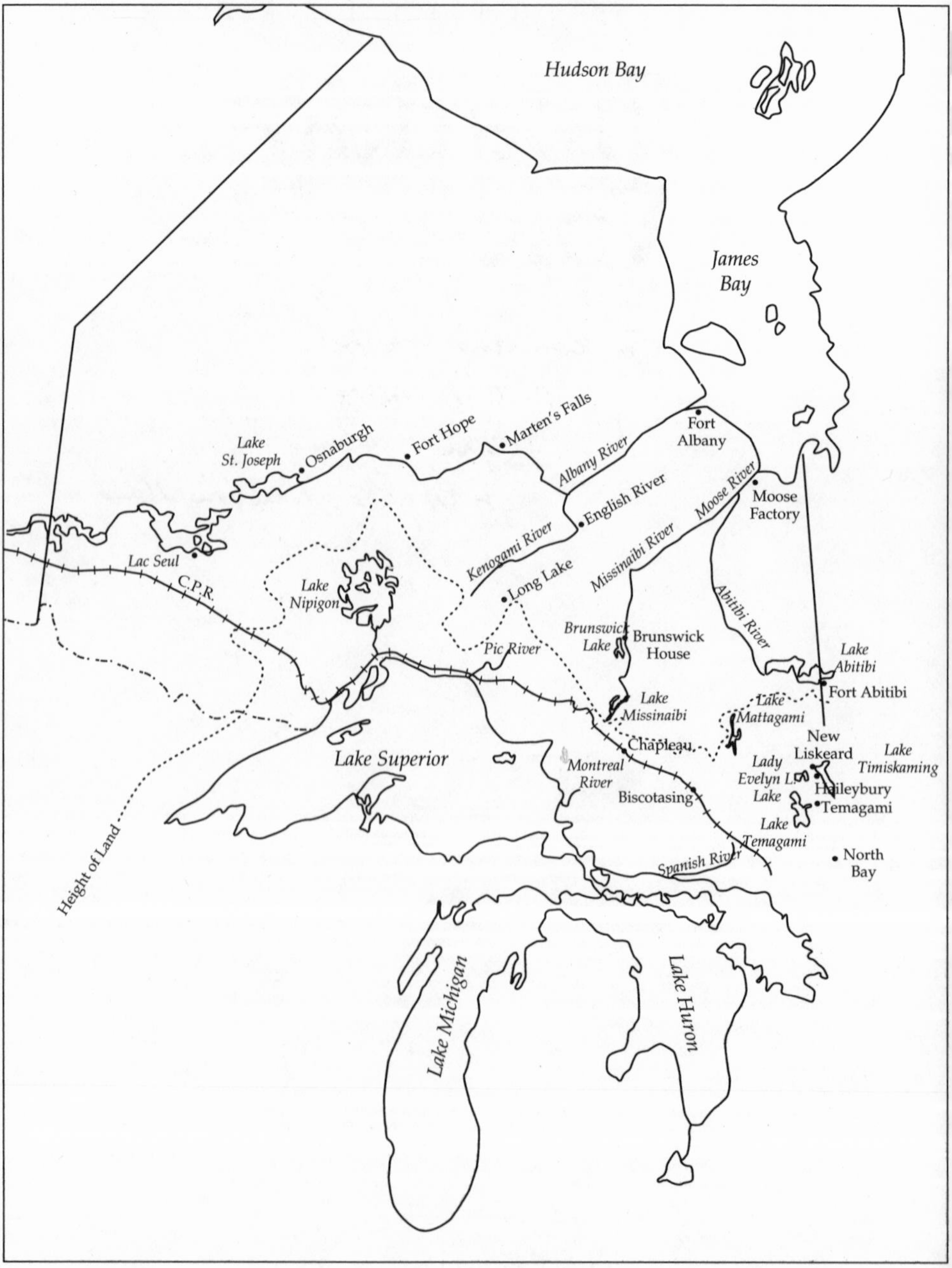
Hudson Bay
James Bay
Fort Albany
Marten's Falls
Fort Hope
Osnaburgh
Lake St. Joseph
Albany River
Moose Factory
English River
Moose River
Kenogami River
Missinaibi River
Lac Seul
C.P.R.
Lake Nipigon
Long Lake
Abitibi River
Brunswick Lake
Brunswick House
Pic River
Lake Abitibi
Fort Abitibi
Lake Missinaibi
Lake Mattagami
Chapleau
New Liskeard
Lake Timiskaming
Lake Superior
Montreal River
Lady Evelyn Lake
Haileybury
Biscotasing
Temagami
Lake Temagami
North Bay
Spanish River
Height of Land
Lake Michigan
Lake Huron

STAN DRAGLAND

Floating Voice

Duncan Campbell Scott and the Literature of Treaty 9

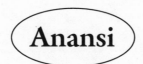

Anansi

Published in 1994 by
House of Anansi Press Limited
1800 Steeles Avenue West
Concord, Ontario
L4K 2P3
(416) 445-3333

Canadian Cataloguing in Publication Data

Dragland, Stan, 1942–
Floating voice: Duncan Campbell Scott and the literature of Treaty 9

ISBN 0-88784-551-7

1. Scott, Duncan Campbell, 1862-1947. 2. Scott, Duncan Campbell, 1862-1947 – Political and social views. 3. Grand Council Treaty no. 9. 4. Indians of North America in literature. 5. Poets, Canadian (English) – 20th century – Biography.* I. Title.

PS8537.C58Z58 1994 C811'.52 C94-930061-6
PR9199.2.S33Z63 1994

Cover design: Brant Cowie/ArtPlus Limited
Cover concept: Angel Guerra
Cover photograph courtesy of the Public Archives of Canada/PA-143064

Printed and bound in Canada

House of Anansi Press gratefully acknowledges the support of the Canada Council, Ontario Ministry of Culture, Tourism, and Recreation, Ontario Arts Council, and Ontario Publishing Centre in the development of writing and publishing in Canada.

Contents

List of Figures

All figures except figure 11 supplied by Public Archives Canada.

Acknowledgements

A PAPER BASED on parts of this book was offered in the University of New Brunswick InterArts lecture series in Autumn 1992.

I am grateful to the Department of English and the Faculty of Arts at the University of Western Ontario for a number of research grants over several years, and to J. A. B. Somerset, former chair of the Department of English, for his support. Sue Desmond gave me valuable computer assistance. I thank the Social Sciences and Humanities Research Council for a Release Time grant in 1989–90. That, and a sabbatical leave in 1990–91, made it possible to build up some research and writing momentum. I am indebted to James Good, Dean of Western's Faculty of Arts, for a Smallman grant in aid of publication, and to John Flood, of Penumbra Press, for an OAC Writers' Reserve grant.

I would like to acknowledge the kind assistance of the staff at the Northrop Frye Library, Victoria University, and at the Thomas Fisher Rare Book Library, University of Toronto; of David Hume, Trish Maracle, and Pauline Charron of the National Archives of Canada; Richard Huyda and Joy Houston, National Photography Collection; Eugene Martel, Greg Brown, and Bennett McCardle, Archives of Ontario; Arni Brownstone and Basil Johnston, Royal Ontario Museum; Judith Beattie, Hudson's Bay Archives; Peter Denny, Department of Psychology, Regna Darnell, Department of Anthropology, and David Maracle, Centre for Research and Teaching of Canadian Native Languages, all at the University of Western Ontario.

Research assistants Peter Georgelos and Susan Lu were most helpful. And thanks to Earl, Louise, and Phillip Meeks for the use of their cool basement room in the summer of 1990.

I thank Mr. John G. Aylen for kind permission to quote from the works of Duncan Campbell Scott.

THIS BOOK has been much improved as a result of the response and encouragement of readers of the manuscript in part or whole at various stages: Pamela Banting, Don McKay, Richard Stingle, Michael Ondaatje, James Cullingham, the anonymous readers at House of Anansi Press, Marnie

Parsons, and my editors at Anansi, Michael Carroll and Martha Sharpe. Some of those named here and above don't always agree with me, though, and the appearance of their names doesn't imply endorsement. In the margin of an early version of my anti-assimilationist argument, for example, Richard Stingle wrote that assimilation "is what happened to other groups, like the German speaking Stingles and my mother's Gaelic speaking MacMillans. But perhaps I should lament the passing of Druidic human sacrifices, Highland dancing, kilts & no underwear. There's a little rebellion against political correctness for you." No underwear: that made me stop and think, but it didn't change my mind. I return to Marnie Parsons, who has had good reason to wonder whether I was married to her or this book and yet was fool enough to read the manuscript twice, invent most of the titles, create the index, and offer deeply sustaining support at all stages. This book is for her.

Bibliographical Note

ARTHUR S. BOURINOT'S COLLECTIONS of Scott letters are cited when he represents them accurately; archival sources are cited otherwise, as they are for letters Bourinot omits and for letters he didn't collect. Scott was not a careful end-stopper, so quotations from his Treaty 9 journal and from certain letters are punctuated with periods, dashes, or spaces in an attempt to be true to the "system" he is using in each instance. The method of citing archival sources by abbreviation (in brackets after passages quoted or referred to) sacrifices some specificity for economy. But as a consequence of the fairly wide dispersal of Scott papers and the classification of Indian Affairs papers in different files, none of these sources is labyrinthine. Samuel Stewart's journal being lengthy, page numbers are added to dates to facilitate location. Abbreviations of archival sources are as follows (for a more detailed listing, with complete locations, see Works Cited):

ASB A. S. Bourinot Papers
CBC Canadian Broadcasting Corporation
HBC Hudson's Bay Company
PA/DCS Duncan Campbell Scott Papers (Public Archives)
PA/EKB E. K. Brown Papers
PA/S-A D. C. Scott — E. Aylen Papers
Q/DCS Duncan Campbell Scott Papers (Queen's University Archives)
Q/EM Edmund Morris Papers
Q/LP Lorne Pierce Papers
Q/RK Raymond Knister Papers
RG10 Department of Indian Affairs Archives
TF Duncan Campbell Scott Papers (Thomas Fisher Rare Book Library)
V/EKB E. K. Brown Papers (Victoria University Library)
V/PE Pelham Edgar Papers

The scene is the Berne Patent Office, 1905, the desk of the technical expert third class, who wears no socks. He is daydreaming his way through a Gedankenexperiment, *a thought experiment, in which he imagines himself a light wave. Einstein, since the age of fifteen, has teased himself with the notion of catching a light ray. He now realizes this dream as he places himself alongside light, running; he overtakes the wave, becoming in fact a light wave himself, only more fleet, and discovers something impossible has occurred. Everything for him has stopped; even light stands still, though oscillating minutely; his own mass has compounded itself infinitely. Einstein, light ray* manqué, *concludes that the speed of light is a constant, c, and that the unlimited acceleration of mass, thinkable under classical physics, is impossible. Light everywhere, for everyone, has the same velocity. By an experiment of empathy, by an act of love in which the knower dwells in his object, an important tenet of relativity theory is set in place.*

Tim Lilburn

I couldn't see it for wearing it.

Zora Neale Hurston

PART 1

Bricks Without Straw

Introduction: A Dance of Molecules

To discover the truth in anything that is alien, first dispense with the indispensable in your own system.

F., in Leonard Cohen's Beautiful Losers

THE MOST ELOQUENT PHOTOGRAPH of Duncan Campbell Scott is not by Karsh, though Karsh's side view of the poet smoking in an easy chair that opens the *Selected Poems* has its appeal, and so does Karsh's Scott at the piano, frontispiece of *The Poet and the Critic.* Other portraits taken over the years, stills from the crumbling of that severe face from youth into age, say that smiling cannot have come naturally to him, but little more. No, the most fascinating photograph, to my mind, is the one taken by a member of the Treaty 9 party in 1905 at the source of the Root River, the height of land portage, in Northern Ontario (figure 1). Scott shares the middle ground with Samuel Stewart. Both are civil servants with the Department of Indian Affairs. They are in the North as treaty commissioners charged with arranging the surrender of land from the Ojibway and Cree to the Canadian government. The background of the picture is rather bleak — low scrub and the odd scruffy evergreen. The Root River scarcely qualifies as a creek at this point, much less a river. It seems narrow enough to jump over, and this impression is confirmed by the July 9 entry in Scott's journal account of the trip: "Engaged with the many portages of the Root River. At last it degenerates with a creek nowhere more than 20 feet wide and tortuous as a corkscrew. [Sentence or fragment illegible.] In one place one of the Indians leaped across" (RG10b). Any canoeist would recognize the Root in the photograph as a problematical stream even for a 16-footer, and the treaty party crew was paddling a 32-foot birchbark and two large Peterboroughs carrying men with their gear and food for three months. The canoes are probably being portaged as the photograph is taken. Some of the unloaded cargo waits to be portaged — tents, by the look of it, boxes, a suitcase. One of the boxes could be a "treasure chest" full of treaty money.

Both human subjects of the photograph, the reasons it was taken, are casually dressed for travel, but Stewart stands out from his surroundings

Figure 1, PA-143064

much less than Scott does. The Wellington boots are his only obvious concession to the rough locale. The watch attached to the fob in his vest might mark him as a southerner; certainly as a white man. But, to white eyes at least, there is nothing remarkable about that. In any eyes Scott would stand out. His hat looks like millinery, even when the veil is identified as mosquito netting weighted with lead shot. There was reason enough to be wearing a bug hat in the North. Scott began a poem on blackflies in the notebook he had with him:

> Imagine a million surgeons
> Each with his amiable knife
> As dapper as any dragon [this is crossed out]
> Each (TF)

Blackflies and mosquitoes notwithstanding, the hat still looks odd, particularly when the ensemble includes such gloves, gauntlets really, and the white shoes with the long tongues. The camera hung over the shoulder doesn't look much like a purse. The impression Scott creates is not really feminine, but there almost seems to be a touch of what we might nowadays call a fashion statement — dark diamonds in the light-coloured band around the tops of his dark knee socks — very incongruous in the circumstances. Not feminine, just out of place; he looks freshly outfitted by some wilderness store in Ottawa. He looks like a greenhorn, which he was not. He seems both dressed for the wilderness and at odds with it.

Much of what I see in the photograph could be detected by anyone asked to read it with care, but knowing something of Scott and his work (both gainful and creative) probably makes an interpretation like mine all but inevitable. Scott was *not* comfortable with the wilderness, though his imagination was roused by it and by the people who lived there. He also felt in some respects out of place in Ottawa, among his peers in the civil service and in public life generally (a dreamer stranded among practical rationalists), but he was very successful in both spheres. He was on terrible terms with himself, at times, though it may be that very few even of his close friends knew how deep his self-loathing could go. Insofar as it expresses tension, division, E. K. Brown's classic encapsulation of Scott's writing as a mixture of "restraint and intensity" (*On Canadian Poetry* 122) might apply to the man himself. Scott is himself in that photograph at the height of land, then: not ridiculous, just disconnected. An oddity, a puzzle. I can imagine Margaret Atwood looking at him with a sense of déjà vu, remembering her drawings in *The Journals of Susanna Moodie,* those childlike distillations of unbelonging, of Mrs. Moodie, "a word / in a foreign language" (11), floating in white space.

This is a little too easy, though, this emphasis on Scott's precariousness in the northern part of his own country, because long before *The Journals of Susanna Moodie* he wrote some wonderful poems and a few stories energized by the irresolution, the hesitations, of a country and a mind that are not yet made, not made up. Scott's image in the photograph is slightly unsettling, slightly puzzling? Well, everything about him is that way. The most difficult puzzle of all is normally seen as an exercise in resolution: how to reconcile Scott's attractive and apparently humane poems and stories about Indians — Indians will be "defined" in chapter 1 — with the dreadful legacy of his administration of Indian Affairs. That problem is what this book, especially part 1, is about.

Here is the problem stated another way: the very authenticity that makes those poems and stories so appealing was bought at the expense of Native people themselves. Scott gathered much of what he knew about them from first-hand contact in the field, not from a desk in Ottawa, at least before he became powerful in the civil service. He saw with his own eyes what they looked like, where and how they lived, beginning with the Cree and Ojibway of Northern Ontario, and this experience removed a veil of illusion that debilitated virtually all white writing about Canadian Natives up until Scott's time, and much of it after. Indians in this early work, to split Rousseau's oxymoron, are either noble or savage.[1] Scott's Native people are neither; they are physical and emotional casualties of European contact. For many years Scott's critics assumed that he knew Indians intimately because his work about them has the ring of truth. But which truth, we now have to ask, Native or white? Perhaps the work feels authentic not because the Indians in it are "real" — in the sense that they could be accepted as such by a Native reader — but rather because they are passionate projections of the incompleteness of white adaptation to this country, of Scott's own argument with his immigrant soul. The source and the nature of this work's authenticity have not yet been sufficiently discussed, and it is important to do so because, despite certain opinions to the contrary, its power is not cancelled by an understanding of the disastrous Indian Affairs policies that Scott administered. Not cancelled, but — because writing, reading, and criticism are not pure acts performed in a vacuum — compromised. This book is also about the struggle that must take place within anyone, like myself, who tries to recognize and write about poems and stories *both* as autonomous and as contaminated by their existence in the world, in history.

SCOTT WAS NO MERE OBSERVER of First Nations people, gathering images for poems; he was no minor government functionary who happened to take an interest in their ways. He was for many years an effective administrator who rose through the ranks to become deputy superintendent general of Indian Affairs. That is the top civil service job in his department and practically the top post period, since the superintendent general is the elected, impermanent Member of Parliament-become-Cabinet-minister assigned to the portfolio, not necessarily in recognition of his or her particular knowledge or interest or expertise. Scott spent his whole working life (1879 to 1932) in Indian Affairs, growing in importance and influence. For the last 20 years of his career he was effectively in charge of the department. He has become the most visible representative of a government whose Indian policy was based on the definition of an Indian as a ward of the state — as little more than a child.

The assumption that the Indians, as virtual children, were not capable of controlling their own lives has been so literally acted on throughout the history of non-Native control over Indian affairs (the Indian Act, incorporated in

1876, codified colonial administration practices dating back to the late 17th century) that the First Nations have almost literally been seen and not heard for all that time. These people whose culture is characterized by the spoken word have been rendered voiceless in determinations about their own affairs. That is what Elijah Harper was telling Canada when he blocked the Meech Lake Constitutional Accord: it was high time First Nations were consulted on their own affairs. That Indians have for so long been wards of the state is at least as large a problem as, and indeed is connected with, the assimilationist policy that Scott administered and for which he is now the one who is usually blamed. The attitudes and policies he is associated with all but guaranteed government inertia with respect to the Indians. When your policy is to take care of the Indians until, in Scott's words, they "disappear as a separate and distinct people" ("The Administration of Indian Affairs" 27), at best you abandon any incentive for encouraging the preservation and continuation of aboriginal ways; at worst you step in with educational and other policies intended to accelerate the assimilation process. (In chapter 5 I trace the evolution of opinion in Scott's nonfiction writings toward approval of such acceleration.) You duck a big problem — the right to otherness of Native cultures and their rights as human beings and citizens — hoping that it will go away. You create a population of foreigners in their own land, people who await a Native voice to speak the nightmare of their estrangement.[2] Robert Bringhurst is recognizing the enormity of this tragedy when he refers to "the holocaust suffered by the Haida" ("This Also Is You" 32). Their real selves swallowed by a leviathan called progress, their languages dying,[3] Native people have lived in poverty, have dived into drink or drugs, have filled up Canadian jails, have committed suicide in terribly disproportionate numbers. Their degradation has been seen as proof of their inferiority. Those Natives who have "made it" away from the reserve are applauded for having had the good sense and the gumption to rise to the level of civilized people. Ingrained white attitudes die hard; intolerance remains. Naturally there has been talk of red power, of seizing rights by violent means, but a more usual response has been astonishingly gentle. That there have not been more Okas is surprising. The better these people understand white culture, the more a great many of them value their own ways and reach out to us with a plea to consider seriously the virtues of their attitudes to life on Earth. What could be more frustrating than to feel confirmed and strong in identity and to remain powerless to act on the basis of that strength?

To read Scott's poems simply as works of art independent of all this is beyond me. In the second part of this book I clear some space to focus on Scott's poems as poems, but even there I don't for long hold off the surrounding circumstances, the contexts of composition. They are too interesting, for one thing, but principally the issue of racism is not one that can be dealt with and then shoved aside. In this way or that way I find myself on both sides of this difficult issue, compelled to see double as I admire Scott's writing and despise so much of the situation that made it possible. Of course, literary history is haunted with such tensions and the terrible questions associated with them. Where in his or her mind does a lover of Lewis Carroll's books hide those nude photographs of young girls? What does one do with the fascist Pound? Paul de Man's anti-Semitic past? One might simply skim off the literary for separate consideration, as Northrop Frye seems to do when he says that criticism, as mediator between literature and society, "has to take account of the difference between the ideological and the mythological. For one thing, that's the only way to account for the fact that so many great writers have been ideological fat-heads: Yeats, Pound, Lawrence — you name them" (Salusinszky 33). It certainly is important to be alive to the difference between the verbal events that make literature literary and the ideological content that writers and writing may share with any sort of discourse, but conscience often makes it hard to know where to draw the line. And because of a sentimentality that one might distrust and still embrace, such questions are more involving the closer they come to home.

"WHERE IS THE BLACK BEAST?" That question opens Ted Hughes's poem, in *Crow*, entitled "The Black Beast." The asker of the question is not identified, nor can a reader tell for certain to whom it is addressed. The one who hears the question is Crow, Hughes's trickster persona. Crow's reaction ("Crow, like an owl, swivelled his head") is not to answer, not verbally at least. Crow's response shows him jumping to the conclusion that the questioner is naming him in the question. He does happen to be black but a question is not necessarily an accusation. Never mind; Crow takes no risks. He co-opts the question which, in his voice, becomes a refrain, a shout that rises by the last stanza to a screech. By then Crow has committed a slaughter of innocents in search of the black beast, an escalating series of atrocities that climaxes with the Earth roasted to a clinker and even space having fled in every direction. What remains is the still unanswered question: "Where is it? Where is the Black Beast?" Oh, and Crow remains. Has the question been answered by a process of elimination, then? Only in a sense; the process has *made* Crow the only possible answer. Before it started there might have been other answers; Crow might not even have been it. If not, that was a wasteful rampage. Desolation is having no possible answers but one.

The deflection of guilt for the ills of the world is not usually presented in such apocalyptic terms. "Crow" clarifies what always happens by showing what never does, never so simply and clearly and literally. Who is to blame for the plight of the Canadian Indians, then? Perhaps the goats should be the politicians, the ministers in charge of Indian Affairs whose tenure depends on the will of the prime minister and sometimes on that of the voting public.

But these people are temporary, and many of them have been little more than figureheads or mouthpieces. The continuity in policy and administration was supplied by the Indian Affairs civil service. All right, perhaps this body is to blame. But where's the satisfaction in blaming a faceless mass? If we choose out of that body a representative, we give it a face, and now we feel we're getting somewhere. It's easy to choose the representative. Scott was *there* all those years, supplying much of the continuity himself, and by his own admission he was in charge of the Indians for many of them. If the blame is going to fall on one person, Scott is the one.

That is E. Brian Titley's conviction. The title of his book summarizes the current view of Scott as an administrator: *A Narrow Vision: Duncan Campbell Scott and the Administration of Indian Affairs in Canada.* Titley's view is more than tempting; it is irrefutable. And yet there is something missing from his book. It lacks a sense of Scott as a warm-blooded, multidimensional human being. There is, furthermore, no sense of sharing, however uncomfortably, Scott's mind-set. Something both tougher and more compassionate than this remoteness seems needed — an exfoliation of the imagination capable of comprehending, not distancing, the dark side. A fictional character who would never evade the question "Where is the Black Beast?" is Catherine Earnshaw in *Wuthering Heights.* Among other things, that is what she owns up to when she declares, "Nelly, I *am* Heathcliff." I hope the reader will find in the course of this book that I am no apologist for Scott, even when I offer him the benefit of the doubt. I hope the reader will feel that I have been able to add something to the debate about Scott and the Indians because I have managed to put some distance between him and myself. But my considerable reluctance to overdramatize is not enough to keep me from saying, about this matter of guilt, that I *am* Duncan Campbell Scott.

In the dialogue with Terry Goldie that forms the introduction to their *Anthology of Canadian Native Literature in English,* Daniel David Moses offers the opinion that white people want to hang on to their guilt. He doesn't elaborate. I suppose he's thinking of self-indulgent liberal wallowing, which must be a tiresome dependency. Who wants to host a former oppressor's parasitical need? But whites aren't all like that, if only because many of them believe that the past is the past. I suspect there are about as many contemporary whites conscience-stricken about Indians as there are males who feel guilty about the repressive effects of patriarchy on women: by no means all even of those who hate racism or sexism. I'm aware of a certain irony in saying this, inheritor that I am of a long white tradition of generalization about Indians, but Daniel David Moses's generalization doesn't hold up. It's not for him to say what white people should do with their guilt. But perhaps all he means is that mere acknowledgement isn't worth much. Better to get out and *do* something, learn something, rather than sit around chewing on guilt. Inadequate as it is, this book is what I did, what I've done so far. Also, this book admits that a wrong was done, and perhaps it may contribute something to the healing that Daniel David Moses calls for. After all, an official apology was far more significant than financial reparation for injustices perpetrated on Canadians of Japanese descent during the Second World War.

TO GAIN PERSPECTIVE on the Indians who are Scott's subjects, one is naturally drawn to ethnographic material. There are all sorts of pitfalls in the path of studying Native peoples, whether to illuminate Scott's work or merely to find out about them. Deep difficulties have to be faced, especially when it comes to writing about them. The tendency of the dominant culture or sex or race is to feed on, and extend its power by absorbing, the vitality of the oppressed other. The most effective instruments of this absorption, paradoxically, may be just those disenchanted members of the dominant culture who drift in dismay to the margin, looking, if not for a way out, at least for somewhere to rest a lever whereby to shift their own mind-set away from the world into which they were born. In 1989 and 1990 the Writers' Union of Canada newsletter hosted a debate on the question of "structural racism" — the assumption by whites of the right to adopt the perspective of a minority race, of males to speak for women — and the debate extends across the world; it is held wherever there are oppressed minorities. Does Keri Hulme, who is only part Maori, have the right to speak as from the inside of that culture in her novel *the bone people*? Even Canadians, specialists in Commonwealth or postcolonial literature at some distance from the locus of the problem, are participating in that debate.[4]

The majority of Writers' Union members decried the imposition of any limitation on their creativity. Well, yes: real writers translate themselves into the other by an act of imagination, of love. To defend the right of lesser writers to try and fail is to endorse the spirit of honest attempt as well as to support the attempts that do succeed — speaking for the moment as though literary value and social obligation coexist unproblematically. But where do we draw the line between the honest failure and the cultural rip-off? Rudy Wiebe would draw it somewhere between himself and W. P. Kinsella.

If he had written nothing but *The Temptations of Big Bear,* I believe Rudy Wiebe would have earned the right to criticize Kinsella for his six books of stereotypical stories about the Ermineskin band of Hobbema, Alberta, Cree. Kinsella's Indian stories have always made me uncomfortable. But what if the Cree were to act on Wiebe's suggestion (in the *Globe and Mail,* February 18, 1990) that they should "gain a court injunction against the proud, good name of their community and their people being misused and exploited in this manner"? Would the Writers' Union, perhaps with a nasty taste in its collective mouth, not have to defend Kinsella's right to publish that stuff?

(Daniel David Moses quite rightly ironizes the whiteness of the whole controversy in "Native People Should Tell Native Stories" [7], but I think the most telling contribution has been the most oblique. Thomas King is fighting fire with fire when he appropriates the key phrase — "If you build it, he will come" — from Kinsella's baseball novel *Shoeless Joe* and works it into "A Seat in the Garden," a terrific de-stereotyping story of his own.)

This debate ought to be going on inside everyone's mind. It is never far from mine as I write about the work of a man who writes about Indians. The best response I can make to the inner voice that accuses me of knowing about half of what I'm talking about, the white half, is to make the effort never to forget that there *is* a Native perspective and, whenever possible, to allow Native voices to speak in their own words. There may be for me no way around the danger of participating in a discourse of power; there may be no way through it, either, but the latter seems a more responsible course.

In his 85 years Scott created a small body of poetry and fiction, as well as some essays and a couple of plays. The proportion of his writing that is of enduring value is smaller yet, but he nevertheless deservedly gained a reputation as one of the most important writers of what is known as the Confederation period of Canadian literature (roughly 1867 to 1910). And, with some exceptions, the best or at least the most distinctive of his best work was written about Indians. For most of his life, and for quite some time after he died, the fact that he was a civil servant who was actually competent was considered an interesting sidelight on the more significant literary career. As Titley says, though, Scott would have been "a significant historical figure had he never penned a stanza of poetry" (vii). The balance of interest, even that of many literary people, has been shifting toward the record of the civil servant, and the question that is always asked by those who read his Indian poems in the light of his administrative record is: how could the same man be responsible for both?

There is no shortage of opinion on the question, as we'll see. For the time being it will suffice to say that the extremes are represented by those, at one end of the scale, who say that Scott's record is reprehensible and that his poetry in no way compensates, and those, on the other, who find that his "narrow vision" is no obstacle to appreciating the poetry. By polarizing the contending sides of the Scott/Indian question, I may seem to be setting the stage for a mediating opinion, perhaps even a reconciliation of the two sides of Scott in the good old Canadian spirit of compromise. The word *reconcile* hovers over much of the discussion of the relationship between the official and the poetic Scott, as I have suggested, and it sometimes expresses an unarticulated and questionable assumption that things do fit if you look at them long enough, or that they can be made to fit if you are ingenious enough to find a way. I have attempted something more difficult, more interesting, and I believe truer to life. The reader who hopes to see the apparently contradictory sides of Scott slide together, the problem solved, might as well stop reading now. It is impossible to strip from Scott his portion of guilt without concluding that what happened to First Nations people under him does not matter, and yet it is impossible to condemn him as a mere culprit when so much of the evidence of his whole life and the era he lived it in, not to mention the writing, suggests the superficiality of that judgement. He and his work, both literary and official, may at least be better understood than they have been heretofore if a difficult act of love is performed that involves staying near him even when his company is hard to stand. For better or worse, then: a bumpy, book-long marriage. I haven't tried for objectivity at every point, feeling that the stresses of a study like this ought not to be concealed, feeling that I can trust the reader to weather the turbulence.

THE CHAPTERS THAT FOLLOW offer a personal view of Scott and the problems involved in interpreting his Indian poems and stories. All books are personal, of course, even those that lay claim to authoritativeness by presenting themselves as objective, but perhaps this one is more personal than many in that I have been drawn or driven to write it. I have not been studying Scott uninterruptedly since I encountered his work 20 years ago, but I have not abandoned him despite realizing that he is a minor poet much of whose work is forgettable. There is an old theory among poets that the way to make your literary mark is to work your way through the genres from minor to major, from lyric to epic, like Spenser or Milton. Or Joyce, in terms of fiction. The careers of Canadian artists as different as James Reaney and George Bowering show something of that trajectory. A corollary for critics, not that often spelled out, would be that one proves oneself by taking on the major writers, engaging literature at its most intense and least exhaustible. In terms of this sort of thinking, Duncan Campbell Scott, a minor Canadian poet who never found his centre, is a waste of time. There is something in that opinion. For myself, a lover of poetry who happens to be a practising critic, life is too short to spend all of it on Scott. One of my great pleasures has been to read and write about contemporary Canadian writing while it was coming into its literary majority, and that has certainly been challenging enough. But something in or about Scott has kept me interested over the years since I first encountered his poetry at the end of Malcolm Ross's anthology, *Poets of the Confederation*. I have since found ways of appreciating Roberts, Carman, and Lampman, the others in that anthology, especially Lampman, but it was Scott's poetry that really woke me up. Scott's work needs the selection that anthologizing performs, since the quality thins out quickly, but there it is: he did write some work that needs no apology — "The Height of Land," "At Gull Lake: August 1810," "Lines in

Memory of Edmund Morris," "Powassan's Drum," "A Scene at Lake Manitou," not to mention certain others. In part 2 of this book, with a chapter on each of these poems, I make what return I can for the gift of their existence. There are some Scott stories I reread with pleasure, as well, but Scott achieved more in poetry than he did in fiction, and I devote only a chapter to the latter.

The work that attracts me most, then, is about the Natives and the North — or, in a few instances, the West. This has been a common experience of Scott readers, so much so that there is cause for complaint about the neglect of his other work. My own feeling is that there is no denying the fact that much of Scott's best work was stimulated by the experience of travelling through the Canadian North and meeting the Ojibway, the Cree, the Hudson's Bay Company traders, and the others who lived there, encountering the "wilderness" itself. Scott did create conventional stories and poems based on this unforgettable experience, some of them extremely accomplished. "Spring on Mattagami" is an example. But there were times when putting his northern dream into words required a formal stretch that took him a step outside of the limit he unconsciously set for himself as a poet and, more consciously, for Canadian literature, which was to be no more than an offshoot or continuation of the British tradition. In literary terms (see his essay "Poetry and Progress"), Scott was an imperialist, and therefore temperamentally opposed to radical originality.

Much has been written on the adaptation to this country of literary forms born elsewhere, of reasons for the failure or relative success of such "transitional" works. *All* of these works are or should be in some ways interesting to a Canadian reader. As Northrop Frye says, reviewing A. J. M. Smith's 1943 *The Book of Canadian Poetry,* "in what Canadian poems have tried to do there is an interest for Canadian readers much deeper than what the achievement in itself justifies" (*The Bush Garden* 132). James Reaney gives this idea a heart when he endorses "the dear bad poets / Who wrote / Early in Canada / And never were of note" ("Letter One" 211). This accepting attitude feels right to me. On it may rest a vision of the nation as a family, willing to embrace the marginally interesting as well as the repugnant but fascinating Beast, both the mediocre and the first-rate. From this sort of building John Metcalf excuses himself in *What Is a Canadian Literature?* There is nothing dear about badness to him. Of course, it isn't Reaney he attacks for getting behind mediocre books; it's "professors" like myself, those tasteless enough to see merit in writing like Duncan Campbell Scott's *In The Village of Viger and Other Stories.* But despite the fact that he normally gets the answers wrong, there is some point to the questions Metcalf raises. Allowing for differences of taste, it is possible to make qualitative judgements about literature. There is a real lift to be felt reading an ordinary writer like Scott when his work rises above the obstacles of adaptation, rises out of badness or mediocrity and into an accent at once his own and the communal property of his fellow citizens — and thus exportable. That accomplishment in a few of his works is what I celebrate here.

Since I am especially interested in the Indian poems, I have looked everywhere in the records relating to Scott for evidence to clarify his relationship with Indians. I have found that the only true recorded meeting of the whole man with individual Natives takes place *in* those poems. His job at Indian Affairs was just that, a job and not a vocation, so much of his life was lived without reference to Native people. That has to be taken into account, and I try to do so in two chapters, one a portrait of the man "at home" and another of the civil servant at work, a man whose problems were by no means confined to his Native "charges."

In chapter 1 I argue that there no longer is any such solid entity as Duncan Campbell Scott. The investigations of chapters 2 to 5 turn up only further masks. When all of Scott's words, and all the words that have been written about him, have been analyzed in terms of their rhetorical packaging, their style, the occasion of their writing — not merely in terms of content, in short — their authority has a curious tendency to dissipate. If there is no Scott to be found, if there are only masks, then there can be no certainty regarding his attitude toward Native people. Contemporary theories of the constructed self undercut opinions like Tom Marshall's (Scott's "sympathy for the Indians is beyond question" [28]); analysis that addresses more than content does the same. Even the content is not always reassuring, though. One conclusion that emerges from the chapter 5 examination of all of Scott's nonfiction on Native peoples (some of it previously unknown) is that he cannibalized his own prose on several occasions. Even without other evidence of low commitment to various of these projects, these essays and reports on Native subjects, the self-plagiarism suggests that Scott could not be said to be inhabiting those words in any significant sense. The real Scott, wherever he might be, is not there. Mine is the first examination of Scott that substitutes a fluid and indeterminate textual personality for a "real" person. The consequences must be something like those that entered physics with the theory that matter is a dance of molecules rather than the sum of its appearances: no more than matter does Scott completely evaporate, but thinking about him and his work crosses a new threshold of difficulty and interest.

THINKING OF PERSONAL IDENTITY as a construct has its parallels in thinking about other sorts of identity, like the national identity that Scott and his contemporaries conceived of as a solid intelligible unity that the future would eventually produce. When Scott speaks of beauty being fugitive from our lives in his "Ode for the Keats Centenary," I think he must have in mind something more than the narrowly aesthetic, something political. Or perhaps I think he *should* mean something more. Beauty and truth were reciprocal for Keats, or at least for his speaker in the "Ode to a Grecian Urn." What Keats meant by them and their relationship, however, is expressed in a koan that will never quite unlock, so the literary world has been probing it ever since.

In Scott's poem a personified Beauty, unaccompanied by truth, has fled a materialist culture and taken refuge (rather incongruously, given her sylphish delicacy) in the Canadian wilderness. Scott thickens up the concept of beauty in "At Gull Lake: August 1810" by associating it with specific incarnations of both peace and terror — truth still between the lines, if present at all — but that opens other questions. The reach of Scott's Keats ode far exceeds its grasp when it strives to express abandonment in terms of abstract personified Beauty alone, but there is a cultural loneliness in the poem that I don't recall Scott expressing quite so broadly and directly anywhere else. I have the feeling that if the terms were shifted a little, perhaps if Keats's truth were yoked with beauty still and expressed in Canadian terms, we might be looking at a local figure for something complex in modernity. It would involve the modern abandonment to nihilism that George Grant finds in the development of liberalism to its technological end. This is the scheme that Dennis Lee, adapting Heidegger, elaborates in *Savage Fields*. It would also take in what Lee finds in the poetry of the deep-rooted Al Purdy, an expression of "*mysterium tremendum* — the encounter with holy otherness" (32) that the modern often seems to lack.

Scott once wrote, rather grandly, that he had walked away from his Methodist faith into the wilderness, where he did not feel alone, but he contradicts that confidence elsewhere,[5] and in any case the wilderness was not his permanent home. There is a thread of loneliness that runs through all his writing. It might be the expression of his consciousness of living in an unformed and second-rate nation of the imagination. Does he want us to remember the exiled Hebrews when he says in 1901 that writing in this country is like "moulding bricks without straw" ("A Decade of Canadian Poetry" [158])? Did he mean to suggest that we might never belong in this strange land? More likely he was trying to convey the magnitude of the task facing writers unable *yet* to write out of the grain of the place, suffering from a colonial position that Northrop Frye calls "a frostbite at the roots of the Canadian imagination" *(The Bush Garden* 134). This is, in fact, a persistent complaint of Canadian writers. "It's only by our lack of ghosts we're haunted," said Earle Birney in 1947. Our postmodernist writers are still obsessed with regional and/or national beginnings, but by choice and out of energetic opposition to most kinds of political or literary settlement. And they are anything but lonely.

MEANWHILE, IN THE NORTHERN ONTARIO Scott was crossing in 1905 and 1906, the Cree and Ojibway could still communicate with the spirits who share their world. Books like *Killing the Shamen* by Thomas Fiddler and James Stevens show that the people were by no means culturally deprived, even though their material existence was often, especially in winter, extremely precarious. Their religion and their stories share the assumption, common to folktales around the world, that metamorphosis is the norm. Physical identity is fluid; animals speak and people assume the form of animals. Some of the First Nations are nonhuman. One of the most dramatic expressions of the node where physical and spiritual worlds meet is the shaman's shaking tent. There are many accounts of the shaking tent in operation; among the most fascinating are those in the journal kept by George Nelson in 1823.

Nelson was a Hudson's Bay Company trader in northeastern Saskatchewan who observed and wrote down, in a sort of journal/letter to his minister father, a great deal of information about Cree culture, both material and spiritual. He was a Christian and would have preferred not to witness the exercise of "pagan" powers, but he could not doubt their existence. "Many things related of these Conjurings," he says, "I acknowledge to be [absurd and idle stories]; but at the same time I am as positive and as firmly persuaded of the truth of the assertion 'that they have dealings with some supernatural spirit,' as I am convinced that I live and breathe in air. . . . And I am by no means inclined to acknowledge myself as superstitious: I am convinced of this from reason, argument, comparison; in short from *analysis*" (82). What Nelson says about these "dealings" may be read in Brown and Brightman's *"The Orders of the Dreamed": George Nelson on Cree and Northern Ojibwa Religion and Myth, 1823,* but I borrow an account of the shaking tent from Thomas Linklater of Sandy Lake. His story is translated from the Cree by Edtrip Fiddler and appears in *Legends from the Forest,* edited by James R. Stevens:

> Talking about my grandfather's powers, there was a certain time of the year that something would come to tell him to perform the shaking tent. He would tell us to go in the bush and get sixteen different kinds of trees — imagine going out and trying to find sixteen different trees to make his shaking tent because it's time for him to perform again.
>
> This is how we bring back our dead: talk to our dead people with the shaking tent. If you want to talk to somebody, you just ask for it. People were pressured to do that because they wanted to talk to those loved ones that passed away. This is how we used to communicate with our dad — my dad.
>
> From the shaking tent our dad would say that he was still watching over us and stuff like that. A lot of things we would ask him and he would answer us. It was amazing how my grandfather did it. I mean no man could physically shake that tent. The poles were driven two and a half to three feet in the ground. Sometimes that tent would loosen right up out of the ground. One time I remember, we took a great big rope because that tent was coming off the ground. We couldn't do anything about it. So we tied the rope

> around the top of it to two big trees near it. The shaking tent made the trees go crazy. Great big trees, not small ones, great big spruce trees. They shook just like little trees.
>
> Before my grandfather, Marten would go in the tent and he would go twice around it, clockwise. Before he reached the point he started from around the tent and before he entered, that thing would start moving. Then he goes in and lays down in there. That tent would really shake then.
>
> There is one person that always comes into the tent. There is always a joker in there. He is the Lynx. He's always there and he calls the dead. He's a sort of a messenger there. He tells jokes too — this is the way he is, entertaining. He can be serious at times. He will call the dead people that a person wants to come in there.
>
> Now each person has a different kind of a song. This is how we used to know it was real in the tent. Like my father, he used to sing on the drum. There's a certain song he sang for his own self.
>
> When you go fasting, you have a certain power that nobody knows — and you have your own way of singing it. And people would know if it's the real him that comes into that shaking tent because he would sing that same song. But grandfather didn't know the other people's songs. This is how we used to know my father was there. He would remember my mother and all the things we did. We would ask him all kinds of questions and he would tell us what we wanted to know. (92–93)

Linklater's account might be supplemented (Nelson heard the distinct voices of most of the Native spirits as they entered the tent), but it corresponds with other versions. It agrees with the story I heard from one of my students in the 1970s, a Mohawk from the Six Nations Reserve who attended a shaking tent ceremony in the North with his Cree wife. Not knowing Cree, he couldn't follow the voices in the tent, didn't know what was making the others laugh. But his eyes couldn't miss the violent shaking of a tent that his own hands had not been able to budge.

When he speaks of the conjurer's "dwarf wigwam" in "Powassan's Drum" is Scott referring rather poetically to the shaking tent? The shaman could use the shaking tent either for healing or sorcery, after all. Perhaps the power of the shaman to curse at a distance is what Scott has in mind in "Powassan's Drum." If so, how does the rescue of the image from the realm of the free-floating picturesque affect what we make of that poem in which the "pulse of being," the conjurer's drumbeat, is demonic? There are general questions that arise from such specific ones: how far could Scott see beyond the appearance of the Indians; how deeply could he see into Native cultures? He was fascinated by what they appeared to be in 1905 — not merely the "weird and waning race" of "The Onondaga Madonna," an early poem, but a collection of individuals caught in the turmoil of the conflict between two lives, almost, in Matthew Arnold's terms, "two worlds, one dead, / The other powerless to be born" ("Stanzas from the Grand Chartreuse" 302). Arnold might have felt well off had he known of Native peoples having to make the transition between eras and incompatible cultures at the same time, and with no acknowledged voice for the pain, no white ears to listen to it. How much did Scott know of what these people had been and therefore, at least in part, still were? The underlying question is whether Scott had any way of knowing that the (to us) remote Indians of Canada, like the northern Cree and Ojibway, still had direct links to their gods: their material and spiritual lives were not severed. Such questions are important, because you cannot value what you do not know.

If the questions I have raised about the depth of Scott's knowledge and understanding of Natives can be only glancingly answered by his nonfiction, what of the fiction and poetry? Are we on even more slippery ground examining the ethnographic content of stories and poems? Yes and no. We are at once at our most oblique and most relevant when analyzing the place of ethnographic detail in the poems in which Scott is least "himself," in the ordinary literary sense that the voice of the poems is that of a persona or "speaker." For what he says when he is beside himself, only the inner man is responsible. Out of reason's reach there is a deeper understanding. This is sufficient motivation in itself for writing poems. How far "out" did Scott reach? While he was writing, when he was negotiating the spirit in himself, did he find ways of accepting the spirit of the creator as understood by Native peoples? It would be naive to expect solid answers to such questions, but analysis that treats such questions as valid may have something different to offer than analysis based in reason alone. There are varieties of knowledge and subtleties of thought in some of Scott's creative work that he never matched in discursive prose. Dramatic evidence of this is the sketch of his philosophy that he sent to Elise Aylen before they were married. This fascinating but low-intensity analogue of the "argument" of "The Height of Land" is introduced and discussed in chapter 11.

THE SCOTT WHO STANDS at the portage on the Root River in 1905, insofar as we can know him, is a civil servant on the rise, a reasonably prolific writer of stories and poems with readers in America and Britain as well as Canada. In 1905 John Masefield wrote his famous letter (quoted in chapter 3) in praise of "The Piper of Arll." Scott seems to have been a reasonably contented husband then; he certainly was a doting father. Especially in 1906, in the company of his friend Pelham Edgar, he was enjoying the experience of a lifetime in the North. He would be decades tapping the literary sources of those treaty-making trips. In 1907 his daughter Elizabeth died. The personal and literary devastation that resulted was in no way compensated for by his steady rise in Indian Affairs. In fact, the climb up the ladder was bad for his writing. It hardly seems too gross an exaggeration to say that Scott's life and work were at a pinnacle of sorts while he was negotiating Treaty 9. He was almost in the middle of his life then, and his life and work in some ways bend around those pivotal years of 1905 and 1906. I think the oversimplification has merit, at any rate, especially for the purposes of a study that is centrally concerned with Scott's life and work concerning First Nations people. Even discounting the pivot theory, though, there should be no denying the usefulness of studying two summers that have been so extensively documented in journals, photographs, paintings, essays, reports and, less directly, in stories and poems. Chapter 1 begins to tell the story of the treaty trips, constructing an armature of information that further chapters will build upon, as I interpret Scott's long life and his writing on Natives and the North, using as fulcrum a detailed scrutiny of those two enormously influential summers.

NOTES

1. It's much more complicated than this, of course. See Leslie Monkman's *A Native Heritage* and Terry Goldie's *Fear and Temptation* for thorough maps of the varieties of white use of Native figures in Canadian (and, in Goldie's case, Australian and New Zealand) literature.
2. In his introduction to the Native writing issue of *Canadian Fiction Magazine,* Thomas King says ("Introduction" [xi–xii]) that Natives have generally avoided the historical period in their fiction, preferring to concentrate on contemporary times, the period of what might be called the aftermath. Ironically the field has been left open to white writers. King's own *Coyote Columbus Story* (for children) and *Green Grass, Running Water* (a novel whose title is drawn from treaty promises) address in ironic terms the origins of contemporary Native problems.
3. In "One Generation from Extinction," Basil Johnston says that "there remain but three aboriginal languages out of the original fifty-three found in Canada that may survive several more generations." Losing their language, he says, Native peoples "lose not only the ability to express the simplest of daily sentiments and needs but they can no longer understand the ideas, concepts, insights, attitudes, rituals, ceremonies, institutions brought into being by their ancestors; and, having lost the power to understand, cannot sustain, enrich, or pass on their heritage. No longer will they think Indian or feel Indian. . . . They will have lost their identity which no amount of reading can restore" (10).
4. In her article "Why C. K. Stead Didn't Like Keri Hulme's *the bone people:* Who Can Write as Other?" Margery Fee explores the basic questions: "First, how do we determine minority group membership? Second, can majority group members speak as minority members, whites as people of colour, men as women, intellectuals as working people" (11)? The Writers' Union debate issued in a feature in *Books in Canada,* entitled "Whose Voice Is It Anyway: A Symposium on Who Should Be Speaking for Whom."
5. At least he wrote as follows to Elise Aylen in 1930 from New England: "This morning I walked & sat & the same this aft. I am not likely to explore. You know my feeling about being alone in the woods. Fear of that Demon that lurks in the wilds keeps me close to the 'huts & haunts of men'" (PA/S-A).

1

What Fish Are Able to See: The Summers of 1905 and 1906

In this landscape every rock had a name, and most names had spirits, ghosts, meanings.

Peter Carey, Oscar and Lucinda

ON FRIDAY, JUNE 30, 1905, Duncan Campbell Scott and his treaty-making party left Ottawa for Dinorwic, a Canadian Pacific Railway stop near Dryden, north of Lake Superior. This was a moment that could be traced back at least as far as 1899, when Scott and T. J. MacRae, according to a memorandum written by the latter in 1901, had "visited New Brunswick House at the head waters of the Moose River, north of Lake Superior, for the purpose of meeting certain Robinson Treaty Indians, and there met a number of Indians who do not participate in the benefits of that treaty" (RG10d). The Robinson Treaty dated from 1850. It included Ojibway and Saulteaux Indians living south of the divide or height of land. It was not requests from the Indians to be included in the treaty that provoked MacRae's 1901 memo; it was the fact that Northern Ontario was on the verge of opening up to railways and thus to settlement. "If there were a scenario which could be said to apply to nearly all . . . extinguishments of native title," says J. E. Chamberlin, "it is surely this. Even the most certain of theoretical experts on the future of the Indian has tended to find the problems of reconciling native and non-native civil structures intractable, and the desirability of obliterating one by enforcing the other fairly difficult to establish until such time as economic interests interfered" (101). Surveyors had already been at work in the North, making the inhabitants nervous; they had the same effect, though more dramatically, in the Red River Settlement, 1869, and Saskatchewan in 1883.

Had the making of the treaty been up to the federal government alone the preparations to do so would already have been complicated enough. A census of Indians occupying the territory in question would have to be prepared, and other information would have to be assembled to permit the presentation of the matter to the government for passage by order in council and for inclusion in the budget. But a federal law had been passed in 1894 that for the first time required provincial concurrence in any treaty negotiations. In Treaty 9, then, the government of Ontario had to be involved. If, as Pelham Edgar says, "Governments move with slow dignity" ("1200 Miles" 255), two governments (with two civil services) must move about four times as slowly. Had there been no other related bones of contention between the two levels of government there would only have been the difficulty of deciding such things as who pays the costs of the expedition and who bears which continuing costs incurred by bringing the Indians into the treaty. But there were unresolved disputes over the fact that Métis living in Keewatin (Northwest Territories) were recognized as having territorial rights, while those in Ontario were not. The government of Canada was also plaintiff and the provincial government defendant in a continuing case seeking definition of what Aubrey White, assistant commissioner of Crown Lands, termed the "rights and obligations of the parties under the B.N.A. Act, with special regard to the terms of Treaty No. 3, dated 3rd October, 1873" (RG10d). Treaty 3 involved the Ojibway and Saulteaux in southern Manitoba and in western Ontario south of the height of land, or watershed, dividing the flow of waters south (into Lake Superior) and north (into James Bay and Hudson Bay).

Perhaps because he had been a member of the 1899 party visiting Brunswick House, perhaps because he was significant in the Indian Department, Scott's initials appear on many flakes in the snowstorm of memoranda that flew between Ottawa and Toronto over the treaty, and he was the one to hit on a compromise that permitted the governments finally to suspend their differences. The federal government had been ready to move in 1904, but Ontario was still dragging its feet as late as March 18, 1905, the date of a memo from Scott, accountant, to Frank Pedley, the deputy superintendent general of Indian Affairs:

> It is suggested that if the Ontario Government will not enter into a specific agreement with this Department under the terms of our letter of the 30th April last that they might agree to a convention whereby the Dominion Government would be allowed to make the treaty on the maximum terms set forth by that letter, the whole case to be considered in the same category as the outstanding differences between Ontario and the Dominion. Unless this matter is decided within the next two weeks it would hardly be possible to make the treaty this year as the Indians will have to be notified almost immediately. This is the second year that funds have been voted without any action taken. (RG10d)

The next item in the Indian Affairs Red Files relating to Treaty 9 is a telegram from Pedley to White, also dated March 18, requesting a meeting on Monday. Agreement to go ahead was secured within a couple of weeks.

At Dinorwic the treaty party — two Dominion commissioners, one Ontario commissioner, a doctor, and two North-West Mounted policemen — joined with Chief Trader Rae of the HBC. He was in charge of transport by canoe north through ancient fur trading routes in a great arc of Northern Ontario all the way to Fort Albany on James Bay, and then south along the bay to Moose Factory. The last leg of the 1905 trip was up the Abitibi River to Lake Abitibi and on to Haileybury, where the railway was rejoined. The northward stage of the journey, begun on July 4, took the party through Treaty 3 territory, into the Lac Seul and Lake St. Joseph systems. On this stage of the arduous trek against the current until the height of land was reached on July 9, one event stands out to readers of Scott's poetry. The experience of hearing a drum across Lac Seul and of visiting the site of a White Dog Feast in order to stop it (by amendment to the Indian Act passed in 1895, the government had outlawed certain religious and social ceremonies like the Sun Dance and the Potlatch) emerged long years later in "Powassan's Drum," one of Scott's most powerful poems.

The treaty was first signed at Osnaburgh Post on July 12. Here the Indians who joined the treaty were paid $8.00 each, $4.00 for signing and the first $4.00 (unindexed) annuity that is still paid yearly to every man, woman, and child. A chief and two councillors were chosen by election, and a feast followed, with speeches on both sides and the presentation of a 12-foot Union Jack to the chief. The reserve — one square mile for every family of five — was selected the following day. The Dominion also agreed to supply schools for Indian children. The terms of Treaty 9 were not quite so rich as those of Treaty 3 ($5.00 per year, with agricultural implements, nets, livestock, and seed thrown in), but the form of the treaty was the same as in the more storied earlier ones by which the land of the Plains Indians was ceded, and Scott was acting in the tradition of Alexander Morris, who negotiated those treaties. "So long as the grass grows and the water runs": the poetic formula was used again in 1905 as before. The edge of the romance — either of expansion and progress, to take one view of it, or, to take another, the innocent selling of souls — is dulled in the North by the absence of any hint of Native power or hostility, the absence of picturesque Indian garb. Since the treaties were, or turned out to be, confidence tricks, perhaps they ought to be deromanticized.

The Osnaburgh pattern was repeated at all the other posts that Scott and his party visited: Fort Hope (July 20), Marten's Falls (July 25), English River (July 29), Fort Albany (August 3), Moose Factory (August 9), and New Post (August 21). Abitibi Post was reached after most of the Indians had left for their winter hunting grounds, so their signing was deferred until the following summer.

A map of Northern Ontario gives little sense of the variety of landscape that Scott and his party passed through. In the inland stretches, between lakes, they encountered rapids and falls requiring long and numerous portages, sometimes the poling or tracking of canoes while the passengers walked along the bank. This was particularly true of the eastern approach to the Albany, and there was a rough section up the Kenogami to English River Post, the most isolated and bleak of all those encountered. The Abitibi River was also difficult, and it was followed by a 17-mile portage to Klock's Depot at North Timiskaming which Samuel Stewart calls the "worst experience" of the trip (RG10e 46). The more beautiful the country was, in many cases, the more difficulty it posed for the crew. The great Albany, flowing through country that became, to non-Native eyes, more desolate the nearer it approached James Bay, was relatively easy to negotiate below Marten's Falls. On Wednesday, August 2, Scott's journal records "about 90 miles" of sailing. "One night," he says in his essay "The Last of the Indian Treaties," "the canoes were lashed together and floated on under the stars until daybreak" (119). Between Fort Albany and Moose Factory, along the coast of James Bay, the party travelled by HBC sailboat *Innenew,* a transportation novelty for them.

The treaty commissioners were passengers in canoes paddled by crews of Indians and Métis arranged by the HBC. They were being paddled on routes known intimately by the likes of Jimmy Swain, head man of the crew that left from Dinorwic. The way lay through land known even today as wilderness, but every foot of it was familiar to the people who, generation after generation, had plied that route. This intimacy with the country is occasionally hinted at in Scott's journal, as when (on July 14) he writes:

> Mkd. names of points on the Albany
> Pull & Be damned Rapid
> Hughie's Creek
> Deep & Shove Lake

But this naming is more dramatically recorded on the 1906 trip by a different diarist.

In his journal of 1906 (having taken Scott's place as "secretary"), Pelham Edgar wrote down Indian words for lakes and rivers and even rapids and portages. It's interesting to follow the treaty party in Edgar's journal between August 5 and 8 as they work their way up the Pic and White Otter rivers north of Heron Bay on Lake Superior, over the height of land on their way to Long Lake Post, and then back the same route between August 10 and 13. Edgar's journal entries on the way up are annotated lists of named and numbered rapids, lakes, and portages. August 12 merely counts backward down the list of stages previously negotiated:

Start 7:15 & 7:45

15 Bochuwassin Through at 9 Water goes between the rocks

14 Weikobigeanigen 9:10 Pulling portage Willow

13 Kawawogigining 9:30 Crooked

Turning Portage

12 Sagiwatanogogeegie 10:45 Cat Rapids

11 Kusigenkskibawati Kasigenksikihbawati

10 Smooth Rock Waweeteeoskadanapawaj Where the Frenchman was soaked in the water

9 Eeskerebawatig

Ageeyakoming

8 Wikawiginigen

7 Sageeboate 1:45 PM Aug 12

6 Kedawskabishigining Left at 4:10

5 Hebusadapekiyag Hebusadapekyago Huckleberry Portage

4 Akeewabeemageenakynn Arrive five Camp 6:30 (RG10b)

Edgar does not annotate all of the stages because he has done so on the way up. "Four" is Dead Man's Portage, 6 is Split Rock Portage, 7 (spelled Sangabow) is "rapid which runs into a lake," 8 (Weikwabiboogun) is "rapid where the boat is pulled up by a rope," 9 is Cedars Portage, 10 and 11 are both called Cat Rapids. "Water goes between the rocks portage" is called Kinnidicaday on the way up.

Edgar is struggling with the language. Some of his words bamboozled Peter Denny, an expert in Cree and Ojibway from the University of Western Ontario. Others seem wrongly translated. There is no Frenchman and no smooth rock in 10, no cedars in 9 (this is probably "low water portage"), for example, so the list is not reliable. "Pelham Edgar's names are a mixed bag," Denny says.

> Some look like English names. The Ojibway terms are not necessarily names, but may often be just descriptions. Since every native person knew all geographical features of his district by memory, it's not certain that they needed anything like names, but they certainly could describe them all. In a narrow enough conversational context, a description such as *booji-assin* "broken rock" will point to only *one* broken rock, and therefore *serve* as a name. However, names are probably more valuable to the outsider, an administrator like Scott. (note to the author)

What could be more intimate than a route that needs no names? This may not be the *Through the Looking Glass* "wood with no names" that unalienates Alice and the fawn, but it's a far cry from the obsession that generated place names along the CPR in advance of any settlement or even experience of the locales. That is the logocentric naming of which Howard O'Hagan's narrator makes so much in *Tay John:* "It is physically exhausting to look on unnamed country. A name is the magic to keep it within the horizons. Put a name to it, put it on a map, and you've got it. The unnamed — it is the darkness unveiled" (80). Scott's journal shows less interest in the Indian names than Edgar's does, Scott's poem "Indian Place Names" notwithstanding, but we can tell from Samuel Stewart's diary that the 1905 route could have been similarly baptized. The particular series of entries on which I have focused shows the "wilderness" to be as familiar in its own way as a complex of city streets, insofar as naming is an index of familiarity, but it has an additional fascination. At Split Rock Portage (accurately named) Scott wrote the poem called "Ecstasy" that he published later that year in *Via Borealis.* And, more important, the route described, passing as it does a "Water Lily (Mud) Lake" (August 7) and a forest fire (August 10), is the particular one Scott recalled when he wrote "The Height of Land" many years later in 1915.[1]

Although Edmund Morris does not figure in that poem (whose exclusions — see chapter 11 — are as interesting as its inclusions), the painter was a temporary member of the treaty party at this point. He also kept a journal, which would supplement Edgar's account even more than it does but for the terrible handwriting, famous since Scott began his elegy on Morris with that detail. Samuel Stewart's diary is much more helpful, being a neatly written consecutive narrative of 270-odd pages.

THE LONG LAKE JUNKET was the second-last stage of the 1906 journey, which was different from that of 1905 in many ways. Much of it was more southerly, for one thing (though still remote from southern "civilization"), and it took much more advantage of the railway, especially for westerly travel. The trip began in Ottawa on May 22 when the commissioners left for Timiskaming via Mattawa on the CPR, and thence by boat to New Liskeard and North Timiskaming to begin retracing their route to Abitibi of the summer before. The Abitibi band was admitted to the treaty on June 7 and 8. Here the commissioners had to explain to Indians who hunted principally in Quebec (these were the majority at Abitibi Post, which is actually situated in Quebec) that they could not enter the treaty because the federal government had made no agreement with that province. In the official report of the 1906 treaty-making there is a brief discussion of the historical and contemporary differences between French- and British-based Indian policies. Ontario, the writer says, "recognizes the title of the Indians to the lands occupied by them as their hunting grounds, and their right to compensation for such portions as have from time to time been surrendered by them," while Quebec "has followed the French policy, which did not admit the claims of the Indians to the lands in the province, but they were held to be the property of the Crown by right of discovery and conquest" (JB 13). It could not have been easy to make this distinction sound sensible to nomadic people, but the report records no difficulty. The Quebec Cree were left with the understanding that a "conference would be held with them later," and that the federal government would try to negotiate land for them. Samuel Stewart made the Abitibi trip for that purpose in 1908.

The party then retraced its steps to Haileybury and the Timiskaming and Northern Ontario railway for Latchford, the jumping-off place for Matachewan, via the Montreal River, where the treaty was concluded on June 21. "Instead of tamely retracing our route to Latchford," Pelham Edgar says, "we decided to make a detour through Lady Evelyn Lake and Temagami, connecting with the T. and N.O. at Temagami station" ("1200 Miles" 62). Doing so, the group was following a route that was by 1905 already famous with recreational canoe trippers. It would be interesting to know Scott's thoughts along this route, close to the one on which his poet friend and sometime canoeing partner Archibald Lampman had strained his weak heart in 1896. This was also, beginning in 1906, Archie Belaney — not yet Grey Owl — country. And the area has since been made famous for another reason, an indirect legacy of the treaty-making, the dispute between loggers and Teme-Augama Indians over control of the Temagami Forest.

From Temagami Station the treaty party went by rail to another jumping-off place, Biscotasing. From here they canoed to Mattagami via the Spanish River, concluding the treaty at Mattagami Post on July 8. "At present," Edgar writes in "Twelve Hundred Miles by Canoe," "our northern country is almost impenetrable, save by the regular water routes. These lie almost north and south. Therefore to go, for example, from Mattagami to Flying Post, one cannot comfortably strike westward. It is necessary to retrace one's steps to Bisco and strike north-west again from that point" (157). Biscotasing regained on July 11, the party (now joined by Edmund Morris) left on the twelfth for Flying Post, where the treaty was made on July 16.

On Friday, July 20, the party left by train for Chapleau, and then Missinaibi, the start of the canoe trip to Brunswick House where Scott had been in 1899. The treaty was concluded there on July 25. Back at Missinaibi on the twenty-ninth, the group departed for Heron Bay and the expedition, already described, up the low waters of the Pic and White Otter rivers to Long Lake where the treaty was signed on August 9. By August 16 the party had reached Ottawa again.

THESE TWO VENTURES OF WHITES into the "wilderness" are almost paradigmatic encounters between what Scott and his contemporaries called civilized and primitive peoples. Some at least of the northern Ojibway and Cree were living in 1905 (if the huge influence of the HBC could be discounted) very much as their forebears had lived, time out of mind, despite three centuries of European contact. The northern lands that the Cree and Ojibway occupied were part of the last Canadian frontier, as well, and something of the old Canadian pioneering pattern may be seen being played out again. Again officialdom, the law, arrives before the main influx of settlers. Again the aboriginal inhabitants of the land are dealt with "fairly," at least in the light of terms (like legal ownership of the land) totally foreign to them, at least when the negotiations are compared with harsher strategies pursued in the United States, South America, and elsewhere. The patterns are Canadian, but they were also worked out with variations in other countries that were colonized over the backs of an indigenous population. Students of many postcolonial literatures find themselves dealing with the image or the place or the absence of the aborigine, or "indigene," according to Terry Goldie's semiosis (*Fear and Temptation: The Image of the Indigene in Canadian, Australian, and New Zealand Literatures*).

Let me be more specific about the sort of encounter that took place 14 times during the two summers of 1905 and 1906, dealing first with the treaty party and then with the people they were treating with.

To describe the official treaty party of 1905 is to describe a group of men who are not merely individuals. They are symbols, each one of them representing an entity larger than himself. And as they travelled in relative harmony, so the institutions they represented are interlocking and for the most part mutually serving. I describe the men as they arranged themselves for the camera in front of a tent and under the Union Jack at Albany Post (figure 2). Standing at attention and framing the civilians are Constables J. L. Vanasse and James Parkinson of the North-West Mounted Police. They are along to guard the treasure chest full of treaty money ("thirty thousand dollars in small notes") and for the sake of what Scott called in "The Last of the Indian Treaties" "the wholesome fear of the white man's law which they inspired" (111).

Figure 2, PA-59549

Seated on the ground, on the left, is T. C. Rae, chief trader of the Hudson's Bay Company. He is the coordinator, the facilitator, of the journey. He sees to the details of transportation, arranges for the Native crews, and so on. The route taken by the commission is not only an ancient Indian route, but an important trading highway also, still in 1905 a theatre of competition for furs between the HBC and Revillon Frères. But the HBC owns the forts along the way where the treaty is made. Having become the summer centres of the lives of people dependent on HBC goods for their very survival, these are logical stopping places for the treaty party. T. C. Rae is acting for a Winnipeg-based company more than willing to help the treaty commission, knowing that a great many of those small notes will purchase merchandise at its stores. At Abitibi, according to Samuel Stewart, food for the feast was also purchased from the HBC store. This must have happened at other posts, as well, though no journal confirms it.

Dr. A. G. Meindl of North Bay sits to the right of Rae. He acts as medical officer. He will examine and inoculate and treat the Indians to the best of his ability, and will supply an appendix to "The James Bay Treaty" concerning the medical conditions he encounters in which tuberculosis is tragically prominent.

In seated dignity are the three treaty commissioners themselves. Daniel G. MacMartin, of Perth, Ontario, is in the middle. He is keeping an eye on things for the Ontario government whose agreement to make the treaty had to be sought and in whose jurisdiction reserves will be chosen and surveyed. MacMartin is to make sure that no reserves are located on future sources of water power or mineral resources. On either side of MacMartin sit the two Dominion commissioners, Samuel Stewart and Duncan Campbell Scott of Indian Affairs. They are the official negotiators, or would be if there were anything to negotiate. They have only fixed terms to offer and no authority to bargain.

Moreover, the commissioners are presumably not mentioning another set of terms that already bind the Indians and restrict their control over their own affairs. The 1876 Indian Act defines them as minors. What is the relationship between the Indian Act and the treaties? It seems that the original document, fashioned without consultation of the Indians, takes overriding precedence. At least amendments to the Indian Act progressively eroded certain promises that were supposed to have had the permanence of the very elements. "Indians are never slow in making demands," says Scott in "Indian Affairs 1763–1841," "and a promise sinks into their minds and becomes as perdurable as an index of brass" (707). That must have been inconvenient, since the same could not be said of the whites. According to Brian Titley, Scott's minister Frank Oliver, addressing the Commons in 1906, "conceded that, while Indian rights ought to be protected, they should not be allowed to interfere with those of whites — 'and if it becomes a question between the Indian and the whites, the interests of the whites will have to be provided for.' He assured the House that the department was making every effort to secure the surrender of 'surplus' Indian land" (21). So much for treaty promises of stable reserves made to Prairie Indians. The question of land surrenders returns in chapter 5, where I examine Scott's nonfiction.

Here are commissioners Scott and Stewart in 1905, at any rate, making Treaty 9 against the background of an Indian Act that was probably unmentioned because it was invisible to them, not a factor. They will give the government's speeches and respond to the speeches of the Indians. They will supervise the signing of the treaty and hand out the treaty money. Perhaps they are seated one on either side of MacMartin for the sake of symmetry, a prominent feature of the photo as a whole, but there is evidence that the two didn't always see eye to eye. If Scott's oblique comments about Stewart in a letter to Pelham Edgar can be credited, the two are opposite sorts of civil servant, one of them (Stewart) self-serving and the other idealistic. Such was the treaty party in 1905.

There were some changes to the party in 1906. Constable Parkinson was promoted and so not available. The policemen seem to have been merely symbolic, anyway, perhaps never more so than when Vanasse, carrying the

Union Jack, led the disgruntled treaty party through a group of Ojibway gathered for the White Dog Feast in 1905 (see chapter 7). There is no mention of police services really being needed, no hint that the treasure chest was ever in danger. Vanasse does stand out from Parkinson in two small but interesting ways. There is his article "The White Dog Feast, Relating an Incident of the Visit of the James Bay Treaty Commission to the [Lac Seul] Ojibway Indian Reserve," two-thirds of which actually describes quite sympathetically Ojibway beliefs and ceremonies. Also, writing to Pelham Edgar on December 11 of 1906, Scott mentions that "Joe Vanasse was here a moment ago — has bought 200 acres near Ville Marie [on Lake Timiskaming] and is full of energetic plans" (ASB). It sounds as though Vanasse became friendly with Scott, and also with the North he was travelling through.

In his useful summary of the treaty trips, James Morrison mentions that in 1906 Scott "brought along Henry Dunneth, the athletic son of an Ottawa friend, as an extra paddler" ("The Poet and the Indians" 5), but another change was much more significant, at least for Scott. Pelham Edgar replaced T. C. Rae. So it is diplomatically put in the official report to the superintendent of Indian Affairs, at least; Edgar-for-Rae was not an even substitution. Edgar was a professor of English at Victoria College at the University of Toronto and would not have been replacing Rae as trip coordinator. He was also one of Scott's closest friends. The report says that Edgar "acted as secretary." He was given the task of writing the official journal that Scott had kept in 1905. But one hardly needs Scott's expression of glee in a letter to Edgar ("You've been appointed. Ain't it bully!" *More Letters* 31) to suspect that he had negotiated a once-in-a-lifetime holiday for his friend, and good company for himself.

We have to stretch a point to take Edgar seriously as an official member of the treaty party, but privately he seems to have made a deep difference to his friend. Scott had two notebooks with him in 1905 and 1906. One contained his official journal; the other was the three-by-five-inch notebook in which he had since 1899 made drafts of poems. In the latter there are signs of activity in the summer of 1905, but during the summer of 1906 there is a poetic explosion fascinating to imagine happening at such a distance from a study in Ottawa, in such unorthodox writing conditions — the canoe travel, the blackflies and mosquitoes, the general roughing it. If Scott had written only the lengthy "Spring on Mattagami" on the trip, that would have been remarkable enough, but there was also "The Half-breed Girl" and a number of the other poems that were privately printed as *Via Borealis* late in 1906 and dedicated to Pelham Edgar. Scott was probably working on some fiction that summer, as well. He had brought a few stories along, at least, and Edgar's journal says that he read them aloud. Information about the particulars is lacking, but internal evidence and publishing history point to "Vengeance Is Mine," "Spirit River," and "Expiation."

I linger on Edgar and his influence on Scott to highlight another respect in which those journeys are symbolic. There is no particular need to subdivide the pair of friends into poet and critic; together they represent the sophisticated cultural achievements of their time and place. And they bring with them and read aloud from *The Oxford Book of English Poetry,* an anthology of the literary tradition of which, to them, Canadian poetry was a branch. This has always created for me a fabulously incongruous image, much of it supplied by photographs like that of Scott and Stewart (the latter giving place to Edgar in 1906) sitting side by side in the middle of a huge Peterborough canoe that has its own birchbark ancestry, while a Native crew paddles them up a northern river that to the passengers at least is the essence of the wild (see figure 3). Other than the scenery the entertainment might be a reading of poems like George Meredith's very European "Love in the Valley," Scott's model for "Spring on Mattagami." Scott was not unaware of such incongruities. An earlier trip had produced "Night Hymns on Lake Nipigon" whose sapphics are as novel a container of the wilderness subject as the cultural opposites of the poem itself, the Indian and white canoeists and their simultaneous rendition of "Adeste Fideles" in Ojibway and Latin. Scott had in 1901 described the coat of arms of Donald Smith (better known as Lord Strathcona, the elevation being his reward for HBC and CPR entrepreneurship) as a "voyageur's song played upon a sackbut." He must have been aware that such wonderful incongruities are part of the paradoxical nature of being Euro-Canadian, new and old at once: "*Arms, gules* on a fesse argent between a demi-lion rampant in chief, and a canoe of the last with four men paddling proper, in the bow a flag of the second, flowing to the dexter, inserted with the letters N.W. of the last. *Crest,* on a mount, vert, a beaver eating into a maple tree proper. *Motto,* perseverance" ("Lord

Figure 3, PA-59516

Strathcona" 552). I can imagine Edward Lear, creator of "The Heraldic Blazon of Foss the Cat," chortling in recognition.

The posed travellers, then, are members of an overarching institution miscalled civilization, the latest leading edge of imperialism and progress. In themselves they do not represent quite all of the white network in the North, but they encounter the others on their way. Clustered near the Hudson's Bay Company post are the missions, or churches, or in some cases their representatives. Reverend Holmes, the bishop of Moosonee whom Scott first met at Moose Factory in 1905, crossed the treaty party's path a couple of times in 1906. These meetings are made to look less than accidental by almost identical comments in the journals of Pelham Edgar and Edmund Morris that the bishop remained behind after the departure of the treaty group "to obtain his tithe." At some of the older and more important centres like Fort Albany and Moose Factory there are also schools and teachers of Indian classes. The schools and the churches can scarcely be separated, in the matter of Indian education, and both are acting in the North as arms of the Indian Department for which Christianizing and educating are barely distinguishable aspects of the civilizing process. At the end of the 1905 trip the treaty group also met township surveyors working for the Ontario government, and surveyors for the Timiskaming and Northern Ontario Railroad. They met prospectors, as well, not to mention tourists and adventurers of various sorts. Just how dramatically progress was encroaching on the North is clear from Samuel Stewart's description of the scene at the foot of Couchiching Falls in his 1908 journal:

> There was a very great change in this place since our last visit. Then the district was in its natural state, and we had enjoyed the walk along the river, and had no difficulty in getting a good view of the beautiful falls. Now a tramway runs from the foot to the head of the falls, & a large log house has been erected near the first fall for the accommodation of the men engaged in construction work. The timber both for the tramway and for the house was cut in the woods near the falls, and the brush from the trees make [*sic*] an almost impassable barrier between the road and the river. (149)

On the more southerly 1906 journey, that series of north-south canoe trips stitched together by the CPR railway running east and west, new northern towns like Cobalt and New Liskeard were encountered. This was far from Ottawa still, but never for long distant from the "line," the tracks that tie the country together.

ONE OF THE FASCINATIONS of those treaty-making trips, then, is the unusual concentration of Euro-Canadian institutions discovered in the act of perpetuating themselves, this civilization expanding and consolidating its territory. The instruments of progress are very much in evidence, the tools by which the surveyors laid their abstract grid over the land, preparing the foundation for the mapping that made the North intelligible to foreign minds, and the incredible amphibious "alligator boat" — part vessel, part stoneboat — designed to winch itself up rapids or even smack through the forest. But more important than these technological wonders were the core technologies of writing and calculating that underlay them.

One reason so much information survives about those journeys is that so much trust was placed in words and figures during them. It's interesting that one of Scott's early causes, in the Toronto *Globe* column "At the Mermaid Inn," was the establishment of a national archive where the Canadian past could accumulate until it amounted to something, because that is where one goes now to follow his career and to seek context for it — in fact, to various archives in Ottawa, Kingston, Toronto, Winnipeg, and so on. I first found Scott's photographic record of the trips in the National Photography Collection (the Ontario Archives has a set and they also appear in Scott's own album preserved in the National Library's A. S. Bourinot papers). And I have been haunting libraries, those storehouses of words and figures, to find the periodicals and the books that contain the reports and articles and essays and poems and stories that contribute to the rather full account of the treaty journeys it is possible to assemble — drawing on the vast network of interlocking information systems that is so second nature to those of us brought up in it as to be practically invisible. The key to this labyrinth is the secret of making it visible. Threading it may not then be easy, but it is not impossible. In this context, far from being merely the passive, uncomprehending signatories of the treaty, the dupes of the whites, the Cree and Ojibway Indians are the key.

So they became for me, anyway, spending my days in libraries reading all I could find about Treaty 9, amassing material, building up the picture I am sharing here; then feeling more than hearing a murmur that gradually rose to intelligibility, a resounding silence created by the absence of documents detailing from their perspective the part played by the Indians in the treaty-making. That documents should be scarce is not surprising, of course. For the most part lacking the white communication technologies, having little use for them in 1905–06, the northern Indians could not have been expected to leave many traces where a researcher would inevitably find them. It may be more surprising that some documents do now exist in oral memories (some of these to be found in the Ojibway–Cree Cultural Centre in Timmins) put into English by latter-day educated Natives, but that is not the point. The point is this: the huge imbalance of power between the two parties negotiating Treaty 9, leaving behind such a one-sided view of the negotiations, also creates a vacuum of desire, a silence or emptiness that cries out to be filled.

What of the Indians, then . . . ?

BUT WHAT ARE INDIANS? I'm not asking whether it makes sense to think of Indians as members of a "red" race, or as those who in Canada possess legal Indian status, there being a large population of nonstatus "red" people in the land. These important questions come up in chapter 5. I'm raising a question of terminology at the moment. Indians would be simply nationals of India but for certain uncorrected European fancies of which Christopher Columbus's voyage ("history's most stunning accident," according to the TV documentary, *Columbus and the Age of Discovery*) was the bravest (or most publicized) expression. We now understand Indians, or Amerindians, to be members of the many cultures indigenous to the New World. Despite the vast differences between them, it makes sense to regard all these cultures as resembling each other more than any of them resembles one or another of that complex of European cultures often miscalled white. The understanding makes the word useful enough to retain, even though it's the wrong word. Rather than emphasizing the contingency of the word by placing it in quotation marks each time I use it, I print it here under erasure, borrowing a stratagem (though not a system) from Jacques Derrida:[2] ~~Indian~~. Also: ~~white~~, though this second cancellation highlights an ethnicity that has been a sort of skin — unconscious, ignored, and thus too easily universalized. I present the words this way once, expecting the reader to see a shade of the X each time the word reappears.

For "Indian" or "Indians" I also use some of the newer substitutes, like "Natives" (capitalized to avoid the sense in which I am native to this country) or "First Nations Peoples." "Amerindian," Olive Dickason's preferred term (see her discussion of "The Problem of Interpretation" in *Canada's First Nations*), might do if the word "Indian" were not so embedded in my sources. I find "indigene" (from indigenous) off-putting, though it does answer the need for a general term in such studies as Terry Goldie's *Fear and Temptation* and, to a much lesser extent, Arnold Itwaru's *The Invention of Canada*. On the CBC (*As It Happens*) I heard a moderate (Brian Maracle) and a militant (Lenore Keeshig-Tobias) agree that the most accurate and least offensive general term for "Indian" would be "Turtle Islander." Turtle Island is the globe that grew on Turtle's back from a pat of mud that Muskrat dived into the great flood to find. The origin myth is widespread among North American First Nations peoples, and Turtle Island often appears, without explanation that it means the world, in their writings. But the best word belongs to the First Peoples. The whole question of terminology encapsulates the wider problem of cultural invasion or appropriation risked by anyone who writes on this subject. Even though I refer with relative relief to Cree and Ojibway whenever possible, these tribal names are white labels, too. But Ininiwag and Anishinaabe, the Cree and Ojibway names for themselves, belong in my vocabulary no more than Turtle

Islander. I return to my argument no further ahead, then, though I have made my mark: X.

No further ahead, but not necessarily floundering. There are good reasons for not getting locked into one safe term like "Amerindian." Some lines in a poem by David Bromige, anticipating the political correctness debate by almost 20 years, come to mind:

> Car stopping — negress, if one can say so,
> Afro-American? A lady with dark skin —
> just say, *a woman* — some loss of accuracy. . . . (80)

Some loss of accuracy, yes. Sometimes "Indian" is the right term, as when I refer directly or obliquely to the views on First Peoples of Scott and his contemporaries. Beyond that, using a variety of terms may be a way of recognizing the present flux of thinking in the areas of culture and race.[3]

WHAT OF THE CREE AND OJIBWAY, then, objects of the combined resources of so many tentacles of white civilization? There is no single Treaty 9 photograph that might ground the difficult explanation, for a white man, of what they were about, nothing like the one of the treaty group, although the photographs dispersed through this book (artifacts of the European "gaze") will supply some visual impressions. Neat parallels are impossible, and that is just as well. The photograph of a group of men at Fort Hope (figure 4), certainly doesn't do it. This picture appears on the cover of Paul Driben and Robert S. Trudeau's

Figure 4, PA-59539

When Freedom Is Lost: The Dark Side of the Relationship Between Government and the Fort Hope Band, a book that makes the name of the post, now a desperate community plagued by unemployment and religious division, seem terribly ironic.

The men in the photograph are a small arc of the inner circle formed by the men for the feast that followed each treaty-signing. Women and children may be dimly seen in their outer circle just in front of the palisade. One obvious thing about these men is that they have no experience in posing for cameras. The selves of the men in this group seem much nearer the surface than those of the whites in the other photograph, not that they can be read. They are mysterious to me because their culture is Other, and anonymous because their names were not considered important enough to record except in band rolls. It is most likely Scott these people are looking at, though his presence in some of the photos, camera case strapped around his neck, proves that someone else occasionally took pictures. Their poses seem at first glance almost abject — sitting on the canvas groundsheet, hands clasped between knees — but unguarded is a safer word. They appear anything but happy, as do most of the subjects of the photographs taken on the trip, which may just mean that Scott had the sense not to ask them to say "Cheese." These men are not dressed like the Indians of popular conception, most of whom were Plains Indians. Their clothing was probably bought from the HBC. Only one of Scott's photographs features a man in traditional costume. This is Chief Espaniol, who is definitely posing outside of the Hudson's Bay store at Biscotasing in 1906 (figure 5). The treaty-making may have been a proud moment for him; he was one of those who had petitioned for the treaty in 1901. Many of the women, in other photographs, are dressed almost exclusively in plaids: shawls, dresses, and skirts. These garments themselves would almost have been enough to suggest "the gleam of loch and shealing" and the rest of the Scottish heritage of "The Half-breed Girl," a poem I discuss in chapter 9.

According to an 1890 report on the northern Indians prepared by E. B. Borron, "to draw the line between whites and Indians, with any degree of precision, is in my humble opinion, simply impossible. Quite a large proportion of the natives of the territory, that I have seen, appear to have more or less European blood in their veins" (HBCa 2). The commissioners apparently felt they could draw the line. "When the treaty party visited Moose Factory, they refused to allow 25 families to participate in the treaty. The Commissioners said that these people were 'half-breeds' and were not living like Indians" (*Nishnawbe-Aski Nation* 37). A glance at these people in the photographs shows the European influence on their dress; their garments in turn testify to the white influence on their lives, their economy, their material culture, in some cases on their spiritual orientation. It's not hard to understand how a man like Scott might look at them and feel that the process of assimilation was irreversible.

Figure 5, PA-43561

"Have you any notion," Virginia Woolf writes in *A Room of One's Own,* "how many books are written about women in the course of one year? Have you any notion how many are written by men?" (27). I can imagine a very similar question being asked by a Native: "Have you any notion how many books about Indians are written by whites in a given year?" And Woolf's analysis of why it is that men who possess all the power are yet obsessed with powerless, "inferior" women has its relevance to the parallel obsession of "civilized" people with "savages." Indeed, she approaches the analogy herself:

> Women have served all these centuries as looking-glasses possessing the magic and delicious power of reflecting the figure of man at twice its natural size. Without that power probably the earth would still be swamp and jungle. The glories of all our wars would be unknown. We should still be scratching the outlines of deer on the remains of mutton bones and bartering flints for sheep skins or whatever simple ornament took our unsophisticated taste. (35–36)

Woolf's irony has its own power. With its moderate tone, scarcely dipping into sarcasm (rage boiling between the lines), *A Room of One's Own* has outlasted Woolf and become a manual of feminist sense. It is a seduction so beautifully suave and lucid as to conduct the reader irresistibly inside itself. "Genuine and thorough comprehension of otherness is possible only if the self can somehow negate or at least severely bracket the values, assumptions and ideology of his culture" (65), says Abdul JanMohamed. Woolf's is one of the riskier ways of conveying otherness: so brilliantly and effortlessly occupying the language, the style of the oppressor, as to render oppression palpable. I know of no more effective equivalent in Native writing than John P. Kelly's address to the Royal Commission on the Northern Environment.

The Treaty 3 area adjoins the southwesterly border of that of Treaty 9, as I have said. Treaty 3 Indians in the Lac Seul area were the ones whose ceremonies Scott interrupted. It is as their grand chief that John Kelly speaks to the royal commission in 1977. His address begins with some truths about the treaty, how little time the Ojibway were given to consider it, how badly the terms were kept. "Governments create commissions only when they must," he says. "Governments then use commissions for their own purposes" (Ondaatje, *Ink Lake* 583). These are not naive words. Their equivalent have been spoken about Treaty 9, as I will show.

One of the fascinations of Kelly's address is how it mixes such direct statement with the technique of teaching obliquely through storytelling. One of his legends is about "a stranger from somewhere in the sunrise beyond the lakes" who appeared during a terrible period of hunger-causing storm. The stranger mastered the wind, cutting off its arms and legs, producing a period of calm and plenty, even gluttony. But eventually "a mysterious curse spread over the earth," a worse pestilence than the former turbulence. The Midewewin[4] elders sang and prayed to Manitou. Then came "a tumult mightier than all the storms that have clapped in the heavens since the beginning of time" (584). This fury, interpreted by a "Midewewin Elder of the Fifth Order," signified that "Man may never try his wiles and power against the Spirit of the Universe, nor is it good to reap from the acts of those who pitch their minds against Manitou" (584–85). The story is no less powerful for its familiarity, and Kelly's eloquence carries on into an adaptation of the story to present times:

> Mr. Commissioner, it seems to me that the stranger from the sunrise beyond the lakes just keeps coming back. Each time he promises us perpetual repose and gluttony, and leaves us with famine and disease. It also appears that, as the years go by, the circle of the Ojibway gets bigger and bigger. Canadians of all colours and religions are entering that circle. You might feel that you have roots somewhere else, but in reality, you are right here with us. I do not know if you feel the throbbing of the land in your chest, and if you feel the bear is your brother with a spirit purer and stronger than yours, or if the elk is on a higher level of life than is man. You may not share my spiritual anguish as I see the earth ravaged by the stranger, but you can no longer escape my fate as the soil turns barren and the rivers poison. Much against my will, and probably yours, time and circumstance have put us together in the same circle. And so I come not to plead with you to save me from the monstrous stranger of capitalist greed and technology. I come to inform you that my danger is your danger too. My genocide is your genocide. (585)

I quote only three more sentences from this powerful speech that was swallowed up with other such material in the mass of briefs to the commission until it came to Michael Ondaatje's attention while he was collecting material for *From Ink Lake: Canadian Stories:* "We have shown that we can survive as a race. We have proved that we will not be assimilated. We have demonstrated that our culture has a vitality that cannot be suppressed" (587).

Were the Indian speeches this eloquent in 1905 and 1906, that of Missabay at Osnaburgh, say, or Moonias at Fort Hope, or Esau Omakess at New Post, with whom Stewart was "favourably impressed" (35)? It seems not, but then we only have bits of them filtered through the words of white men who were not paying much attention. It would be unlikely that any Cree or Ojibway spokesman could at that time have expressed himself as John Kelly does, in terms both traditional and modern, based at once on legend and on research into documents. But who would doubt that the elders Scott met had their share of wisdom? Scott, apparently. His essay "The Last of the Indian Treaties" is full of warmth for his "charges," and it certainly registers the irony in the imbalance between the treating parties, but the warmth turns patronizing in the implicit adoption of the terms of the Indian Act ("the Indian is a minor under the law") as Scott's own:

> To individuals whose transactions had been heretofore limited to computation with sticks and skins our errand must indeed have been dark.
>
> They were to make certain promises and we were to make certain promises, but our purpose and our reasons were alike unknowable. What could they grasp of the pronouncement on the Indian tenure which had been delivered

> by the law lords of the Crown, what of the elaborate negotiations between a dominion and a province which had made the treaty possible, what of the sense of traditional policy which brooded over the whole? Nothing. So there was no basis for argument. The simpler facts had to be stated, and the parental idea developed that the King is the great father of the Indians, watchful over their interests, and ever compassionate. (*Circle* 115)

The government believes these people are children, then, but a treaty, like any legal contract, is an agreement concluded between adults. That buried fact has not gone unnoticed by present-day Treaty 9 Indians. Inevitably the treaty came up often in the Native submissions to the Royal Commission on the Northern Environment.

Speaking for the Moose Factory Band Council on February 2, 1978, Chief Munroe Linklater shows that, like John Kelly, he has done his research; he has read Scott's journal and maybe "The Last of the Indian Treaties" as well. He also quotes one of his grandfathers who signed Treaty 9 at Fort Albany. Since he addresses the treaty directly, he is worth quoting at length. First, about the treaty and its commissioners:

> In their travels of the watersheds of James Bay, His Majesty's treaty party was explicitly instructed to carry out one specific mission, and that was to acquire this vast tract of land mass for a handful of coins annually and place the native in a parcel of land to pursue their one way of life until interruption came along, which it has. It was apparent.
>
> a) that the treaty party was not to alter its specific terms as laid down in Ottawa whether they were accepted or not.
>
> b) that the officials representing the king fully well knew the value of the land requested to be ceded to the Crown.
>
> c) that they were aware that the natives were not able to communicate with them in the full sense of the word.
>
> d) that the natives had no counsel.
>
> e) that the natives were impressed by the pomp and ceremony and the authority of the officials.
>
> f) that they were dealing with uneducated people in the legal sense of the word.
>
> g) that the treaty party capitalized on the occasion by exploiting the accompanying clergy, which the natives had respected, to gain their own needs.
>
> h) that the natives really did not know or fully understand the meaning and implications of the treaty.

i) that the father image was being advanced by the authorities.

j) that the alleged consideration that was being advanced by the treaty party to the natives in exchange for the ceded land was not totally appreciated by the natives, nor could they understand the concept binding their heirs and assigns to these documents.

k) that respect and the ceremony with which the officials were dealing with the natives lulled them into a passive mood as the journals of the party would indicate.

l) that forever and a day for all intents and purposes it is obvious to whoever reads these journals of the treaty party and history in the making, that His Majesty's treaty party commissioners perpetrated legal fraud in a very sophisticated manner, upon unsophisticated, unsuspecting natives. We have well recognized and undisputed rights to these aboriginal lands. (11–12)

Linklater's conclusion arches around to his elders at the turn of the century and introduces the wisdom of his grandfather, appropriately named Solomon,[5] "who signed the treaty," and is part of a conversation with "the late Bishop Renison." The source of the quotation is not given, and I was not so convinced of its unmediated authenticity as I was of Kelly's prose, even before I located most of the passage verbatim in Robert John Renison's *For Such a Time as This,* but the grandfather's authority is at least partially restored by the grandson's underwriting of what he says:

> Solomon had commented, "wherever the whiteman goes he makes work and trouble, he is not happy himself and therefore cannot make others happy." Renison replied, "But surely, Solomon, you must admit that civilization is a good thing, for without it the human race would not progress." Solomon rolled his black tobacco between his palm and asked, "But what are you progressing to? The wonders you are making do not change the body of man nor contribute to his happiness.
>
> "I have been in Cochrane and I once went with the Governor of the Hudson Bay Company to Montreal. Along the height of land the trees were dead and burned by the whiteman, the moose and beaver are gone forever, the flowers and the moss have been scraped off the hills when there [*sic*] were looking for gold, the lakes where the ducks used to breed are green with poison from mines. The railroad train is great Medicine, but it is not half so terrible as the lightning of an August storm. Kitche-Manitou would never have made these things to pass forever from his world. The whiteman makes a god of himself. In your cities men live in

> cliffs, like swallows in the river bank, and many cannot see the sun. I am even told that men are awakened by a devil's machine before daybreak year after year, and they work all day, every day from home, never seeing their own children by daylight.
>
> "As for me, I work and I rest as I please, when the sun rises in the morning, if the day is fine I call to my wife and we pack our tent and load our canoe. We paddle forty miles downstream. When the sun returns to the tops of the trees in the evening, I push the canoe ashore with my paddle and in a half an hour, there is a new tent site and a new fire. And when the stars come out at night, wherever they find me I am at home." (13–14; compare *For Such a Time* 93–94)

This is enough to make the deskbound writer pause at his computer keys and look out the window, envisioning through the cityscape spread below him some personal version of northern peace and respite from the welter of research. Scott must also have tuned out of his Indian Affairs office, aching for Lake Nipigon, "that most heroic of all the lakes," as he called it, writing to Pelham Edgar (ASB), or Lake Achigan where he camped with Archibald Lampman, and which E. K. Brown says "was one of the special places for his imaginative life" ("Memoir" xix). Solomon knows enough about "civilization" to regard his home as a natural refuge from all "the welter of the lives of men" that Scott wrote about in "The Height of Land." Whether one takes Solomon literally (in which case the next question is "What on earth is keeping me here?") or recognizes that Bishop Renison has slipped him into the convention of the perfectly balanced and sensible norm of satire, living as he does the rich simple life that we need to believe we have lost (and that men often seek in unempowered women), the fact is that Solomon and Scott, speaking respectively from north and south of the symbolic height of land, have a lot in common.

Perhaps Solomon had not experienced enough of the difference between plain and sophisticated lifestyles in 1905 to speak to Scott as he did to Bishop Renison but, in any event, there would have been no occasion for such conversation. Scott and his party had a deadline and a tight schedule. They had to arrange the cession of 90,000 acres of Northern Ontario in 1905, 40,000 more in 1906. That left little time for listening and discussing, even if Scott had had the impression that the Indians could understand him. Widely differing attitudes to time, in fact, do much to separate the two races. The commissioners felt liberal in allowing the Indians overnight to deliberate over the treaty, but their descendants say that "Usually these matters were considered for a very long time, at least five years" (RCNE submission by Cat Lake Reserve, December 6, 1977). Apparently overnight was at least relatively generous. Representing the Kishechewan Band at the

RCNE, Moose Factory, 1978, James Wesley says that "These commissioners, that were representing the Crown in the negotiation process, gave our people one hour to make a decision. In that short hour our people did not have a chance to understand or discuss much of what was going on because of the language . . ." (4). Not all of the Indians were hesitant, of course; some of them had been requesting the treaty for more than five years, whether or not they knew what it would involve.

"WHAT COULD THEY GRASP . . . ? Nothing." This question and answer is the nub of the passage in "The Last of the Indian Treaties" where Scott expresses his sense of helplessness before the cultural gulf between the treating parties. Thomas Linklater reads this admission as invalidating the treaty, and how could anyone not seduced by realpolitik disagree? Scott was mistaking cultural difference for cultural inferiority; he was treating men as children, and it's easy for us to see how his own culture invisibly conspired against *his* seeing that. It's easy to wish that he had been vouchsafed the internal distance that time has granted us, but he can't be plucked out of this 1905 encounter, like an Ebenezer Scrooge by some consciousness-raising ghost, and retroactively granted the power to understand before it's too late. "One thing about which fish know exactly nothing," says Marshall McLuhan in *War and Peace in the Global Village,* "is water, since they have no anti-environment which would enable them to perceive the element they live in. . . . What fish are able to see bears a close analogy to that degree of awareness which all people have in relation to any new environment created by a new technology — just about zero" (175). When the *Titanic* went down, it most likely didn't occur to Scott that an Indian might have advised taking icebergs more seriously. ("Our ancestors had learned to live with nature, not against it," says John Kelly. "An elder once said to me: 'Do not fight against the cold, or you will freeze'" [587].) As will be seen, Scott did have serious doubts — in fact, he was a tortured man — but they seem to have been personal doubts. He seems not to have formulated for himself any critique of the cocoon of culture in which he led his life.

History has rolled in a new set of assumptions, a new enlightenment about the human status of Native peoples, that ironizes even "The Last of the Indian Treaties," Scott's most liberal nonfiction text about Indians. It's easy to point out the essay's limitations, impossible to produce a text that is not in its turn wide open to ironizing by another revolution of the wheel. How to catch oneself out before history does: an anxiety addressed by theory. It causes the "problematization" of stances. It makes of self-doubt an active principle of probe, infects critical texts to their benefit, fosters "an humilitas sufficient to make [one] of use" (Olson 25). It leads me back to that passage about cultural gap in "The Last of the Indian Treaties." The passage emits an energy of frustration that suggests Scott felt the gap keenly. The rest of his Indian Affairs career was devoted to eliminating the gap entirely. If he had succeeded, it's worth remembering, the historical irony would be harder to see. That he didn't lends poignancy to an openness he was only afterward to demonstrate in fiction and poetry.

NOTES

1. Scott had been up and down the Pic River on the 1899 trip. "A great many miles I have been paddled in canoes," he wrote to his daughter Elizabeth on August 13, 1899, "and my bum got very tired of it sometimes." He went on to deal thus with the Pic: "One river I travelled is called the Pic and it is quite as crooked as this line [Scott's pen zags its way down the right-hand margin of the page] and the water is very thick with mud so I made up a little nonsense verse about it.

    There once was a stream called the Pic
    A stream so exceedingly thick
    That when you go through
    With a boat or canoe
    You carry a shovel and pick"

2. This is something simpler than "the strategy of using the only available language while not subscribing to its premises" (*Of Grammatology* xviii), as Gayatri Spivak puts it, because substitutes for "Indian" are available.
3. According to Marie Annharte Baker, it is necessary to go beyond terms into names: "It is not enough to have the outer trappings of being Indian or Native, such as braids or beads. I claim my identity through my motherline. My mother was fluent in the language and spoke to me in it when I was a child. I identify as Anishinabe because of the way I was treated by my mother and relatives. I don't take the racial designations to be as important. Some people even prefer terms for themselves and not names. I think terms such as 'Aboriginal,' 'Metis,' or even 'First Nations' do not tell as much as the name of a people. In addition to the legal designations or anthropological terms applied to Anishinabeg, there are the many distinct names for the various bands, clans, or family groups that lived across the country" (64).
4. Midewewin (Mi-day-we-win) means Grand Medicine Society, according to Selwyn Dewdney (*Indian Rock Paintings* 12). Basil Johnston introduces the chapter of his *Ojibway Ceremonies* on "The Society of Medicine" as follows: "The term Midewewin could mean The Society of Good Hearted Ones (from mino 'good,' and dewewin 'hearted'). It could also mean The Resonance (from midewe 'the sound'), as a reference to the drums and the chants that were used in its ceremonies" (95).
5. Appropriately in the Christian tradition, at least. In "This Also Is You: Some Classics of Native Canadian Literature," Robert Bringhurst says of the Haida poets and storytellers that "their native names are almost always lost to us, like the rich sound of their voices. We know them instead by bizarre colonial labels like Moses and Abraham, Albert and Charles, Stevens and Sydney, gifts of a missionary culture that promoted European social conventions as zealously as it promoted the Christian religion" (38).

2

Knotted G String: "The Last of the Indian Treaties" in Context

Perhaps we can only read a narrative, any narrative, by reading with or against a meta-narrative that is assumed, often unconsciously, by the reader or by the culture or by the writer.

Robert Kroetsch, The Lovely Treachery of Words

THE ONTARIO NORTH that Scott and the others passed through in 1905 and 1906 still exists. All those rivers and lakes in the grand water system that Eric W. Morse calls "the really amazing feature of Canadian geography" (holding "half of the whole world's fresh water surface" 27) is all still there. Not untransformed, of course. The surveyed reserves appear on maps, but they do not alter the face of the land as certain of the dams did, those hydro-electric sources the treaty commissioners were careful to exclude from the reserves. The legacy of the treaty party is still felt in the North; stories, not very happy ones, are still told of their passing. The real North: Ontario highways now reach into it. Secondary Highway 599 reaches beyond Osnaburgh; tertiary highway 808, shading off into gravel, reaches north of Windigo Lake, halfway between 52 and 53 degrees north latitude. The Ontario Northland Railway runs its Polar Bear Express from Cochrane to Moosonee, a modern town just across the Moose River from the ancient Moose Factory. The remoter settlements — Fort Hope, Ogoki (Marten's Falls), and those much farther north — are accessible by plane. The real North still exists. The descendants of the people whom the commissioners brought into the treaty still live there under the paternalistic system whose effects they could not have anticipated in 1905 and 1906.

In "Local Wilderness" Don McKay writes that "most people can sense, almost taste, that boundary in our minds and lives beyond which lies something completely other, something undomesticated by the mind's categories"

(5). Gingerly he calls this untamed something wilderness: "At a basic level it may be seen as simply the persistence of otherness, the disturbing thrilling awareness that there really is a world outside language, which, creatures of language ourselves, we translate with difficulty" (5–6). One wants to hold on to a real North, as one wishes to maintain connection with wilderness in McKay's sense, and especially so in a book like this that is based on a textual North. All of the information assembled in chapter 1, even Native sources once oral, was written down.

Textual sources are always packaged in words and sentences; they fall into genres; they are "voiced" in accents not necessarily native to the writer, but achieved. I have not so far emphasized this constructedness in the material I have used to present a composite outline of the treaty-making summers. From now on I will be stressing the presence, sometimes palpable, of the created or constructed personae that mediate every text. Revealing the mask that conceals the writer from the reader is hardly news as critical technique, but it hasn't yet reached Scott studies, not of the nonfiction, at any rate. Pointing out the mask relativizes the text. The effect on the image of the Scott that I am tracing is a blurring. At times he almost disappears into the black of words on a white page. I argue in chapter 3, in fact, that there *is* no Scott, only textual opacities contradictory and fascinating. What is left of Scott *is* in a sense wilderness, is other. Writing *toward* Scott, I never arrive at the truth of the man who bears the name, so from here on my own text will be marked by a play of presence and absence. As fashionable as this may sound, to literary critics at least, I am not interested in playing theoretical games. If I accepted that *"Il n'y a pas de hors-texte"* (Derrida 158), I wouldn't be quoting McKay about the wilderness beyond words, but I still feel the force of the theory of all-embracing textuality. When Albert Camus's Sisyphus concludes that his universe consists of himself and the rock he must perpetually push uphill, he is freed from tormenting metaphysical distraction to concentrate on the rock he has been so intimate with but has not known. A new universe slides into focus. Camus's reading of the myth moves me; it seems both true and partial, clarifying and resistible. Theories are probes, not truths, and no one applies a theory very successfully who doesn't remember that. Textual theory in this book is generated by raw material and not by other theory.

The raw material for this chapter, a composite textual setting for Scott's essay "The Last of the Indian Treaties," is principally the official report(s) of the Treaty 9 trips and Samuel Stewart's 273-page journal (so much fuller than the skimpy diary Scott kept in 1905 and the slightly more ample one Pelham Edgar kept in 1906). There are also Edgar's lengthy serial essay "Twelve Hundred Miles by Canoe," a sequel of sorts to "The Last of the Indian Treaties," and Edmund Morris's 1906 diary. In fact, there is version after version, in whole or part (Morris's newspaper piece "Old Lords of the Soil" and J. L. Vanasse's "The White Dog Feast," not to mention modern-day versions by James Morrison, John Long, and the anonymous writers of *Nishnawbe-Aski Nation*), and the versions differ dramatically enough to remind a comparatist of the words of John Berger that Michael Ondaatje adopted as one of the epigraphs of *In the Skin of a Lion:* "Never again will a story be told as if it were the only one." The exulting resolve in those words is a welcome reminder that multiple narrative is adventure as much as frustration. Approaching the question of Scott's relationship with the Indians from this angle and from that and another, and never finding a single satisfactory answer, one may be sustained by an appetite for irresolution cultivated by postmodernist fiction. Or, being *obliged* to "remain content with partial knowledge," one might just as well find solace in Keats's "negative capability."

In order to keep the potential confusion to a minimum, I will consider at length only the three texts first named. Others, at any rate, make their appearance naturally in other chapters: Vanasse's article in chapter 7 on "Powassan's Drum," Morris's journal in chapter 8 on "A Scene at Lake Manitou," and so on.

"The Last of the Indian Treaties" is a narrative scattered with the seeds of later works that Scott was to write about the treaty trips. It fleshes out what we know about the journeys from other, sketchier sources, though it is much shorter than the narrative furnished by Samuel Stewart's diary narrative. The essay's style makes it clear (as Scott's journal does not) that a human being, not a cipher, was dealing with the Indians, and the content shows that the Native people he was travelling with and some of those he met were individuals, and not *mere* representatives of the Native population, though in some measure Scott renders them that way. Without "The Last of the Indian Treaties" we would have very much less sense of the human texture of the treaty commission's experience in the North.

The word *last* had to be footnoted in *The Circle of Affection,* when Scott gathered the essay into his final collection. As the note says, "treaties were afterwards negotiated with other Indians" (109).[1] But the word could not be dropped without sacrificing an association with the momentousness of the passing of an era or a race ("The Last of the Mohicans," "The Last of the Curlews," "Custer's Last Stand"). The word carries some of the thrill of resignation to disappearances that are picturesque, because literary and distanced.

Scott's introduction to the story of the 1905 trip is a brief version of the sort of history of "The Indian policy of the Canadian Government" that prefaces a good many of his articles on Indians. He picks up the Indians in "the early days," but well into the postcontact period during which they "were a real threat to the colonization of Canada" (109). The "tragic savage" of "The Onondaga Madonna," with the child "paler than she" that is ironically "The latest promise of her nation's doom" is here, generalized, in the second paragraph of the essay:

> The Indian nature now seems like a fire that is waning, that is smouldering and dying away in ashes; then it was full of force and heat. It was ready to break out at any moment in savage dances, in wild and desperate orgies in which ancient superstitions were involved with European ideas but dimly understood and intensified by cunning imaginations inflamed with rum. (110)

These are only in a general sense the ancestors of the Indians with whom Scott is making treaty; they are not the northern Cree and Ojibway, that is, but "Brant's People" of 1790, Six Nations Indians of Southern Ontario. They are held up as examples of the success of treaty-making in a sort of oblique answer to Scott's father who, as we shall see in the next chapter, had occasion to express a typically white frustration that the Indians were sitting on so many fertile acres of land: "all down the valley of the Grand River [by 1905] there is no visible line of demarcation between the farms tilled by the ancient allies in foray and ambush who have become confederates throughout a peaceful year in seed-time and harvest" (110). The parallelism in both sound and sense of "foray and ambush" with "seed-time and harvest" reinforces Scott's sense of progress. The second has replaced the first. (The harmony in Scott's image was illusory, of course. Never having signed away its territory by treaty, the Six Nations Confederacy is an independent state unrecognized by the Canadian government. Scott's department quashed a militant sovereigntist movement headed by Deskaheh in the early 1920s.)

The 1790 Indians of Scott's envisioning are not precontact Indians, then, but those who have already come under European influence. Scott has few illusions about the immediate effect of whites on vulnerable Indians. He has no illusions about the Hudson's Bay Company, so hospitable to himself and his treaty party because the treaty-making was so good for business. Scott knows that the fur trade has bound the Indians to the HBC posts, on which they depend for their very lives. The Indian "enriches the fur-traders," he says, "and incidentally gains a bare sustenance by his cunning and a few gins and pitfalls for wild animals. When all the arguments against this view are exhausted it is still evident that he is but a slave, used by all traders alike as a tool to provide wealth, and therefore to be kept in good condition as cheaply as possible" (114–115). Like Pelham Edgar in his article on the 1906 journey, Scott remarks on the purchases made by Indians at the HBC post: "soon the camp was brightened by new white shawls, new hats and boots, which latter they wore as if doing a great penance" (117). The picture of all this new incongruous finery is meant to be amusing, but there is something sad about these shopping sprees that Scott doesn't register.

In his 1890 report E. B. Borron had suggested that

> the [treaty] annuity should be paid entirely in flour, which is already (with many of these Indians) one of the necessaries of life, and will be of still more vital importance, when game becomes scarce and difficult to obtain. There is not an Indian family in the territory, but will require yearly, a quantity of flour, equivalent in value to the five dollars per head, or whatever sum the annuity agreed upon may amount to. Food is the Indian's most pressing want, and starvation during the winter season their greatest peril. (37)

Flour was one of the food introductions that undermined the health of the Indians. They were made "sad with flour and beef," according to the narrator of Scott's story "Charcoal" (*Circle* 221). The concerned Mr. Borron may not have been aware of that, but it adds another layer of irony to native shopping with treaty money at HBC posts. Expecting to sell a great deal of flour after the treaties were signed, the HBC laid in extra supplies, and perhaps extra flour was sold. But many of the Indians, being left the proprietors of their own money (which, on the face of it, is only fair), were not able to resist the temptation of luxuries when staples were desperately needed. "Took in nearly $600.00 today" (HBCa), writes Jabez Williams, the HBC trader at Osnaburgh in his daily journal for July 13, 1905. He added $500 the following day. No other entry for the whole year mentions daily receipts. "Busy in store selling for cash," writes G. W. Cockram of the Albany HBC in his journal for Thursday, August 4, 1905. "Sold $1072.00 worth of goods" (HBCb). Had journals survived for the other posts visited, they would doubtless continue the pattern.

The cunning by which the trapping Indian is said to "gain a bare sustenance," in the passage about HBC treatment of Indians, is not the cunning of "cunning imaginations inflamed with rum" in the passage about Indian nature. The former means possessed of lore (as it does in "A Scene at Lake Manitou," where the words *cunning* and *lore* are equated); the latter means something like malevolent. It's not easy to read words like *savage, orgies, superstitions,* and *cunning* without sensing the stereotype of the Indian as pagan antagonist, though at least Scott is not depicting Indians as "themselves," but as already affected by white interventions in their culture. He is talking about Indians who have been subject to the "puerile negotiations," the "rude," and "gross diplomacy of the rum bottle and the material appeal" of insubstantial presents. This is a "control," Scott says, "that seemed to be founded on debauchery and licence." The only thing Scott finds to applaud in this early contact, ironically, is "the principle of the sacredness of treaty promises" (110).

Scott does not elaborate on the "fire" of his version of Indian nature at a time when Indians, one might say, were Indians. But a related image appears in "The Onondaga Madonna" in the woman's face "Where all her pagan passion burns and glows." The stereotyping image of high temper and irrationality is extended, in the essay, into "inflamed," though Scott may have meant something more positive by it. Passion would be positive, like vitality and (one of his favourite words about the North and those who met it face-to-face) virility.[2] The rum whips up the heat of a nature already subject to few of the mental curbs of unacceptable behaviour as defined by the "civilized."

Savage and even the more neutral *primitive* are words we flinch from in these days of de-hierarchizing, of centralizing the marginal. Scott's use of the word *savage* has been taken as a sign of prejudice against the Natives, but he doesn't reserve the word for them. He uses it as a synonym for primitive when he introduces the *Traditional History of the Confederacy of the Six Nations* as a document having parallels in other cultures: "It was in recognition of the fact that all nations have a traditional history which originated while they were yet in a savage state, that this small fragment of Indian traditional history was written by the Chiefs, so that they might preserve it as other nations have done theirs" (197).

A nation is not exactly a race, of course, though there is slippage between the two, a traffic of essentialisms, in Scott's thinking. "[T]he Gesners were an intellectual race," Scott writes of Archibald Lampman's maternal forebears in the "Memoir" for Lampman's *Poems,* and he calls the Lampman side "a valiant, loyal race" (xii), just as he refers to one of his 1905 guides as "a fine type of the old half-breed race of packers and voyageurs . . . (*Circle* 112). None of these notions of types being in doubt in Scott's time, the terminology is allowed to cross indiscriminately. Still, granting Scott his outmoded view of stable races, he is differentiating between whites and Natives only in historical terms: *they* are what *we* used to be, rudimentary in social and mental organization. "The Half-breed Girl," written in 1906, makes an interesting selection from Scottish nature for the white component of a divided mind:

> The reek of rock-built cities,
>   Where her fathers dwelt of yore
> The gleam of loch and shealing,
>   The mist on the moor,
>
> Frail traces of kindred kindness
>   Of feud by hill and strand,
> The heritage of an age-long life
>   In a legendary land. (*Poems* 55–56)

The primitive, the savage, aspect of this woman is not necessarily or only the Ojibway side. Given the rudimentary psychology Scott assumes, she might well be inflamed by bagpipe music, though probably without knowing why. Scott's notion of Scots/Ojibway cultural, if not racial, intersection is echoed by Maria Campbell in her autobiographical *Halfbreed.* And in *The Book of Jessica* she talks about the research she did to try to place her white grandfather, and her own identity in relation to him. "I went to the [Celtic] societies," she says,

> and found that they had all the same things [as Native peoples], storytellers, music, sacred stones, mother earth, little people. They told me that when the British came they took the bagpipes away, banned them, because they knew that their music was sacred, gave them strength. (36)

Scott's Indians in "The Last of the Indian Treaties," as elsewhere, are not simply good or bad, nor do they divide neatly into the primitive and the civilized. They are people in transition who could be affected for either good or ill by the white people they met.

There is a limit to Scott's enlightenment, though. His assumption seems to be that Indian nature is not like white nature. In 1906 white nature is presumably full and actively self-realizing and does not need moulding into something else or better. It just needs policing to keep it up to the moral mark. White nature, or at least the "best" of white behaviour, is the norm by which Indian nature is measured and found lacking in development. Indian nature is implicitly essentialized, as feminine nature has so often been, as passive, to be acted upon. If the rum traders get the upper hand, the effects are bad; if the missionaries do, the effects are good. A double standard permits Scott to feel that religious institutions like the Methodist Church he had himself abandoned would be the best influence on his charges, much as an apostate father might send his children to Sunday School under the general principle that religion is okay for kids.

Scott's ideal transitional Indian is a person of the wild who has been gently modified by contact with the Church. At the end of his essay he describes "an Indian who came in from Attawapiskat to Albany just as we were ready to leave":

> He seemed about twenty years of age, with a face of great beauty and intelligence, and eyes that were wild with a sort of surprise — shy at his novel position and proud that he was of some importance. His name was Charles Wabinoo. We found it on the list and gave him his eight dollars. When he felt the new crisp notes he took a crucifix from his breast, kissed it swiftly, and made a fugitive sign of the cross. "From my heart I thank you," he said. There was the Indian at the best point of a transitional state, still wild as a lynx, with all the lore and instinct of his race undimmed, and possessed

> wholly by the simplest rule of the Christian life, as yet unspoiled by the arts of sly lying, paltry cunning, and the lower vices which come from contact with such of our debased manners and customs as come to him in the wilderness. (122)

Here is the word *cunning* again, now describing the deceptiveness of low white people. The word's meaning metamorphoses in the text and joins Indians and whites in common, ambiguous, humanity.

The portrait of Charles Wabinoo is meant to be very attractive and is reminiscent of that of "Mizigun, the mighty hunter" and devout Christian of Scott's poem "The Mission of the Trees." Perhaps the reader is even intended to contrast Charles Wabinoo with the debauched Indians earlier described in much more general terms. They seem to have the worst of both worlds while he, poised between the wild and the civilized, the pagan and the Christian, appears to possess the best. He is a far cry from Watkwenies, the Half-breed Girl Keejigo, and the Onondaga Madonna, among Scott's Indian heroines (it's curious that so many of them are female, and thus doubly other to Scott), all of whose lives have been scrambled by various combinations of mixed culture, mixed consciousness, or loss of Native context — they are neither one thing nor the other. But Scott's portrait of Charles Wabinoo has a misleading toughness about it. White people are seen as corrupters of Indians, but they are also implicitly regarded as sole shapers of the Indian future, as if the Indians had little of cultural significance to contribute to their own evolving identity. To put it another way, "the Indian" is not regarded as human enough to have in his own racial makeup either a spiritual base for morality or even a natural capacity for cunning (the bad kind) of his own.

The verbal portrait, the characterization by description that the essay as a genre shares with fiction, is one of the techniques Scott uses to focus the story of his trip. One would scarcely know either from the journals or from the Treaty 9 report that any of the people Scott travelled with, or any of those he met, were anything other than generic people, like those representatives of institutions I described in chapter 1. In the report, individuals are singled out only in terms of their usefulness to the treaty party (each HBC factor is thanked for hospitality and interpretive services, as is the odd churchman who filled this function; each spokesman for the Indians is named and something of his speech paraphrased). No characterized individuals appear. In the essay, by contrast, not only Charles Wabinoo but, of the crew, David Sugarhead, Oombash, Simon Smallboy, and Daniel Wascowin are all described, and Jimmy Swain (see figure 6) gets a whole paragraph. He is "the old Albany River guide, sixty-seven years old, who ran to and fro over the longest portage carrying the heaviest pack" (112). Jimmy Swain must have been unusual. He also earns a paragraph of description in the journal of

Figure 6, PA-59538

Samuel Stewart, who is generally admiring and appreciative of the efforts of each of the Indian crews, but seldom singles anyone out. Swain reminds me of mixed-culture heroes in Scott's stories, Petit Bonhomme and Clute Boulay, those old men in the declining years of once-prodigious strength. In the essay Jimmy Swain is a figure much like Charles Wabinoo. Both are presented as disappearing ideal types, among the last of their sort:

> He is a fine type of the old half-breed race of packers and voyageurs which is fast disappearing; loyal and disinterested, cautious but fearless, full of that joy of life which consists in doing and possessed by that other joy of life which dwells in retrospect, in the telling of old tales, the playing of old tunes and the footing of old dance steps. (112)

The strategy of characterization is the same as it was with Charles Wabinoo, though in Jimmy Swain's case the details follow the generalization. Some of the most interesting details have to do with Jimmy's playing of his old fiddle whose "G-string had two knots in it" (113). From this essay, and from Stewart's diary, one discovers that the northern air around the commissioners' encampments rang in the evenings with "all the jigs popular on the Albany for the last fifty years," as well as "curious versions of hymn tunes" and other melodies.

The portrait of Jimmy Swain is, again, a warm one. Scott was clearly as taken with the man as he was with Charles Wabinoo, though there is again that patronizing subtext. There is nothing overt about white superiority in "The Last of the Indian Treaties," but a superior attitude lurks even in Scott's sympathetic regret, quoted in chapter 1, that the Indians could grasp nothing of the meaning of the treaty. The superiority spreads throughout the essay in an irony created by the fact that the persona or voice of the essay is established as being more sophisticated than the people he writes about:

> "Oh, it's a fine fiddle!" Jimmy would say. "It's an *expensive* fiddle. Dr. Scovil gave it to me, and it must have cost ten dollars." He had scraped the belly and rubbed it with castor oil, and the G-string had two knots in it. But what matter! When Jimmy closed the flap of his tent and drew it forth out of its blue pine box, I doubt whether any artist in the world had ever enjoyed a sweeter pang of affection and desire. (113)

But what was the music like? Scott must have been listening to authentic folk music, and I wonder if his trained musician's ear could appreciate it. His manner of writing about it is noncommittal. Jimmy loved to play jigs and "curious versions of hymn tunes" (113); that's all we hear. By choice, Scott would probably have preferred the violin music his wife was playing in England while he toured the wilds: Locatelli's Sonata in G minor, Mozart's Concerto in E flat, Tartini's "Larghetto," Leonard's "Gavotte" and "Conte de la Grandmère," and Marsick's "Tendre Aveu." The program is derived from four appreciative notices of a Thursday night performance at the Aeolian Hall in London (PA/S-A), one of them from the *Times,* July 7, 1906. Mrs. Scott wrote her husband on August 13, 1906, from Grand Hotel des Bains in Heyst, Belgium: "I know you would like it here & what a difference from where you are" (PA/DCS)! Scott must have been continually aware of the difference. He wrote it into "Spring on Mattagami," that sophisticated poem composed in a canoe; the difference was the residue of his entire oeuvre for Northrop Frye:

> Whatever one thinks of the total merit of Scott's very uneven output, he achieved the type of imaginative balance that is characteristic of so much of the best in Canadian culture down to the present generation, when altered social conditions are beginning to upset it. On one side he had the world of urbane and civilized values; on the other, the Quebec forest with its Indians and lonely trappers. He could write a poem on Debussy and a poem on a squaw feeding her child with her own flesh; he was at once primitive and pre-Raphaelite, a recluse of the study and a recluse of the forest. (*The Bush Garden* 9)

Perhaps it's unimportant to know how Scott the classical musician reacted to Jimmy Swain's folk fiddle. Placing Scott and Swain side by side, we have an epitome of cultural opposites (the set of George Meredith's sophisticated novels Scott discovered in remote Moose Factory is another) that found expression again and again in the poetry and fiction. In fact, it's tempting to think that Jimmy Swain and George Meredith combine to create "Spirit River." In this Scott story the naive Parto has somehow come to own a Maggini violin, which the new priest Father Pascal, connoisseur of violins as Scott was of classical music, is able to identify. The passages in which the cultured priest considers the differences between the Maggini and a "common half-breed fiddle" (73) reveal a technical knowledge for which he can have expected to find absolutely no use in the North. Only the strings are faulty, and the worst is the one that was knotted on Jimmy Swain's fiddle: "the wire on the 'G' string was loose and snored horribly" (*Elspie* 75). Father Pascal tries to rescue the violin by offering to find a purchaser, as Scott carried the Merediths away with him. (Meredith was one of his favourite novelists, and perhaps he was right to feel that they would grace his own shelves better than they did the HBC library.)

Scott uses the verbal portraits as a means of dramatizing by particularizing the treaty trip, and he similarly singles out for discussion experiences at three of the several posts his party visited: inland Osnaburgh and the James

Bay posts of Albany and Moose Factory. Here again the essay differs from the official report, which is much more of a "chronicle," though Scott uses that word for the essay (112). The report plods from one post to another, describing in much the same terms the activities that took place at each, and describing also in a formulaic way the journey between posts. In the essay Scott focuses first on Osnaburgh (ignoring the bad start on Lac Seul) because what happens there is typical and because it had "all the importance of a beginning" (114). Moreover, Osnaburgh is an inland post and one at which the Indians, Ojibway speakers, have had less exposure to Christian ways than the Cree speakers on the bay. Albany and Moose Factory were nearer "civilization," not geographically but in terms of the white institutions that had been drawn to these northern places. Both had been established "within fifteen years from the founding of the [Hudson's Bay] company" in 1670 (Innis 119). The Indians here knew the syllabic alphabet that Scott says was "invented by Rev. James Evans, a Methodist missionary about the middle of the last century" (121) for the easier teaching and conversion of the Indians. (The last visual component of the essay as it appeared in *Scribner's,* liberally illustrated by Scott's photographs, is "Part of the Albany address in Cree syllabic.")

Unversed in writing, by contrast (though in *The Sacred Scrolls of the Ojibway* Selwyn Dewdney reveals how they stored history and legend on birchbark scrolls), the Ojibway at Osnaburgh have their powerful memories: "Everything that was said and done," Scott writes, "our personal appearance, our dress and manners, were being written down as if in a book; matter which would be rehearsed at many a campfire for generations until the making of the treaty had gathered a lore of its own; but no one could have divined it from visible signs" (114). Scott's valorization of the written over the oral culture shows in the graphic metaphor he chooses; "recorded" would be more accurate than "written down."

He was right, though, and touchstone glimpses of the treaty-makers from without can now be found in such documents as submissions to the 1977–78 Royal Commission on the Northern Environment. Some of the Cat Lake Ojibway were absent from the signing at Osnaburgh, for example, but had met the treaty party on the way there:

> It was during the winter of 1905 that a mysterious death occurred at a campsite near the post of Cat Lake. The following spring, in the same year, a policeman arrived from Kenora. He took back with him ten to twelve canoes of our people who knew of what had happened.
>
> It was on this return trip to Kenora, between the Lac Seul River and Lake St. Joseph, around Root Portage, that the Cat Lake group encountered another canoe party heading north. They set up camp together for the night.

> The white people travelling in the other party said that they were on their way to Osnaburgh to make a treaty with the people living there. The commissioner talked about the treaty and asked the people to think about it and give him their decision by the following morning. Our people were very reluctant to give an answer to such a serious question. Usually these matters were considered for a very long time, at least five years.
>
> The following morning, although the Cat Lake party could not give their answer to the signing of this important paper, the commissioners gave them their first treaty payment from a chest of money. The commissioners then headed for Osnaburgh and our people continued on to Kenora. When Missabay signed the treaty in Osnaburgh he did so on behalf of all the people from Cat Lake area. . . .
>
> Other than the annual treaty payment, our elders can remember very few benefits we received from the government for signing the Treaty. We did receive balls of twine for net-making. Farm tools, potatoes and other seeds were sent to each family, although no-one knew how to farm and these things went to waste.[3]

By contrasting the inland post and the two James Bay posts, Scott highlights each of them. For transition between the inland and coastal experiences, he writes an impressionistically generalized account of the Albany River journey full of hints and suggestions of experiences that he would later fashion into poems and stories. "Occasionally the sound of a conjurer's drum far away pervaded the day like an aerial pulse" (119), he writes. While the seed for "Powassan's Drum" may have been planted back on Lac Seul, the word *pulse* (which appears in the poem) suggests that it has already begun to sprout. In Scott's account of travel on the Albany, spiced by stories of "Indian cruelty and superstition" like those of the wendigo, there are suggestions of other poems: "the lonely spirit of the stream becomes an obsession," he says. "It is ever present, but at night it grows in power. Something is heard and yet not heard; it rises, and dwells, and passes mysteriously, like a suspiration immense and mournful, like the sound of wings, dim and enormous, folded down with weariness" (119).

A "region-spirit" like that of "The Height of Land" (where "suspiration" becomes "susurrus") seems to be making itself heard. The image of wind and wings appears explicitly in *Via Borealis* poems like "An Impromptu" and "Night Burial in the Forest," especially the last stanza of the latter:

> Then, as we fare on our way to the shore
> Sudden the torches cease to roar:
> For cleaving the darkness remote and still

> Comes a wind with a rushing, harp-like thrill,
> The sound of wings hurled and furled and unfurled,
> The wings of the Angel who gathers the souls from the
> wastes of the world. (*Poems* 58)

The mysterious "Something" that sounds in "The Height of Land," and in the essay, is much more dramatic and involving than this taming image of angel wings. As Gordon Johnston points out, "there are a surprising number of angels in [Scott's] poetry" (267). Sometimes they seem less out of place than this one. Assigned to the wasteland detail, it must be low on the hierarchy.

I ONCE SHARED with John Flood, Gerald Lynch, Brian Titley, and others the assumption Scott wrote the official Treaty 9 report. He was a writer, after all, and moreover a notch higher in the Indian Affairs hierarchy than Samuel Stewart. But perhaps one advantage of being higher up is that more work falls to the lower man. Actually, the report was probably the result of a collaboration featuring a division of labour. Passages on pages 8, 9, 13, and 17 of the report appear verbatim in Samuel Stewart's journal, while the "Schedule of Reserves" (for 1905, at least — Edgar didn't keep these notes for the surveyors in his 1906 journal) appear verbatim in Scott's diary. Whether each commissioner was solely responsible for the part of the report that can clearly be traced to him is impossible to say, especially given that what looks like Scott's hand appears in Stewart's journal text, adding a few annotations, clarifications of a word or two. But in terms of style and substance "The James Bay Treaty" proper resembles Stewart's journal much more than either Scott's journal or "The Last of the Indian Treaties."

"The James Bay Treaty" is a sort of letter, or rather a pair of letters. The first is dated November 6, 1905, the second October 5, 1906. Like all of the annual reports in the Government Sessional Papers in which they first appeared, the "letters" are addressed to the minister: "The Honorable The Supt. General of Indian Affairs Ottawa," in this case.

As I have said, internal evidence makes it seem safest to attribute the report to Stewart, though it's just possible that Scott borrowed his fellow commissioner's words. Either way, there are significant differences between "The Last of the Indian Treaties" and the Treaty 9 report, many of them traceable to the difference in genre. The essay is warm and engaging in tone, the report neutral, objective. The one is persuasively composed and uses figurative language and fancy sentence structure, mostly to good effect; the other is stylistically competent but flat, and its structure is mechanical. For the entertainment and mild instruction of his cultured equals, readers of the *Scribner's* article, Scott creates an avuncular persona to carry his tale of remote places and simple people. The readers stand side by side with this

Scott, as it were, looking down on his subjects. In the official report Stewart (with Scott perhaps at his shoulder) looks up to his superior in the hierarchy of a department for which Indians are not exotic curiosities but rather political and administrative problems, potential obstacles to business. No verbal portraits of Indians need be sketched for the minister, who is addressed in something like the manner of an eldest son giving an account of his activities to his father. The report's emphasis on explanation and justification of the commissioner's activities, bordering on servility as it does, reinforces the implicit hierarchical assumptions that underpin it (and, much less overtly, Scott's essay). The authority of the commissioners to negotiate is referred to as confirmed by other documents, orders in council and statutes of Canada. There is no place here for such reservations about the inequality of the treating parties as appears in Scott's essay.

In "The Last of the Indian Treaties" Scott accounts for the presence of the treaty party in the North by saying that the Indians had sued for the treaty (which was true of some of them at least) and that this "unregarded region . . . contains much arable land, many million feet of pulpwood, untold wealth of minerals, and unharnessed water-powers sufficient to do the work of half the continent" (111). But there is no indication in the essay that the government of Ontario wants control of these resources for itself; rather, it is said that the pressing need to clear a right of way for the new transcontinental railway "made a cession of the territory imperative" (111). The conclusion of the report of the 1905 journey displays the agenda of the commissioners as agents of the government:

> Throughout all the negotiations we carefully guarded against making any promises over and above those written in the treaty which might afterwards cause embarrassement [*sic*] to the governments concerned. No outside promises were made, and the Indians cannot, and we confidently believe do not, expect any other concessions than those set forth in the documents to which they gave their adherence. It was gratifying throughout to be met by these Indians with such a show of cordiality and trust, and to be able fully to satisfy what they believed to be their claims upon the governments of this country. The treatment of the reserve question, which in this treaty was most important, will, it is hoped, meet with approval. For the most part the reserves were selected by the commissioners after conference with the Indians. They have been selected in situations which are especially advantageous to their owners, and where they will not in any way interfere with railway development or the future commercial interests of the country. While it is doubtful whether the Indians will ever engage in agriculture, these reserves, being of a reasonable size, will give a secure and permanent interest in the land which the indeterminate possession of a large tract

> could never carry. No valuable water-powers are included within the allotments. The area set apart is, approximately, 374 square miles in the Northwest Territories and 150 square miles in the province of Ontario. When the vast quantity of waste and, at present, unproductive land, surrendered is considered, these allotments must, we think, be pronounced most reasonable. (96–97)

Here is a theme of the Reverend William Scott's 1883 report on the Oka Indian situation (yet to be discussed): potentially productive land is going to waste. The native inhabitants thought otherwise of this land, of course; it was anything but unproductive to them[4] — even though life in the North could be extremely hazardous, especially when game was scarce.

Occasionally the commissioners took their directions too literally. In 1911 James S. Dobie, the official surveyor, pronounced the reserve set aside for the English River Indians to be "absolutely useless" (RG10c, letter to J. D. Maclean, August 2, 1911). On his own, though not without some authority to make changes as he saw fit, he surveyed a better reserve. (This was the second hitch Dobie encountered: the Osnaburgh Indians also claimed that they had chosen a different area than the one contained in his verbal directions.)[5] If the commissioners had been engineers, they might have foreseen the backup of rivers, the creation of lakes, that occur with the building of dams. The site of the treaty signing at Osnaburgh has been drowned by the waters of Lake St. Joseph.[6] Locating reserves away from water powers didn't ensure that they wouldn't feel the effects of harnessing those powers.

The 1906 report is virtually identical with the 1905 report in terms of form, though there is less preamble and no real conclusion. Perhaps Stewart felt that these niceties, done once, would stand for both reports. In both of them the stance is that of the dutiful servant of the government, friend of the Indians only within severe limits. This is clearest in the 1906 report when, in one of the passages taken directly from his diary, Stewart records the request of Chief Newatchkigigswabe of Long Lake "that provision would be made for their sick and destitute, as even in the best seasons the Indians found it very difficult to do more than make a living, and were able to do very little towards assisting one another" (103). The response to this reasonable request reminds me of Brian Titley's view of Scott as "an almost obsessive penny-pinching book-keeper" (202): "In reply the chief was informed that the government was always ready to assist those actually requiring help, but that the Indians must rely as much as possible upon their own exertions for their support" (103). The reply may have been designed to prevent Indians from expecting too much from a government whose budget was given to fluctuation, in which case it is only decent, a forestalling of false hope.[7] But it sounds rather heartless. It sounds like what a superior would like to hear.

In the passage just quoted from the James Bay Treaty report and, in fact, in the account of each set of treaty deliberations, there is assumed a very different opinion of the ability of the Indians to comprehend what the treaty was about than appears in "The Last of the Indian Treaties." Of the few Indians who were met at the desolate English River Post, some 60 miles off the Albany up the Kenogami River, Stewart says

> it did not take long to explain to the Indians the reason why the commission was visiting them. . . . The terms of the treaty having been fully explained, the Indians stated that they were willing to come under its provisions, and they were informed that by the acceptance of the gratuity they would be held to have entered treaty, a statement which they fully realized. As the morrow was Sunday, and as it was important to proceed without delay, they were paid at once. (73)

There is no ceremony and no feast for these Indians because they are considered "but a branch of the Albany band." They are offered not even the night to think things over. No wonder the reserve chosen for them was so little suited to their needs. No wonder contemporary Natives and others have been unconvinced of the legality of some treaty negotiating.

The only event singled out for special comment in either of the 1905 and 1906 reports is the feast given at Moose Factory. Once again drawn from his journal, Stewart's praise for the success of the Christian church in the James Bay area might well have been shared by Scott, though Scott (not writing for an official audience) at least made Indians the focus of his essay.

> In many respects [says Stewart] it was a unique occasion. The gathering was addressed by Bishop Holmes, who began with a prayer in Cree, the Indians making their responses and singing their hymns in the same language. Bishop Holmes kindly interpreted the address of the commissioners, which was suitably replied to by Chief Mark. It may be recorded that during our stay at this point a commodious church was crowded every evening by interested Indians, and that the good effect of the ministrations for many years of the Church Missionary Society were plain, not only to Moose Factory but after the immediate influence of the post and the missionaries had been left. The crew from Moose Factory which accompanied the commissioners as far as Abitibi held service every night in camp, recited a short litany, sang a hymn and engaged in prayer, a fact we think worthy of remark, as in the solitude through which we passed this Christian service made a link with civilization and the best influences at work in the world which had penetrated even to these remote regions. On Friday, August 11, the question of a reserve was gone into, and settled to

> the satisfaction of ourselves and the Indians. A description of the location is given in the schedule of reserves. (9)

I leave the last two sentences of this to show how Stewart spoils the unity of his paragraph on the sort of cultural incongruity that is at the heart of Scott's "Night Hymns on Lake Nipigon," something Scott would presumably not have done even in a report.

The 1905 journey had that unpromising beginning on Lac Seul when Scott was obliged to go out of his way, following his ears to the site of a drum dance, to prohibit the ceremony he found in progress. Stewart's journal makes it clear that it was Scott, "speaking for the commissioners [who] demanded to see the conjuror" (25). Since all native drumming is religious, the drum itself being the gift of the Creator, an agent of prayer, Scott as agent of the law and (believer or not) of Christianity suppresses the indigenous "pagan" religion. Approval of the Christian church's work at Moose Factory is consistent with attempts to suppress Cree and Ojibway religion elsewhere. What Stewart wrote, Scott signed; what Stewart wrote about, as at Lac Seul, Scott did. Insofar as Scott is implicated when he signs the report, in the substance if not the style of it, there is again the sense of constructing a stance (a self) based on the expectations of the audience it must be presented to. Preparing "a face [one might say] to meet the faces that you meet" (Eliot 4).

THERE WOULD PROBABLY be little debate about Scott's opinion of Indians if "The Last of the Indian Treaties," so apparently warm and compassionate, were the only prose text we had to go on. Perhaps the essay is where his opinion *should* be sought, if anywhere in his prose, since it's the only essay he wrote to please himself on a subject involving Indians. Even the illustration of the piece with his own photographs is a personal touch. All of the photographs he took were turned over to Indian Affairs, of course, with a set of prints saved for his own album. Like the journal, the photographs apparently occupy a grey area between private and public property. In the essay, at any rate, the opinions expressed should be divided into two categories: of the Indian in general, and of Native individuals.

Scott appears to feel that "the Indian" has scarcely emerged from a North American version of the Dark Ages; he is ignorant and innocent and vulnerable to calculating, worldy whites. His heat, or "fire," might be seen as freedom from the superego of civilization, but (the assumption is) civilized norms are those by which he should be judged and in whose image he should be cultivated. About all the individuals he names in the essay, Scott is warm, even affectionate. The individuals he chooses to portray are admirable. They are nevertheless patronized. They are not equals. If it is granted that Scott felt warmly about some individual Indians, what does that tell us about him? Only that he was in a position to be caught tightly in the bind that makes a modern reader feel ambivalently about E. B. Borron's paternalistic 1890 report.

Like Scott in the essay, Borron sounds like a knowledgeable, compassionate man, but one of his paternalistic recommendations was to remove the Indians' freedom to direct their treaty annuity where they chose. His motive is the hardly reprehensible one of trying to prevent them from starving, of saving them from themselves, believing as he does that long-term planning is foreign to their natures. Well-meaning people can be dangerous. Scott might have *loved* Indians and still have administered the paternalistic system in good conscience. Some parents never know when to let go, either. I'm not suggesting that Scott's conscience *was* clear, merely that establishing his feelings about the Indians, even if that could be unequivocally done, resolves nothing.

And doubts must remain about the authority of the essay as a repository of Scott's feelings. The account is severely limited to what Scott presumably assumed the readers of *Scribner's* would be interested in hearing about: the exotic northern landscape and its aboriginal inhabitants. Not the white treaty party, which is introduced with stark brevity: "Our party included three commissioners, a physician, an officer of the Hudson's Bay Company who managed all the details of transport and commissariat, and two constables of the Dominion police force" (111). The Mounties get a little play because their uniforms inspire so much awe, but no white person is introduced by name or described. Only one white presence can be made much of — the narrator of the essay, whose name appears only in the credits. Otherwise, he is merely "the writer [who] was appointed one of three commissioners" (111). Would we be justified in thinking of this writer and Duncan Campbell Scott as having a simple and direct equivalence? I doubt it. That Scott has created a voice in which to tell his narrative is confirmed by the difference between his writing in it and in the other less "literary" prose that is examined in chapter 5.

Scott was 44, not a callow and unformed youth, when he wrote "The Last of the Indian Treaties." Perhaps the essay was not only his first but also his last expression of "personal" views on Natives; perhaps he maintained his rather compromised enthusiasm for Native people all his life, though the basis of what he was to *say* on the subject from this time on was already expressed in the Treaty 9 report, which he did not write, but which he signed. He was never again to be such a friend of the Natives in print, except obliquely in fiction and poetry; his public stance was almost always to be that of apologist for the official view. In 1906, in the meantime, there appears to be some distance between the private and the public opinions. We might even say there was a tension, though there is no evidence that Scott felt it as such. Had he given the matter any thought he would probably have found nothing odd about addressing the general reader differently than the superintendent of Indian Affairs. He was neither the first nor the last to adjust his voice to his audience; for such adjustments hypocrisy is too strong a word.

According to Brian Titley, "Scott's pronouncements" on Indians in "readily comprehensible prose" do not vary and are "by far the best guide to what the private and public man really believed" (32). In 1906 there is already a problem with this equation of the private and public man and, in fact, there *is* a variance of "pronouncements." In chapter 5, at the end of an examination of the remaining official and semiofficial prose on Native subjects, I trace the evolution of Scott's expression of assimilationist policy, a "progress" from laissez-faire to social engineering. In none of this material, early or late, does Scott ever set out to deliver opinions on the subject of Native people. His readers have gleaned such opinions, often by selective reading. The gleanings may not be without substance, but the picture they make blurs when the particular occasion and/or context, not to mention the style and structure, of each work is taken into account. There are, in fact, no "pronouncements" as such; every assemblage of Scott's opinions is an artificial construction and ought to be acknowledged as such. When the assembler's process is disclosed, the accuracy of his or her own pronouncements may then be more accurately assessed. When all of Scott's writing on Native subjects is interrogated, the conclusion is nearly inescapable that his opinions about Indians, how he really felt about them, are simply not to be found anywhere in his work.

The reader may wonder why so many chapters follow this one if the writer has already abandoned one of his essential quests. I have not given up; I have simply redefined the problem to incorporate its problematics. What I have discovered is far from nothing, though none of it is simple, nor does the wished-for neat kernel of solution ever appear in it. After the present chapter, the answering takes what may seem to be a detour, away from the Treaty 9 material (though the containing view is still the years 1905 and 1906), but the contexts of Scott's life (chapter 3) and of his civil service career (chapter 4) are impossible to ignore — even if, looking into them, we find still more puzzles.

NOTES

1. Treaty 9 itself was not concluded in 1906. The "Quebec" Indians were treated with in 1908, and a further Treaty 9 trip was made in 1929, this time by airplane, when Commissioners Cain and Awrey brought many of the Indians of far northwestern Ontario into the treaty.
2. "When [Walter J. Phillips] came to this country he had had a varied experience but he adopted our roughish life, our fierce climate, and our uncultivated landscape which had no romantic or traditional associations as a natural home for a genius that was virile enough to contend with them and, insofar as they can be overcome, to conquer them" (*Walter J. Phillips* 10; see also page 12).
3. This memory is the more interesting because it may be something of a composite. The encounter with the Cat Lake group is not recorded in report, essay, or journal. It's unlikely Scott would have omitted noting such a meeting in the journal, since he did make a point of mentioning other stray groups the treaty party met and the reserve they were to be attached to. However, he does say in an entry for July 12: "At Cat Lake there are 30 families of [?] Indians. Will try to get these into Tr. next year." The mention of farm tools is odd, since such items were left out of Treaty 9. But Osnaburgh is not far from the area of Treaty 3, whose terms included farm implements, seeds, and ammunition, and, in fact, Scott was worried that the Osnaburgh Indians would object to their treaty terms being less munificent than those of their neighbours. Evidence favouring the Indians' memory — if "the following spring" is still 1905 — may be found in the Osnaburgh Post journal for May 28, which contains a very full report of the murder of Peter Peetwaykeesicouse who was found dead in his wigwam on April 8. The suspect, Tuzhwaykee, "had been living with the deceased's sister who had left him sometime during the winter and he had been heard last fall beating a drum and singing the deceased's death song."
4. The difference in opinions (not to mention styles, literary and colloquial) can be demonstrated with two passages, one from "The Last of the Indian Treaties," the other from James Locke's 1978 submission to the Royal Commission on the Northern Environment. Of the low, flat, marshy environs of James Bay, Scott wonders, "Can these be called shores that are but a few feet high? The bay is vast and shallow; ten miles away the fringes of red willow look like dusky sprays brushed in against the intense steel-grey of the sky-line, and the canoe paddles will reach the sandy bottom! No language can convey the effect of loneliness and desolation which hangs over this far-stretching plain of water, treacherous with shifting sands and sudden passionate storms, unfurrowed by any keels but those of the few small boats of the fur traders" (120). "Almost every body in Moosonee and Moose Factory live off the land in some way," says Locke. "'Awna Cawawna is nothing but a big swamp' so say the mining industry. But their wrong. My parents and I went out in the so called swamp. We saw ten grouse one Saturday and more than that on Sunday, not counting the two magansers and some moose tracks and some bear tracks. and the trees and the bog, ugly, rotten, swampy, so called but some of them are hundreds of years old and the bog probly developt futher the glacier melted." Locke is referring to the Onakawana River a few miles south of Moosonee, the site of an environmental assessment recommended by the Royal Commission on the Northern Environment in 1978. Onakawana Development Limited had signed a lease with the Ministry of Natural Resources permitting it to mine lignite coal in the area.
5. W. H. Galbraith, the previous surveyor, had found that "the Reserves expected by [the chief and council] do not agree with those specified in the Treaty" (RG10c to J. D. Maclean, July 29, 1909).
6. Eloquent testimony about the result of flooding appears in a submission to the 1977 Royal Commission on the Northern Environment by the Treaty 3 Lac Seul band. The speaker presents the commissioner with pictures of "the bodies of my ancestors," and comments:

> Every day, of every month, for the past few years, the remains of my forefathers have been washing up from their sacred burial grounds. There they sit on the edge of our lake, disturbed from what was to have been their eternal resting place. The remains act as a constant reminder that Indians pay a harsh price when the white man and the white man's power company visit the lands of my people.
>
> Over forty years ago, Ontario Hydro flooded my people's land to produce Hydro electric power. We were never told of the full extent of the flooding. We were never given full compensation for the flooding. And were never given the resources to move our ancestor's graves and save them from a watery destruction.

7. Perhaps Scott was not niggardly himself but simply resigned to the realities of the civil service's dependence on the vagaries of the Ministry of Finance and its annual budget. In the section of "The Administration of Indian Affairs in Canada" entitled "Indian Health Supervision," he says no less than six times that need for medical care has outstripped the amount of funds available. Perhaps there is a sign here of the lumps Scott had taken from P. H. Bryce, the medical inspector for the Department of the Interior between 1904 and 1921. Bryce embarked on a personal campaign to fight tuberculosis among Indians and, as Titley shows, came into conflict with Scott who, partly for budget reasons, did not support him. "Bryce blamed Scott personally for sabotaging his proposals, and in 1922, many years after the event [the submission in 1909 of Bryce's tuberculosis plan], he published a scathing pamphlet, *The Story of a National Crime*, in which he denounced the deputy superintendent for his vanity and his indifference to the health problems of the native population"(85).

The 1927 Annual Report, parts of which are borrowed for the 1931 address, also has a section called "Indian Health Supervision," which, while concerned about tuberculosis, is much less defensive about it: "While it is well known that tuberculosis is prevalent among the Indians, steps are now being taken to ascertain its actual incidence with some degree of accuracy, and every effort is made to encourage the natives in following hygenic modes of life which tend to strengthen the powers of resistance to disease"(12). Scott, or some mask of the man, is obviously not looking right at this problem. He is drawing a veil of words over it. Figures about the "actual incidence" of tuberculosis appear in Bryce's medical report for 1906, which, ironically, precedes the Treaty 9 reports in the sessional papers for that year. Scott had observed actual incidences of tuberculosis with his own eyes in 1905 and 1906. According to Dr. Meindl's 1906 medical appendix to the treaty commissioner's report, "Tuberculosis was generally prevalent, and I can safely state that nearly all these Indians have been or are victims"(305). One doesn't have to listen to Bryce to wonder at the discrepancy between what Scott says about the tuberculosis problem in 1927 and what he knows, or knew, about it.

But Bryce's pamphlet would have been a stronger "Appeal for Justice to the Indians of Canada," to quote its subtitle, if he had left off the "Epilogue," in which he complains of an injustice to himself: "To my disappointment the position of Deputy Minister of Health to which I had a right to aspire after twenty-two years as Chief Medical Officer of Ontario and fifteen years as Chief Medical Officer of Immigration and Indian Affairs was given to another, wholly outside the Federal Civil Service and in violation of the principle of promotion, which was supposed to prevail when the patronage system was to be done away with"(15).

3

A Life of Drift: The Man, Family Relations

Being stretches from thought to thought in much the same way the thin thread of the wasp's waist connects thorax and abdomen. In much the same way the siphuncle of the chambered nautilus winds through the spirals of its growth. This being is perceived as soul and threads the phenomena of mind in a special sequence known as personality. The beginning and end of each thought is marked by a gap. Existence implicates a thread through the gap which cannot be proven.

Christopher Dewdney

IF THEORIES OF THE UNSTABLE SELF, of the fiction of identity, had not developed by now, what we know of the life of Duncan Campbell Scott would be reason enough to develop one. A surprising thing to say about a man whose life E. K. Brown called (writing to Arthur Bourinot, April 11, 1948 TF) "not very *mouvementé*?" I think I can make good the claim. To follow me through this chapter and beyond, all you need to accept is that there is no Duncan Campbell Scott.

No D. C. Scott as we usually think of him, that is, accepting without hesitation what others have told us, but rather a series of notations made by his actions and his words, his letters, his essays, his poems and stories, by the spoken and written comments of people about him. It is so difficult to reconcile many of these notations with one another, especially in the absence of the living man who lent a physical focus to the idea of a core of identity, that a coherent, linear account of the man's life requires a lot of telescoping. What if one wishes to remain alert and alive to the nuances, the contradictions, the holes in the record, wishes to allow these full play? Even if the search were as much as ever driven by a desire for wholeness, it would still make sense to proceed with negative capability for a watchword and without expecting to reach the core or solve all the mysteries of Scott's personality.

Even if one sees him as having been formed while a child into the austere, reticent adult he became, Scott was a personality in process all his life. No matter what the formative years lodged in his makeup, he still had to *deal* with that cluster of traits as long as he lived. His life was hardly an untroubled dictation of his particular genetic and early environmental coding. Perhaps there are such easy lives, lived by people who have no difficulty accepting themselves and their lot, but Scott had trouble doing both, and his life must at times have been more *mouvementé*, psychically speaking, than was at all comfortable to him. Scott was in process during his life, then; he is still in process, though his own participation has been superseded by that of others, by those of us interested in him, both fascinated and frustrated by the incompleteness of the information.

If one accepts as a method of probing the matter the proposition that there is no solid Scott, then it follows that the Scott we think we know was created in two subdivisible stages. The first stage was Scott's. It's doubtful that he ever thought of himself as a self-construction, though he must have regretted at times the fact that he grew into a man obliged to wear a mask everywhere, a man whose manner of restraint concealed deep emotional turbulences that had little outlet except obliquely in poetry and fiction. He was shaped, and he shaped himself, as most of us do: merely by living in his time and place. Few of us buck the current of our times, and Scott was in this respect one of the many. Late in his life he suffered from a sense that he had let himself drift where he might have stood and fought. The second phase of the construction of Scott (and of his work) began, in talk and writings about him, while he was still alive. A sort of summary of that phase is the "Memoir" of E. K. Brown, who met and talked with Scott late in his life. This essay has seemed so authoritative that no one except Robert McDougall has suggested that it is a construction. It is based on "hard" fact, to be sure, but also on Brown's best hunches, and even on honest suppression of material that could not be authenticated or simply did not fit.

Regarding Scott as a fluid entity makes possible (in fact, is partly generated by) the reading of style as well as substance in both the words of Scott and those who write about him. A method of approach that assumes there are no neutral or transparent presentations, that the identity of a person, as of a text, is composed as much of manner as of content, disciplines the inquirer to examine the packaging of every pronouncement. What follows in this chapter, then, is not another memoir, but a new reading of the sources of a life that almost bends in two: before and after the death of Scott's daughter in 1907. It's a reading intended as context for the experience of the treaty trips and the writing that issued from them and, in fact, for everything Scott wrote about Native people. A detour from that territory will help us to see it better. If it has been hard to make Scott's Indian Affairs career fit with his poetry on Indians, is it partly because what we know of his life hasn't helped us much? Have we been looking in the wrong places? Asking the wrong questions? The whole of my approach to his life (private in this chapter, public in the next) has been determined by a wish to illuminate that central problem. This chapter is a hall of mirrors in which Scott's friends, his parents, his daughter, his two wives, are held up by turns in an attempt to explain him. The reflections of Scott that return are multiple, and they aren't always as clarifying as one might wish, but they do turn out to be useful.

WHAT WE SEEM TO POSSESS are the basic facts of a long life, unsurprisingly fewer of these for the early years than for the later ones, when some people were paying more attention to Scott, and when he himself was thinking to save and order papers that might be important some day. We owe to such consideration for latter-day collaborators on his biography the knowledge that Scott occasionally assumed the mask of a pseudonym. As Silas Reading in 1895, he published "An Open Letter to a Member of Parliament" in the *Ottawa Journal;* as Oliver Gascoigne he published a satirical poem in *Toronto Saturday Night* in 1937. The true author of these pieces is identified as DCS in Scott's hand on his own copies preserved in the Scott-Aylen papers. From about 1899, when he began to correspond with Pelham Edgar, it would be possible to create a much more detailed chronology of Scott's life than the useful one that Glenn Clever assembled for *The Selected Poems of Duncan Campbell Scott.* From the extant letters we could put together an account of Scott's movements almost monthly, if not daily. We know what sorts of activity he engaged in when he was in Ottawa, and we know when and for what purpose, whether business or pleasure, he left the city he lived in all his adult life. What we do not know is who he was.

To those who try to construct a portrait of him from the traces he left behind, never having so much as caught a glimpse of the man, never having heard him speak, except on tape,[1] Scott would be a mystery even if there were no problem in squaring his Indian Affairs work with his poetic life. One envies E. K. Brown his opportunity to meet the man whose memoir he was to write. The value of personal contact can hardly be overestimated as a basis for quickening information and as governor of the unaided imagination — which will not be absent from any account worth reading. Imagination is certainly present in Robert McDougall's article, "D. C. Scott: A Trace of Documents, a Touch of Life," the first signal of it being the title, with its pun on trace, meaning both a small amount and a search. The search refers to McDougall's tracking down of the Scott material now known as the Scott-Aylen papers that make up so much of the source material for any archive-based study of Scott. His article provides a basis for the "Introduction" to *The Poet and the Critic,* his edition of the letters between Scott and E. K. Brown.

McDougall's brief portrait of Scott the old man is a mere touch of his life, enlivened by vivid writing replete with telling detail, as in this brief account of Scott's physical appearance:

> He is tall, or seems so at 5' 10", because he holds himself erect despite his four-score years, and as he comes into the light we can see that his sandy hair has thinned to reveal a large and prominent forehead. His eyes, behind rimless glasses, may seem cold, but they can light up quickly with a twinkle that is both impish and warm. He dresses conservatively and wears an English broadcloth shirt with a tab-collar. ("Trace" 128)

McDougall is not remembering Scott in this passage; he is dramatizing an imaginary appearance of the poet, bringing him up close, onstage, into the present tense. *Today* he has on the broadcloth shirt with the tab collar. What the man wears has something to do with who he is, of course, but the function of that detail in McDougall's portrait is to convince a reader, as circumstantial detail does in realist fiction, that the writer knows his subject and that the reader may trust him.

McDougall would probably be the first to admit, and it's no reproach to suggest, that his techniques are those of fiction. McDougall would also admit that his biographical work, like anyone's, must be read with an eye for narrative point of view if he is not to be granted more authority than he possesses. Having been over most of the sources myself, I know almost as well as McDougall the biographical problem that Scott presents. As he puts it, comparing the critic with the poet, "Brown is one man . . . not two or three men as Scott seems to be" (*Poet and Critic* 3). McDougall's article is a clearing of the throat, a discussion, with dramatized set pieces, of the problems facing Scott's biographer.

McDougall rightly admires E. K. Brown's memoir, "a piece of work so deft and perceptive and well informed that it was and remains difficult for one to imagine how it could be bettered" ("Trace" 134). At the same time he knows that the memoir, particularly its final sketch of the octogenarian poet, "has become in some respects the authorized version of the Scott image" ("Trace" 129). McDougall knows that he is contributing a version of his own to which could be added others of Scott in his "'perfectly tolerable, perfectly beautiful old age'" (Brown, quoting Walter Pater xli), versions like those of William Arthur Deacon and Arthur S. Bourinot. *Version* is a word carefully chosen by a man aware that the biographical definitive is infinitely elusive, even with apparently plainer subjects than Scott.

I THINK IT MAKES SENSE, stressing rather than ignoring the gaps in our knowledge and the component of invention in what we do know, to regard Scott as a fluid rather than a solid entity, but there is nothing very mysterious about this in at least one respect: he was not exactly the same person to all those who knew him. This is clearly so in his letters, where we can observe him showing different masks to different people. In July 1946 he wrote to Arthur Stringer, then working on a biography of Rupert Brooke, that he was "glad to think you are undertaking this difficult task" (PA/DCS); in October he asked E. K. Brown, "confidentially, was the choice of A.S. for this work not extraordinary, for there seems to be no sympathy between the work of the two men, placing them side by side . . ." (*Poet and Critic* 177). Scott was also a friend and admirer of Lorne Pierce when he was addressing Pierce as the head of the Ryerson Press, and an occasional detractor behind his back. Pierce was unlucky enough to find this out.

Nothing Pierce had heard from Scott told him anything other than that he and the poet held each other in mutual esteem. In fact, Scott wrote to him warmly on September 27, 1943, saying "I note from your last that you think of preserving my letters to you; I don't think they contain much wit or wisdom but they will show I think a constant friendliness which still continues unimpaired. I hope this letter will be included for it is written to acknowledge the Memorial Address for Marjorie Pickthall and to give you great praise for it. It seems to me entirely adequate and it revived all my admiration for her work and led me to take out her Collected Poems and reread them" (Q/LP). If there is any hint in this letter of reservations withheld, it would be in the faint praise of "entirely adequate." The flattery is further undercut by references to Pierce in Scott's letters to E. K. Brown. In February 1943 Scott had commented to Brown on the "advance notice of the Sir Charles Book" (Elsie Pomeroy's biography of Roberts), saying that it "sounds like our national criticism at its worst," and adding that "L.P. has been one of the chief offenders and I dread to read his contribution to this biography" (*Poet and Critic* 54).

While Scott and Brown were collaborating on the edition of Lampman's new poems that Pierce's press was to publish, Scott was quite often testy on the subject of Pierce's ideas and practices. His tone was not consistent with unimpaired friendliness, and that was quite clear to Pierce when in 1959 Scott's opinions became public in Arthur S. Bourinot's *Some Letters of Duncan Campbell Scott.* Pierce's displeasure overflowed onto Bourinot: "When you collected the first DCS letters," he wrote on June 15, 1960, "I should have appreciated a look at the Ms before publication. Scott's attitude, as revealed there, is so contrary to all that his letters to me showed that I was astonished" (ASB). He goes on to give his own perspective on problems with the Lampman book, and says that "Scott was impatient, as he was when the Royal Society Medal was slow in coming." If Pierce had seen Bourinot's manuscript, would he have asked for equal time? His letter has a whiff of censorship about it.

The archival preservation of letters to, from, and about Scott facilitates this cross-referencing, the detection of inconsistencies and small deceptions.

Did Scott really have so little use for Pierce? Clearly he did not admire Pierce hugely, as he did Lawren Harris (*Poet and Critic* 106), but he probably had mixed feelings about the publisher, feelings that may well have varied with his mood. One of the letters to Brown even takes back a previous outburst: "You will have begun to understand me and know that I sometimes yield to irritation; but you know I have no such strong feeling against Pierce as my remark would imply; so forget my censures" (*Poet and Critic* 188). Well, few publishers are constantly popular with their authors. Tracing something of the ups and downs between Scott and Pierce reveals an irony: an expression of apparent cordiality could mask quite another attitude.

In fact, as I have said, Scott seems to have been wearing a mask almost all the time. One of Brown's informants, "the wife of one of his most intimate friends [identified as Mrs. R. H. Coats in Brown's drafts for his memoir PA/EKB], used to say that Duncan Scott's habitually fixed and melancholy expression was 'not his real face,' but a mask that had formed upon it" ("Memoir" xviii). The mask was not only melancholy but austere, and Scott knew that he wore it. He confessed to intimates like Pelham Edgar and Elise Aylen that he was able to speak about himself only with great difficulty. Close friends knew that the mask of coldness was just that — a mask. But how many of them can have known that Scott was not only a witty, warm-hearted friend when you got to know him, a good mimic, a man with a rich sense of humour tending to the dry, but that underneath the austere mask was a troubled soul, melancholy indeed. If his letters to Elise had not been preserved (she claimed to have burned them,[2] and perhaps intended to; did she incinerate Pelham Edgar's letters instead?), there might have been no way of knowing how little he sometimes thought of himself.

How much did E. K. Brown know about this self-doubt, this self-recrimination? It would be interesting to find where the "authorized version" came from, how it was formed. Brown was a scholar, so his drafts of the "Memoir" for *Selected Poems* bear marginal notations of his sources (and a list of informants precedes the published version), but most of this is factual. My impression is that the principal source must have been Scott himself, no free revealer of intimacies. That Brown "knew" more than he could or would say in his memoir is suggested by a couple of details. One is a letter from Pierce to Bourinot about Scott's relationship with his parents and other members of the family.

> The last time E. K. Brown was in my office, we discussed it. He himself regarded it as a mystery and told me a number of things about the relationship that he had heard in a casual way, that are rather startling. Something needs to be said about that period of his life and his relationship with his parents and family. Just what happened? (ASB May 21, 1951)

These startling things didn't appear in Brown's "Memoir." Perhaps he left them out on the grounds that a "Memoir" of quality should give little credence to hearsay. It's hard to blame Brown for suppressing what sounds like speculative testimony about Scott's relationship with his family, though it's a loss not to know it. What else did Brown find out about Scott that he could not or did not say, and how did he find it out?

A manuscript leaf of Brown's "Memoir" quotes a passage from J. B. Yeats's *Early Memories: Some Chapters of Autobiography* that Scott wrote into his notebook for 1921: "To be cut off from sin and evil is to be cut off from so much that, entering into our intricate being, is necessary to mental power and effectiveness" (77). Brown comments: "but [Scott's] contemplation of sin and evil was chiefly in books or in his dreams where guilt, vengeance and terror were rife. In his conscious hours there was an embarrassment in being preoccupied with himself" (PA/EKB). Those remarks, edited out of the final version, are immediately followed by the quotation from Scott that remains: "'The trouble is,' he writes 'that the moment I endeavor to write or speak about myself something intervenes and I become shy and inarticulate and anything that I write or say seems affected and banal. I suppose this makes ordinary intercourse with me difficult but I cannot change my spots now.'" Scott's remark about his shyness appears in an undated letter to Pelham Edgar (ASB), but where did the other provocative information come from? A preoccupation with dark matters might be projected from reading certain poems and stories, and that might be what Brown is going on. The scholar in him notes in the margin of his draft, beside a generalization about Scott's early years, "deduced from his unpub. novel."

I don't want to make too much of a passage in a draft of Brown's "Memoir" simply because it's interesting, but I don't want to ignore it, either, especially because Scott did try his best to "change his spots," or at least to remove the mask, with Elise. He was able to bring himself to write to her regularly on that painful subject, himself — painful not only because the mask had become fixed but also because it covered a self he did not like. "I would like you to understand me better if there be anything to understand," he wrote on July 7, 1929. "I find it most difficult to say anything about myself. Whenever I begin, something stops me. Some ancestral emotion I suppose — afraid to give anyone power over me? Is that it?" (PA/S-A). Scott's letters to Elise cover a period of five years. Many of them were written when he was on business trips or on vacations and she in Ottawa. The earliest letters were quite formal, but intimacy gradually developed and it peaks in a six-page love letter combining silliness and rapture in apparently unprecedented release. The letter is undated, but it was sent to Elise from Victoria, probably in 1929. Here is part of it:

> This does not conform to the model [for love letters] but it is just as full of love as any of yours — as this is almost my first love letter I don't mean my first to you but *really* my first I feel as if I am not doing badly. I have cultivated reticence too long & I am so perfect in this kind that it does not come easily for me to spread my strongest, most secret feelings on this blue page, as when I write I love you dear Elise I feel all the restraint back of it & the confession is or seems to me, richer than if I could give myself up to repetitions. It is like a flower that grows out of the rock — the granite is proud of it and you, even you, who pluck it may find some greater beauty in it because it found difficulty in blooming but you take it root & all. This may be obscure but there is something in the idea. If I (as you say) give you the companionship you have lacked — What Joy! for I truly believe that your heart and mind are worthy of all devotion so I give myself to that destiny in all simplicity. (PA/S-A)

"Root and all" may have been unconsciously pulled from Tennyson's "Flower in the Crannied Wall," but the image is turning into something else that Scott knows he hasn't yet grasped. The fact that he leaves it as is, including the slightly incongruous editorial comment, is evidence of his spontaneity. To adapt two of Scott's lines from "The Height of Land," Elise has cast a spell that "gives the inarticulate part / Of [his] strange being one moment of release."

Scott had, in fact, been writing undeclared love letters to Elise before this crucial outburst; he had been sharing more of himself than he seems to have shared with anyone else. In one letter, of March 16, 1929, he encloses a page he "did a few days ago." In what seems to be a response to something a depressed Elise had written him, he tried to work out his philosophy in prose. The substance of those words will be considered in chapter 11, where I deal with "The Height of Land" as an orchestration of thought, but Scott's comment on what he had just written is important here:

> I feel foolish in writing this as I am not bringing help with full hands. My philosophy after a life of drift is no consolation to one who is young & who wants sweetness & activity. I know now that I have never fought against anything nor worked for anything but just accepted & drifted from point to point — I have dimly felt that if I worked & protested & resisted I should be wrecked — So maybe you will understand why with some gifts I have done so little. (PA/S-A)

These are precisely the damning words one might delight to find if building a case against Scott the civil servant in Indian Affairs, though Scott does not specify that aspect of his public life in his confession. On the other side, anyone wanting to defend him would find these words difficult to work around.

How defend a man who confesses his guilt? At one point I had thought to delay introducing this passage until late in the book, for dramatic reasons I suppose. But I have decided to insert it here, without much comment, feeling that it ought to hover over all that is to come. Eventually I will have more to say about the passage. When an intensely private person confesses his inmost self-doubts before strangers, as I have in effect induced Scott to do, it seems to me that those strangers owe him the consideration of not rushing to judgement before as much as possible of the context for his words has been put into place. It should also be remembered that the perspective of this book is the view, so to speak, from 1905–1906, many years before Scott assessed his life as a "life of drift."

SCOTT'S RESERVE MAY HAVE STEMMED from his family's having moved from town to town, from charge to charge of his father's Methodist ministry. E. K. Brown speculates that this might have been the case. One might also expect to find an overbearing father somewhere in the background of a shy man constitutionally unable to talk about himself, but there is no sanction in Scott's letters or anywhere else for believing that the unflattering portrait of Firmian's minister father in the untitled novel is based on life. E. K. Brown thought that the novel as it stood was not worthy of publication, according to an unaddressed report he wrote after Scott's death, but he did consider it a biographical source. "The interest," he says, "would be less in the book itself than in the light it threw on the author. From that point of view it is a fascinating thing" (PE). Unfortunately, again, he wasn't specific about what he meant. Robert McDougall speculates a little further on the novel as

> a tempting source for biographical readings, and especially in its early scenes, which is where we most need help and which take place in the 1880s in a community very like that of Smiths Falls,[3] the community of Asheville where the young Firmian Underwood makes his start. Later in the novel, when Cornelia says to Robin Garrabrant, "I was brought up with people who would never speak out and I was infected by it," are we justified in attributing this bitter recollection to Scott's own experiences as a boy? I have hearsay evidence of his having used, in conversation with a relative, almost the exact words Cornelia uses. But one must be wary of the devious ways of fiction, and I think wary especially of Scott himself when in fiction he seems most autobiographical, for it is characteristic of the man that with acquaintances and even with friends he remained throughout his life uncommunicative about these early years. (139)

Late in his life Scott remembered his parents warmly in connection with the woodcuts in *Good Words* and *Good Words for the Young*, magazines that came into the Scott household monthly. "The bound volumes of those periodicals," he says, "were the possessions of happy children brought up by indulgent parents whose influence was ever for the best in letters, music and in art, who encouraged every evidence of talent" (*Walter J. Phillips* 34). Otherwise, he had little to say about either of his parents, except in a general way, and it's hard to read from their son back to them. This is really what Pelham Edgar is doing when he discovers the source of each "side" of Scott's character in the stock characteristics of nationality and gender: "No doubt from his mother, rich in all wisdom gathered from the islands of the highland sea, there came his music and poetical gifts. From his father perhaps the great capacity of taking pains, his powers of management, his ability to get things done." (This appears in a draft of Edgar's *Dalhousie Review* article, "Duncan Campbell Scott" [PE]. In the article itself only one ancestral strain is stressed: "Those who discover the 'natural magic' of the Celt in the work of their poet son are permitted to attribute this to the infusion of a Highland Scottish strain into his blood" [38]). "No doubt" and "perhaps" create a dubious parallelism in this sentence, this apparent stab in the dark. I say apparent so as not to dismiss out of hand a theory of national or racial origin of personality that may now look naive, but which Scott shared with Edgar. "The Onondaga Madonna," "The Half-breed Girl," "At Gull Lake: August 1810," and other poems and stories portray people inwardly torn between ancestrally determined aspects of themselves.

Scott does say that his father was a well-read man, and that his well-stocked library was open to his son. The Reverend William Scott was himself something of a writer. He had a competent, occasionally vivid prose style, as we can tell because some of his prose has survived. His two-page "Introductory Remarks" to "Fragment of a Tragedy [*Cromwell*] by Lord Lytton" is pasted into his son's scrapbook (ASB). There are also his pamphlets on the Oka situation, on educational matters, and on Wesleyan Methodism, not to mention the introduction to his *Teetotaller's Hand Book* (using strong drink: "the most gigantic evil of our times" iv). Scott's creative side may not have been inherited solely from the wild Highland Scots background of his mother, even assuming a one-to-one relationship between personality and place; his father was Celtic, as well, albeit from Yorkshire. At any rate, it's surely relevant both to Scott the poet and Scott the civil servant that his father spent so much of his life ministering to the Indians in Southern Ontario and Quebec, and that he always took a special interest in their welfare while remaining very much a believer in progress and white civilization.

According to William Scott's 1891 obituary in the *Ottawa Citizen,* the public highlight of his life was the investigation of the controversy surrounding the situation of the Indians at Oka in Quebec. A fascinating glimpse of William Scott comes from his report on the Oka Indian controversy, and the correspondence preceding and following it, that has been preserved in the Indian Affairs Red Files. The controversy is well worth dwelling on not only because it affords an opportunity to construct something of a father to Scott's son, but also because it seems in some ways like a paradigmatic land claims dispute. The disputants were the Sulpician Brothers who claimed to own the Seignory of the Two Mountains and those (not all of them Natives) who held that the Indians were living as tenants on land that was properly their own. There were local factors in the dispute, of course, like a conflict between English and French, Methodist and Catholic elements that were pressing their own predispositions in the name of the Indians, but the core issue was who had the right to the land.

Mr. Scott had secured for his son a patronage appointment to Indian affairs. "Nobody deserves more at my hands than you," wrote Sir John A. Macdonald on November 14, 1879. "I shall have great pleasure in helping your son to a position in the public service at an early day" (ASB). One might then expect the choice of William Scott as investigator to have been a biased one, and it was, but the bias was in this case toward the Indians. William Spragge, then superintendent general of Indian Affairs, felt that the French Crown must have intended that "a reserve of this Tract, for the benefit of the Indians in all time to come, should be established" (RG10a). It was Spragge who in February 1882 asked William Scott for "the benefit of your views" (RG10a). Scott's response certainly was impressive.

Not content with offering his personal opinion, which Spragge might reasonably have expected to favour the Indians, Scott came to Ottawa and researched the whole matter through government documents reaching back 200 years into the French era. Judging by a slight defensiveness in the preamble to his report, he knew that the verdict he rendered was not the expected one: "Some of the results of my examination may not be gratifying to many with whom I have been accustomed to co-operate, but there is only one path open to me, and that is fairly and impartially to present the case as it really stands, according to my candid opinion" (*Oka* 5). The gist of a very long report is that the Gentlemen of the Seminary of St. Sulpice did indeed own the land in question. Their proprietorship dated from 1663, according to the deed of donation that Scott located. He gives the impression throughout of being unswayed by anything but the truth; he seems like a decent man with a lively concern for the welfare of the Indians that, as he says, goes back 40 years to the time when he appeared before Lord Metcalfe and proposed measures to Lord Elgin on behalf of the "Western" Indians (probably those of Manitoulin Island among whom he did missionary work between 1841 and 1847).

The elder Scott also visited and reported on the Muskoka reserve where some of the Oka Indians had relocated and where it was his recommendation that the others would do well to move, given that there was no legal basis for expecting their situation at Oka to improve. In the summer of 1990, when the long-standing conflict took a dogleg into golf course expansion, a great many authorities were given reasons for wishing that Scott's recommendation had been accepted. First Nations people may have reason to be thankful they were not. "Elijah Harper and Oka changed everything for us," says John Bird. "The relationship between the First Nations and the rest of the people in what we now call Canada is no longer as it was before the summer of 1990" (xvii). The confrontations at Oka, together with Elijah Harper's scuttling of the Meech Lake Accord, begin to look like the turning point in government-Native relations in this country.

We can't learn what the son was like by examining the father, even assuming that we are seeing the father clearly in a couple of essays and some letters. In fact, we know of some ways in which the father and the son diverged widely. William Scott was a strong enough temperance man to have served as editor of the *Canada Temperance Advocate*, while his son enjoyed a social drink and didn't think much of prohibition. Scott abandoned his religion, as well; at least he severed institutional ties. "I was born into the Methodist Connection," he wrote to E. K. Brown in 1946, "when the adherents were called Wesleyan Methodists and were close to the revered founder of the sect; they seem to have forgotten him in their union [the United Church] and I have forgotten them all having wandered far away and am lost in a wilderness, but I have a strong Faith of my own, you see I spell Faith with a capital" (*Poet and Critic* 180–181). It is very unlikely that Duncan Scott would have quoted scripture to establish authority in a land claims question, as his father did, though the son undoubtedly carried Christian ideological baggage.

Notwithstanding his genuine concern for what he took to be the Indians' needs, William Scott believed it was absurd to think there could be any question of Natives owning the land when the earth belonged to God. He quotes scripture ("The earth is the Lord's and the fullness thereof" [*Oka* 48]) to prove it. Native elders might, in fact, agree: there could be no question of whites owning the land that was given by the Creator as a trust to be shared. William Scott does not see that natural extension of the argument. He reveals instead some of the blinkered assumptions that made the churches and the government such companions on the road to progress.

Genesis is William Scott's authority for differentiating between good and bad sorts of occupation of God's earth. In the account of the creation of man there is an injunction not only to take care of the earth (to "replenish" it) but to tame and take control of it, to "subdue it, and have dominion over" all of the creatures. It ought to be a nice theological question whether or not all God's directions to unfallen man remain in force after the contract-breaking disobedience and the exile to stony ground. At any rate,

William Scott sees in Genesis moral support for pioneers, who are much better than Indians at subduing a country in desperate need of it:

> Meanwhile there are millions of acres of unsubdued lands, and millions of people willing and able to fulfill the original decree. Discovering these immense tracts of land, of no value to the aborigines, except as hunting grounds, and required by the necessities of augmenting civilized populations, it is quite natural that an effort should be made to colonize the unsettled territories. The only question is how to do this on principles of justice and equity. (48–49)

Land takes on value, in William Scott's terms, only when it is "improved." The Indians being unlikely to do that, uninterested in subduing as they are, the land is thought to have no value for them. J. E. Chamberlin's *The Harrowing of Eden* eloquently shows the system of private ownership, usually rooted in agriculture (with or without scriptural backing), being imposed on North American Native peoples by governments ignorant of their culture, the capacities of the land they occupied, their real adaptational needs. Malice had a smaller part to play in this harrowing than well-meaning blindness. William Scott's report is typical. It's easy now to see his argument circling within the white value system (just as his research takes him through white documents only), but hindsight is 20/20. The younger Scott didn't have it, either.

E. K. BROWN'S INQUIRIES about the Scotts turned up little about Mrs. Scott, though there was this, in a letter to Brown from Jessie Colby of Stanstead, where the Scotts had lived for a year in 1877: "I am sorry I do not know anything more about the Scott families save that Mrs. Scott struck me as having good background & upbringing as well as good sense and charm and was somehow connected by marriage with McCallums in Montreal who were R.C.'s & had some sort of distinction" (PA/EKB). (Scott's uncle, Dr. Duncan Campbell McCallum, "was a well-known physician of Montreal and a Professor in McGill University" [Edgar, "Duncan Campbell Scott" 39].)

That we know so little about William Scott's wife, Duncan Scott's mother, is partly a function of the relative positions of men and women at the time. What we know about William Scott is preserved in records of his public life. Mrs. Scott had no public life, so hers is one of those untold stories of mothers in society almost until the present generation: invisible, unheard, like Native people and children. Of course, more might have been heard of Scott's mother had not that rift opened up between herself and her son over or after his marriage to Belle. This is presumably the family problem about which Brown heard the startling things. The estrangement extended to Scott's two sisters, as well, but he was reconciled with them in later years.

The cause of the trouble and the date of its beginning is lost. The most one can do is speculate on the basis of what is known, and that is little enough. Part of the problem might have been the differing backgrounds of the Scotts and the Botsfords. There must have been money in the Botsford family; perhaps it paid for such things as Elizabeth's education abroad. It seems unlikely that Scott's salary in 1905 would have stretched that far. Perhaps the salary would have had to be supplemented to accommodate European trips with Belle in 1902, 1904, 1907, 1921, and 1925, though Scott was often abroad with Elise in the early years after their marriage in 1931. One of the reasons Scott gave Pelham Edgar for not having attended university (he was thinking of taking medicine) is that his modest clerk's salary made a significant contribution to his family's income. Between the Boston Botsfords and the Ontario Scotts there must have been a wide economic gap.

Would the economic gap have been a social gap, as well? — not so much in that the Botsfords might have been or considered themselves "better" people than the Scotts, as in that different priorities might have obtained. One of the most interesting documents in the A. S. Bourinot papers is Belle Scott's social scrapbook. It gives a totally different impression of what the Scotts' Ottawa social life must have been like than anything Scott wrote or said on the subject. He seldom mentions anything in the social line except the visits of friends, and small gatherings of a slightly more formal sort, which he seems to have enjoyed. With friends he could unbend a little and exercise his lively wit. But Belle clearly circulated in the higher social spheres of Ottawa. Her social calendar was astonishingly full, as the periodically clipped-in, neatly written notebook pages recording her engagements show. Her teas and euchre parties were reported in the papers. She played violin at the Women's Morning Music Club. She kept souvenir cards of the "at homes" of others, including those of six successive wives of governors general. She kept tickets for the opening and prorogation of Parliament, and invitations to private theatricals at Rideau Hall. Scott would presumably have been, at the office, clear of the morning and afternoon activities, but the social ambition that radiates from Belle's scrapbook must have affected him.

On the evidence of Belle's scrapbook and the absence of any stress on social ambition in the letters of her shy husband, it would appear that Scott and his wife presented very different faces to the world. This is not proof of incompatibility, of course. And Scott might not have minded floating with his wife, in some ways. One of his letters to Elise in 1930 reports a gathering where he encountered "a lot of very ordinary folk . . . not our kind of people"; another written home from their honeymoon in 1934 suggests that they found too many "vile" people on the beaches of southern England. Perhaps there was a touch of snobbery in Scott's famous aloofness. Madge Macbeth suggests another way in which Belle and Duncan might have agreed. She "was an epicure if there ever was one" and he "had very discriminating taste in food" (*Over My Shoulder* 143).

Was the alienation of Scott's mother the product of a social gulf between the two families? Perhaps the cause was merely a conflict of personalities. Whatever the reason, Scott seems to have had to keep references to his mother out of 108 Lisgar Street. It's extraordinary to hear how Scott refers to her death and funeral in an undated letter to Pelham Edgar: "I wrote you a note last night — But this is to say that my mother died this week and we buried her yesterday. I thought you might hear of this and write me a letter of condolence — I don't want you to do that and I will explain why when we meet — so pass the event by without a written word" (ASB).

Whatever explanations Scott made must have been verbal; only rumours of rumour survive, because even to friends Scott was closemouthed about the problem. R. H. Coats was Scott's friend for 40 years. "Beyond saying to me a couple of times," he wrote to E. K. Brown on October 17, 1950, "that he had had a 'hell of a time' occasionally in his domestic life he never referred to the fight between Belle and his family" (PA/EKB). This at least omits Scott from among the combatants. Brown was less frank in his "Memoir" but still quite direct about Belle's influence on her husband's life:

> Belle Scott was energetic, high-strung, and imperious. She had much of the characteristic New England zeal to remould persons and circumstances nearer to her heart's desire. She was a stimulating companion, and she cared about poetry; but a man of Duncan Scott's disposition, shy and slow to mature, might sooner have come to a full self-understanding if he had not lived in the shadow of so dominant a wife. (xviii)

When Rupert Brooke stayed with the Scotts, he found Scott "a very nice chap (especially away from his wife, who's nice enough)," good company over a drink at a "club in the country," and anxious to talk poetry (*Letters* 487). So he said to Wilfrid Gibson; introducing Scott to Harold Monro (*Letters* 492), Brooke simply wrote of Scott, in a boys' club sort of way, "He has a wife." "Of course we all rather walked on eggs with Belle," R. H. Coats says in the letter already mentioned, "though I have heard him 'jump' on her too." Might the "high-strung" Belle have suffered from hypochondria? Scott fairly often writes to Edgar of her indisposition and his resulting inability to get much done.

There is one other bit of evidence of Scott's feeling for Belle that is perhaps worth introducing: Scott's love letter to Elise — almost his first, he says. The implication is that he feels for Elise something that no other ever inspired in him. It's best not to build too much on the words of a man whose sensibilities are inflamed, but the little we know of Belle Scott suggests that her husband would never have been able to drop his defences so completely with her. (If he had not been unguarded to Elise, I repeat, we would have lost the most revealing comments Scott ever made about his life; we might never have been able to lift that austere mask.) Perhaps Scott never wrote love letters to Belle; perhaps something other than passionate love had brought Belle and himself together. Brown makes her sound as if she would have been capable of doing the proposing and supplying the acceptance. But with Belle Scott, as with William Scott, there is not enough evidence to permit a full view. What looks on paper like a bad match might have been anything but. R. H. Coats says that "Elizabeth . . . was an unbreakable bond between them. I don't know which of them was the more wrapped up in her." He also backpedals on the matter of marital conflict in an undated letter to Brown that refers to the one quoted above: "I hope I did not give the impression that he was unhappy with Belle. She was devoted to him and he to her" (PA/EKB).

I doubt that Scott was an "ordinary guy" compared to his first wife. An appetite for social status does emanate from her social scrapbook, and society may be what, unlike Scott, she was bred to. But there are various indications that Scott was not uninterested in associating with the powerful. He belonged to a private dining group, male by the sound of it, the one for which he wrote his irreverent "Byron on Wordsworth, Being Discovered Stanzas of Don Juan." Private clubs are not for the hoi polloi. It's curious that Scott and his western rival for the post of deputy minister, W. H. Graham, both lost their Indian Affairs jobs over a teapot tempest stirred up about a private club.[4] Scott did some hobnobbing with prime ministers. He was friends with Robert Borden, a sometime golf partner, and Borden worked an inspirational passage from "Fragment of an Ode to Canada" into his 1929 convocation address at Queen's University.

Of course, Scott may have been obliged rather than eager to socialize with first ministers from time to time. His letters show that he was no fan of Mackenzie King as far back as 1905 when King was interfering with the Makers of Canada biography of his ancestor, William Lyon Mackenzie King, but he must have had some social contact with the man. There are two accounts of a social engagement at King's residence, Kingsmere, which would not have improved Scott's opinion of King: an anecdote of Arthur Bourinot's (TF) and another in Madge Macbeth's *Over My Shoulder.*

Precisely what happened on the evening that Scott appeared on the same program of entertainment with Pat, King's Airedale, is not clear. In Bourinot's version he read from *The Green Cloister;* in Madge Macbeth's he played the piano. Bourinot says that Pat's vocal stylings were accompanied by his master on the piano, Macbeth that Pat supplied his own accompaniment. Both versions agree that Pat was not an accomplished performer. "I took second place to the dog," Bourinot quotes Scott as saying, still astonished but appreciating the comedy of the situation. "It was a bit of an anti-climax!" That's one way to look at it, but at least Pat was the warm-up act. The story is irresistible for the comic *mouvement* it adds to a quiet life. It also shows that Scott had a place near the seats of the mighty. Perhaps he was not totally unlike his wife in his ambitions. And as for her, a new dimension of her character shows in her devastated reaction to the death of their daughter Elizabeth in 1907. There are no entries in her social scrapbook between 1907 and 1912. That hiatus tells me she was no mere superficial social butterfly.

IF SCOTT'S LIFE was temporarily broken by Elizabeth's death, his literary life was almost broken into two stages by it. In 1907, at 45, Scott was roughly halfway through his life. Behind him were three books of poetry, *The Magic House and Other Poems* (1893), *Labor and the Angel* (1898), and *New World Lyrics and Ballads* (1905). The chapbook *Via Borealis* appeared in 1906. His book of short stories, *In the Village of Viger,* had been published in 1896. Scott had, in fact, been anthologized in W. D. Lighthall's *Songs of the Great Dominion* (1889) before publishing a volume. Other stories and poems had been published in magazines. He had been working on the novel that is usually dated circa 1905, though he mentions it in a letter to Pelham Edgar of 1902 and was still at it in 1911. He had published essays here and there and had collaborated with Archibald Lampman and William Wilfred Campbell during 1892 and 1893 on the weekly column entitled "At the Mermaid Inn." With Pelham Edgar, in the early years of the new century, he was editor of the Makers of Canada series of biographies. His own contribution to the series, *John Graves Simcoe* (a "potboiler," he called it to R. H. Coats), was published in 1905. If all of his sorts of literary work are considered, the first few years of the 20th century were quite productive for Scott. He would have had reason to think he was getting somewhere. Since he had been writing for 18 years (having started under the stimulating example of Archibald Lampman in 1887 or 1888), he could not be called prolific, but he hadn't been rushing immature work into print, either. For Copeland and Day, the American publishers of *Viger,* he could put together a long list of favourable English and American reviews of *The Magic House.* He was publishing regularly in American periodicals.

"The Piper of Arll," first collected in *The Magic House,* had been published in the American magazine *Truth.* That was where John Masefield saw it. He was then working in a New York mattress factory and reading hugely in his spare time. His autobiographical *In the Mill* somewhat dilutes the minor Canadian myth that "The Piper of Arll" made a writer of the laureate-to-be. Here, Scott's poem has to share the credit with other works. Chaucer's "The Parliament of Fowls" is "something deeper" (95), Masefield says, but

"The Piper" was still "the first poem by a living writer to touch me to the quick" (58). It was on November 8, 1905, that Masefield wrote Scott to repay the debt of awakening to poetry that "The Piper" had accomplished, and to ask permission to include the poem in *A Sailor's Garland,* an anthology he was editing. "I can hardly hope that you will know my name," he begins, and goes on as follows:

> Ten years ago, when I was in America, as a factory hand near New York, I read "The Piper of Arll" in the Christmas number of a paper called "Truth." I had never (till that time) cared very much for poetry, but your poem impressed me deeply, and set me on fire. Since then poetry has been the one deep influence in my life, and to my love of poetry I owe all my friends, and the position I now hold. (PA/DCS)

This is the beginning of a lasting friendship between the two, all of it apparently conducted in letters, though Belle Scott visited the Masefields in 1906. It was Masefield who sent Rupert Brooke to visit Scott, and Brooke who arranged introductions for Scott to the other Georgians, of whom Lascelles Abercrombie and the anthologist Edward Marsh became correspondents.

Masefield was not poet laureate until 1930, of course, and it was not until then that his awakening by the Canadian poet became a legend repeated almost without fail whenever there was an occasion to write about Scott. If Scott eventually got tired of hearing about that typically Canadian claim to fame (only foreign appreciation counts), he could only have been gratified in 1905 to know he had caught the attention of a fellow poet in another country, and that this man thought well enough of his work to spread the word. Scott heard from Masefield of other admirers abroad. In an undated letter probably written early in 1906, because it refers to the second treaty summer as upcoming, Masefield sent Scott "a little book about death [probably not one of his own], for you to read by your campfires at the back of beyond. It is too tiny a volume to make much difference to your pack, and the cover ought to be great medicine for the Indians." He went on:

> Since I first wrote to you, William Sharp (Fiona MacLeod) has died; and, as he was very well known in America, I expect that the Celtic poets have all of them a certain popularity on your side. He was a great admirer of "The Piper of Arll," and of the charming lyric "Afterwards" in Labor & the Angel. I remember one night at Yeats's rooms, when they read the poem aloud, (& the Dirge for a Violet) & talked about your delicate rhythms, saying how beautiful they were after the mechanical, metallic rhythms of the school of Kipling. I thought you might like to know this. (TF)

Most likely Scott did, though he would not have been overwhelmed to know it. He never did muster much appreciation for the Celtic Yeats and, in fact, remained grudging in his praise for the Irish poet throughout his life.

This connection with Masefield tells us that Scott was already a literary somebody in 1905. Roberts, Carman, and Lampman, the other important poets of his "generation," had gotten the jump on him in terms of general reputation, and that would not begin to change until E. K. Brown's *On Canadian Poetry* picked him and Lampman out of the group, but Scott could not complain. He was a quiet perfectionist, always scornful of uninformed boosterism of a Canadian literature that had no dependable critical conscience. He was content not to be lionized. He was doing all right, but the death of his daughter caused a 10-year hiatus between books. Part of what is meant by thinking of 1905 and 1906, the treaty-negotiating years, as watershed or pivotal years, is that they just preceded Elizabeth's tragic death in 1907.

While Scott was in the North, Elizabeth and Belle were in France, where Elizabeth was attending a convent school in Paris, the Convent du Religieuses du Très-Sainte Sacrement. (The name appears on the letterhead on which Elizabeth regularly wrote her parents.) According to Pelham Edgar and others, she was a gifted piano student and that was the reason for study abroad. Her parents were both musicians, having met when Scott was piano accompanist for a violin recital of Belle Warner Botsford in Ottawa. Belle had also studied in Paris before beginning a career as professional violinist. She made her English debut as Belle Botsford at the Aeolian Hall in London on July 6, 1905. I have already mentioned four brief but favourable reviews of the event. Scott was corresponding with Elizabeth during both of his summer trips, though with what regularity it's hard to know. When mail caught up with the treaty party, it was worth a mention in Scott's journal. In 1905, Elizabeth's birthday (September 22), was also mentioned. The most poignant of Elizabeth's letters, given that she was a year away from death, is the following (I quote two excerpts), written on June 14, 1906:

> How are you getting on with your treaty this time and are you allowed to have what you want to eat now that you haven't got Mr Bray [T. C. Rae] with you. . . . Isn't it nice for you to have Pelham with you please give him my love. How do you feel having a baby named after you? — My Grandmother told me that if my mother was like anybody else we could spend the summer togeather [*sic*] and I just thought, if you were like anybody else we might. The big black cat is still at the convent but both the yellow one and the canary are dead. (PA/DCS)

The offhand comment about spending the summer together must have given Scott a twinge even in 1906 when he didn't have the reason of her death to lament the loss of such valuable time with her. Elizabeth had been in France for two school years, the 11th and 12th of her life, before she died. The Scotts visited her at the convent in 1907 and left her apparently hale as they proceeded to Spain. The first telegram from the convent that reached them at the Hotel Orient read: *"Elizabeth malade fièvre probablement scarlatine Inquietante Revenir."* Before they could act there was this: *"Madame Duncan Scott est-elle chez vous Elizabeth Morte."* There is no sadder letter in all of Scott's correspondence than the one he wrote to Helen and Pelham Edgar on July 17, 1907. It makes the summer of 1906 look not only like a high point in Scott's life, but like a time of relative innocence and unreflective happiness:

> I have both your notes and can only write a word in reply. We have both suffered too much. I think every fibre of our souls was ingrown and tangled with hers. In no merely rhetorical way I say it seems impossible for us to go on. How can we? My poor dear wife has been prostrated. Do you remember Pelham how I used to say when we were so happy together last summer "I wonder where we will be this time next year?" Well here am I — and there is still a next year and a next year — How happy we were and how thoughtless. I have thought much about it and have said to myself "If I might be there now by one of those still deep lakes with my friend as it was last summer I might get some rest." — I should like to have a talk with you both; it seems necessary in truth but we are far separated — and it cannot be. My wife sends best wishes and thanks for good words. We are coming home as soon as we can — I don't know just when. (Bourinot, *More Letters* 34–35)

Lundy's Lane and Other Poems appeared in 1916, dedicated to Elizabeth and with a section of playful and elegiac poems as a sort of memorial to her, including both "The Closed Door," a mourning lyric, and "By a Child's Bed," the lyric of a father's fears for his precious and vulnerable child. Remarkably both had been written in 1902, well before Elizabeth died.

WORKING WITH TOO LITTLE INFORMATION on a very recalcitrant biographical subject who shows us aspects, faces, masks, rather than a solid continuum of self has its frustrations, but it is something other than floundering in the dark. Each bit of information carries not exactly the same value as each other bit; motifs do recur, carrying more weight than isolated testimony. Let me try to round out this glance at Scott by introducing what Madge Macbeth says about Scott's public life. It has a fascinating resonance with what he says to Elise about his life of drift, his failure to fight for anything. "He was a fierce though unaggressive individualist," Macbeth says:

> He never sought an argument and never took part in one if he could help it. A genuine humanitarian, he loved his fellow men in small doses and was always willing to extend a helping hand to those who asked him. He refused, however, to become involved with crowds, with joiners, with movements. He dreaded the inescapable differences of opinion that invariably merged into bitter recriminations and poisoned personal relationships. If a matter of principle produced disagreement he armoured himself against the hostility of those who held divergent opinions. But he would not enter into unimportant controversies although by evading them he was called high-handed or snobbish. Once, I asked him why he was not a member of a certain organization. He answered: "Because I can't adjust myself to a crowd of people. I don't expect them to accept my ideas, but neither can I accept the ones they hold. So there's bound to be friction, and —" he smiled at me "— I never learned to quarrel." (*Over My Shoulder* 136–137)

What sort of "genuine humanitarian" loves his fellow man "in small doses"? Macbeth's unintentional oxymoron makes Scott seem more niggardly than he may have been. For a man who was not a joiner, moreover, he was not only a member but an executive member of a goodly number of groups of quite various sorts, from his country club to the Royal Society. Still, with the reinforcement of Scott's self-condemnation as a nonfighter, we are probably justified in putting some faith in Macbeth's less negative version of the same motif. In fact, her version may supply a needed corrective to Scott's own.

I have said that Scott was no saint, but there is a beatitude for the man of peace: "Blessed are the peacemakers, for they shall be called the children of God." As a member of the Royal Society and a longtime member of the executive, Scott may have been working against the grain, but he may well have served a valuable function. At a 1919 National Conference on Conservation he delivered a brief paper entitled "Relation of Indians to Wild Life Conservation." Under attack by the provincial game guardian of Saskatchewan in the ensuing discussion, Scott remarks that "This subject should not be discussed in a controversial way" (28). It sounds like the man who "never learned to quarrel." Lyle Weis suggests ("A Sense of Order" 66) that the heat of hearing testimony over a 1920 bill might have been what provoked Scott to his most colourful expression of the assimilationist views that I examine in chapter 5:

> I want to get rid of the Indian problem. I do not think as a matter of fact, that this country ought to continuously protect a class of people who are able to stand alone . . . that has been the purpose of Indian advancement since the earliest times. . . . Our object is to continue until there is not a

> single Indian in Canada that has not been absorbed into the body politic, and there is no Indian question, and no Indian Department, that is the whole object of this bill. (RG10f)

WE APPROACH SCOTT BY INDIRECTION. Certain possibilities firm up into probabilities, like this reluctance to get involved with disputes, which seems to have made him invaluable as a sort of diplomat at the Royal Society, and which may have smoothed the waters in his civil service department, as well. However, we have also probably found out that Scott was no Norman Bethune, that scarcer kind of Canadian willing and able to buck the system. It takes an effort to imagine Indian Affairs, with its "kow-towing and bootlicking" (Macbeth 138), under a Bethune. The suggestion is not meant to devalue the sort of contribution made to the civil service and to human affairs generally by administrators with qualities like Scott's. If, whatever the psychological explanation, Scott was a peacemaker who also had administrative capabilities, then it's easy to imagine Indian Affairs in much worse hands than his. But I can't see any radically new policy originating from such a man. To combat the celebrated civil service inertia alone, he would have needed an idealistic energy of heroic proportions.

NOTES

1. CBC Radio Archives has a 1947 recording of Scott reading "A Song." It was part of a National School Broadcast that aired on September 16, 1947.
2. "Perhaps I did wrong to burn the ones Duncan wrote to me. But I burnt the ones I wrote to him, and he said in his laughing way that he didn't think it was fair to keep just one side of a correspondence!" (December 12, 1959)
3. McDougall doesn't say why he singles out Smiths Falls where the Scotts lived in 1874 and 1875, when their son was 13 and 14. The Methodist itinerancy took them through several small towns in Ontario and Quebec.
4. Lyle Weis puts it this way: "In January 1932 newspapers in Saskatchewan and Ottawa carried a story describing the discovery of liquor sales at a private club on Indian land, a club to which Graham belonged. The sale of liquor on Indian land was, of course, in direct contravention of the Indian Act and Graham was accused of having knowingly allowed the practice. Graham panicked and, in an attempt to avoid some of the responsibility for the error, produced Scott's signature on the lease approval form. The controversy spilled over into the House of Commons question period and, within thirty days, both men had tendered their resignations" ("A Sense of Order" 70). Weis says that Scott's uncharacteristic lapse from "strict adherence procedure" (69) made him vulnerable to elements in the R. B. Bennett government that wanted him out.

4

Filing Cabinets, Magic Casements: Scott in the Civil Service

> *[T]he heart of the matter is always somewhere else than where it is supposed to be.*
>
> *Trinh T. Minh-ha,* Woman, Native, Other

SCOTT'S FIRST FULL-SCALE READING of his own works took place on April 22, 1925, in Victoria College Chapel at the University of Toronto, with Pelham Edgar presiding. "Poet Is in Big Demand While Visiting Toronto," reads the caption under the picture of Scott illustrating the *Globe*'s coverage, a fairly standard appreciation of an event apparently distinguished by introductions to and readings from "Lines in Memory of Edmund Morris," "The Forsaken," and "Powassan's Drum," the latter delivered "with much dramatic feeling" by Bertram Forsyth.

The review in the *Toronto Daily Star* could not have been more different. The author of the column called "The Spotlight," in which it appeared, has almost nothing to say about the reading. His real agenda is to satirize the civil service by stressing the poet as anomaly within it. That he lacks complete control of his approach is suggested by the mixture of flippancy and seriousness in the opening of his third paragraph: "His long face notwithstanding, Dr. Scott is not an Indian, but he has a marvelously wide and deep knowledge of the race to all Canadian branches of which he has been immediately in loco parentis since Frank Pedley resigned." There is no concern for Indians in this writing, but genuine appreciation of Scott's work is not quite obscured by the man's cynicism about the civil service:

> It is exhilarating to know that another Canadian poet is being dragged from his lair to read his verses to admiring compatriots. Duncan Campbell Scott is the present hero, and, as he is an Ottawa official, his appearance

> in our midst must be all the more gratifying to those highly literary persons who would fain believe that thence no good can come. Can a deputy minister be also among the poets? He can, and is, and the truth is glorious enough to wish it could be brought home to a deeply religious business man who said that poets were efficient enough, among the stars, but he would like to see one of them on the Manchester Exchange, among the cotton. Dr. Scott is far better than the impossibility longed for by this Lancastrian. For twelve years he has been superintendent of Indian Affairs, over half a continent, working daily on a political rialto where whole armies of clever beings practice the art of pulling wool over each other's eyes.

This is an irreverent version of a Scott curiosity that went long unexamined: he was both good poet and highly competent bureaucrat. We have only recently become interested in what Scott's competence was being used for.

Deconstructing written accounts of Scott's life and character leaves Scott's identity much less solid than one might wish. Contemporary assertions of his skill as civil servant, when not simply accepted at face value, come to seem similarly insubstantial. Ignorance did not disqualify many from offering an opinion, and there are degrees of ignorance. Even so intelligent and knowledgeable an observer as E. K. Brown apparently brought to his writing on Scott no more than the average Canadian's knowledge of the North and of First Nations peoples. In the 1940s and 50s that would be negligible. And many praisers of Scott the bureaucrat are much less shrewd than Brown. To read their accounts knowing even a little of Native peoples is to hear again and again a hollow echo. It sounds in the perfunctory praise of Scott's administrative work by people who felt obliged to mention it in passing to the poetry and fiction, people like Pelham Edgar, Leonard Brockington, and Madge Macbeth who knew Scott and thought he was good at his job but who, again, show no particular knowledge of or interest in Native people. Nobody, in fact, not even Brian Titley, suggests that Scott was incompetent or lazy or otherwise reprehensible in non-Native terms. But no praise of Scott's administrative record can be swallowed by anyone who knows that his competence was not serving Indians.

There is some point in trying to think about Scott as civil servant period, though, suspending for a time the unavoidable complication that his department was responsible for the Indians, because the civil service is an environment as well as an occupation, and Scott chafed in it. He lacked the perspective on Native peoples that hindsight gives us, but he certainly knew that the civil service was far from perfect, and he might even have chuckled over the review of his reading in "The Spotlight." The "vast inertia" of military bureaucracy he refers to in *John Graves Simcoe* (224) was not outside his own experience. In fact, his pseudonymous "Open Letter to a Member of

Parliament" is a critique both of the service as a whole, with no special reference to his own department, and of the parliamentary forces that made it what it was — hardly a springboard for radical change. Scott may well have found dealing with Indians a relief after dealing with his fellow bureaucrats.

He must often have wished he were free of the office, again for reasons having nothing directly to do with Indians. The longer Scott spent in the service, the more its demands interfered with his writing, the occupation of his desire. He tended to blame himself for not accomplishing as much as he should have, but no man who hates his job (not an exaggeration) can do it wholeheartedly, and a job that has to be suffered depletes the energy needed for a demanding discipline like writing.

FRIENDS OF SCOTT THOUGHT he was a wonderful civil servant. Perhaps they were right in their way. His activities outside the government prove that he was a good organizer, and there is ample evidence that he would have felt it his duty to do a good job even when his heart was not in it. But he was probably not the bureaucrat-saint proclaimed by broadcaster Leonard W. Brockington:

> He brought order out of chaos and human and humane understanding to the problems of the Indian wards of the Federal Government. I suppose it is too much to hope that all Government officials in their hours of ease could weave tapestry out of red tape and fashion statues of Venus out of sealing wax. Duncan Campbell Scott belongs to that bright company of public servants who found in their leisure the opportunity to enrich our literature with imperishable possessions . . . Charles Lamb, Walter Bagehot, Austin Dobson, Archibald Lampman, Walter de la Maire [*sic*] and the rest of those happy brothers who, in spite of filing cabinets, were able to dream of magic casements.[1] (ASB)

Not a long list of writers, and not as impressive in our day as it was in 1941 when Brockington spoke those words over the CBC in a "Tribute to Duncan Campbell Scott." Whatever their literary achievements, moreover, some of those mentioned hardly shone as civil servants. Lampman's lack of enthusiasm for the post office branch is well known. According to the author of "The Spotlight" (apparently a connoisseur of literary civil servants), Charles Lamb "flowered in the India office and said that he made up for coming late by going early." But Brockington's effusive prose is hard to swallow, anyway, at least on the page. Maybe his famous resonant voice carried more credibility over the air. Pelham Edgar's prose has a disappointingly similar tendency to flap off away from his subject on pseudo-poetic flights.

The flights lead me to feel, about his "Twelve Hundred Miles by Canoe" essay, for example, that about seven-tenths of the substance might remain if the stylistic excess were skimmed off. Examples of his runaway style, reflecting I think an obedience to convention, also appear in "Duncan Campbell Scott." Between the biographical notes that Scott supplied and the biographical section of Edgar's *Dalhousie Review* article, there is a literary transformation for which a reader of both the plain 1906 diary and the adorned "Twelve Hundred Miles" essay is prepared. Here is Scott on his entrance into the civil service:

> On 15th Dec. 1879 I entered the Civil Service in order to earn enough money for one or two years at college & study for my matric — As I was offered a permanent apptmt. at what seemed a large salary to a family that was accustomed to the small stipends then in vogue, after a family consultation, I decided to remain in the service. (PE)

Edgar cranks this up: "[He] decided with enthusiasm, fortunately as the sequel showed, to connect himself with a branch of the Service which was then in its interesting formative stage" (39). Enthusiasm is prominent neither in Scott's statement nor in what he says about how the job worked out for him: "I was in the acc'ts Br. where the business management of the Dept. centred — a retentive memory, a sincere interest in the work & in the welfare of the Indians enabled me to gain a grasp of the business and as time passed to assist in formulating policy & in carrying out innovations and improvements in educational methods." In Edgar's version Scott's flat assertions are metamorphosed into the portrait of a man of talent and ambition entering and then rising in a job worthy of his qualities: "He had no intention of limiting his ambition to the perfunctory duties of a routine clerk. Much of the work was necessarily mechanical, but its larger human aspects appealed to his imagination, and he rapidly mastered the business detail of his office in the interests of this wider scope" (39).

Scott's own versions make dull reading, but Edgar's enthusing would render what he says suspect even if there were no originals to ground the soaring. Here is how Edgar brings Scott up to date as deputy superintendent general of Indian Affairs:

> He is thus, under the Minister, the permanent head of a great Government service, commanding the confidence of his chief and the utmost loyalty of his staff. He is resourceful, firm and considerate, and has the born executor's faculty of knowing precisely what is to be done and finding the right way to do it. (39–40)

"Born executor" is a surprise, coming from this friend of Scott's for so many years. Were there things Scott did not or could not tell him? Or could Edgar simply not write plainly what he knew, labouring perhaps under the impression that certain matters should be expressed in certain ways? Edgar gives no impression at all that there was any conflict between Scott the individual (never mind the poet) and Scott the civil servant, and there certainly was. The reason it's so important to separate this issue from the question of Scott's official contact with Indians is that his encounters with Indians were always, as far as I can tell, official ones. His meetings with Indians, his entire relationship with them, must have been coloured by the connection with a civil service that he would have disliked whatever his department.

In 1898 Scott could mention his job obliquely and mildly in a letter to Archibald Lampman: "I think if the positive need for money did not prod me I would sit as idle as a monk on Athos contemplating his navel. I seem to have within me quite infinite possibilities for contemplation. However there seems to be no immediate chance of my withdrawing from the world to a seclusion in the Gatineau Hills" (Bourinot, *Some Letters* 8). The immediate context of this, in the previous sentence, is that Scott has "not been adding to the useless store of literature of the present day," so contemplation is associated for him with writing, or at least with stimulating the creative juices. He said much later in his life, after election to one of the presidencies that he seemed to be offered with dismal regularity (of the Ottawa Country Club, in this case), "what folly when I should be dreaming or thinking of something else" (ASB). He meant writing, as another letter confirms, this one written to Elise Aylen in 1928: "I am not making good progress with the poem I'm working on as I cannot get my mind settled — or my dream faculty working continuously . . . " (PA/S-A). Scott was not a complaining man, but the odd note does creep into his letters from time to time about being "driven" with work (to Pelham Edgar, May 5, 1920 [postmark date] ASB), or about the pressure of work being "severe" (to Elise Aylen, March 24, 1929 PA/S-A).

It wasn't long after the northern trips that the routine once more dropped between Scott and his writing: "The familiar [Indian Affairs] crest should tell you that I am waiting for estimates," he wrote to Edgar in February 1907. "The annual weary grind waiting for a few hours of questions. . . . I am interested in working at a new story and would prefer to be at home" (ASB). He wrote to Raymond Knister (September 9, 1928 Q/RK) that "I might have written more fiction, maybe, under other conditions and even now my mind is full of fictional and dramatical [fragment]. But the essential stretches of time are absent now as they ever were, and so the characters and plots go 'up the chimney' where Tennyson said so many of his fine lines went." Casting his mind back to the early stages of his writing career, he wrote in a 1947 newspaper column called "The Readers Take Over" that "I continued to be a contributor both in verse and prose to *Scribner's* and other American magazines until my official duties became *responsible* and I had no strength after office hours for constant production" (PA/DCS).

There is a good deal of evidence that Scott's job interfered with his creative work, then, though the work may not have been continuously demanding. The silent piano Scott kept in his office to practise on (in his "few leisure moments," according to A. S. Bourinot [*More Letters* 2]) tends to be introduced as evidence of his great love of music, without any reflection that it proves no great devotion to his work. Madge Macbeth introduces the piano after remarking that there was not much for Scott *to* do: "With a highly-trained, efficient and devoted staff — Indian Affairs was not one of the Government's most exacting departments — Duncan had quite a little leisure during office hours" (142). It would not be hard to imagine a Cree or Ojibway reading about Scott's work on his fingering and remembering the fiddling of Nero — a strained analogy, maybe, given that Scott was a bureaucrat neither mad nor theatrical, who was, in fact, highly responsible, but then the burning of a city is (or ought to be) a mere blip of history beside the slow destruction of a people. The office would have kept Scott very busy at certain times of the year (as when the House was in session and he had to be available to answer questions), but the large amount of literary and other correspondence he wrote on Indian Affairs letterhead tends to support what Madge Macbeth says. Scott was an incredibly hardworking person, but when he was busy at the office it was not always with Indian affairs.

We don't have to rely on reports of Scott's behaviour in the office to know how he felt about his job, though. When he began to unburden himself to Elise Aylen he made it clear enough that he felt trapped in his offical life among people whose minds were foreign to him. "This business life would kill me," he wrote from Winnipeg on November 15, 1930, "the men I meet all splendid fellows bent on making money seem so far away from me. I can only tolerate the Dept. at home by forgetting it and living that other life, ineffectual enough I suppose but a little more natural" (PA/S-A). Ironically, Scott's initial appointment and early success in the civil service were owing to his competence in handling money. He was an accountant for much of his early career. He seems to have been good at various occupations he did not like: strong enough to toil effectively in the wrong furrows, not strong enough to step out. "A life of drift." When Scott divides his own life in two, with the "Dept." in one compartment and the "other life," presumably the literary one, in another, Natives do not figure in the equation. We can't forget them, but Scott may have had to, for the sake of his own sanity. It doesn't sound as if he were trying to escape Indians when he went home and did his best to occupy that other life, which is properly a career in itself. Instead, it sounds as if he were escaping "the welter of the lives of men" that in "The Height of Land" he associates with the settled South and contrasts with the peace to be found in the North — where, especially in 1906, he did such a good deal of writing.

Archibald Lampman is the Confederation poet usually thought of as out of place in the civil service, but Scott might well have been personally touched by Lampman's 1892 statement in "At the Mermaid Inn" that "A life spent in an occupation out of harmony with one's natural bent can never be quite happy or genuinely faithful even in the most fortunate circumstances; while a life of congenial labour, unsubjected to any exceeding pressure, is really the supreme happiness" (113). Scott's more specific, more laconic, version of this appears in a letter to B. K. Sandwell (September 22, 1945 PA/DCS): "If one is cut out for a literary life and [*sic*] official life is no adequate substitute. No matter what good work is done by an executive as soon as he leaves his chair it is forgotten or misrepresented." No supreme happiness for either of these poets.

Lampman's words got truer and truer for Scott the farther up the bureaucratic ladder he climbed, but they would probably have seemed relevant at least as early as 1893 when, on February 21, an "Open Letter to a Member of Parliament" appeared in *The Evening Journal*. It was signed, pseudonymously, "Silas Reading." The issue was the consideration in the House of a bill intended to improve the civil service.[2] "Reading" has a few things to say about changes that ought to be made to the service, but that he thinks unlikely to be encouraged by the bill. His remarks would be interesting even if they were not written by someone who rose so high in the service. They are the words of an idealist frustrated both with what the civil service is and with the ignorance of the MPs who are considering changes to it:

> [O]ver the portals of these Departmental buildings might well be written the lugubrious words which greeted Dante and Virgil at hell gate, "All hope abandon ye who enter here." You smile; but did you ever reflect that the majority of the service is composed of men who can never earn more than one thousand dollars a year and only attain that salary after twelve years' work . . . ?

By the index of salary Scott was not among the majority. His yearly salary was $1,100 five years after he began. In 1893, he was making $1,800. Clearly he was not speaking merely of his own case. And money was not the only or the main problem, anyway. The entrant into civil service hell would discover that "the chances of his making the best use of his faculties are one in one thousand, that there is absolutely no chance for the development which comes to men in other walks of life, that the never ending routine breeds an apathy of mind, a special disease I might say, which makes a man useless for the other employments of life." There is more in this line, but I pass on to Scott's recommendations:

> There is a way and a very simple one to cure all the disorders of the civil service which is held to be in such an alarming state that a medicine so

> drastic as the new bill must be administered at once. It is merely to strike at the evils where they exist, to dismiss the loafers, to cancel the antiquated and cumbersome methods of transacting public business, to put some trust in the public servants and if they betray it to let them feel the hand of the law; to make the service as a class, know that its honest efforts are appreciated and that it exists for more reasons than as a refuge for political intriguers; to allow promotion to follow merit and not influence; and without pampering to permit the so-called privileges, which are really the only compensations of a life which breeds inability to battle with the world.

Being sensible, these are utopian proposals. Scott seems to have held to these ideas in private as well as in public, though, and not only for the sake of a particular issue affecting his workplace in 1893. We are back to those treaty trips, I think, when we read Scott writing to Pelham Edgar probably in December 1907, in a letter still heavy with the sadness of Elizabeth's death, "I am not writing anything new — but cobbling a few old things, improving them perhaps and perhaps not — office work very heavy and futile — our Dept should be filled with idealists and enthusiasts and philanthropists — instead — well. You know what we have, having had some experience of it" (ASB). This appears to refer to Samuel Stewart, the most likely recent exemplar to Edgar, other than Scott himself, of Indian Affairs types.

Was Stewart one of the dogs? That is what Scott calls unscrupulous bureaucratic climbers in a 1922 letter to the explorer Vilhjalmur Stefansson:

> I see that some of your friends are trying to get into the limelight again. I think the true inwardness of that is that we have had a change of Government and they think if they bestir themselves they may get some attention. This always happens, and in my own Department there are fifty people trying to bring forward old and fake claims of all kinds. There is only one thing to be said about these people: they are Dogs! (ASB)

In one of Scott's 1900–1910 notebooks there is a sonnet called "Some Men," which satirizes human males as "dogs, dogs to the very claws" (TF).

A department populated with sloths at best and dogs at worst is made up of people unlikely to have their minds focused on the business they are supposed to be doing, whatever that might be. Whenever Scott alone is blamed for what Indian Affairs did or failed to do during his jurisdiction it might be remembered that more than a "born executor" would be needed to urge a huge bureaucracy off its collective inertia, even if the goodwill of its members could be counted upon.

Scott's open letter may have exaggerated the horrors of belonging to the civil service, but he is not alone in identifying difficulties peculiar to the job.

To rise to the position of deputy minister, moreover, is not to escape those difficulties. Rather, it means assuming the responsibility for administering and motivating one's staff subject to the frustrations outlined by A. W. Johnson in his essay "The Role of the Deputy Minister":

> When he enters the public service, he may be an unqualified enthusiast for his program — be it highway building or social welfare. But sooner or later he will meet with one or both of the frustrations which are typical of government. First, he may find that despite the logic of his recommendations concerning his program, there are political factors to which his political masters give greater emphasis than they do to his logic. Alternatively, they may accept the validity of his proposals but decide in making their budgetary choices that some other program is more important. This will seem inconceivable to the program enthusiast but there it is. (355)

Johnson's conclusion refers more specifically to the fix of the deputy minister:

> So the deputy minster finds himself in the curious position of being exposed to the political process, without at the same time being part of it. He must not permit himself the luxury of becoming too attached to ideas or positions. Somehow he must find a way of maintaining a cordial relationship with those who assist and advise him without ever losing sight of the fact that his first loyalty is to his minister. His first loyalty can never be to his staff or to the public affected by his minister's policies. (356)

The deputy minister has no real power, failure doesn't stick to him personally, it's a product of the system. Does this mean that there is no black beast, no blameworthy Scott? There are those who think so. One is S. D. Grant. "Assuming that criticism of his administration of Indian Affairs is just," she says, "the blame cannot rest on a single individual whose beliefs were shared by a vast majority of Canadians and their elected representatives in Ottawa. Equal responsibility must rest with our ancestors who believed in white supremacy and Anglo-Saxon imperialism" (37). Another is Lyle Weis, who works from the assumption that idealism was what motivated Scott in the civil service, that he "found in the Department of Indian Affairs a clear articulation of Victorian aims, and, by giving concrete form to these aims, he became a kind of cultural representative figure" ("Order" 72). Like me, Weis finds some evasiveness in Scott's assertion that he was never unsympathetic to aboriginal ideals, but he prefers to accentuate the positive. It might almost be concluded, he says, that "Department policy was actually from Scott's desk."

> Moral opinion today might find this interpretation attractive, since earlier Indian policy is commonly held to have been misguided, and if blame is

> to be assigned it is more satisfying to point to an individual than to an abstraction like the Law, or a cultural belief. It is more likely, though, that Scott's convictions arose not from the formulation of original ideas, but from his unquestioning subordination of self to a social and cultural ideal. ("Order" 66)

My argument is not that it's fair to blame Scott, just that it's necessary. The price of pointing the finger is sharing the blame. And Scott does seem — see below — to have made things happen in Indian Affairs.

WHAT OF E. K. BROWN on Scott as civil servant? I take his opinion seriously for various reasons. Brown knew Scott, and he had an original mind. He was almost the first critic of substance to tackle Canadian poetry in a measured way, expecting it to be no more than he found it. The man could think, and his thinking was independent enough to redirect the course of Canadian literary criticism with *On Canadian Poetry*. Of course, he knew Scott late in life, long after retirement from Indian Affairs, and he lists people rather than texts as the sources for his remarks on Scott the civil servant in the "Memoir" written for *Selected Poems*. One of his sources was R. H. Coats, head of the Dominion Bureau of Statistics between 1908 and 1942. Coats would have known something about Scott as a civil servant, though the extant letters from him dwell on family matters. A greater authority would have been T. R. Loftus MacInnes, Archibald Lampman's son-in-law who had worked in Indian Affairs with Scott for, as Brown says, 20 years. Loftus and Natalie (Lampman) MacInnes are known to Scott scholars since they had to be consulted over the potentially embarrassing poems addressed to Kate Waddell, Lampman's extramarital interest, that Scott and Brown were preparing for publication in *At the Long Sault and Other New Poems* (1943).

Whatever his sources, at any rate, Brown says that Scott's position as deputy minister was earned, that his was not a political appointment like the previous and the following ones — examples of the sort of abuse Scott had complained of in his open letter:

> He was not a party-minded man — he preferred the Conservatives to the Liberals mainly because they were sounder in all that had to do with the British connection — but in his own round of activity he had an acute political sense. He knew how to defend the interests of his department when it came into conflict with others, and his own interests within the department. His conception of the national duty to the Indians was simple and sound. It was the result not of close ethnological study, but of immense experience and imaginative understanding. The poet in him and the civil servant agreed in believing that the future of the Indians, if it were

> not to be extinction or degradation, depended on their being brought more and more nearly to the status of the white population. Special safeguards were a temporary necessity; but meanwhile by education and encouragement the Indians were to cease being interesting exotic relics and practise trying to hold their own in a society which could not be bent in their direction. Sometimes Duncan Scott felt that he should stress the special safeguards, the peculiar status, but it was to the end of bringing the Indians into the national society that he strove with that mixture of guile and idealism that is the mark of the highest sort of civil servant. (xxv–xxvi)

Brown's portrait of Scott the administrator seems more rational than Pelham Edgar's, and miles from magic casements among filing cabinets. The view is external, though, and inevitably static, being a summary. It might even be accurate as a generalization, though it hazards no opinion regarding inner conflict between the idealism and the guile. Common sense makes it seem unlikely that those qualities or abilities can run along in perfect balance all the time. We need to look between Brown's lines, need to open up some space between his words, and Scott himself supplies the crowbar.

Scott was anything but cheerful about the guile shown by people in his department whenever the government changed, as we have seen. There are occupational hazards for an idealist regularly obliged to compromise his ideals: either cynicism or self-reproach. Scott was prey to the latter when he was deputy minister. His letters to Elise make that clear, though his depression had other sources than feeling out of place in Indian Affairs. He felt a hypocrite "going to all the 'rubric mummeries' attendant on the Making of a Bishop tomorrow morning with a heart full of unfaith" (PA/S-A), he wrote to Elise in an undated letter (probably of 1929). He also wondered what on earth he was doing apart from Elise in New England, visiting the Botsford in-laws: "You know everything is very comfy here and I cld have everything I wanted but there is nothing *material* I want. There is a lack of inward harmony when I am here and I seem on this occasion to be even more definitely playing a part" (PA/S-A). The part would be that of son-in-law, a role that must have been doubly uncongenial to a man on his way to a second marriage. Scott had a conscience; he didn't like pretending, and it would have chafed him to play the role of the civil servant, for that is what he was doing — playing it very well, in fact. For years and years.

The only indication in Brown's passage that Scott had any second thoughts is the comment that he sometimes felt he should stress the peculiar status of the Indians. Brown may have been thinking of a letter Scott wrote in July 1941 in response to Brown's article "Duncan Campbell Scott, an Individual Poet":

> Your remarks about the Indians are very good. I had for about twenty years oversight of their development and I was never unsympathetic to aboriginal ideals, but there was the law which I did not originate and which I never tried to amend in the direction of severity. One can hardly be sympathetic with the contemporary Sun-dance or Potlatch when one knows that the original spirit has departed and that they are largely the opportunities for debauchery by low white men. (*Poet and Critic* 26)

I have always found the above passage a curiously defensive statement to volunteer, with its striking "but" indicating some conflict between sympathy for aboriginal ideals and obedience to the law. If Scott was truly sympathetic, then the Indian Act ("the law") must at times have grated, must have been a source of inner conflict. On a more official occasion he gave other reasons, economic ones, for opposing the Sun Dance.[3] And he never strikes me as having achieved a stance deep enough within Plains or West Coast Native cultures to be a good judge of the presence or absence of the original spirit in their ceremonies — even allowing that it was his business to make such judgements. In Brown's paragraph there are no doubts, though, only a few niggles detectable on close scrutiny.

There is nothing in Scott's annual reports to tell us whether or not he found official policy personally grating, but we can tell which amendments he sponsored. Do these tend "in the direction of severity"? Not if the underlying assumptions of the annual reports are accepted. In Scott's writing about these amendments, a sort of refrain, "for the benefit of the Indians," appears and reappears. It would seem that very little was ever done by Indian Affairs except for the benefit of the Indians. Scott attributes Indian recalcitrance about certain of these beneficial measures to a failure to see where the best interests of Indians lay. These interests, spelled out for the Indians without their consultation, seem fortuitously identical with government policy. "The rhetoric of power," says Edward Said, "all too easily produces an illusion of benevolence when deployed in an imperial setting" (*Culture and Imperialism* xvii). Examining Scott's advocacy of enfranchisement in the early 1920s, we find out more than whether or not he was "severe"; we see a typical segment of the long one-way street of Native–Indian Affairs relations.

Enfranchisement refers to the process by which, as Scott put it in his essay "Indian Affairs 1840–1867," an Indian ceases "in all respects to be an Indian" (353) and joins the Canadian community at large. Scott's first report as deputy minister in 1915 calls for reform of a cumbersome enfranchisement policy (enfranchisement was tied to membership in a band and either residence on the reserve or a "location ticket" conferring technical residence, and these requirements were difficult to meet by Indians living off reserve), and he repeats the call annually until in 1919 he is able to record an amendment that simplifies the process. Then he begins in 1920 to point to the numbers of applications for enfranchisement as proof of the wisdom of the policy, though he also mentions those who "cling to the benefits and protection attendant on their wardship" (20) and he calls for a further amendment to permit representatives of the superintendent general to inquire into the fitness for enfranchisement of individuals "without the necessity of obtaining consent" (32). This amendment has passed by the 1921 report, along with another making attendance at day and residential schools compulsory: "The recent amendments give the department control and remove from the Indian parent the responsibility for the care and education of his child, and the best interests of the Indians are promoted and fully protected" (13).

All of this — whether enfranchisement or education — is about assimilation, a subject I will address from a different angle in chapter 5 and from yet another in my conclusion. Enfranchisement, assimilation: this was Indian Affairs policy when Scott came into power. The amendments he presided over might then be seen as mere technical adjustments to make the policy easier to administer or, to put it in a less neutral way, to give the policy teeth. There is nothing more severe about Scott's amendments than there is about the Indian Act itself, and until recently that seemed severe only to those inconvenient, unconsulted people unable to see where their own best interests lay: in loss of identity and absorption into the Canadian nation.

"The poet . . . and the civil servant agreed," says Brown (there is no contradiction between the roles for him), and he goes on to the mildest possible expression of assimilationism, which he calls a "sound" policy. Brown is not neutral, then; he agrees with Scott and implicitly presents himself as one who knows what he is talking about. If that were actually the case, he would understand what "education and encouragement" meant in practical terms: the residential schools, for instance, operated by the religious denominations. Perhaps he did know something of the means adopted by the Indian Department to "civilize" the Natives. His "Memoir" as a whole gives the impression that he knows more about some matters than he has the space to write.

But there is knowing and there is understanding, which is impossible when the heart is not engaged as a third eye, a visionary organ. The government's assimilationist policy *was* rational. If reason were enough, few of us would be complaining about assimilation. There would be no ache in the heart about the effect of the residential schools (and, later, of day schools) on Indian children and their parents, personal tragedy after tragedy, amounting to a racial tragedy of diaspora.

In Fort Albany in 1987 a man named Laurence told me about the terrible cruelty he and others had suffered in what he called the "orphan school" at Moose Factory. "Somebody has to tell this story," he said, and the telling has finally begun. "It was a dark landscape," says Tomson Highway. "When the stories come out, people will be shocked. A lot of my colleagues from those days are dead, by suicide, by alcohol-related violence that they leveled at each other. Few of us made it through" (Wigston 8). In Basil Johnston's touching *Indian School Days* the controlling metaphor is the prison. Johnston makes his residential school, St. Peter Claver's School at Spanish, Ontario, sound less cruel than the one at Moose Factory and those others where sexual as well as physical abuse took place, and his book is not an entire condemnation of the system, but it records without rancour the arbitrary injustice of wresting children away from their parents with no explanation and, in many cases, no hope of escape until graduation many years later. Being children, the inmates of residential schools were completely powerless, and their parents were as powerless as children before the law. On the children were pinned the hopes of the civilizers.

Brown may have talked to Loftus MacInnes and others, but he can't have asked a Native person how sound Scott's policy was. Once again Scott is praised for his work in Indian Affairs on the assumption, evolved entirely within white culture, that a white man may know what is good for the Indians. "The national duty" has a slightly ominous ring, with its faint echo of "white man's burden." The point of this analysis is less to put Brown in his place (inside the bubble of white culture) than to observe that this smart and sensitive man was making statements corroborated only by his considerable professional authority. He was a good literary critic who probably knew little of Indians, but his clout in the former sphere has allowed him to go unchallenged on what he was implicitly saying about the latter.

Brown could not have realized how damaging the afterthought of his "Memoir" on Scott the civil servant would become. At the end of an argument about Scott's clearsighted understanding that poetry was, especially in Canada, the passion of a very few, and that the many were philistines, Brown remarks that

> His work in the civil service interested him; but the centre of his life was not in his office, where he seldom came early, and never stayed late. After he retired his conversation did not run on the Indian department. The centre of his life was the search for illuminations, and for the expression of them. The search and its occasional reward was enough. (xxxiii)

It is a shame that the centre of Scott's life had so often to be pushed to the periphery by his work in an uncongenial job, but that's not what strikes Brian Titley about Brown's words.

The first two of Brown's sentences just quoted are the last words of Titley's *A Narrow Vision,* where they illustrate the view that Scott's "position in the government was to [him] a mere source of income rather than an abiding passion" (204). "Mere source of income" seems extreme, but Titley is right. Brown is portraying Scott as a work-to-rule civil servant. The climate in which Brown wrote did not require that he examine what he was saying on that score.

THE CLIMATE HAS CHANGED so markedly that Scott is now charged with narrow vision and with, in John Flood's term, "duplicity." In "The Duplicity of D. C. Scott and the James Bay Treaty," Flood concentrates on Treaty 9, in a sort of forerunner to Titley's book on the whole of Scott's record in Indian Affairs. Both writers respond with healthy indignation to the practical dilemmas in which Indian Affairs policies stranded Native people. They supply some needed bite on the subject of Scott and Indian Affairs.

Flood is actually quite intemperate, but his vituperation is not unsupported. He deserves the credit for really breaking open the poet/civil servant controversy (so gently broached by Keiichi Hirano and E. Palmer Patterson III) by researching the relevant documents, principally Scott's prose on Indians and Indian Affairs. If I thought that Flood had said everything that needed to be said, or that axe-grinding had made him unfailingly sharp, I might not be writing this book. He writes out of firsthand knowledge of the North and the assumption that Indians must be listened to. His article needs to be seen as a part of his literary advocacy of the North. For many years he edited *Northward Journal* and he still publishes books about the North under the imprint of Penumbra Press. He has also written a volume of poems about Scott and the negotiation of Treaty 9, in which a more hospitable view of the man emerges. Perhaps this is another case of conflict between private and public views — not of the Indians, in this case, but of Scott.

I need more discriminations than Flood makes in his article, and that is my attitude toward S. D. Grant's work and Titley's, as well, though for different reasons. When Grant credits Scott with believing that "the final resolution [of the Indian problem] might not be reached for centuries" (37), she is referring to "The Last of the Indian Treaties," in which he advances an unexceptionable early view of assimilation, a view (as the next chapter shows) that unfortunately changed. *A Narrow Vision,* by contrast, is a very unsympathetic account of the Indian administrator derived from many of the same sources Grant consulted — the official or semiofficial prose record left behind in Indian Affairs archives and in Scott's writings about his Indian work — though Titley's research is more exhaustive. If Scott had been nothing but an administrator, Titley's negative characterization of him as a cold penny-pinching bureaucrat might be quite accurate. But bureaucrat was an identity he assumed at the office.

In Scott's own location of the centre of his life elsewhere than at the office (in the letter to Elise), he invites a characterization of himself as neatly split in two like Dickens's Wemmick in *Great Expectations,* although without Wemmick's motivation of insulating himself from social horrors his heart could otherwise not abide. But even though Flood and Titley both create one-dimensional portraits of him, Scott is hard to catch in such a clean split — cold and careful at work, warm and caring at home. That is tempting, but too easy. All we have left of Scott is masks, and trying to see the man is not so much a matter of examining the one mask and then the next and so on through the repertoire; it involves seeing how this one tends to dissolve into the other, and so on and on. Tempting though it is at times to look fixedly at one of the masks and declare it the true face, as Flood and Titley have done, too much else about the man crowds in to complicate the matter. I don't find Scott's writings on the subject of Indians as uniform as Flood and Titley do, because I don't regard technique as transparent. So a pronouncement like this of Titley's seems to flatten out a good many distinctions:

> Scott's poetry is a highly unreliable guide to his feelings regarding the native population. Nor is it really necessary. Scott's pronouncements on Indians in readily comprehensible prose, in both an official and unofficial capacity, are legion. Because of their frequency and unwavering consistency, they are by far the best guide to what the private and public man really believed. (32)

Titley is a historian, not a literary critic, and he is not comfortable with Scott's fiction and poetry in the chapter he devotes to them. I can understand the temptation to split off the creative work from the workaday prose, in the hope of establishing what Scott believed, but I think it's a mistake. The poetry and fiction *is* difficult to quarry for ideological content, but it's still his best and most intense work on Indians. It can't be right to privilege the mainly feeble nonfiction I examine in the next chapter just because an unambiguous Scott seems to emerge from it. And, in fact, there *is* much more difference between Scott's various writings on Indians and Indian Affairs, not all of them "pronouncements," than Titley detects. We find what we look for. Titley has found his Scott of "unwavering consistency," and one of those is enough.

NOTES

1. The ellipsis is Brockington's. I quote from a typescript of his CBC address, "Tribute to Duncan Campbell Scott," dated August 2, 1941. "Maire" is corrected and the filing cabinets and magic casements are dropped in the *Saturday Night* version.
2. Scott is probably reacting to a bill "further to amend the Civil Service Act" introduced by John Costigan on February 13, 1893. The Journals of the House of Commons records that introduction, and the withdrawal of the bill on March 27, 1893. The actual bills for that period were lost in the 1916 House of Commons fire, but another civil servant, writing pseudonymously as "Critic" in the February 18 Journal, reveals that the controversial clause of the bill would have extended the civil service day (9:30–4:00) by an hour and a half (9:00–5:00) and removed the Saturday half holiday, as well. "[T]o take away our time in the way proposed," the "Critic" fulminates, "without a word of compensation is an act of brigandage."
3. "It may seem arbitrary on our part to interfere with the native culture. The position of the department, however, can be readily understood, and it is pointed out that Indians will spend a fortnight preparing for a sun-dance, another night engaging in it, and another fortnight to get over it. Obviously this plays havoc with summer ploughing" ("The Administration of Indian Affairs in Canada" 25).

5

Indian Affairs Nonfiction: The Habit of Superiority

> *It is the mission of new theories in the arts, and particularly of new theories that come to us illustrated by practice, to force us to re-examine the grounds of our preferences, and to resist our accepted dogmas. Sometimes the preferences are found to be prejudices and the dogmas hollow formulae.*
>
> *D. C. Scott, "Poetry and Progress"*

FROM A LITERARY STANDPOINT "The Last of the Indian Treaties" is Scott's only interesting nonfiction about Indians. It also stands apart for its literary integrity. With a few exceptions the rest of his nonfiction about Indian Affairs almost asks to be regarded not as a series of discrete essays, introductions, reports, but as a fluid pool of material, parts of which were recycled again and again over two decades. The self-cannibalizing habit that shows in this material is one of the snags in the search for the "real" Scott, the Scott who at heart was either callous or compassionate or indifferent toward Indians. With the discovery of his labour-saving, his going through the motions, the portrait blurs again; in fact it smears. Here is another mask to contemplate, one that is amateurish, ill-made.

It's not hard to see a possible origin of the recycling habit in Scott's annual reports, beginning with those written between 1909 and 1913 when he was superintendent of Indian education. When from one year to the next there is no new information in certain areas, last year's words serve well enough. Scott's first education report introduced a somewhat revised format (the new man putting his mark on the old office, something he was also to do in his first report as deputy superintendent general); thereafter, what he wrote in certain categories changed very little for three years. Much of what he wrote about education in the Treaty 9 area is repeated verbatim. Recurrences of this sort are anything but unusual in the annual reports; no doubt they reduced the tedium of the reporting exercise. And I suppose one would expect to see variance only in response to new information. But what explains the fact that about half the preamble to the 1927 report is an essay repeated verbatim from the report for 1920? The title has been changed from "The Indians of Canada" to "The Canadian Indians After Sixty Years of Confederation," and the introductory paragraph of the earlier report turns up as the penultimate paragraph of the later one. The secondhandness of the piece is concealed by its new introduction as "a brief summary of the development of Indian Affairs during the past sixty years," apparently composed in recognition of "the Diamond Jubilee of Confederation" (7). Much of the same piece, this time entitled "The Red Indian," also appeared verbatim on May 25, 1920, in the *Times* of London, raising a question about which publication, the annual report or the newspaper, it was originally written for. Some of this same material, again verbatim, is still present over a decade later in "The Administration of Indian Affairs" (1931), as are passages from the 1927, 1928, and 1929 annual reports and one from the 1923 essay, "The Aboriginal Races." (The same passage from "The Aboriginal Races" also appears in Scott's unpublished 1944 introduction to Mildred Valley Thornton's *Indian Lives and Legends,* though Scott there acknowledges the self-quotation.) So Scott's last official essay, prepared for the 1931 "Fourth Bi-Annual Conference of the Institute of Pacific Relations," is something of a pastiche of earlier work.

This cannibalizing practice began early. A passage from "The Last of the Indian Treaties" that I made much of in chapter 2 (the one beginning, "The Indian nature now seems like a fire that is waning") appears in *John Graves Simcoe* (1905) with a minor adjustment in the second sentence: "In Simcoe's time it was full of force and heat" (76). A section on day schools from the 1910 education report appears in the third part of Scott's long historical essay on Indian Affairs published in Doughty and Shortt's 1914 *Canada and Its Provinces: A History of the Canadian People and Their Institutions by One Hundred Associates.* Paragraphs from all three parts of that essay then appear verbatim in the 1922 annual report. The bare bones of the research for the *Canada and Its Provinces* essays are visible in the 1921 report, introduced in these words: "It is probable that no department of the public service can trace the policy which has actuated each administration from the earliest times in such detail as the Department of Indian Affairs, and, it has occurred to me, that a record of the organization which has rendered our administration successful throughout the years would be of interest to the public and particularly to students of Canadian history" (8). In the outline that follows a few familiar passages occur, although there is also documentary material that was not quoted in the essays. The 1923 report contains a history of "Our Indian Treaties," possibly another spinoff from the research done for Doughty and Shortt, as well as a brief history of the Records Branch of Indian Affairs. Two paragraphs in Scott's foreword to the 1932 *Catalogue of the Manoir Richelieu Collection of North American Indians* (portraits) are derived from the Doughty and Shortt "Indian Affairs 1840–1867."

A few of Scott's pieces of prose on Indians are onetime productions, untouched by any trace of recycling: the 1909 introduction to Amelia Paget's *People of the Plains,* the very short note prefacing *The Traditional History of the Iroquois Confederacy,* and "Relation of Indians to Wild Life Conservation," a brief address to the 1919 National Conference on Conservation of Game, Fur-Bearing Animals and Other Wild Life. Scott wrote to Pelham Edgar in March 1911 that his work for *Canada and its Provinces* was "a pure task, nothing more" (ASB), and it seems that he felt the same way about most of his writing on Indian Affairs. Certainly his prose almost never rises to the level of vitality and polish achieved in "The Last of the Indian Treaties," and brief exceptions are not sustained.

What do we make of all this? It's probably best to stay off the high horse. Having written it, Scott is, after all, the proprietor of all of this material. (What would have been supplied by the "Research Committee" acknowledged in "The Indian Affairs of Canada?" Statistics?) He did put a great deal of effort into research and writing for Doughty and Shortt: almost 100 pages of prose in three installments. Still, I couldn't help but feel, as cross-checking began to explain the déjà vu I kept experiencing when I first read this material, a tinge of the bad taste that comes from catching a student in plagiarism. The desire to save on work for these "pure tasks" is understandable, but the signs of going through the motions do Scott no credit and, in fact, suggest a disinclination for rethinking matters that, like assimilationist policy, had become (according to the old, fossilized saying) as if carved in stone.

Surely this evidence of bureaucratic document-shuffling counters Brian Titley's argument that Scott's *own* opinions on Indians are readily available in his nonfiction writing. To refigure the image of the mask: there is in this writing so much evidence of labour-saving (which, said about words, means thought-saving) that its writer comes almost to look like no individual at all but a sort of generic Indian Affairs administrator, a man who wears the mask of his role. He looks quite like William Johnston, the man he calls "the great prototype of all Indian officials" ("Indian Affairs 1763–1841," 698). Comparing Johnston's 1767 vision of the future of Indian Affairs with Scott's of 1931 reveals fewer differences than one might expect, or wish to find, given the passage of a century and a half. In Johnston's words:

> [T]ime, intercourse with us and instruction in religion and learning would create such a change in their manners and sentiments as the present generation might live to see; together with an end to the expense and

> attention which are yet so indispensably necessary to attain these great purposes and to promote the safety, extend the settlements and increase the commerce of this country. (699)

In Scott's:

> It is the opinion of the writer . . . that by policies and activities such as have been outlined, the Government will in time reach the end of its responsibility as the Indians progress into civilization and finally disappear as a separate and distinct people, not by race extinction but by gradual assimilation with their fellow citizens. (27)

Assimilationist policy is implicit in Johnston's words, explicit in Scott's. Much had changed between the two administrations and, ironically, little had changed. Little "progress" had been made. Not in Johnston's generation, not in Scott's, not in mine has the distinctness of the Indians disappeared. The present generation may, in fact, be the one to enshrine aboriginal self-government in the constitution, at which time presumably the disastrous policy of assimilation will become a ghost: dead but still capable of haunting. Two centuries of painful marginalization by a policy with its origin in an 18th-century idea will not just evaporate. Still, reading Scott's words 60 years after they were written and considering all the factors of personal and bureaucratic inertia that were outlined in chapters 3 and 4, and given that any radical rethinking of assimilation as policy would have had to be provoked from *inside* Native cultures so devalued as to be invisible, many of them so demoralized as to be voiceless — one would have to forget all that to see oneself doing better in Scott's place.

MOST OF THE WRITING DISCUSSED in this chapter is not mainly or directly about Indians. Much of it is about Indian Affairs (the branch of the civil service), a name which was never identical with the affairs of Indians, a term that certainly has not aligned with the *interests* of Indians, though (as I have suggested) Scott's official writing assumes complete congruence. In those essays preliminary to the annual reports, in the Doughty and Shortt chapters in "The Administration of Indian Affairs in Canada," Scott is looking at the history of the institution he serves. That is often the centre of his interest, at any rate; the Indians inevitably figure as content, as the wards of a huge and expensive bureaucratic Fatherhood. Whatever doubts Scott may have had privately, his public mask is complacent, even boastful. This, from "Indian Affairs, 1867–1912," is typical:

> As may be surmised from the record of past Indian administration, the government was always anxious to fulfil the obligations which were laid

> upon it by these treaties. In every point, and adhering closely to the letter of the compact, the government has discharged to the present every promise which was made to the Indians. It has discharged them in a spirit of generosity, rather with reference to the policy of advancement which was long ago inaugurated in Upper Canada than in a niggardly spirit as if the treaty stipulations were to be weighed with exactitude. (600)

"The Administration of Indian Affairs in Canada," Scott's last essay, is the smuggest of all, quite self-congratulatory about the success of the department, but complacency is not absent from the annual reports. In fact, like the rhetoric of progress — it is never in a bureaucrat's interests to report any backward slippage — self-justification is a convention of the genre. Nineteen fifteen was a banner year for that sort of thing. Scott's report for the year begins with an account of the fact-finding visit of F. H. Abbott, secretary of the Board of Indian Commissioners of the United States. Scott takes pleasure in reporting that Abbott liked almost everything he saw, and he includes the "Summary of Recommendations" through which the secretary hoped his own government would be able to profit by the Canadian example.

George Orwell didn't invent the concept of doublethink from nothing, which is why it has proven such a handy index of bureaucratic and political duplicity. Of course, doublethink is official policy in the world of *Nineteen Eighty-four, unofficial* "policy" in the world of politics at large. Beyond the conscious duplicity that has become associated with the name of Machiavelli, there is a much more insidious, unconscious sort that was in the very grain of thinking about Indian Affairs. "From its initial promulgation," says J. E. Chamberlin,

> there have been those who have questioned the sanity of a piece of legislation [The Indian Act] which actively discouraged and indeed in some areas positively prohibited, the assimilation of the Indian into the social and economic life of the non-native population, while at the same time being the centrepiece of a broad policy of moving the Indians toward full citizenship and full participation in Canadian life. (90)

Scott meets the norm of sanity in these matters, then, unaware as he is of any inconsistency between amending the Indian Act and saying that the government has never broken any of its treaties. He must be forgetting or suppressing his faculties of logic or memory, never to see (never, anyway, to *say* he sees) that the sacredness of treaties that are to hold as long as the sun shines and the waters flow is profaned by a mutable Indian Act. One of the categories of the Indian Affairs annual report that did not originate with Scott, but which he continued, was that of land surrenders. Always "for the benefit of the

Indians" (that is, swelling a trust fund over which the Indians had limited control), reserves across Canada were "legally" eaten away, especially in those areas where the choice of a reserve location became retroactively inconvenient. As with enfranchisement and alterations to traditional Native governmental structures, surrenders were arranged without the need for anything but token consent from the individuals or bands whose land was involved.

Nowadays it's so simple to gain an elementary grasp of Native perspective on such things as land surrenders as to be correspondingly easy to be astonished at the general blindness about such matters in Scott's time. Hindsight again. One has to keep reminding oneself that, for Scott and most of his contemporaries, the Indians *do not exist* as a people that must be reckoned with. Scott might respond if he could that this nonexistent people certainly caused him and his department its fair share of headaches. The day-to-day welter of administering Indian Affairs would certainly have distracted him from the point that seems so obvious today: powerless people *are* invisible. In any crunch they don't count.

When Scott says in "Indian Affairs, 1763–1841" that "The Indians are never slow in making demands, and a promise sinks into their minds and becomes as perdurable as an index of brass" (707), he is referring to collection by Six Nations people on promises made for their loyalty to the British during the American War of Independence, but the generalization hints at firsthand experience. A long and accurate memory could be inconvenient when it came to unilateral alteration of laws that govern the very conditions of one's existence. Here is the entire entry under "Six Nations Election System" from the annual report of 1925:

> Until the present year the Six nations Indians, who are located at Ohsweken, Brant county, Ontario, had from time immemorial selected their chiefs and councillors by an ancient hereditary system in which the voting power lay with the women of the different tribes and clans. It had been for some years obvious that this obsolete system was wholly unsuited to modern conditions of life and detrimental to progress and advancement. There has unfortunately developed, moreover, during the past few years a retrogressive and obstructive agitation on the reserve which has so impeded progressive administration that it was felt that an improvement in their political system must be effected without delay. In March, 1923, the Government appointed a Royal Commission in the person of Lt.-Col. Andrew T. Thompson to investigate the affairs of the Six Nations. The commissioner in his report, among other important recommendations, strongly urged the abolition of the old tribal system of choosing the councillors. This recommendation was promptly put into effect by the department. An Order in Council, dated September 17, 1924, was passed

> applying the election provision of Part Two of the Indian Act to the Six Nations. The election was held on October 21, 1924. Under the new method, the Six Nations will have a measure of local autonomy largely corresponding to that of a rural municipality but subject to the supervision of the department and the Government in Council. It is felt that the change that has been made will assuredly further the development of these Indians and hasten the time when they will become a fully responsible and self-supporting community. (11)[1]

"A measure of autonomy largely corresponding to that of a rural municipality" might sound enlightened enough, even prophetic given current discussions of Native self-government, but this high-handed erasure of an ancient system of government with a one-person royal commission/rubber stamp smacks of self-interest. So does the use of passive voice to minimize the selfhood of the writer and disown the opinions expressed. The latter is reminiscent of the sort of manipulation of language in the interests of the spread of European culture that Mary Louise Pratt analyzes in an essay on explorer-writers in Africa. "To the extent that it strives to efface itself," she says, "the invisible eye/I strives to make [the contents of travel reportage] natural, to find them there uncommanded, rather than assert them as the products/producers of European knowledges or disciplines" (125).

Followers of developments in the Oka crisis of 1990 will have recognized in Scott's words the source of jurisdictional problems of a sort that Tom Siddon, the minister of Indian Affairs, blamed for dilatory resolution of the situation: with whom do we negotiate? he asked through the media. Perhaps it was not in the government's interests to explain how the grip of the hereditary system is still strong among the Mohawks, because that would have involved admitting that "improvement" of the Mohawk political system has split them, much as the status/nonstatus distinction has split bands all over the country. When you have two jurisdictions, one hereditary and one imposed, each having a different sort of authority, no wonder there is confusion. It was either disingenuous or ignorant of Siddon not to acknowledge his department's historical part in producing that confusion.

NOT ALL OF SCOTT'S NONFICTION about Indians is mere white self-serving, though it *is* white only. "Civilization the Ideal" is the opening section title of Scott's first essay for Doughty and Shortt; whiteness and civilization are, like Indian Affairs and Indian affairs, implicitly interchangeable terms for him. Allowing for this severe limitation of view (so clear in postcolonial hindsight), Scott's writing on Indian Affairs should be placed in the context of his general cultural commentary in books and essays not only on literary subjects but on historical and political ones, as well. This category would include (besides the columns of "At the Mermaid Inn") "Canadian Feeling Toward the United States" (1896), *John Graves Simcoe* (1905), "The Tercentenary of Quebec, 1608–1908," and "Notes on the Meeting Place of the First Parliament of Upper Canada and the Early Buildings at Niagara" (1913). The essay on Quebec contains the nation-building rationale for writing them all:

> Especially for such a young people as ours, it is wise to perpetuate old deeds and to treasure what is, after all, our chief possession — the actions of those who were all unconsciously framing our destiny. Our lives should be blown through and through by historical memories and national ideals, otherwise we live in a fen country without vistas, or in stifling air, like old people in a workhouse. This is what civilization means in its highest sense. (*Circle* 154)

These contributions to constructing the nation ask to be seen in a positive light, and that includes some of the writing about Indians. Some of the Indian Affairs prose, like the annual reports, was part of Scott's job; not so the semiofficial writing that fell to him because he was high up in Indian Affairs and also a respected writer.

Scott felt it his national duty to spend so much of his time on activities of the Royal Society, on the editing of The Makers of Canada series, on the board of the Ottawa Little Theatre, on the writing of occasional patriotic poetry, and so on and on. Two essays already mentioned, those on "Indian Affairs" for Doughty and Shortt and "The Aboriginal Races," were part of projects intended to raise the historical consciousness of the Canadian people in changing times, and both were something like reprises of his and Edgar's own Makers of Canada series. The handsomely produced, multivolume *Canada and Its Provinces* (1914) arose out of a felt need to consolidate the image of a country in transition. "Canada has been concentrating all her forces on the conquest of nature for the use of man," say the editors in their introduction, with evident approval, "but it is not to be forgotten that the national character is not moulded exclusively by economic causes." This series was to have a patriotic purpose:

> To the end that a broad national spirit should prevail in all parts of the Dominion, it is desirable that a sound knowledge of Canada as a whole, of its history, traditions and standards of life, should be diffused among its citizens, and especially among the immigrants who are peopling the new lands. (viii)

Underlying this seems to be a certain nervousness of a sort still common in the 1990s, a concern that new Canadians are likely to see the country as a blank slate, rather than a place with traditions and ways of its own that merely need to be better known to be effective in shaping the new arrivals.

"The Aboriginal Races" was contributed to *Social and Economic Conditions in the Dominion of Canada* (1923), a volume of *The Annals* of the American Academy of Political and Social Science. Of this collection the editor writes: "Recent years have intensified and developed the organized social and industrial life of Canada, and, with that development, problems — some of an international nature, some peculiar to the Dominion — have forced themselves to the front and demanded consideration" (np). Scott's essay is one of nine in Part I — Population. There are eight sections in the volume, 300 pages of problems reminding one of the national complexities of which Indian Affairs was and is an aspect. The volume is more detached and analytical than *Canada and Its Provinces;* the purpose is to discuss, rather than shape, the nation. But Scott's presence in it seems not unrelated to his own patriotic purposes.

For all the emphasis on process and becoming in Scott's poetry, he seems to have held a common and once-defensible view of the country's future as a monolithically stable entity, an identity that he would have liked to be able to take for granted in his own time. It was the freedom of a later generation, clearing space for an uncompromising new sort of beginning, to assert that Canada had no identity. This is how Margaret Atwood hyperbolized it in *Survival:* "there is no new 'Canadian' identity ready for [an immigrant] to step into: he is confronted only by a nebulosity, a blank; no ready-made ideology is provided for him" (150). Outside of the whole context of *Survival,* and disregarding the hyperbole, that statement certainly looks naive. Ideology is never absent, as Arnold Itwaru understands. He objects to the way Atwood monologizes identity in *Survival.* His own *The Invention of Canada* emphasizes the constructedness of Canada, a nation that has, even in the name of multiculturalism, kept immigrants (like people of First Nations) on its margins. Itwaru and those of like opinion see strength in plural identity; still others exult in the fact that the very pluralism is in process: there are good reasons why Canadian identity is hard to grasp. "It may be that we survive on a very low level of definition," says Robert Kroetsch (7–28). If the shapers of the constitution were to listen to Canadian writers, the closure that seems to be expected might come to seem suspect. In the contemporary short story writers he anthologized in *From Ink Lake,* Michael Ondaatje sensed a version of the country that sounds superficially like Atwood's, but is actually celebrating glissando identity:

> And when we look at the stories, from Rudy Wiebe to Alistair MacLeod to Austin Clarke to Leon Rooke, there is the preoccupying image of figures permanently travelling, portaging their past, still uncertain of where to settle in this country which, in Elizabeth Smart's phrase, is "waiting, unselfconscious as the unborn, for future history to be performed upon it." We are all still arriving. (xvii)

Why *not* be always uncertain, why *not* be always somewhat lost, a little between things? Having tried on static, stable, essentialized identities (national, racial, sexual, ethnic), we are in recoil from them now. Why not try something more uncertain, something fluid — but emphatically not without understanding this as a model or an invention, to avoid drifting into the belief that it coincides with reality. Unselfconscious exchange of one model for another is no solution.

This has not been the digression from Scott's nonfiction writing on Indians that it may have seemed. In that writing, linked with Scott's other cultural commentary, a national insecurity appears. It needs to be added to Scott's personal insecurity as part of the field of resistance to change in which he existed. Writing Canadian literature was "making bricks without straw" to him. Having no strong sense of national/literary identity, and embracing an essentialized notion of what a nation is, his efforts were understandably bent much more toward making one than toward challenging it. Revisioning, tearing apart a political and cultural fabric to make something new, is even for later generations no easy task, and the difficulty of seeing outside of a mental edifice not yet constructed should not be underestimated.

INDIANS ARE NOT ABSENT from the rolls of heroes in the Doughty and Shortt essays, which occasionally draw some vitality from sketches of individuals. Scott writes not only of William Johnston, General Brock, and Sir Francis Bond Head, but also of Da-ga-no-we-da, the lawgiver of the Six Nations (whose peacemaking story is told in "Traditional History of the Confederacy of the Six Nations"), Joseph Brant, and Tecumseh, the latter under the heading of "Tecumseh, A Great War Chief." Of course, these great Indians are allies, and not difficult for a white bureaucrat to admire. Scott's version of the 1885 "half-breed rebellion" (598) is introduced as "the only breach in the mutual regard with which the treaties have been observed" (599), the breach being on the Indian side. Louis Riel's name is not even mentioned in Scott's account, perhaps because Métis affairs are not Indian affairs; Big Bear *is* mentioned, but barely, not having then the high profile that, thanks to Rudy Wiebe and Hugh Dempsey, he has now. Now it seems ironic how little sympathy Scott has for the rebellious Indians, how one-sided his view is:

> These [rebellious] Indians for the most part belonged to bands that had not settled on their reserves, but had continued to wander about the country, hunting and trapping and leading the aboriginal life. The most revolting of the atrocities which followed the first overt acts were perpetrated by such Indians — by Big Bear's band, for example. This band ruthlessly massacred two Roman Catholic priests, the Indian agent, the farming instructor and several other white people at Frog Lake. The

> change from apparent friendliness to deadly enmity was sudden. The last reports which had been received from all points before the outbreak spoke of the contented state of the Indians. They had small cause for rebellion; owing to the failure of their crops a large supply of provisions had been sent to the districts which afterwards became disaffected, and the Indians had before them no fear of starvation. (599)

In 1885 Scott had been employed by the Indian department for six years. He might have had some inside knowledge of the rebellion from the department perspective. But, by 1909, before he wrote the above, he had also read Amelia Paget's *People of the Plains,* a book that conducted him into a Cree perspective. Interestingly Paget's book says nothing whatever of her capture, with her family (her father was Hudson's Bay Company trader J. D. Maclean) by Big Bear's band. Her sole concern is to describe the ways of the people she came to know quite intimately,[2] and not only while she was a prisoner. It is left to Scott, introducing the book, to fill the reader in on Mrs. Paget's authority for writing. He does so in a defensive attempt to counter the positive view of Indians that emerges from her book:

> Captured at Fort Pitt in April of [1885] by Big Bear and his braves, they were held until the 17th of June following, sharing all the hardships of his shifting camp. During this experience Mrs. Paget's knowledge of the Cree language and her intimacy with all the ways of the Indians, even the very fashion of their thoughts, proved a constant defence for the whole party. The following pages must be read by the light of these facts; they account for the tone of championship for all Indians, and for the idealistic tendency which places everything in a high and favorable aspect. If there were hardship and squalor, starvation, inhumanity and superstition in this aboriginal life, judged by European standards, here it is not evident. All things are judged by the Indian idea of happiness, and the sophistication of the westerner disappears. The real felicities of the situation are heightened by the glow which might be spread over the reminiscences of some ancient chief whose lines had been cast in pleasant places, and to whom everything in the old days had become transfigured. This animating spirit is pleasant; there is no reason why the arrogance of our so-called civilization should everywhere prevail. . . . (13–14)

Something, probably his position of authority (Indian Affairs had funded the publication of *People of the Plains*) and perhaps his gender, as well, released Scott from the responsibility of taking Mrs. Paget's book as anything more than a pleasant diversion. Scott sees no contradiction in talking up her credentials and then presenting himself as the one who really knows the story. This is the only place I am aware of that Scott speaks of "our so-called civilization." He so regularly uses the word *civilization* as equivalent to white culture that the step into irony here feels merely rhetorical. Mrs. Paget's book did little to modify Scott's opinion of the 1885 uprising, at any rate. Why would a woman who had been dragged around the countryside by Big Bear's people hold such a positive view of the Cree if there weren't something to it? If Scott had asked that question, he might have written differently about Big Bear for Doughty and Shortt. He might have seen the Riel Rebellion in less polarized terms. The "good Indians" (not Scott's phrase) were the chiefs who "were able to control their followers and maintain their loyalty. A roll of honour might be written with such names as Pakan, Mistawasis, Ahtahkakoop, Moosomin, John and James Smith, Blue Quill and Sharphead" (600).

LESS DAMAGE CONTROL is being exercised in the introduction Scott contributed to Mildred Valley Thornton's *Indian Lives and Legends,* a volume of verbal and painted portraits of members of various British Columbia and Prairie tribes. Scott's introduction, written in 1944, did not appear in the book when it was published in 1947. A typescript survives (PA/DCS), as does a letter from Ms. Thornton thanking Scott for writing it and expressing pleasure in what he says. She was right to be pleased with the end of Scott's introduction, where he accurately observes that the book is inadvertently the self-portrait of a remarkable woman. Otherwise there is again a disjunction between Scott's self-justifying stance and the contents of the book, which is an amateur's attempt to preserve what can be preserved of attractive Native ways that are passing. As Amelia Paget writes with understanding of the Sun Dance, Mildred Thornton writes approvingly of the Potlatch, the two most famous ceremonies that Indian Affairs had banned and whose survival Scott himself pronounced in "The Administration of Indian Affairs in Canada" to be unwarranted.

One of the most poignant images in Thornton's *Indian Lives and Legends* is of the anthropologist Franz Boas returning to visit the Kwagiuth (Kwakiutl) he had studied as a young man:

> When Boaz first went to Fort Rupert at the request of the Smithsonian Institution 700 Indians were living at the ancient village, and the old ceremonials with all their color and fantasy were in full swing. He made several trips and spent many months among them, learned their language, respected their customs, and loved the people. When he was an old man he went back to visit them once again. Meanwhile the great houses had been torn down, most of the mighty totem poles were gone, and a mere remnant of the population was left. He stood before them, horrified, weeping openly and unashamed over the cataclysmic changes that the years had wrought. (49)

Boas opposed government proscription of the Potlatch, showing where his intellectual and professional sympathies lay, but there is room for doubt about this public display of feeling. No lamentation appears in *The Ethnology of Franz Boas: Letters and Diaries of Franz Boas Written on the Northwest Coast from 1886 to 1931*. Thornton may have needed those tears too much to let the literal truth impede their flow. The weeping Boas is a simple figure for the elegiac impulse that gathers and gathers to a single sentence about Big Bear late in Rudy Wiebe's *Temptations:* ". . . his heart staggered for all the great goodness now gone, gone forever" (397). The grief that Thornton attributes to the pioneering cultural relativist shouldn't be discounted because it represents heart's truth rather than historical fact. It seems natural to me, if sentimental, to search everywhere for some such expression of regret from Scott, some inkling that his private views of the Indians and of assimilationist policy were different from those he espoused and acted on in public. Even if one would then have to conclude that he had sold his soul to his job.

Mildred Thornton's book seems to have affected Scott no more than Amelia Paget's did. At least his writing (not necessarily identical, it should be remembered, with his inmost reflections) bears no signs that he regretted the effect of his policies on the people Mildred Thornton writes about. The introduction to *Indian Lives and Legends* is of interest now and worth quoting at length as (outside of letters) Scott's last statement about Indians and his official relationship with them. The interest is increased by the unrepentant affirmation in it of opinions expressed in "The Aboriginal Races" and repeated in the notorious "The Administration of Indian Affairs in Canada." His retrospective view, based on a reading of Thornton's book, seems to be that things have turned out for the best:

> Once I wrote that the policy of the Canadian Government is to protect the Indian, to guard his identity as a race and at the same time to apply methods which will destroy that identity and lead eventually to his disappearance as a separate division of the population. The Indian has proved that he can withstand the shock of contact with our civilization, that he can survive the manifold evils of that contact, and transfer his native energy into the channels of modern life. Mrs. Thornton's book might be regarded as a discursive and detailed treatment of that statement. This sensitive and sympathetic artist, roving from the Pacific coast to the prairies and meeting Indians everywhere without ceremony or official guidance found them in varying degree approaching this manifest destiny. There are here and there in these pages memories of the vanished aboriginal life, but they are few and indistinct. Manners, costume and even physical distinctions have changed under the constant pressure of imposed conditions; and I find records now and then of the popular fallacies regarding Indians which are

> inescapable and which will be hard to eradicate. The painter did not observe a different outlook on life by the Coast and the Prairie Indians; so far as I can gather from her pages there is acceptance of social conditions and an effort to make the best of the present without any hankering after the past. As for myself that past, often so highly colored by our writers, seems by comparison less happy. Then there was the opportunity to fight and starve, the extremes of that liberty which is always held up to us as ever-present in an ideal existence. Now there is no reason for tribal warfare or for scalping white men and a better chance for most Indians of a stable maintenance, and moreover, not infrequently, opportunity for the individual Indian to get the best of a bargain with the white man. (PA/DCS)

That Mildred Thornton wrote Scott to say she liked his introduction is perhaps a measure of the unselfconsciousness of her procedure, which is partly elegiac. The passage about Boas is by no means the only expression of her own sadness that the old Indian ways had all but disappeared. Whatever the reason, Scott misrepresents the book he is introducing. Ironically, his own early story of "Charcoal," the Plains Indian who "regressed" to "savagery," killed for revenge in the old way, and eluded white authorities for weeks, resembles the story of Simon Gun-a-noot that Thornton tells ("It was murder according to the white man's Law, but simple justice from the Indian point of view" 104; "For thirteen long, gruelling years he played the game of hide and seek with the police, living the life of a hermit . . . " 105). These men were certainly not sliding peaceably into an assimilated present. Of course, one needs to probe into the reasons why the rebellious few are of so much interest to white writers and readers. Are *they* the ones who most truly represent their culture, or are they being sentimentally assimilated to a white vision of tragic heroism? We need Native writers to tell us.

IN LESLIE MONKMAN'S GUIDE to white treatments of Native subject matter, *A Native Heritage,* Duncan Campbell Scott's work is discussed most thoroughly in the chapter entitled "Death of the Indian." Monkman places Scott in the category of those white writers drawn nostalgically to the image of a heroic Indian past far superior to their present. He says of "Charcoal" that it "evokes the same sense of inevitability as Scott's official despatches; the principles of progress and social Darwinism which underlie white policy are accepted rather than attacked" (73). Aside from the odd use of the term *despatches,* if he is thinking about essays, Monkman is right. Resignation to Native decline abounds in Scott's fiction and poetry; "The Last of the Indian Treaties" fits the pattern, as well. What about the claim that Scott was a social Darwinist? Answering the question will take us once again through Scott's writing about Indians (at least through those widely separated passages in which he directly introduces assimilation), this time attending to the "progress" in them of the policy. Now we need to look harder at that oddly contradictory passage from "The Administration of Indian Affairs in Canada," with its linkage of preservation and destruction. I have been able to find no sign in the nonfiction of any special feeling *for* Natives; what about the other extreme? Was Scott a racist?

Social Darwinists believed in stepping into evolution to speed the inevitable. "Survival of the fittest" became a watchword for them, if not for Darwin; the slogan became grounds for racist action based on the belief that a (self-chosen) few could identify not only "the superior race" but the superior members of a race and on such grounds were justified in contributing to its purification. Is this what is expressed by the well-known passage about the disappearance of the red race at the end of "The Administration of Indian Affairs"?

After Peter Haworth's presentation at the banquet of the Scott Symposium in Ottawa in 1979, Vincent Sharman asked a question that nobody could or would answer. Haworth's introduction had broken the news about P. H. Bryce's attacks on Scott for his handling of the preventable tuberculosis epidemic that was killing so many Indian children out West. The audience was in shock. Perhaps that was why Sharman's question took us by surprise. He said: "What's wrong with assimilation?" This is a fair question, and I think I'm ready to answer it after more than a decade.

Nothing is wrong with assimilation if by it is meant the creolization of races at whatever rate is natural when merging is unforced. Assimilation in that sense is celebrated by Salman Rushdie in an essay setting into context the novel for which he has been forced onto a reservation of one. When a self-described "mongrel" endorses racial mixture, you listen:

> *The Satanic Verses* celebrates hybridity, impurity, intermingling, the transformation that comes of new and unexpected combinations of human being, cultures, ideas, politics, movies, songs. It rejoices in mongrelization and fears the absolutism of the Pure. *Mélange,* hotchpotch, a bit of this and a bit of that is *how newness enters the world.* It is the great possibility that mass migration gives the world, and I have tried to embrace it. *The Satanic Verses* is for change-by-fusion, change-by-conjoining. It is a love-song to our mongrel selves. (*Imaginary Homelands* 394)

Mongrelization in something like Rushdie's sense seems to be what Scott was thinking about when, speaking as a private citizen (and without mongrel authority), he wrote "The Last of the Indian Treaties." Here he points out that "the effect of education and of contact with a few of the better elements of our civilization were noticeable at Albany and Moose Factory" (121). After offering some examples of what he means, he goes on to say:

> But any forecast of Indian civilization which looks for final results in one generation or two is doomed to disappointment. Final results may be attained, say, in four centuries by the merging of the Indian race with the whites, and all these four things — treaties, teachers, missionaries and traders — with whatever benefits or injuries they bring in their train, aid in making an end. (121–122)

Four centuries seems generous enough to qualify as a schedule of noninterference on the Bo-Peep model: "Leave them alone / And they'll come home." With assimilation in this sense, with "the merging of the red and white races by marital unions" (*Manoir Richelieu Catalogue* 3), there is nothing wrong. But a distinction has to be made between this natural process and the policy of forcing it, and even the policy is not so harmful as the means of implementation. What is wrong is a policy that pushes assimilation onto a people many of whom might, in fact, embrace it if the say were their own.

All writing on this subject treads on thin ice. Anti-assimilationism in some parts of the world has fed loathsome forms: the holocaust, apartheid, ethnic cleansing. Where is the line dividing all that from support for the restoration and maintenance of separate First Nations identities? I can't draw it, though I can feel it, just as I feel its perviousness as a boundary. What would such support amount to without guaranteed continuance of those roots of Native cultures, their languages? Window dressing. Pro-mongrel/anti-assimilationist: people like me will have to stagger along as best we can with the burden of our contradictions. I think we should stagger on out of the picture, taking unconflicted members of the dominant culture with us, and leave Native peoples to decide their own future. That means self-government, whether or not it means assimilation.

Nothing is wrong with assimilation; assimilation is the way of the world, "a metaphor for all humanity" (Rushdie 394). It's when assimilation means genocide that the heart rebels. Sadly, Scott's earliest expression of the policy is his most relaxed.

The schedule for assimilation has been accelerated, by 1912, according to the section of "Indian Affairs, 1867–1912" entitled "The Future of the Indians," a section parallel to the "Transition" section of "The Administration of Indian Affairs." Here Scott boasts about the progress toward absorption already made by Indians in Ontario and Quebec, and concludes:

> The degree of general progress which makes it possible thus to divide and classify the Indian population of the older provinces has been developed within less than a century, and in this relatively short time we have arrived within measurable distance of the end. The happiest future for the Indian is absorption into the general population, and this is the object of the policy of

> our government. In the Indian communities now under discussion we see the natives advanced more than half-way towards the goal, and the final result will be this complete absorption. The great forces of intermarriage and education will finally overcome the lingering traces of native custom and tradition. It may be some time before reserves disappear and the Indian and his lands cease to be marked and separated. (622–623)[3]

It has to be remembered that Scott is not necessarily talking about the disappearance of Indian physiognomy. The Indian Department does not deal in such matters; it deals in words, in definitions. "Under certain somewhat oppressive regulations an Indian may become enfranchised," Scott says in a passage already quoted from "Indian Affairs 1867–1912." "He then ceases in all respects to be an Indian" (619). "In all respects" does not square very well with the psychology implicit in, say, "The Half-breed Girl." There a Native girl has Scottish "blood," and some of the Scottish aspect of her mental tension is centuries old. The girl could not be called a Scot, but the Scot is alive in her. The view of race that grounds this psychology may be obsolete, but the point is that assimilationism is inconsistent with the assumptions implicit in the poem and in much of Scott's other poetry and fiction. Nothing in his writing overtly says that dominant Celtic blood would be capable of surviving while recessive Indian blood would not, but Scott was clearly not free of the common white assumption that assimilation could never absorb the white races (Appiah 37).

Of the two "great forces of intermarriage and education" Scott speaks of, the former has been less forced than the latter. Indian education was one of his portfolios on the way to the top in his field. This meant that he was responsible for the residential schools, for the policy of separating children and parents in the effort to cut the young ones off from their roots in one generation, then (in the most extreme of such experiments) to unite the graduates of those schools in marriage and to set them up on farms as a sort of dowry confirming the detachment. Outlawing Native ceremonies was part of this effort. In short, this was social engineering or social Darwinism.

In "Indian Affairs 1867–1912" Scott cites as an example of successful assimilation the situation at Metlakatla in British Columbia. Brian Titley summarizes:

> Here Scott was referring to the radical experiment in social engineering conducted by the Anglican missionary William Duncan following his arrival at Fort Simpson in 1857. Appalled at most aspects of coastal Indian life, Duncan resolved that total cultural transformation would be required. Having secured a small following, he decided to create an isolated community.

> In 1862 Duncan led his "catehumens" [*sic*] to Metlakatla where the new zion was established. It became a model village in which almost everything, from rules and regulations to architecture, and [*sic*] was based on the standards of Victorian England. Indian customs were forbidden, and strict rules were imposed requiring religious observance, school attendance, cleanliness, industriousness, abstinence from alcohol, and other trappings of the Protestant ethic. Duncan ruled Metlakatla in an autocratic manner with the assistance of a force of Indian constables and succeeded in imposing astonishing behavioural changes on those under his sway. In fact, the transformation was so dramatic that it drew the wondrous admiration of visitors, one of whom remarked that they were no longer Indians, but white men. (35)

High praise. This description reminds me of nothing so much as a hymn to the wonderful potential for creating urban-style suburbs in Northern Ontario sung by a mining company presenter to the 1978 Royal Commission on the Northern Environment. One sure indication of difference is horrified reaction to a plan advanced with pride by someone else.

The attitude implicit almost everywhere in Scott's prose on Indians surfaces only once. He presumably wrote it once, that is, though it was published three times: in the 1920 annual report, then as "The Red Indian," and finally in the 1927 annual report. In these pieces (or this piece) Scott calls whites "the superior race," a phrase like a red flag when waved before readers of a later time. Here is the phrase in its context in the opening of the *Times* article:

> It may be conceded that the typical Canadian Indian is the hunter and trapper, and, when one thinks of him buckskins and beadwork and feathers still cloak him with a sort of romance. But these are rarely seen, except in pageants and on holidays, when the superior race must be amused by a glimpse of real savages in war paint. The Indian hunter and trapper follows the craft of his ancestors clothed as you and I, his wife and children likewise. His domestic surroundings grow less and less savage. The rabbit skin robe yet holds its own, and the snowshoe, but the birch-bark canoe is supplanted by the basswood or cedar variety; as likely as not he has a sewing machine and a gramophone in his tent.[4]

I shouldn't have been shocked to see "the superior race" in black and white. Scott is generally more circumspect, but so much of what he says, even in "The Last of the Indian Treaties," grows out of the hierarchical elevation of the "civilized" over the "primitive," as the superintendent general is over the lesser bureaucrats, that the attitude, the *habit,* of superiority is hardly news.

Still, the overtness is disappointing enough to make me wonder if Scott might have been trying for and missing an ironic effect (in which case "the superior race" would be meant to be understood by sophisticated readers as a joke). That line of thinking would be more tenable if the phrase were in quotation marks, or if there were some other indicator that irony was on Scott's mind. What *is* ironic is that the very feature of the article (the so-so prose) that makes one wonder about the effect Scott was trying to achieve frustrates any answer.

Racist is not a word to be flung around lightly, but it seems to fit. It fits the words I have been discussing, at any rate; how well those fit Scott, how much they belong to him, is a question more difficult to answer. Minorities in his day were neither so visible nor so vocal as they are in ours. There was much less of the troubling and clarifying pressures exerted by the current assault on the centre by the ranks of the marginalized. In Scott's time no one was calling race a "dangerous trope" (Gates 5); nobody was saying "The truth is that there are no races: there is nothing in the world that can do all we ask 'race' to do for us. The evil that is done is done by the concept and by easy — yet impossible — assumptions as to its application" (Appiah 35–36). Scott was never pushed to take a stand on race. His prose opinions on the subject, like his own stance, if he had one, inevitably remain soft, blurred, a sandy foundation for any critic to build on. Of course, we haven't exhausted quite all the sources of answer to the question of Scott's stance on race.

WE CAN'T ALWAYS be sure of having the authentic Scott in his letters (those written to Elise excepted), but we are surely much nearer the man and his opinions in letters than we are anywhere in the nonfiction. That being accepted, what do we make of Scott's outburst about the "Jap" scare in a letter to Arthur S. Bourinot written from Vancouver on March 2, 1942? Racism is palpable here; does it reflect in any way on Scott's feelings about Native people? Here is the pertinent part of the letter:

> If we are exposed to the Jap menace one does not feel it much. There is a justifiable, bitter feeling against this treacherous race but it is truly a difficult matter to get rid of them. We have taken away their radios, motor-cars & cameras but as they didn't invent any of these things they can get on without them & they have to be in their holes, shacks & houses from sunset to sunrise & I have no sympathy for them. In fact my ruthless will would submerge their cursed island & all their fleets & crash all their air-planes. We have no blackouts but are prepared. As for protection there is much talk & some work but everyone with a grain of sense must know that the japs could land & establish themselves at places on the B.C. Coast whenever they felt it was worth while.

It's both ironic and saddening to see Scott invoking sense when his reaction to a crisis that history has proved to have been illusory is simply irrational. Scott's outburst is the sort of raw material on which Doris Lessing bases her 1985 Massey Lectures, published as *Prisons We Choose to Live Inside.* "Whenever," she says, "things seem to be going along quite smoothly — and I am talking about human affairs in general — then it is as if suddenly some awful primitivism surges up and people revert to barbaric behaviour" (11). She feels that "writers are by nature more easily able to achieve . . . detachment from mass emotions and social conditions" (14), but she makes no distinction between the writer as represented by his or her work and the writer as average citizen. In some cases this distinction seems minimal; in others it is crucial. When A. S. Byatt says, "My opinions on the Gulf War, or how to arrange social security in my own country, are worth no more nor less than any other member of the general public" (8), she is distancing her ordinary self from the engaged artistic self that commands the sort of knowledge, the kind of analysis, that Lessing sees as one of the most valuable tasks of the novelist: "to enable us to see ourselves as others see us" (14).

Is it Scott's ordinary self speaking those offensive words about Japanese Canadians? Is it then his Arnoldian best or artistic self that is on display in the fiction and poetry? So simplistic a statement of a subtle distinction that is surely not stable even for an individual, let alone from artist to artist, sounds altogether too schizophrenic. If Scott had written fiction on the subject he addresses in his letter, the result would hardly have been an *Obasan.*

One uncharacteristically vicious letter in a long lifetime — but it can't be reassuring about his orientation to Native peoples that he should leap so blindly to blame a whole race for what happened at Pearl Harbor. That is to answer one barbarism with another. There were a very few more rational white minds in Canada in 1942, and part of the complexity of *Obasan* is that Joy Kogawa lets them speak in her novel, but Scott's reaction was typical. Nothing of the much that might be said of the confusion and paranoia of what Scott calls later in his letter "these terrific times" justifies such blind racism. But the reason his letter must not be cited as proof of flaming racism with respect to the Indians is that his blindness about the Japanese clearly stems from fear fed by an ignorance about the distinction between Imperial Japan and Canadians of Japanese descent. I think it could never be said of Scott what Sweetgrass says to John MacDougall in Rudy Wiebe's *The Temptations of Big Bear* ("when you speak, I hear my own voice" 45), but he was by no means ignorant of his charges. In the interests of presenting as rounded a picture as possible of Duncan Campbell Scott, his position on the "yellow peril" must neither be suppressed nor overstressed.

THIS CHAPTER IS NOT the first to put into play the idea of a difference, a distance, between Scott the ordinary citizen and Scott the writer. If the theory of such a distinction is employed with tact and subtlety, so that the writer "writing beyond himself" in fiction and poetry is neither sentimentalized nor romanticized, it may be of use in extending the discussion of Scott's orientation to the Indians. The figure they make in the fiction and poems is surely not *irrelevant* to his personal views, though how to squeeze those literary artifacts so that Scott's opinions run out is something I have not learned and do not expect to.

My procedure, as I move into the contextualized readings in part 2 of this book, is oblique and, in a sense, arm's-length. That is, I discuss the stories and poems, especially the poems, *as* poems, as works of art, rather than as arguments about Native identity or assimilation. This means restoring the ethnographic content of each text to the position critics have often wrenched it out of: as a sometimes but not always important *aspect* of the whole. The ideological content of fictions that have been written in response at least as much to the making impulse as to the impulse to say something must be teased out of an environment from which ideology can never be completely detached. There is no way to find out what Scott thought about Native people in general by looking directly at the poems in which they figure — not when the poems are almost all about individuals or, much less often, about one of the Indian nations. The reader might feel some resistance to being asked, from here on in, to watch for the continuation of my argument about Scott and the Indians out of the corner of his or her eye (with the intuition, as some like to call it), but criticism going about its business properly ("with great love and great coldness" Ondaatje, *Rat Jelly* 58) will always have more to say than meets the eye. In any case, all of the writing that I go on to discuss has been in need of a fresh look. I will introduce further perspectives on the matter of Scott's relationship with Native peoples, and a good deal more information about the Treaty 9 trips, but my not-untroubled admiration of his art at its best is what will be driving me through part 2 of this book.

NOTES

1. In his "The Six Nations Status Case" chapter of *A Narrow Vision,* Brian Titley offers a full account of Scott's involvement in "one of the most intractable difficulties which plagued Indian administration during the 1920's. Its underlying assumptions posed a direct challenge to the very foundations of federal policy. The Department of Indian Affairs operated on the premise that it knew what was best for the native population. Its policies were therefore formulated and implemented without real consultation with its charges. The Six Nations Indians not only opposed specific federal regulations, but actually rejected the authority of the department and of the act it administered" (134). The last chapter of Ronald Wright's more polemical *Stolen Continents* covers much the same ground, although Wright minces no words: the 90 square miles on the Grand River remaining to the Six Nations is a nation, and Scott was the "time-serving mandarin" who in the 1920s stood "[a]gainst Deskaheh — against all Indian leaders at odds with the settler government . . . " (321) .
2. In a marginal note in his 1909 western journal, Edmund Morris says of "Mrs. Padgett" [*sic*], whose book he had just received, that her "grandmother was one of the Dog Ribb (Dene) Indians. She is related to the Campbells & Murrays — half breeds" (192). Mrs. Paget may have been white technically, but if Morris's information is correct, her Native connections may make *People of the Plains* less remarkable (as penetration of another culture) than it would otherwise seem. It depends on whether or not she was raised white.
3. Scott goes on: "It would be foolish to make this end in itself the final object of the policy. The system of reserved lands has been of incalculable benefit to the Indians, who require secure foothold in the soil, and great caution should be shown in regard to any plans for separating the Indian from his land or for giving him power to alienate his heritage" (623). This sounds good, but there are those land surrenders to remember.
4. A gramophone and a "hand-sewing machine" are two of the "treasured possessions" that the Widow Frederic tries to sacrifice to "the Manitou / That lived in the lake" in "A Scene at Lake Manitou."

PART 2

The Flower in the Rock

6

"Civilization Against Savagery": Fiction on Natives and the North

fist *The typographer's fist is not a blunt instrument but a silent, pointing hand. All too often, however, it is overdressed, with ruffles at the cuff.*
Robert Bringhurst, The Elements of Typographic Style

UNLESS JOHN METCALF somehow succeeds in discrediting *In the Village of Viger* ("horribly *wrought* style with its soft focus and imprecise diction," "genre-writing" of "sentimentality, artificiality, and condescension" [53]), Scott's reputation in fiction will continue to stand on that volume, and on two or three of the northern stories I examine in this chapter. "Labrie's Wife" is probably the only Scott story of "world class"; perhaps a few admissions of that sort might have saved Metcalf the considerable effort he expended in tracing the academic conspiracy to establish *Viger* in the Canadian tradition. *Viger* is an uneven book, but it stands out in its time and place as an early example of one of those cross-genre books that Canadians are so fond of writing — the short story cycle that falls somewhere between the story miscellany and the novel. Of course, Metcalf is right that other Canadian writers have paid little attention to *Viger,* and he is right to say that a tradition is generally established by writers building on the work of other writers. *Viger* has been finding readers almost exclusively among academics and their students, and there should be no objection to the asking of some questions about that. Who makes the Canadian canon, after all, and with what motivation? Does the New Canadian Library *In the Village of Viger and Other Stories,* which I edited, represent the recovery of a worthy text that had been virtually lost, or is it an academic make-work project, a stepping stone in an academic career? The reader will be able to guess my answer, in this case, but I don't dismiss the question.

Metcalf's good questions are often more difficult to take seriously than they might be if he were not so palpably wanting to win the arguments he engages in. He is not above falsifying the evidence. He makes no mention of the northern stories that compose roughly half of *In the Village of Viger and Other Stories,* the volume's main evidence for Scott's contribution to Canadian realism. He prefers to transfer that claim to the *Viger* stories, an invention on which he then rests many of his further assertions. That selection of stories (to leave Metcalf behind) was made with the intention of representing Scott as a writer of fiction on subjects both "pastoral and heroic," to adapt the terms for Canadian poetry that Scott advances in "Fragment of an Ode to Canada" (*Poems* 12). This construction of Scott the story writer follows a view of Canada and its writing expressed not only in "Fragment of an Ode," but also in "The Height of Land." The "lonely north" and "the crowded southern land" — those antithetical environments stretch Scott's mind between them, and still exert an organizing influence on Scott's critics. To my mind, Scott's *best* stories do almost fall into two categories dividing along a North-South axis, and there are enough decent northern stories to make a strong, unified, northern counterpart to *Viger.* But the picture is not so clear when the stories that fit less neatly in one or the other category are factored in. Many of the uncollected stories are uncollectable, but they often have to do with mysterious plots involving violence (like many of the northern stories) and they often have a touch, or more than a touch, of the supernatural and the Gothic and the romance coincidence found in some of the *Viger* stories. Published in various magazines, and often illustrated with period wood engravings, each of them merits its own version of the sensationalizing heading that one of them received in the *Globe* of November 23, 1889:

Coiniac Street

A Tale of Love and Sorrow

Duncan Campbell Scott's Latest Production

THE WOODS IN A STORM

The Lair of the Counterfeiters — Presentiments Fulfilled —
A Desperate Resolve — No Life Within and Death Without

An interesting study might be made of the pressures of popular genres on Scott's fiction, collected and uncollected, but this is not the place for that. In fact, I have a number of agendas in this chapter that are somewhat difficult to unify. The argument of the next few pages will therefore be more elliptical than each of the chapters focusing on single poems that follow. This book being partly about Scott's literary handling of Native peoples, their place in his stories needs to be considered, even though, with one exception, the issue of Nativeness is secondary at best. The exception is "Charcoal," which must be discussed for the same reason as "At Gull Lake: August 1810," though neither story nor poem has directly to do with the treaty trips that are my other focus. Neither does Scott's unfinished novel, though the "ca. 1905" attached to the published version suggests that it falls within my temporal frame. The North is an important and symbolic environment to one of the novel's main characters, as well, but I stretch my mandate when I extend myself into some other views of this flawed and fascinating work. The centre may not quite hold in this chapter, then, but one aspect of it will establish a pattern for all those that follow: I introduce the evidence that some of the northern stories (like the poems I go on to discuss) had specific sources in the people, places, and situations that Scott encountered in the summers of 1905 and 1906. The chapter concludes with a detailed discussion of "Labrie's Wife," and that ends with some remarks about the function of Native characters in the story. So at least I end where I began.

"CHARCOAL" WAS PUBLISHED in 1904, which makes it roughly contemporaneous with "The Last of the Indian Treaties." The story and the essay have in common narrators palpably in sympathy with Indians who find themselves, neither choosing nor comprehending, emotionally stranded between cultures. In both essay and story some attempt is made to stand in the shoes of the dispossessed and to look from there at the dispossessors, but "Charcoal" is Scott's only prose work to focus on a Native person *as* a Native, on the question of identity and its dilution. This is one of those historical stories (like those of Simon Gun-a-noot and Almighty Voice) of sudden escape from the straitjacket of new white ways in which the test of responsible Blood manhood is no longer killing enemies and stealing horses, but rather holding down a job and supporting a family. Charcoal's grip on these niceties is relaxed by the infidelity of his wife and lost through talks with an uncle who steeps Charcoal in the old ways.

After his first rebellious acts, Charcoal "called on his gods to strike his enemies. They had taken his country from him, his manners and his garb, and when he rebelled against them, their hands were upon him. Sometimes he felt as if his head was on fire, and he held his hands up in the dark to see the reflection of the flames" (*Circle* 218). Waiting to be hanged, he has leisure for further reflection:

> He had thought of many things which he did not understand. He was to be killed in the white man's manner; to his mind it was only vengeance, death for deaths, which the warriors of his own race dealt to their foes in the old days, and in a braver fashion. They had driven away the buffalo, and made the Indian sad with flour and beef, and had put his muscles into harness. He had only shot a bad Indian, and they rose upon him. His gun had shot a big policeman, and when they had taught his brother-in-law their own idea of fair dealing he was taken in sleep, and now there was to be an end. He did not know what Père Pauquette meant by his prayers, and the presentation of the little crucifix worn bright with many salutations. It was all involved in mystery. (221)

Charcoal's consciousness is extremely rudimentary in this version. Scott makes Charcoal a sort of simpleton, not unlike Charles Wabinoo in "The Last of the Indian Treaties." He has an "infantine curiosity" about the contents of the "medicine-pole-bag" he buys his wife.

The man who appears in Hugh Dempsey's *Charcoal* is very different. He is an Indian of high spiritual attainments, "a member of the powerful Horn Society and the holder of medicine bundles and religious objects — all requiring honesty and fidelity from their owner" (16). He is the owner of "the holy bear knife" from which "he had received all the terrible strength of the grizzly bear" (19). Scott simplifies all of this. Charcoal had also discovered and killed his rival in the act of intercourse with his (Charcoal's) wife, a telling bit of specificity that Scott was not the sort to use. But the emotional core of the story is similar in the accounts of both writers. As Dempsey puts it, "if he had done these things thirty years earlier, Charcoal would have been a great warrior" (70), a hero not a criminal. "It was once more civilization against savagery," Scott's narrator says, overinterpreting his own tale. "Against this one Indian who had dared to follow the old tradition was arrayed all organized law" (217).

Or *is* he overinterpreting? We do have to be careful here, because there is an edge of irony in "civilization against savagery," a formula too easy to apply to Charcoal's rebellion. Scott's Charcoal is not a mere savage. The narrator stands near, though not within, Charcoal. He appears — this mask of the man who later urged the banning of Native ceremonies — to accept "the sacred mysteries of the Mow-to-kee when the centre pole was raised" (213). These are female mysteries, of course; a narrator who remains near Charcoal has no call to enter them. To venture near the mysteries that the historical Charcoal participated in would have made the story altogether different, more difficult for a white man to bring off. Perhaps Scott's narrator comes closest to acknowledging Charcoal's otherness when, without editorializing on his accurate reading of invisible signs of his wife's treachery, he naturalizes something of the man's highly developed instinctual life.

Scott lacks the hindsight of Rudy Wiebe who, in "Where Is the Voice Coming From," can tell the tale of Almighty Voice's rebellion (a parallel case of "civilization against savagery") while interrogating the sources of narrative authority. But, insofar as I, another white man, can tell (leaving aside the question of whether he ought to be doing it at all), Scott doesn't seem to be doing badly in this story that he wrote, according to Leon Slonim (162) sometime between 1898 and 1904.

Not doing badly, but not overpowering the reader, either. Compared to my standard of white fictional investigation into Native reality (Rudy Wiebe's work), "Charcoal" looks rather thin. It feels recounted at secondhand, rather than lived; the imagination is engaged, but not the senses that Wiebe summoned to help him animate historical fact in *The Temptations of Big Bear:*

> Through the smoke and darkness and piled up factuality of a hundred years to see a face; to hear, and comprehend, a voice whose verbal language he will never understand; and then to risk himself beyond such seeing, such hearing as he discovers possible, and venture into the finer labyrinths opened by those other senses: touch, to learn the texture of leather, of earth; smell, the tinct of sweetgrass and urine; taste, the golden poplar sap or the hot, raw buffalo liver dipped in gall. ("On the Trail of Big Bear" 132)

"[It] is obviously silly to hope by the simple massing of facts to arrange for art" (133), Wiebe says. Scott did more than mass the facts, but he certainly didn't set himself a challenge anything like Wiebe's. He wrote in response to John Masefield's appreciation of "Charcoal," which had been included in *The Circle of Affection,* that the story was little more than an adaptation of the transcript of Charcoal's trial.[1]

There is another way to look at Charcoal. He is not only a historical type (the "regressive" Native); he is something of a Scott type. The reader can plot the rebellious Charcoal at one extreme of a gamut of characters that Scott is fond of presenting. He is often interested in the dramatic possibilities of "civilization" confronting "savagery," as in this encounter between an Ojibway patriarch and a new priest in "Spirit River":

> They faced one another, antipodes as they were. The old man was as uncouth as a bear, almost without facial expression, with strange little tufts of grey hair scattered on his rough face. He was clothed in a pair of moleskin trousers and a red and black checked shirt; a broad leather belt went around his waist and on his feet he wore a pair of shoe-packs. He was unlearned in any of the world's methods, but in his massive head there was stored a subtle lore that was part instinct and part acquirement, a knowledge of the wilderness that had made him a supreme hunter among

> a race of hunters. The priest faced him clad in his long soutane, a uniform that placed him in the army of the schoolmen, sophisticated by long study for a special mission, bred under the tradition of the Society of Jesus. He was as incomprehensible to Petit Bonhomme as Petit Bonhomme was to him. (*Elspie* 68–69)

Clearly the potential for misunderstanding, and therefore for drama, is great — not that Petit Bonhomme and Père Dugas are the principal antagonists in this particular story. In fact, the deceased priest whom Père Dugas succeeds had achieved a perfect understanding with Petit Bonhomme, so we get a "civilization versus savagery" opposition only by ignoring aspects of the story that soften its edges.

In the northern stories the word "savage" means brutal or out of control as often as it means primitive. The word "savage" clearly triggers Scott's imaginative adrenaline, though; many of the stories set in the North involve some tremendous release from the strictures of law, whether external or internal. All this passion of lust or vengeance or physical prowess (the white face in the North, according to Elizabeth Waterson, is "contorted by frightening and terrible passions" 224) supplies an opposite to calm and balance in the characters of Scott's unpublished novel, many of them walled within themselves. In the Underwood family, for instance, "Feeling would be restrained until upon some occasion it would break bonds and a scene of passion would ensue" (45–46). This would be verbal passion, of course, and nothing like that found in the scenes of physical violence in the stories, or of release from the bonds of old age (a favourite Scott theme) in the stories and poems, but it does make me wonder if Scott was living out again and again in his later fiction a freedom that his upbringing made impossible for him to live in person. Scratch the deputy minister of Indian Affairs and reveal the repressed savage? Archibald Muir, of "Labrie's Wife," as something more than a literary mask of Duncan Campbell Scott? This is tempting, though psychoanalyzing a writer on the basis of his/her works must be chastened by recalling the power of the imagination to take a writer outside him or herself.

WHAT DID SCOTT FIND on the treaty trips that would be of use for his fiction? What aspects of his fiction are illuminated, at least, by what we know of the trips? Some of the evidence that Scott was the writer-bee in the North (gathering pollen/material) is more circumstantial for the fiction than it is for the poems, but not all of it. The real question is not, *did* some of the stories originate in the trips, but rather *how* did Scott use what he found, because artistic licence must be inferred from the differences between the stories and their demonstrable sources.

There were a lot of campfires on the waterways of the North in the summers of 1905 and 1906. We know there was traditional music on those evenings. There was Jimmy Swain's nightly concert, at least as far as Fort Albany in 1905. Were stories also exchanged? On some of the colder nights when firewood was plentiful, Samuel Stewart says, there were fires in front of each tent — not a scenario for intercultural sharing. We don't know who told the story that Scott turned into the poem "Night Burial in the Forest," but Pelham Edgar says that his friend was so struck by it as to leave the campfire and paddle to the spot where it took place. Other stories must have been told. Scott indicates in "The Last of the Indian Treaties" that he heard some, though he credits no particular teller: "When one has heard even a few of the stories of Indian cruelty and superstition which haunt the [Albany]," he says, "of the Crane Indians who tied a man and his wife together, back to back, and sent them over the falls because they were sorcerers, of the terrible windigo of Marten's Falls, the lonely spirit of the stream becomes an obsession. It is ever present, but at night it grows in power" (*Circle* 119).

The Albany is lonely and desolate near James Bay (at least to white people), but not haunted by any lack of ghosts. The windigo (or wendigo) is mentioned in "A Legend of Welly Legrave" as Welly's antagonist in another phase of the Welly Legrave cycle.

The core of at least one other "historical" story must have been communicated by the crew on the way up the Abitibi in 1905, because there was a ritual attached to it. Shortly after a 5:30 a.m. start on August 29, Stewart tells of the party's reaching "Granny's Rock," the place on the Abitibi now known as Iroquois Falls, "a high rock or bluff at the foot of which our canoemen stopped to enable each member of the party to throw a piece of tobacco into the water to benefit in some way the spirit of an old, blind Indian woman who had been pushed over the rock by a war party of Iroquois Indians to drown in the water below" (RG10e 149).[2]

But the stories that Scott found of use for his own writing — especially those of fur traders — were mostly neither Native in origin nor oral in treatment. Stewart fairly often mentions that stories were told by the white people who acted as hosts for the treaty party, factual stories by the sound of them, but he never says what was in them. Some of the traders seem to have been great talkers. Mr. Mackenzie, at Moose Factory, told stories of the early days of the Hudson's Bay Company. "Mr. Barrett [of New Post] had formerly been a member of the North West Mounted Police, and had many stories to relate of adventures while doing duty with the force" (124). "During the evening [at Abitibi]," Stewart says, "we were entertained by Mr. Drever with many stories relating to Indians, their traditions, habits & C. Mr. Drever has lived among the Indians for many years and has a thorough knowledge of both Cree and Ojibway languages. He is also an authority on all matters relating to the manners and customs of the Indians so that we listened to what he had to tell us with much pleasure" (157). Drever's store was not exhausted in 1905. He entertained the treaty party with similar fare for two evenings in 1906 when they returned to finish the work of the previous summer. In 1906 Stewart otherwise mentions only Mr. Loudet, inspector of Revillon Frères who, at New Liskeard, told stories of his adventures in the Far North (and who may have lent his name to the Northwest Company trader in "Expiation," as Chief Espaniol may be connected to Mme. Espaniol in "Spirit River"), but there were others.

James Miller of Mattagami Post becomes something more than a mere name, unlike the northerners Stewart records, because in "Travelling with a Poet" Pelham Edgar recounts a little of what the man actually told. In it we can feel something of the spirit, if not the literal content, of Scott's fur trade stories. Edgar writes:

> Half a century ago James Miller said a final farewell to his Hebrides home, and serving as boy and man in various posts of our remote interior reached at last by slow and arduous stages the rank of trader. Like most of his class he has practically lived the Indian life, and married a woman of the tribe. His elder brother retired five years ago, and a yearning seized him to pass his last days in his Hebrides home. So he called his Indian sons and daughters about him, shook hands with them with no more sign of emotion than if they were going on a fifty mile journey to return in a week, and sailed across the sea with his old squaw. It is a strange story and not without its pathos. The brother spoke to me about it with a twinkle in his eye. "He'll pine like enough for the old life again, you bet, and I'm thinking that the wife will be wanting a smell of the woods and a wee bit camp-fire in the cool o' the night." Miller of Mattagami desires no more civilization than a week of deep potations once a year at Biscotasing with his old crony, Macleod of Flying Post. The distant Hebrides stir no regrets in his heart. He has lived in the wilderness, and there he chooses to end his days. (64–65)

Of course, the "neat little gasoline yacht" that Stewart mentions may have influenced Miller's decision to stay in Canada. No man who operates a yacht is inhabiting a true wilderness.

The most poignant tale of a white trader in accounts of the 1905 and 1906 trips is that of G. B. Cooper in Samuel Stewart's journal. If some northern heart of darkness had been reached in 1905, it would have to have been at English River (or Kenogami) Post, the remotest, loneliest post on the route, where Cooper was the clerk. In Stewart's description the approach to Marten's Falls Post on the Albany feels like a deep penetration into the interior of the North. The Albany *is* a highway, but here it must have seemed just a mighty, wild river. Here the loneliness was thick enough to provoke the prosaic Stewart into quoting poetry for the only time in two summers of verbose journal writing:

> Mile after mile was travelled without any sign being discovered that there were any other human beings in the district but ourselves. More than once the words of the Ancient Marriner [*sic*] occurred to us:
>
> We were the first
> That ever burst
> Into that silent sea. (62)

Leaving the Albany to enter the Kenogami was the beginning, Stewart says, of "one of the *worst* stages of our journey. We were then travelling up stream, as the Kenogami runs south to the Albany" (71). "The water of the river is a dark, dirty brown, and has a very unpleasant smell" (72). The crew's carelessness nearly caused a forest fire. The mosquitos and black flies were "beyond words to describe" (73), which is saying something, because Stewart usually tries. Insects and Native dancing were the chief objects of his thin vein of irony. Then the HBC post was not where the map put it. And Stewart describes the Kenogami Post, once located, as

> the most desolate one could well imagine. It is as much out of the world as if situated in the heart of Labrador. The clerk in charge Mr. G. B. Cooper is quite a young man, apparently not much over 20 years of age, but looked as if all his energy had been taken from him. He came to this place from Aberdeen by HB steamer by way of Hudson's Bay about three years ago and this wild uncivilized district is the only part of Canada he has seen or will probably see for years to come. The house in which he lives is little better than a dog kennel, and in this he will have to live alone or nearly so until the Indians return at the opening of navigation. Cooper has only a few books, but expects to get some from Albany in the spring. We left him a few that we had on hand which we hoped would enliven some hours for him. Cooper's last mail was received by him five months ago, and the news that he then rec'd is the last that he has received from the outside world. This visit of ours is one event to be spoken of both by the Indians, and by Mr. Cooper for a long time to come. (74–75)

Since, as usual, the twain of Indian and white do not meet in his sentence, one wonders whom Stewart imagines Cooper is to speak of the visit *to.*

Which stories can we pinpoint as having origins in the treaty trips? In "Travelling with a Poet," Pelham Edgar quotes one of his "home letters," saying that on June 1, 1906, Scott "read two splendid stories to me that he has written lately" (60). Since the 1906 journey had just begun, "lately" must mean in the recent past. That is all Edgar has to say about fiction, perhaps because much of what Scott wrote during the 1906 trip was poetry. Probably the two stories he refers to are "Vengeance Is Mine" and "Expiation," both published in 1907. "Vengeance" is set in Winisk, much farther north on James Bay than Scott ever got, but the landscape is probably the one he saw and shuddered at in the Fort Albany area. And it may be that something of young Cooper shows up in the young, broken Evan McColl:

> If he had not long ago wrung his heart dry so that there were in it no more tears he would have wept aloud. But where his heart was there was a feeling of ache and terror; and where his soul should have animated him there was deadness. He had been only two years in that land, but it was enough. To one sensitive and subject to the longing for things home-like, and with comfort at the core of them, two years of that land were equal to ten of strange cities. He had signed for five years, and three of them lay before him. (*Elspie* 48)

Solitude might be more pleasant than the company of Black Ian Forbes, if that were all Winisk Post had to offer. Forbes "expected nothing of God or man. The country and the trade, loneliness and disappointment, had seared his heart, and having met with kindness nowhere for years and years, he paid his debt by hardness, studied and determined" (50). McColl and Forbes are opposites in terms of the effect the environment has had on them: the one is invaded and made softer, the other sharpened like flint. Forbes does have a milder side that he plans to show to Evan in his own good time. It takes the form of an unacknowledged homoerotic attraction, and makes a love triangle of Evan's love for the Cree girl Julie.

Ian Forbes in "Vengeance Is Mine" is quite like the violent Forbes Macrimmon in "Expiation," set at Missanabie Post. In his northern stories Scott sometimes repeats or varies slightly the names of his characters (Père Dugas appears in "Tête Jaune" and "Spirit River," for example; a minor character named Ogemagebow turns up in "Spirit River," "The Vain Shadow," and "Labrie's Wife." But, besides the publication date, what locates the source of "Expiation" in 1905 is not the two Forbses, but the fact that the other main character, Daniel Wascowin, shares his name with the cook for the 1905 trip,[3] whom Scott photographed at Missanabie (see figure 7).

The photograph is one of Scott's most interesting portraits. Daniel Wascowin sits on a rock, sideways to the camera, with his head turned slightly toward the lens, his eyes slightly downcast, as if not posing but merely looking at something or perhaps thinking. I have the feeling that

Figure 7, PA-59521

Scott appropriated Daniel Wascowin's meditative attitude for the story's framing description of the guilt-ridden Macrimmon, the figure who "sat there [on a rock] with an inscrutable air, unconsciously expressing itself with such intensity that none dared profane the sacredness of such silence" (102). Whether the actual Mr. Wascowin was a model for the transcendently loyal character of the same name is impossible to know.

Three other stories, not directly traceable to 1905 and 1906, along with "Expiation" and "Vengeance Is Mine," make up a group of fur trading stories — or rather tales of fur traders, since all of them are psychological studies of white men coping with varying degrees of success in the North. These are "The Vain Shadow" (published in 1900 and perhaps written out of Scott's 1899 northern trip), "Labrie's Wife," and "In the Year 1806," all of which appeared in *The Witching of Elspie.* The first two of these are a pair, being excerpts "from the manuscript journal of Archibald Muir, clerk of the Honourable the Hudson's Bay Company, at Nepigon House in the year of our lord 1815."

"Vengeance Is Mine" and "Expiation" originated in 1905. Two others, "Spirit River" and "Tête Jaune," were probably written out of experience gathered in 1906. Both are set in what appears to be the same area. The action of "Tête Jaune" takes place at Heron Bay, where the Pic River flows down toward Lake Superior over the stairs of rapids that inspired "The Height of Land." The village of Spirit River appears to be Heron Bay fictionalized as a "cluster of houses" (63) in a time "before the railroad was built" (64). At least the description of the story's setting almost paraphrases that of the watershed in the poem:

> The north point of the plain [where Spirit River sits] disappears upon the silver thread of a stream that has led many explorers and Indian hunters from the plateau to the long tangle of lakes and rivers rising level upon level to the height of land, and beyond that sinking again, binding with a net of silver the savage and lonely slope of the Hudson Bay watershed. (*Witching* 63)

Both stories may have been written much later than 1906, though "Spirit River" was finished soon enough to make it into *The Witching of Elspie* (1923). "Tête Jaune" certainly was a late harkening back to the experience of the treaty-making days. Scott wrote to G. H. Clark, editor of *Queen's Quarterly,* in June 1939 about it, saying, "It is probably the last I shall write." (Actually "The Circle of Affection," published in 1945, was the very last.) And Scott wrote to John Masefield that

> "Tête Jaune" came from the attempt of a halfbreed guide I had with me once who thought he had a claim to halfbreed scrip and attempted ever so often to give me the names of his fourteen children; but he always stuck when he came

to his favorite, the fair-haired Archie; and he always used that phrase from which my story started, "he was caught in my trap." (TF 10 August 1947).[4]

SCOTT PROBABLY DIDN'T ABANDON *Untitled Novel* merely because he lacked the time to work on it. His output slowed as his career advanced, but he did keep writing into the last year of his life. He was likely aware that the novel suffered from technical defects he could find no way to solve. The novel doesn't have much in common with the other work being done as a result of the 1905 and 1906 treaty trips. Begun probably two years earlier, and set mainly in Ottawa, its basic nature was probably too fixed to be affected by them. Those treaty-making years were important to Scott, but they weren't everything.

The novel does have one important northern setting, on the shores of Lake Achigan which E. K. Brown says is so important to Scott's imaginative life. That is where Robin Garrabrant goes to sort out his problems. The actual sorting out anticipates something of the meditation in "The Height of Land" and will be introduced in the chapter on that poem. Suffice it to say for now that Robin "was restored by the great healer and was cast forth again upon the ocean of deeds" (299). The passage as a whole would be improved if there were less closure in Robin's northern experience — what he takes from it might issue in action rather than statement — but his mental processes are more complex and more interesting than the conclusion suggests. The healer is no divine power; it is the landscape itself, with "the rest, the quiet, the balm of silence" (298) that it offers. Robin is totally alone on Achigan, but he is there voluntarily and temporarily. The same North that weakens or infects white minds in some Scott stories heals or clarifies them in others.

Apostasy from the Methodist Church did not turn Scott into a confidence man, as it did Firmian Underwood (who would occupy Scott's position in the novel if it were autobiographical), but it seems to have been permanent and conclusive. Of course, there was the Faith with a capital *F* of which he wrote to E. K. Brown, perhaps veiled in his last-written story — the last word (because placed at the end of *The Circle of Affection*) of his writing career. Perhaps the source of his Faith is "the unperverted earth-spirit lying at the core of all life" (*Circle* 232). Perhaps that is what he meant when he said he turned from the Methodist Church to the wilderness for sustenance. Perhaps the earth-spirit is the healer of Robin Garrabrant at Lake Achigan; perhaps this is another name for the region-spirit in "The Height of Land," murmuring "inappellable" secrets that soothe the soul without offering it finality.

COULD IT BE THAT "Labrie's Wife" is Scott's best story, his only completely satisfying story, because in it he found a natural way to contain plot and character in the journal form that was so much in use by white people living in or passing through the North? The 1905 Post Journals for Osnaburgh are a fascinating narrative. The account of Peter Peetwaykeesicouse's murder (mentioned in chapter 3) is especially potent, but there is power in a series of melancholy laconic entries about loneliness and the frustrations of trying to resist with too few resources the activities of the "opposition," Revillon Frères. Trading competition is the basis of some of the conflict in "Labrie's Wife" and "Expiation."

The journal kept by James S. Dobie, the surveyor whose job it was in 1912 to apply the laws of geometry to the reserves bounded by Scott's verbal descriptions, is just as strong. Dobie's journal casually presents astonishing acts of physical endurance and expertise: surveying through swamps where even the Indians go with reluctance in the summer, walking for 20 days in December from Moose Factory to Cochrane, he and the other members of his party each pulling a toboggan loaded with supplies; walking on snowshoes that he made from "half finished" materials rather than wait for a new supply to come into the HBC store.

Glancing at the stories of these individuals may seem to be a digression, but I think not. Not if there is anything to the theory that certain literary forms are most appropriate to the rendering of experience in certain places. If there is, I think it will be so not because there is a platonic match between form and landscape (which seems to be the idea in Northrop Frye's speculation in "The Narrative Tradition in English-Canadian Poetry" that "some of the poetic forms employed in the earlier centuries of English literature would have been more appropriate for the expression of Canadian themes and moods than the nineteenth-century romantic lyric or its twentieth-century metaphysical successor" (*Bush Garden* [148–9]). I suspect, rather, that forms, like people (like *language*, Wittgenstein says) become naturalized with use. If there is something to that, it would explain why the journal form, why documentary forms in general, have been so much and so effectively employed by the writers of this country.[5] At any rate, I move into a discussion of "Labrie's Wife" by quoting some passages from the Daily Occurrences Journal 20th March 1904 to 18th November 1906 that was kept by Jabez Williams at Osnaburgh Post.

> Jan 17 — H. Lawson and John Carpenter passed on their way north again this morning. This is getting rank. I asked for a dog train last summer but could not get any. Now I have no means of following these beggars up.
>
> April 27 — Mr. Edwards [of Revillon Frères] came over for a visit. Put in a pleasant evening for this part of the world.
>
> July 11 — Therm min +60 Wind WSW Cloudy. Wm Mishenenir child died this morning. Poor little creature. It was not fully formed being a very exaggerated form of hare-lip. Was unable to nurse. Canoe from Fort Hope

passed just at noon after calling in for a few minutes to pick up their provisions. Report water very low in river having taken 7 days going down but apparently only 4 upstream. Commission Treaty # 9 arrived about 4:15 p.m.

Who are H. Lawson and John Carpenter that Jabez Williams of Osnaburgh Post wants to follow them up? They could be Ojibway who owe the Hudson's Bay Company money; they could be employees of the "Opposition" Revillon Frères trading company. Mr. Williams takes a more sociable attitude to his competition than Archibald Muir does to his (Labrie of the North West Company) in "Labrie's Wife": "We drank healths courteously, that were ready to cut one another's throats" (*Elspie* 147). Jabez Williams records the deaths of a total of five children in his journal for the year 1905, usually without any more comment than Archibald Muir, writing on May 24, 1815: "Ogemah-ga-bow came up to say that one of Needic's boys had died last night, having over-eaten himself after his fast on the Dry Beaver Islands. Rain today" (146). A death; the weather: no distinction in a land where infant mortality is no novelty.

Jabez Williams is a historical character; Archibald Muir is fictional. Correspondences between the content and the style of their journal entries highlight Scott's verisimilitude in "Labrie's Wife." He catches the flavour of the journal as a genre along with the voice of his writer, which is slightly more archaic than that of Williams, as befits the 100-year gap between them.

The matter of voice provides one index of the distance between the two excerpts from Archibald Muir's journal, the first being "The Vain Shadow" (January 9 to February 14, 1815), the second being "Labrie's Wife" (May 22 to June 15, 1815). The first is much more Scottish in feel, because Donald Murchison, Muir's superior at Nepigon Post, speaks with a broad accent ("puir feckless fule," "'Haud,' says he, 'dinna touch it'") and a good deal of Scots diction (of James Boswell: "'a doited body! a clavering idiot!'"; of Hugh Farquarson: "this disjasket, speldering nobody"). Muir himself uses far more Scottish diction ("speering," "dreeful") in "The Vain Shadow" than he does in "Labrie's Wife," though both stories take place in the same year. It is as if Muir had been catching the Scots inflections from his colleague and sloughed them off when the influence was removed. The shift out of dialect from the one story to the other has the effect of shifting Muir nearer the land of his choice, his career. Of course, the difference may also be attributable to Scott's increased confidence with short fiction (he had written the odd so-so dialect story before "The Vain Shadow," which probably owes as much to the genre as it does to the North), but, anyway, Muir's naturalization in the North is also established in "Labrie's Wife" by some of his comparisons: Alec "can no more control his countenance than an otter can help fishing" (142); the "pirates of Frenchmen" "would eat [our trade] like a bear eats honey-comb" (145).

"The Vain Shadow" would be a more effective prequel to "Labrie's Wife" if the plot were not so melodramatically driven toward the epiphany produced by the climactic baring of the dead Donald Murchison's chest. "Over his heart" Muir discovers "the initials M.F. with H.F. above and below a true-lover's knot" (46). So! Donald Murchison is nae Donald Murchison at all, but Hugh Farquarson, who fled Scotland after murdering his rival Purvis! The authorities would have hanged the wrong man had Mary Fraser been unable to talk them out of it. And (violins, please) it is on St. Valentine's Day that Donald's true identity is revealed. The northern setting of "The Vain Shadow" and even the journal form seem incidental to the Scottish tale of rivalry in love that enters the outer story, in the pages of the *Glasgow Herald,* as a serial tale within the tale. Donald Murchison, Muir's superior at the post, decrees that the winter must be passed with a twice-weekly reading, even though the news is from 1814 and the post possesses the whole year's papers. Declaration of serial reading might well be a sensible means of dealing with northern winter isolation and boredom, but it takes an obsessive mind (or an author locked in artifice) to delay discovering the outcome of a story involving himself, one he thought he had successfully fled 25 years before. The failure of Donald's health is hastened by the tension he imposes on himself.

"The Vain Shadow" is not so successful as "Labrie's Wife," then, but the two comprise a unit. The first completes the Murchison/Farquarson story but leaves open that of Archibald Muir, whose last entry in the first story begins: "It is late at night now. I got wrought upon by waiting and thinking what I should do now I have charge of the Post" (45). Much of the drama of "Labrie's Wife" involves the first test of his new authority.

Figure 8, PA-59518

"LABRIE'S WIFE" IS a remarkable character study of Archibald Muir, ironically so, given how little he thinks he is giving away. His journal is all about the trade, his opposition (Labrie and his "wife" — who turns out to be Labrie's niece), his "boy" Alec (that is to say, his subordinate at the post) and, incidentally, the Indians employed in the trade. But it is one of the story's many intersecting ironies that this dour, reticent man, so seldom perceptive about others, is actually at the centre of his own story, self-revealed by what he writes. Muir is interesting because he shows himself to be a cluster, or (in his case) a knot, of human characteristics. The range is narrow, but the cluster is thick. This is psychological verisimilitude.

Partly, as Elizabeth Waterston observes about five of Scott's northern stories, Muir's characterization draws from the Scottishness of his characters:

> All are fatally bound by pride in ancestry, by propensity to drunkenness, and by devotion to manners and rituals. All are Scots also in theological bias, dour Calvinists, duty-ridden, set on by clash of values. The author sets these Scots into situations in which the most dangerous aspects of the national character would be brought out. Perhaps we might say he brought out, through these Scottish protagonists, the most subtle and self-torturing situations in which a northern form of Puritanism might embroil itself. ("Missing Face" 225)

He sets them, that is to say (though Waterston doesn't put it this way), into a North at least as primal as the Scottish North that originally formed that "national character." "It is almost a fearsome thing, when you consider it," writes Archibald Muir on January 10, "to be here so many miles away from home in a land burdened with snow and deep cold, just the three of us, Donald, myself and the boy" (26). Not all of Scott's characters so wrought on by winter in the North are Scots, of course, but the Welshman Pendarvies who loses his mind in "In the Year 1806" is Celt enough to be counted among them. These isolated men are variations on a type, and Archibald Muir is the most interesting of them all.

With his somewhat twisted sense of humour, Muir delights in tormenting Alec by exaggerating his own Scots imperviousness to things around him. "Not to appear interested before the lad," he writes, having been deeply attracted by the unusual sound of female laughter, "I went back to my work" (149). This is as typical of Muir as openness is of Alec (if Muir's narrative view of Alec can be trusted), whose personality is not so bent by the national character. Muir is an accomplished tease, in fact, but only the reader can see this, because the teasing is done deadpan. As far as Alec knows, Muir is some kind of emotional rock. The reader finds out that Muir privately entertains gentler feelings for Alec (as did Ian Forbes for Evan McColl in "Vengeance

Is Mine"): ". . . I reflected that of late I had treated him much as poor Donald used unthinkingly to treat me, and that he must be occupying my old position of complaint, and my heart was softened a bit, and I resolved to be more kind to him in future, who is in much a good boy and canny in a sort about many things" (150).

Muir's reticence is natural to him, of course; it extends to his journal writing where it sometimes conflicts with his truthfulness. On two occasions he sets down an occurrence, though "it be against myself" (153, 157). The first of these is one of the funniest scenes Scott ever wrote, as the stiff Muir is prevailed upon by Madaline and Alec to unbend a little with his pipes. (The second comes the morning after the uncharacteristic overindulgence that prevents him from remembering if he betrayed the route by which his fur packs were coming to the post.)

The bagpipe scene is a link between "Labrie's Wife" and "The Vain Shadow," in which Muir runs through part of his repertoire on the pipes to soothe Donald Murchison's torments. In "Labrie's Wife" the performance is abortive:

> Well, scarcely had I begun to get the skin filled with wind when Labrie's wife began to laugh. Now I am willing to admit that the foreword to a performance on the pipes may be dispiriting, but I charge that what follows after when the instrument is well controlled, and when the melody pours forth in full cry, would serve to obliterate a greatly more dispiriting prelude. But in this case I did not get beyond that stage, for Labrie's wife laughed with so little judgement that I was put about. I saw something in Alec's face which led me to think that the whole matter was preconceived by him, and with that I laid down my pipes on the bench beside me. Not another note would I play (154).

The teaser is being teased, but in a mode he does not understand. Since he feels that not only his own talent but "the national instrument" (153) is being insulted, his sense of humour is not triggered. The laugh on him is louder if one notices that Muir refers to Madaline either as "the young wench" or "the huzzy" before she asks him to play, and as "the bitch" and "yon slut" afterward (though it's "huzzy" again later in the story). The change in terminology slides from the distasteful into the offensive. It's not accidental that his only moment of delicacy toward her, either in his narrative or his speech, comes when he thinks she is impressed with him. "Now I am always at pains to oblige a lady, if it be possible" (153), he writes then; the reader knows better.

Where did Muir find out how to refer to a woman? Not from experience. He is as green with the opposite sex as about running a trading post. He admits his ignorance to Alec, who could scarcely be more different from

Muir with respect to this matter of understanding women. Compared to Muir, he does seem to be a "young oracle" (155) about Madaline. At least he sees very quickly what Muir cannot: that Madaline is attracted to Muir and that his very lack of response whets her interest. Having fallen in love with Madaline, Alec is condemned to watch her falling in love with Muir, and his frustration is increased by the fact that nothing he says to Muir can convince him of Madaline's affections. The whole matter is complicated by the belief of both that Madaline is Labrie's wife. "I would not make love to a married woman," Alec says "hotly" (153) during one of his attempts to warn Muir that this married woman has designs on him. The second last thing Madaline says to Muir before leaving reinforces Alec's claim that he understands women: "Your boy Alec is twice the man that you are" (160).

Perhaps Alec cannot be blamed for failing to understand that this particular "married woman" to whom he is himself so impossibly attracted is innocent. He takes her part against Muir as much as he can, but there is the compromising "fact" that *she* apparently takes her marriage vows too lightly. Ironically he is missing one crucial piece of information. Madaline, in fact, supplies it in a flirting note left at Muir's window one night when he knew she was there but, typically, ignored her. So Alec discovers it after she is gone:

> "Why do you call me Labrie's wife? She is my aunt. Do you think I would marry an ugly fellow like Labrie? They brought me up here to help their plans. We shall see. If you want to know my name it's Madaline Lesage. I learned to write from the Sister St. Theresa at Wikwemikong. Is it not pretty? M.L." (162–163)

Alec's fears that Madaline, unprincipled about her "marriage," must also be a spy (152), have some foundation. Labrie intends to use her so; she has other ideas, whether or not she had them at first. Her loyalty follows her love. Muir himself gave her the means of proving it, having spent the evening of whisky excess talking business, probably gloating over the superiority of the new route, from Osnaburgh via the Mud Lakes rather than via Lake Wabinosh. He is proud of this discovery, a contribution to the trading business at Nepigon House that he is counting on to attract the notice of his superiors. However, only Madaline's loyalty keeps him from losing all those furs to Labrie, whom she directs up the Wabinosh route. Her loyalty is so firm that even after Muir fails to acknowledge what she has done for him, risking her life in the process, she tells Alec that Muir said nothing to her about the fur packs.

One of the many ironies of the story is that in one sense Muir unthinkingly interprets Madaline more accurately than Alec does. He hears her innocence in her contagious laugh (149, 153). Innocence in this context is not the opposite of guilt, but it gathers that meaning to it as the story proceeds.

Alec is betrayed by the incompleteness of his information into generalizations about women that Madaline's actions disprove. "You never seem to understand," he says to Muir, "that a woman's not like a man. The best of them you have to watch, and more particularly when one of them is in love with you" (152–153). "Don't you know enough of women to let them laugh and let them talk?" (155) he asks a day later. But Alec, wrong about Madaline, is also undercut as an authority on women. Such complexities breed multiple ironies recognizable only by the reader.

"Labrie's Wife" has a structural frame of sorts, which is focused by that image of woman as ambiguous causer of trouble/happiness, an image that comes to seem central in more than one sense. The section of the story in which Madaline first appears is opened with the sound of laughter, and that is parallel to the closing sound of sorrow in Alec's sobs. "Now laughter is an uncommon thing in this country, visiting us very infrequently" (149), Muir says, to introduce his first hearing of Madaline's voice. "It was high-pitched and very clear and had something merry and withal innocent about it. It was contagious also and the mere sound of it made my very muscles twitch" (149). Trying to go on with his writing at the end of the story, Muir "was detained by a sound which is as uncommon as that of laughter in these outlandish parts. The sound of sobbing" (163). These opposites are marks of the extremes of a full life, whether caused by love or by something else, a life of rich emotional turbulence of the sort that Muir seems unlikely ever to live. Structural tightness and complexity is difficult to achieve naturally in the journal form, where it would be out of place. But Scott does manage it, partly by indenting the first installment of the frame so that it doesn't stick out too much. Otherwise the story is structured episodically by entries in Muir's journal. Transitional material, as in actual journals, is omitted. The story is a series of small retrospectives, usually of the day just past, but occasionally of a slightly longer period, 19 entries, covering 25 days, between May 22, 1815, and June 15 of the same year.

Unlike the rest of Scott's stories, "Labrie's Wife" is not completely resolved by the ending, an ironically partial two-stage epiphany. The second stage depends on the first, and the first occurs through a trick of Muir's memory. That is to say, first he is conducted by association from the sound of Alec's sobbing into a recollection of his "sister's voice as she sobbed for her lover when they brought him back dead and dripping out of the sea. I had a vision of it as if it were snapped upon my eye in a flash of lightning, she leaning her forehead upon her wrists against the wall" (163). Connecting Alec's loss with his sister's loss of love to death, his genuine feeling for Alec blooms into compassion and self-reproach: "I understood in a flash. I pray God to forgive me for the sin of blindness, and for always being so dead to others in my own affairs" (163–164).

The last words, about the man Muir sees walking away from him where he used to see a boy, form a conventional enough resolution. This is a double resolution, though: Alec may well have been matured by his suffering, but since a veil has suddenly been removed from Muir's eyes, could it be that Alec's new maturity is at least partly a function of Muir's own new maturity of perception? The ending is an active one, in this sense; it gives a reader new eyes to read all of Muir's patronizing of Alec, all that about his being "unable to control his countenance," about his "beard no longer than a pinfeather" (145) — the whole initiation subplot. Part of what Muir pooh-poohed was Alec's assumption of greater maturity on the subject of women. There retrospectively seems to be support for Madaline's suggestion that the apparent man (Muir) is, and always was in one sense, the boy. Alec's maturity has not been that he understands women, or even one woman, but that he knows how to listen to his heart.

In another sense the ending of the story is not only unconventional but piercingly poignant, and in various ways. For one thing, the recollection of the sister is echoed earlier in the story by one other reminiscence of the past. This appears in the June 8 entry of the morning after, which ends with Muir "in mind very much put about" by Alec's certainty that Muir had betrayed the whereabouts of the furs. "Ah, those women!" he muses, "I well remember my father used to say, 'At the bottom of every trouble, there you will find a woman,' and my mother used to retort, 'And likewise at the bottom of every happiness.' Whereupon he would kiss her" (158–159).

There is material in this recollected image for a flash of insight of another sort, a mental picture of Muir and Madaline together, but the timing is wrong for it and so is the point of view — looking out. After all, it is not only the sound of sobbing, but the physical image of Alec "leaning at the doorpost" (163) that places him parallel to Muir's sister. It looks as though a strong appeal to at least two senses at once is what it takes to stretch this self-involved mind out of its confines. On June 8, worried about business failure precipitated by the "slut," Muir is not likely to form an image of Madaline and himself to parallel that of his mother and father. The story's ending is active in another sense, then. I have said that it leaves Muir knowing one thing more than he knew before, able to interpret one strand of the story he was in, that of Alec's thwarted love. The strand of Alec's loss would have tucked in the way it does whatever else happened, because Madaline could not see Alec for Muir, but Muir's blindness prevents the tying up of another loose end: he and Madaline are clearly "made for each other," and nothing comes of that. The very flash of insight into Alec's pain may even confirm Muir's blindness to potential happiness for himself.

IN "NATIVE PEOPLES IN SCOTT'S FICTION," John Flood chastises Scott for relegating Native people to the background of many of his northern stories, and he accuses Scott of stereotyping the Natives in others. I can't bring myself to grind this axe. Does it matter what race Madaline Lesage belongs to? Perhaps she is Métis, perhaps Ojibway. She went to school, probably residential school, at Wikwemikong on Manitoulin Island. Her father is not in evidence, and Muir's patronizing description of her mother, one of "two other women in Labrie's party, rather old and haggish" (151), might be that of a Native woman. Perhaps Native people are not so peripheral as Flood thinks in "Labrie's Wife." He is surely wrong, ignoring Muir's narrowmindedness in other areas, to blame Scott for Muir's ignorance of the Natives. When Muir has a devil of a time reading the white people around him, he shouldn't be expected to be more enlightened about Indians.

In fact, the irony of Muir's misunderstanding, extending into the Native background, creates an eloquent commentary on the relationship between dominant and subordinate cultures. As far as Muir is concerned, there are no questions to ask about this relationship. "[T]hese fools of Indians," Muir fumes, "will never learn not to devour half their rations in the first day out from the Post. They came in looking like wasps, their belts girt so tightly about their middles" (143). But Muir hasn't learned, and never will have to learn (because his is the dominant culture), what living for the moment is like, what habits are bred by the necessity of living off a harsh land. He is conventionally unthinking about the significance of his phrase "our Indians" (meaning those who work for us, those we own). The unintelligibility of the Indians to him is clear in his failure to read even their laughter: "To be sure the Indians laugh, but that to me always has an unmeaning sound, and sometimes a bestial" (149). When the fur packs arrive safely, he throws his employees a party: "Godfrey and the men all well. I mixed a keg of spirits for them and they made a hideous night of it" (161). "Half the Indians are drunk yet" (162), he writes the next day. One remembers Scott himself, in "The Last of the Indian Treaties," on HBC exploitation of the Indians. Muir is a smart man and a shrewd man; if there were a sequel to "Labrie's Wife," it would probably reveal that his insensitivity to the humanity of Natives had taken him far in the fur trade.

I have stressed the difficulties in discovering Scott's own attitudes in anything that he writes, even his personal letters. Scott's stories, with their narrator-personae, are very tricky objects of such a quest. I can see no justification at all for assuming a simple equivalence between Scott and Archibald Muir, the obvious butt of much of the irony of "Labrie's Wife." In fact, "Labrie's Wife" subtly exposes a Eurocentric mentality unlikely ever to appreciate the otherness of his Native customers and employees, unlikely ever to get so much as a whiff of what he might be missing. "Labrie's Wife," with its art of involvement, is a much more telling critique of Eurocentricism than "Charcoal," which sits rather heavily *on* its subject and even leadenly underlines its own theme, "civilization against savagery." The implied author of "Labrie's Wife" seems both enlightened and intelligent, artist enough to leave spaces of irony in his text that a reader negotiates by way of "completing" the story. In my completion the relationship between Muir and "his" Indians figures a terrible cultural imbalance, a huge absence on one side of it. This absence, this space *will* be filled, and a key to how it happens (derived from the thought of Wilson Harris) appears in Ashcroft, Griffiths, and Tiffin's *The Empire Writes Back.* For Harris, "persistent intuitive elements," whether "intended" or not,

> exist in all cross-cultural creative works as significant internalizations of the post-colonial impulse which constantly "seeks to consume its own biases." The surface "historical reality" is of a destructive and continuing imperialism, but its exploration inevitably exposes an underlying imaginative imperative towards cross-culturality, Creolization, hybridization, and catalysis. Imperialism, the prevailing political reality of these works, is thus perpetually undermined by a persisting regenerative seed, masked perhaps as intuition or dream. (152–153)

Or by a structure of ironies? The regenerative potential of "Labrie's Wife" lies dormant until a reader follows the story's ironies as far as they go — into the "subsidiary" Native content. Then the reader can see how to right that cultural imbalance according to a formula that the authors of *The Empire Writes Back* quote from Tsvetan Todorov's *The Conquest of America:* "difference in nature but equivalence in value" (102).

NOTES

1. Perhaps to mask its nearness to sources in actuality, Scott called Charcoal Star Blanket in his magazine publication of the story. The restoration of Charcoal's historical name, his story now safely in the past, removes the superficial appropriation of another actual name. Star Blanket was a Cree chief who at first refused to sit for a portrait by Scott's friend Edmund Morris unless he used his influence to secure permission for a dance. "I promised to speak to Graham & Scott," Morris writes in his 1910 diary. He could actually speak to both of them, since Graham was an Indian Affairs inspector in the West whom Scott was visiting on an inspection tour in the summer of 1910 (140), but he knew enough to hold out little hope. See Leon Slonim's "The Source of Duncan Campbell Scott's 'Charcoal'" for an examination of the story in the context of the trial transcripts.
2. Stewart uses this story rather perversely in 1908, on his return from settling the Abitibi Indian question: "We arrived at 'Granny's Rock' at 10 AM and here I tried to impress upon Bazille [his guide] the fact that his friend Frank Lemaire was one of the descendants of the hated Iroquois who had worked [?] such evil to the Crees and Ojibways at the time when poor old Granny had been thrust over the cliff. Bazille was not at all excited at this however and only lit his pipe, as if to say that these old tales troubled him not a jot" (188-189). One can imagine other interpretations of Bazille's silence. In Lola Tostevin's novel *Frog Moon,* the legend of Iroquois Falls is that a party of invading Iroquois was led over the falls by a single Ojibway. Maybe Bazille knew that version.

3. At least Stewart (journal 76) says he was cook. Perhaps he was an assistant, because a man named Harry Black is depicted cooking in the 1905 photograph preceding that of Daniel Wascowin in the series.
4. "Tête Jaune" was published in the same issue of *Queen's Quarterly* as "A Mountain Journey," a story by Howard O'Hagan. O'Hagan's *Tay John* is set in the Rockies, and his main character is much more mythical than Scott's, but perhaps a case might be made for Scott's having planted the seed that became O'Hagan's novel.
5. Are the journals kept on the 1905 trip in any sense shadowed by David Anderson's Albany River journal, published in 1854? Anderson, bishop of Rupert's Land, began in Red River, ended at Moose Factory, and returned by the same route. It is certainly striking to read Anderson on drifting all night in his canoe, presumably over the same stretch of the Albany that Scott and his party drifted over in 1905. The canoes of both parties ran aground at roughly the same place and even the jokes about slumbering steersman are similar. The 1905 diarists probably knew nothing of Anderson's account, so there is no direct link, no tradition of Albany journals. Perhaps the only link is the one I make myself.

7

An Ache in the Air: "Powassan's Drum"

There's the same tension in the heat tonight. It's been gathering and tighening now for weeks, and this has been the hottest, stillest day of all. It's like watching an inflated, ever-distending balloon, waiting with bated breath for it to burst. Even the thud of moth wings on the lamp — through the dense, clotted heat tonight it's like a drum.

Sinclair Ross, As For Me and My House

ON THURSDAY, JULY 6, the third day of the first treaty-making trip, Scott's party rose at 5:00 a.m. After breakfast they paddled several miles of marshy stream before entering Lac Seul. They were still in the Treaty 3 area and expected to find the Ojibway assembled at Lac Seul Hudson's Bay Post to receive the year's treaty annuity and to offer themselves for medical inspection. To make a strong impression, flags were attached to poles and erected in the front of each canoe, and the three canoes made good speed toward land, the large canoe flanked by the two smaller ones. The illustration (figure 9) gives the idea, although the photograph was taken at Long Lake in 1906 where the treaty party canoes had been joined by others. It must have been disappointing, perhaps humiliating, when this Entrance was greeted only by HBC trader J. D. MacKenzie. Evidence of the whereabouts of the Ojibway (the sound of a drum) had actually been audible for some miles of paddling up the lake. They were engaged in the final day of a three-day Dog Feast about eight miles from the post.

There are three accounts of what happened when the treaty party, anticlimactically, paddled over to the reserve to investigate. Since the episode resulted almost 20 years later in the composition of "Powassan's Drum," Scott's terse journal entry for July 6 has always been fascinating. For years it was the only context available for the poem, but now that Stewart's journal has come to light we have a much fuller account. There is also another complementary and quite detailed version from police constable Joseph Vanasse.

Figure 9, PA-59577

I have wondered about "Powassan's Drum" for 20 years. Nothing of the context of Scott's other writing (not even the dream poems) really demystifies the stance out of which it was written. The poem doesn't seem to be an expression of Scott's attitude toward nature and life, nor can it be said to embody a Native view. Perhaps it bears the sort of relationship to Ojibway religious practice and to nature in the North that Tom Thomson's *Northern River* bears to the landscape he was looking at when he painted that canvas. Until Peter Mellen pointed out the obvious, few people noticed how stylized, how Art Nouveau, that fabulous screen of trees really is (67). It is time to place "Powassan's Drum" in two contexts, those of its inspiration and those of its apparent ethnographic content. The poem bears a one-to-one relationship to neither.

GIVEN THE NIGHTMARE NATURE of "Powassan's Drum," Scott's journal has always struck me as an invitation to read between the lines. His whole sparse journal has to be approached that way, in fact, but on July 6 there is a little more than usual for the imagination to work with:

> Broke camp at 6:45 Up at 5 Bath in lake Lovely morning Reached Lac Seul Post at [blank] Very few Ind Had breakfast with the MacKenzies in charge of the Post Lunched whitefish [?] Learned that Inds were having a dance and making medicine on the Res. about 7 miles away Went down in canoe Mack. Rae & the party Long argument with

> old medicine man — cunning old devil with swollen jaw Powassan[1] the head medicine man had sent them word to make the medicine Conference with MacKenzie about this Warned Ind. not to dance They promised to do what they could to stop it But we must speak to Powassan Returned about [blank] Very hot Taken ill.

According to Basil Johnston, the Dog Feast might take two forms. "One was for warriors," he says without giving details; "the other was for the people in general."

> In the first, the purpose was to test, and by frequent testing to uphold the courage of warriors. In the second, the people were reminded of famine and survival through dance. They re-lived adversity and reenacted their endurance. At the same time, the dance pre-figured future famines and petitioned for courage and endurance. (*Heritage* 145)

It might have been the testing that the government officially found offensive, especially if it took anything like the self-mutilating form of warrior-making that offended white people about the Sun Dance, though as Scott himself elsewhere makes clear there are also political and economic motives for proscribing Native rituals. One of these motives may be felt in the encounter on Lac Seul between Scott and the shaman named Nistonaqueb (Scott doesn't name him, but Stewart does): Native ceremonies inconvenience the white masters. But it was no doubt much simpler to ban these ceremonies from the distance of Ottawa, where the "pagan" was abstract and had no voice, than face-to-face.

"Taken ill" are the two words that snap Scott's journal entry into sharp focus. I have always felt those words to be significant, though my response to them has changed over the years. Part of my mind has always been drawn to a cause-effect relationship between Scott's admonition of the Natives and his illness — which was temporary; Stewart tells us that he spent a bad night but "reported himself well enough to travel" (29) the following morning. "Weak but much better," says Scott. At first I felt that the illness might be owing to a sense of guilt, but that was making much of very little evidence, and not something I would even have put into print 20 years ago. More recently, aware of the power of the shaman, I have wondered if Scott had been subject to a curse. He was the spokesperson, according to Stewart; he was the reprimanding voice of the "great Father the King" (Vanasse 62). If any one of the party were to be cursed, Scott would be that one.

The imagination is active in any such cause-effect formulation, of course. It may be a coincidence that Scott takes ill after his direct experience as spokesperson for one culture with the alien voice of another. Perhaps it still says more about me than it says about the event if I mention Northrop Frye's opinion that "In ordinary life a coincidence is a piece of design for which we can find no practical use" (*Secular Scripture* 47). But that journal entry, read in the context of "Powassan's Drum," gives off more energy than it should if there were no particular significance to it. Whether or not anything ever comes of the theory that cold fusion experiments produce a mysterious surplus of energy, the concept is not strange to readers who often feel something more than meets the eye of reason generated by the association of words.

Like Scott in "The Last of the Indian Treaties" and in his journal, Joseph Vanasse uses that word "cunning" for Nistonaqueb. "The old conjuror was very cunning and non-committal, and answered but equivocally at first" (60), he says, but he goes on to offer a fairly sympathetic paraphrase of quite a lot that was said. He repeats the shaman's declaration "that he was only obeying a superior conjuror, living about fifty miles distant, and whom he feared to disobey, as this superior conjuror was very wise and mighty" (63). But he also explains in detail the healing function of the White Dog Feast, showing a considerable knowledge not only of that particular ceremony, but also of Ojibway cosmology and religious practice. Over half of his article details the Dog Feast in its context. Perhaps he gathered such information as he travelled in the North, but he learned a portion of it directly from the offending shaman himself. Here is the information that Vanasse attributes directly (although he paraphrases) to Nistonaqueb:

> The old conjuror, who at first asked for a few minutes time in which to frame his reply, explained that his ancestors used good and bad roots, and herbs, but he made use of the good ones only. His ancestors were very superstitious, and their descendents, the present generation, had inherited many of these superstitions. They still believed, for instance, that the spirits have a great influence over their fate. This is the reason why, in dispensing his medicines, he sacrifices a dog to the evil spirits, to pacify them, so that they will not prevent his medicines from producing a good effect on the patients. (63)

Was "superstitious" what the shaman, presumably speaking through a translator, actually said? Vanasse does seem to be very interested in all he describes, much of it without being judgemental, but he does say that the conjuror "subsists by mystery" — by keeping all that he does a mystery to the band that depends on him. *Superstition* is a word used to describe an alien religious system either by one who subscribes to another or by a rationalist who subscribes to none. Perhaps it was Vanasse's word. Perhaps the word was co-opted by a shaman, or his translator, trying to explain a difficult concept to naive and ignorant white men.

Rudy Wiebe has Edgar Dewdney say this about Big Bear's Cree theology: "His own system once conceded, within it he cannot be touched" (114). To say that such a colloquy as the fictional one between Dewdney and Big Bear parallels the encounter between Scott and Nistonaqueb on Lac Seul is probably to step once again into the realm of the imagination. But not totally without factual basis, given what Samuel Stewart reports about the meeting. Where Scott and Vanasse speak of "cunning," Stewart uses the words "diplomatic" and "wisdom." He is the only one of the three to record the shaman's name. Here is Stewart's version of what happened when the man was finally located, having made himself scarce while the commissioners strode through the "twenty tents and wigwams . . . pitched on top of the hill" (Vanasse 62), with Constable Vanasse "marching in their footsteps," carrying the Union Jack out of one of the canoes:[2]

> He was a short, stout-built Indian, and it was soon evident that he had all the Indians well under his control. He was very diplomatic in his answers to the questions asked him, and would not commit himself by a promise to discontinue the practice of conjuring. We learned that his name was Nistonaqueb and that he was considered to have great skill in driving out the evil spirits from those afflicted with any kind of disease. We heard that Nistonaqueb made a good living by his conjuring but he professed to be giving his services free and out of compassion for those who were suffering from various ailments.[3] The goods and money received by him were used to appease the evil spirits that were tormenting those for whom his services were called into requisition. He also said that he was acting under instructions from Pow-was-sang the head conjuror of the district who would visit him with divers pains and penalties if he neglected to hold these Dog Feasts. Nistonaqueb showed great diplomacy in the manner in which he conducted his case. We could not but be surprised at the wisdom shown by him in the replies given to certain questions, and the manner in which he avoided answering others. (25–27)

Since Stewart is regularly so free in his use of "we" the pronoun may or may not include all members of the treaty party, but there is no reason to believe that Scott wasn't impressed merely because he uses the pejorative word "cunning" to describe a man who was neither a fool nor a child. It may even be that Stewart understates the wisdom of Nistonaqueb, given that he goes on immediately, with no sense of incongruity, to say "we [meaning Scott] gave the Indians a lecture on the folly of their conduct and told them that their actions for the future would be carefully watched" (27). "So much for my explanations," Nistonaqueb might well have concluded. "These people don't listen."

Figure 10, PA-59501

"OCCASIONALLY THE SOUND of a conjuror's drum far away pervaded the day like an aerial pulse," Scott says in "The Last of the Indian Treaties." There is that heartbeat word, so important in "Powassan's Drum." Otherwise, the arguably traumatic experience of confronting Nistonaqueb has already been generalized. *Were* other distant drums heard on the 1905 journey? If so, none are reported by either Scott or Stewart. And such drumming as went on in 1906 seems to have been heard up close, to judge by Pelham Edgar's unimpressed and ironic account of a drum dance at Long Lake:

> A kettle-drum was improvised — a strip of moose-hide stretched over a tin pail of water — and one of the older men began to this rude accompaniment an incantation which might have been an invocation to the ancient deity of this tribe, or an adjuration to the evil spirits, had he remembered the words of the formula. As it was, he contented himself with the incessant repetition of two or three words, of which I could distinguish "Manitou, Manitou, Manitou," and a hundred youths and maidens drifted round a huge bonfire to the measure of the song. (February 16, 1907 245)

Edgar's assumption is that a real song is extended through variation; it doesn't occur to him that a repetitive song performed to a regular beat might relax the mind open to spirit, that it might be a form of prayer.

Scott may have drawn on other sources of drumming, other evidence of "paganism" than the White Dog Feast on July 6, 1905, but when he composed "Powassan's Drum" in January and February of 1925, it was clearly the drum across Lac Seul he was remembering. In April of that year, when the poem was performed by Bertram Forsyth at Scott's first public reading, The *Globe* reported it as "a hunting [*sic*] treatment of an incident in the Northland with an uncanny drum-beating by an Indian medicine man heard fifteen miles across water" (Thursday, April 23, 1925). Publicly Scott seems to have been stressing the exotic in a pulse that had entered his mind to resurface two decades later. By this time the accountant in the Indian Department had climbed all the rungs to the post of deputy superintendent general of Indian Affairs.

It would be interesting to know whether something in Scott's life in 1925 triggered the retrieval, whether anything particular fished this memory up, because the form in which it returns (or at least the shape it takes) is much different from anything Scott could have experienced in 1905. Insofar as the shaman in the poem may be traced to anyone in particular, Nistonaqueb becomes Powassan (or else the headless emanation of Powassan's dream), and Powassan is removed from all social traffic. There is no White Dog Feast, no communal ceremony of any kind, only a drumming of hatred by a shaman figure isolated in the elemental nature of which his drumming may be the voice. Yes, the poem may be traced to a particular hill on Lac Seul, and maybe Scott was trying to catch what he experienced there (rather than using that experience symbolically to embody stresses and impulses of his own), but an abstraction, a stylization of setting, character, and action, has taken place. To what extent *any* of this is consistent with Ojibway culture is a question to examine after I have offered a new reading of the poem.

MOST OF THE POEMS I will be discussing in detail have attracted critical attention enough so that what I have to add is in the way of (sometimes much-needed) nuancing. That certainly can't be said of "Powassan's Drum," which has been discussed in detail only by Fred Cogswell, and his reading is problematical. Even Gerald Lynch, quite plausible on many of the "Indian" poems, has his troubles with "Powassan's Drum." Scott's "respect for the culture," he says in a leap of logic, "is evident in the powerfully incantatory rhythm of the poem" (54). The only other thing he says also has no sure anchor within the poem that I can see: "[H]is doubt with regard to assimilation is revealed in the question: 'will it [the throbbing of the drum] last till the world's end / As the pulse of Being?'" (54). The issue of assimilation is not addressed in the poem, not even symbolically. Looking not at the question about the throbbing but at the "answer" at the end of the poem — where the throbbing of anger and hatred "lives" — might show us an obstacle to assimilation. But the assumption would have to be that Powassan is expressing hatred toward white oppressors, and no object of anger is singled out. If the moulded image of the headless Indian is seen as an icon representing The Indian — and this too is a stretch — then the combination of power and impotence perhaps takes us a little farther. Perhaps this is what Lynch has in mind without having worried through to it: a power that is impotent is at least parallel to a culture rendered obsolete.

There is no point in being obdurate; the violence in the poem originates somewhere. Still, it seems too crude to conclude, with Tom Marshall, that "Scott seems fully aware of the resentment and hatred felt by the Indian for the forces destroying his world" (31). The same goes for Lyle Weis's assertion that "Powassan is a negative force who conjures the hatred and superstition Scott believes may hinder plans to bring the Indian into the modern, Europeanized world" ("History" 33). Speculation certainly has its place in criticism, but it looks like guessing when unacknowledged as such.

The assimilation issue is about as fundamental to the poem as the symbolic equivalences Fred Cogswell arbitrarily assigns to nearly everything in it. Practical Criticism was not theorized to legitimize such inventions. After his preamble, Cogswell gets off to an unfortunate start, claiming that Powassan is a dwarf (224). The word "dwarf" has associations that somewhat distance the wigwam in the poem from either the "medicine tent" that

Vanasse described as being attached to Nistonaqueb's larger tent, or the famous Ojibway conjuror's shaking tent, but not so far as to make a "dwarf wigwam" the wigwam of a dwarf. Nothing built on that misidentification is going to stand, and Cogswell says nothing else to regain his credibility.

More accurate, I believe, are the general assertions that "Powassan's Drum" has to do with (E. K. Brown) "huge and sinister suggestion" (85) or (D. G. Jones) the "demonic irrational power of nature" (70) or (Weis) "primitive instinct separated from reason" ("History" 31); they are consistent with Glenys Stow's sound thesis that Scott's "best verse presents the violence and passion of natural man, but he continually persuaded himself that he was a writer of classical rationality and balance" (168).

But it is odd, seeing that the poem is one of Scott's best known and most anthologized, how relatively untouched it is. Perhaps critics glance at it, or sidestep it, or employ aspects of it to serve a general thesis, because interpreting symbolic poems — like "The Piper of Arll" or "The Water Lily" — is a hazardous business. The temptation is to allegorize a line of argument through such poems, to substitute stable paraphrase for a shimmer of potential meanings, of play. Milton Wilson's interpretation of "The Piper of Arll" is not vulnerable to the charge of paraphrase because the sure touch of his own writing opens the poem out rather than closing it off. Openness to indeterminacy, whether instinctual or theory-driven, is an impulse best fulfilled in answerable language. Otherwise there are certain secrets a poem will never give up.

WHAT CAN BE SAID about the elusive "Powassan's Drum," then? Quite a lot, if common sense is allowed to walk hand in hand with tolerance for ungraspable suggestion. The design the poem describes in the air, whether read silently or aloud, is an aspect of the poem that means, but to which meaning can't be easily assigned, so a good beginning might be to describe the poem's movement, its verbal choreography. This design is an orchestration of irregularities. Since it never settles into set stanza form or standard metrical pattern, the poem is one of the least regular of Scott's characteristic mixed-form poems, especially those employing what Gordon Johnston calls "the variable line" (254). "In musical terms," Johnston says, "the basic Scott structure is a set of variations" (252). The line lengths of "Powassan's Drum" are irregular; the lengths of the 12 verse paragraphs are irregular also, the longest being the ninth and tenth (20 and 24 lines respectively), as befits the concurrent enlarging of the movements, or fits, in the narrative of the poem. This is free verse, tightly controlled; the poem unfolds as a series of aural and visual variations, of departures from and returns to the poem's onomatopoeic refrain, the "throb — throb — throb — throb / Throbbing of Powassan's Drum."

The refrain's pulsing creates an "ache in the air" of the poem that imitates the ache created by Powassan's drumming. Each beat of the drum is a spondee separated by a caesura, or — in musical terms — a rest. All of the extension and forward movement made by the sentences returns to this static pure sound — the word "throb" so repeated flies away from abstraction almost to pure equivalence between sound and sense. The deployment of the refrain epitomizes the aural variations in the soundscape of the whole poem; while the refrain lines normally appear at the end of each section, they are never approached in precisely the same way. And there is variation in that regularity of positioning. The refrain doesn't appear at all in the short sections 4 and 8, it's displaced (slightly) from the end of section 9, and is shifted to the middle of section 10. The altered location of the refrain in these longer sections, along with their greater length, suggests that something different or something more is going on in them than happens in the other sections. The something more, in one sense, is the appearance of the storm cloud (9) and especially (in 10) the apparition of the headless Indian.

More irregularly regular yet, the whole poem proceeds in terms of a sort of unscripted incremental repetition of sounds and visual motifs that is dispersed throughout the poem. The shaman crouches in his "dwarf wigwam" (2),

> under the poles
> Covered with strips of birchbark
> And branches of poplar and pine (4).

In section 2 he is also "wizened with fasting, / Fierce with thirst." The privation is extended in section 8, when he is "parched with anger / And famished with hatred," then further varied as the statement of section 2 becomes a question in section 8. There is a sense of the words and of each unit rolling, metamorphosing slowly and deliberately through the poem. This occurs also in variations of the sun personified as fisherman in sections 5 and 9, of the image of the shore reeds in sections 3 and 7, of the image of sky as taut bubble (section 6) that bursts in section 12, of the association of the (impotent) sun with a lack of answers in sections 9 and 12, in the questions asked in sections 1, 4, 8, and 11. All of this movement, this shifting, this turning of the world of the poem every time a word lifts off it — all of this is beginning to mean before any of the words and sentences are approached in terms of content (though the mind absorbs such sources of further complexity much more quickly than the pen can spell any of it out). It means: instability. If you just reach out to a little of the atmosphere generated by the content of the images — that of nightmare, of Gothic cul-de-sac — this instability may be seen to produce the frustration of an urgent need to know, to escape, to get beyond whatever pressure of terror is building up. This is the effect of the "powerful, incantatory rhythm" Gerald Lynch names correctly and then leaves alone.

Of the taut rhythm of chastened advance that marks the movement of the poem as a whole, section 10 is the epitome. The word "Then," which opens it, signals something beginning to happen, some intensification in the narrative of the poem. Section 10 is a nightmare within the nightmare, and the inner terror unfolds with predatory deliberateness as the lines all but stick on certain words and seem to move on only with difficulty. The first sentence of section 10 is a complex unit that pulses to its end in spasms of incremental repetition:

> Then from the reeds stealing,
> A shadow noiseless,
> A canoe moves noiseless as sleep,
> Noiseless as the trance of deep sleep
> And an Indian still as a statue,
> Moulded out of deep sleep,
> Headless, still as a headless statue
> Moulded out of deep sleep,
> Sits modelled in full power,
> Haughty in manful power,
> Headless and impotent in power.

There are 58 words in this passage; only 29 different ones (28, counting "modelled" as a variation of "moulded"), and yet for all that repetition only one unit is repeated exactly. The whole poem moves so, as I say, but nowhere else does it turn so slowly through such a severely limited verbal repertoire as in section 10.

The constriction in the poem's technique of advance and return feels to me like a way of enacting what is happening in the poem's content. To put it generally, a vessel of form is filling slowly with words, prolonging the suspense about when, even whether, it will be filled. To put it in the poem's own terms, the form is a bubble blown tighter and tighter until it bursts with the storm at the end of the poem. In terms of this metaphor sections 9 and 10 are large, long breaths blown into the bubble form. The poem *does,* intricately, what it says; or, rather, what it says — what it asks — is partly answered by the way it moves. So it delivers aesthetically while it delays and eventually frustrates the desire for discursive meaning.

The poem is, in fact, about a search for meaning. It posits a situation that is emotionally charged — the puzzle of a shaman whose drumming cannot be ignored because its sound enlarges as the poem progresses, taking in more and more of existence until, in "The sky is a bubble blown so tense / the blue has gone grey," the sky seems to have become a drum. What does this drumming mean? The poem is a nightmare because the possibilities offered are all on the dark side. The meaning of the drumming is not even so open as the drumming along the Congo interior was to Marlow in *Heart* of *Darkness:*

> We penetrated deeper and deeper into the heart of darkness. It was very quiet there. At night sometimes the roll of drums behind the curtain of trees would run up the river and remain sustained faintly, as if hovering in the air high over our heads, till the first break of day. Whether it meant war, peace, or prayer we could not tell. (35–36)

Hatred is the essence of the malevolent medicine made by the shaman in "Powassan's Drum." His power is demonic; it generates fear. The questions that are asked express a nightmare uncertainty not about that hatred, but about the object and the extent of this power, this anger.

Is it the past or the future that Powassan addresses in his discipline (he is fasting his way into power) of hatred? Has this beat always been, will it always be, "the pulse of Being"? Does the darkness control the world? The question could only be asked within a nightmare. Scott's poetry as a whole, and more particularly most of his poems that interrogate the nature of existence, link the darkness and the light in a balance that is out of reach in "Powassan's Drum." Such is the power of this poem that the light-dark balance in other poems and stories ("No resolution of the kind suggested in other Scott poems is attempted here," says Weis, ["History" 31]) doesn't tame it in the least.

Within the poem, though, is this drumming everything? The sun, benign in his activity, throwing his net to catch the star/fish (morning appears in section 5), hauling it again at twilight (section 9) is otherwise passive. "All" of what the sun does is done "to [the accompaniment of] the throbbing of Powassan's Drum." The darkness has not been dispelled by the day; even the sun seems in thrall to the demonic power of hatred generated by one shaman — presumably mortal. Like the reader, the sun waits for answers: "The sun waited all day."

During the waiting, the storm begins to develop. "There was no answer" is repeated, "But" (the word suggests an introduction of some alternative to an answer, some development in lieu of an answer) the storm cloud like a disembodied hand begins to exert its own dark power. Its own? The storm cloud "rears up / To the throbbing of Powassan's Drum." It seems the first sign of something conjured by the drum, an instrument of wild power that will build and build until it bursts at the end of the poem. But something else happens first, as the question is "answered" by a visual riddle. About the decapitated Indian it is asked,

Is this the meaning of the magic —
The translation into sight
Of the viewless hate?

Lyle Weis answers yes ("Powassan's vision represents an impossible return to a dead way of life: he succeeds only in creating an illusion of power based on memories of former Indian greatness" [35]) but, once again, there *is* no answer, neither by sun nor sky. But the storm answers, and presumably the meaning toward which the poem has been nudging the reader is going to be unfolded for us. What is this meaning, though? It is no more intelligible than the image moulded of the Indian, because the storm "speaks" in action, crushing "the dark world," and this is where we are left:

At the core of the rushing fury
Bursting hail, tangled lightning
Wind in a wild vortex
Lives the triumphant throb — throb — throb — throb —
Throbbing of Powassan's Drum.

This is not an unequivocal yes, in answer to the question of whether the sound of the drum is the heartbeat of Being, but neither is it a no. "Lives" and "triumphant" are clear enough, in their way. No counterforce of love or peace has taken on hatred in this poem. Hatred, anger, has prevailed. No "beauty of peace" succeeds the "beauty of terror," as with the storm of "At Gull Lake: August 1810." One of the strengths of "Powassan's Drum" is that the taut bubble of it bursts — something happens — causing a certain release and relief of the pent-up dramatic tensions, while the core of tension remains. To put it another way, there has been a resolution of the inner nightmare, but no wake-up from the outer one. The throbbing that began the poem ends it. The ending is active, sending an uneasy reader back into the poem to search for signs of a milder meaning, a backbeat, or underlying pulse to the demonic pulse of being. Perhaps this reader will be encouraged by the ambiguous impotence-in-power of that symbolic icon. Perhaps there is encouragement to be found — evidence that the triumph of the storm may be temporary — in the patience of the sun, in the persistence of "the live things in the world" who hear Powassan's Drum and are silent:

They hide silent and charmed
As if guarding a secret;
Charmed and silent hiding a rich secret. . . .

Charmed into silence by the drum, to which they, like everything else, are throbbing? Or charmed by some other, more beneficent power? This is another riddle, an answer to which might lurk in the word "rich," which is not in the same key as all the images of anger, hatred, self-deprivation, and death. Perhaps the key word to underscore in section 6, though, is "live," because the moulded Indian of section 10 seems to be a death wish, or a talisman of death, summoned from the sleep or anaesthetization of reason. At least his canoe is compared to death and the water through which he "trails his severed head" is "dead." It's a fearful kind of death that won't die, of course, so perhaps there ought to be some relief when in the final section "the murdered shadow sinks in the water." Going back where it came from? Into some inner unconscious? At any rate, the last sentence of the poem is ambiguous. Yes, the drum throbs on, but it "lives," and the nature of its living is expressed by the tremendous energy it releases.

No "beauty of peace" here, then, but what the "beauty of terror" might mean (a tremendous frightening power in which one might yet exult?) is clarified by this poem as, more positively, by the similar ending of "Night Hymns on Lake Nipigon." In that poem a canoe loses its race with the pursuing storm only to be willingly engulfed by pure, wild energy. In fact, the complex Latin/Ojibway human song — language, form — is what is racing the storm:

> Back [the lonely phrases] falter as the deep storm overtakes them,
> Whelms them in splendid hollows of booming thunder,
> Wraps them in rain, that, sweeping, breaks and onrushes
> Ringing like cymbals. (*Poems* 24)

A storm is not just a storm in Scott. The storm in "Night Hymns" is wonderful, awe-inspiring. The one in "At Gull Lake" inspires the other awe — terror — but is an instrument of vengeance for injustice. A just storm, however terrible, is intelligible in human terms. The storm in "Powassan's Drum" is a voice of darkness. The unconscious, the instinctual, has its day in this poem. It isn't any prettier than the darkness that claims Kurtz and powerfully draws Marlow, and its triumph suggests that it cannot be denied.

I don't see any point in getting lost in a labyrinth of symbolic equivalences — trees hiding forest — as Fred Cogswell does, speculating on what the moulded Indian's head means, what means his decapitated body and so on. None of these items *means* much in isolation from all the other elements of the poem. The ensemble meaning that is generated is surely uneasiness over a force, demonic or dionysiac, that is easier to respond to than it is to name. Call it darkness, the demonic, even evil — no one who thrills to its incarnations in this poem can disown it.

I have one more thing to say about the verbal materials out of which Scott built his salute to the dark powers. With one possible exception — the word "marish," which admittedly combines with "night" to mean something more than "marsh" — Scott uses only plain words. There is none of the poeticizing, with obscure or archaic words drawn from inherited conventions — classical, biblical, medieval, faerie — that vitiates so many of his poems. This poem is powerful not only because of its musical structure, its incantatory rhythms, its terrifying images, but also because Scott allowed the material to come directly, unmediated by fancy-dress words. The poem is a verbal construct; its construction is what one can most surely analyze. What makes it a good poem is that the superstructure of words houses a soul — a dark one, in this case — whose presence is palpable because the effort to contain it is not obscured by a screen of convention.

I HAVE SAID that I don't think "Powassan's Drum" is authentically Indian at all. I doubt that Scott was trying for authenticity. The proof, such as it is, lies in the differences between the "ethnographic" content of the poem and the beliefs and ceremonies most likely to have been Scott's sources. Of these I don't pretend to know the inner significance. Some Native people hold that anything traditional that appears in print is already compromised, and my own sources are mostly print sources. What these tell me, for what it's worth, is that Powassan and his drum, as they appear in the poem, are probably much more imaginary than has hitherto been thought.

I begin with the rather lovely image of the fisherman/sun, because it isn't crucial to the spirit of the poem. Scott's sun is as Native as anything in the Indian mythology of Isabella Valancy Crawford's "Malcolm's Katie." In a literary sense this is a compliment. Crawford makes no pretense that her "Indian" content is anything but literary, and *therefore* she has adapted the general spirit of mythology to this country. As far as I know, the sun as fisherman is not Ojibway, but a personified mythical figure conceived in such local terms, once again, doesn't seem out of place unless the premise is that Scott is hoping to sound Native. Drumming and the "dwarf wigwam" of the shaman, however, are very important in Ojibway society. Does Scott use them in ways that a Native could recognize and accept?

In a sense it seems that Scott is asking the right questions about Powassan's Drum:

> Has it gone on forever,
> As the pulse of Being?
> Will it last till the world's end
> As the pulse of Being?

Ignoring, for the moment, the hatred that is pulsing out of Scott's drum, the answers to both questions could be yes. Yes, the drum is the pulse of Being, the gift of the Creator, and a voice with which First Nations people communicate with the spirit world.[4] Still placing that hatred on hold, and remembering that we are translating the terms of the poem into others — literary terms into social ones — a proper question might well be, will it last forever? The poem makes no direct comment, perhaps no comment at all, on Native cultural identity, so I don't pretend to be addressing the poem anything but obliquely when I suggest that the drum *is* the people. When the sacred drum is silent, the people have no voice. They have voices, rather, social chatter unanimated by the sacred.

This is quite clear in Tomson Highway's *Dry Lips Oughta Move to Kapuskasing,* a fabulously courageous, because comic, examination of Native despair. Highway is like many other contemporary Native artists, perhaps all of them, in acknowledging that his work is political. Whether or not this is the bottom line in all cases, the work is always at least partly remedial in its address to Native audiences. It has as one of its functions the raising of an inexcusably lowered view of their people. Like Daniel David Moses and Lenore Keeshig-Tobias, of the Committee to Restore the Trickster, Highway wants Nanabush the trickster back, or sobered up, to focus his community's healthy self-image. "Without the continued presence of this extraordinary figure, the core of Indian culture would be gone forever" (*Dry Lips* 13). And he wants the drum back, as well.

> **SIMON**: The drum has to come back, mistigwuskeek . . . has to come back. We've got to learn to dance again. . . . I have my arms around this rock, this large black rock sticking out of the ground, right here on this spot. And then I hear this baby crying, from inside this rock. The baby is crying out my name. As if I am somehow responsible for it being caught inside that rock. I can't move. My arms, my whole body, stuck to this rock. Then this . . . eagle . . . lands beside me, right over there. But this bird has three faces, three women. And the eagle says to me: "the baby is crying, my grand-child is crying to hear the drum again." (43–45)

Native drumming is not dead, of course. Perhaps the water drum (the "Midé or water drum, used in the ceremonies of the Midéwewin Society is a sacred instrument and is never used lightly," ["Drums" 11]) is not as common as it was — tuned by changing the water level; "the water in the drum splashes against the drumhead, this adds resonance and helps carry the sound a long distance" ("Drums" 11) — but the old drumming, dancing, and singing techniques are not only preserved but very much alive at festivals and powwows.[5] If Thomas King's *Medicine River* is an accurate reflection of contemporary Blackfoot life (the novel delights in deadpan exaggerations), modern technology has made the drum portable: now it can be beaten in a van driven to and from basketball games. Of course, western movies alone have so assimilated Native drumming to the Gothic tradition of richly terrifying experience that most of us have no other mental slot to put it in. Drumming has all sorts of functions, both social and religious, and one of these functions is, or was, sorcery.

Scott chooses from the spectrum of drumming possibilities an unlikely one, an expression of hatred, given that he was told of the original occasion that it was a healing feast, but then he ties Powassan's drumming to no particular occasion. Perhaps the compelling sound of that drumming over Lac Seul, and then over the years within Scott himself, overrode what he knew, or at least what he was told, of the White Dog Feast. He must have been disturbed by his encounter with Nistonaqueb. If, like Stewart, he felt wisdom where he reported cunning, a terrible tension might well have developed between his instincts and his function as civil servant charged with applying European law in the North. Perhaps we don't need a curse to explain why he was "taken ill." Still, whether he discovered it on Lac Seul or somewhere else, or whether he merely heard about it, shamans were as susceptible to dark spirits as to benign ones, and they sometimes drummed and chanted in deadly serious competition with each other. They could send curses a long distance. There may even have been contrary shamanistic societies. Basil Johnston reports that the Medi-wi-win or Medicine Society was contrary in spirit to the Society of the Dawn, "Waubunowin." "It was said that the Waubunowin was dedicated to the practice of sorcery, and that its members were inspired by evil. No one was quite sure" (*Ceremonies* 115).

Johnston's *Ojibway Ceremonies* has much in common with other writings by Ojibways like his own earlier *Ojibway Heritage,* Norval Morrisseau's *Legends of My People,* and the collections edited by James Stevens — a presenter of Native voices in such books as *Legends from the Forest* — in giving the sense that, as much as is being described of Ojibway ways, much is being held back. *Ojibway Ceremonies* seems to me to work better than *Ojibway Heritage,* because the English prose is more tuned, and the weaving of story and information is more skillfully done. Still, I don't feel moved into the core of this world, whether that's because the attempt to go there is for Johnston himself an anthropological exercise (he was educated, *well* educated — being one of the "lucky" ones — and therefore perhaps colonized at one of those notorious residential schools), or because what he has to say will fit only with the greatest of difficulty into English, into *any* written language. Whatever the reason, something is not coming through. And something is. This is a classically "primitive" world view in which the spirits live and interact for good or ill with human beings. The shaman is the mortal furthest advanced along the spirit road, and thus the one most qualified to channel the powers of the spirit world. The shaking tent is the most fascinating instrument for communicating with the spirit world, at least to me, and it may be somewhere behind the "dwarf wigwam" in which Scott's shaman crouches to make medicine.

Perhaps Scott had only a general notion of the operation of the shaking tent, or perhaps his vision in "Powassan's Drum" required an intensely static distillation of hatred. Whatever the reason, if he did have a shaking tent in mind, he has simplified and stylized it into something iconic, symbolic. There is no Native audience, no spirit performers, no payment of goods, no *shaking* — nothing that makes a shaking tent ceremony so dynamic and theatrical. It would seem unlikely that Scott hadn't heard accounts of shaking tent ceremonies, having spent two summers in the North among people like George Drever, who took such interest in Native ways. But there is no proof. "Dwarf wigwam" sounds unlikely to be drawn from anything else than a shaking tent; there is nothing of the sweat lodge about it. That being so, describing the workings of the shaking tent, outlining the function of the drum, should be enough to show that Scott was inventing his wigwam, inventing his drumming.

I am not finished wondering about "Powassan's Drum." The final chapter speculatively makes the poem a key to understanding "Scott and the Indians," the whole problem of this book. Meanwhile I hope I have cleared the way to approaching "Powassan's Drum" as a poem without guessing about it as a reflection of Native culture. At least it should now be possible to resist assumptions like Tom Marshall's: ". . . the ferocity of Indian hatred seems the paramount theme: the poem is located within the Indian world" (31).

NOTES

1. A man named Powassan has a significant part to play in James Redsky's *Great Leader of the Ojibway: Mis-quona-queb:* "James Redsky, by Ojibway custom, received his Indian name, Esquekesik, Last Man in the Sky, from the dream revelation of Powassan, whose name translates literally as 'fruit falling off the stem or branch.' Powassan was one of the Indian chieftans [*sic*] of the Lake of the Woods who signed the North West Angle Treaty with the Government of Canada in 1873" (13). A slightly different version appears in Selwyn Dewdney's *The Sacred Scrolls of the Ojibway:* "The fifth signature on the list of native representatives was that of Powassan(g), pre-eminent among the Lake of the Woods leaders and Grand Shaman of the Midéwewin at Northwest Angle. Some, if not all, of Red Sky's scrolls were originally Powassan's, for Red Sky's mentor and uncle, Baldhead, learned his Midé lore at the feet of the great Northwest Angle Midé master. Further evidence of Red Sky's family standing among the Midé elite is the fact that it was Powassan, still living in 1895, who dreamed Red Sky's proper Ojibway name, Eshkwaykeezhik (Last Sky)" (23).
2. Perhaps Nistonaqueb is a member of the "Group at Lac Seul Reserve" depicted in the photograph on page 160.
3. Vanasse is very skeptical about this. He implies that Nistonaqueb is profiting from superstition. Other accounts show that payment for a shaman's services was usual and normal; it is white eyes that see something sinister in the practice.
4. This understood, one may grasp the full resonance of the connection between title and subtitle in Boyce Richardson's *Drumbeat: Anger and Renewal in Indian Country.* The writers addressing political realities, arguing for aboriginal self-government in that book, are hardly on the warpath. "Once, in a time before the world changed," according to an item, "Drums," discovered in the Ojibway-Cree Cultural Centre, "the sound of the drums,

pounding like a heart beat, echoed through the forests and over the plains, invading the hearts and souls of Indian people. The people recognized that all living creatures shared the same origins; they recognized the harmony in nature around them, and the beating of their drums symbolized this pulse they felt running through all life and nature. For this reason, drums have always had religious and ceremonial significance for Indian people" (2).

5. "One of my great regrets," says Selwyn Dewdney, "is that as a naive youth I was unable to cast off the inhibitions of my role as student missionary at Lac Seul in the summers of 1929 and 1930. Night after night I lay in my bed in the old mission house listening to the seductive beat of the Midé water drum sounding across the lake. Unwittingly I threw away my chance of watching the last celebration of the White Dog Feast, for at that time the Ear Falls Dam was being built and only a year later the flooding began that permanently dispersed the Lac Seul Band, ending the most active Midé centre on the English River system" (*Sacred Scrolls* 146). So much for Scott's warnings; flooding was what it took to eliminate that "seductive sound."

8

Into the West: "A Scene at Lake Manitou"

In the course of his life [Eshkwaykeezhik/Last Sky/James Red Sky] had acquired considerable knowledge of the Christian lore and rites and could see no fundamental conflict between them and those of his people.
Selwyn Dewdney, The Sacred Scrolls of the Ojibway

HARDLY ANYBODY ANTHOLOGIZES "A Scene at Lake Manitou." It doesn't even appear in Souster and Lochhead's selected poems, *Powassan's Drum,* which gathers a group of Indian poems in a section with the same title. Ever since I first read the poem in *The Green Cloister,* I have wondered why it isn't more popular. Janice Simpson calls it one of Scott's best poems (67), and I agree. In my own Scott canon I place it above "On the Way to the Mission" and "The Forsaken," though, as Gerald Lynch hints, "A Scene at Lake Manitou" is almost "The Forsaken" revisited. The structure is very different, and so is the narrative centre — a mother's grief over the death of her son — but there is a similar focus on the strength, resilience, and endurance of the Widow Frederick, another of Scott's Native heroines. Glenys Stow says that "the passionate energy usually present in the Indian verse is missing" (175) in "A Scene at Lake Manitou"; perhaps such perception accounts for its being so often passed over in anthologies and critical discussion in favour of its companion poem, "At Gull Lake: August 1810." I can understand that, but not the greater popularity of "The Forsaken."

"The Forsaken" is very important in Scott's career as an early success in the free verse variable line, with occasional rhyme, of which "A Scene at Lake Manitou" is a later example. But "The Forsaken" is not a better poem. In fact, there *is* a surge of passionate energy in the narrative of "A Scene at Lake Manitou" when the Widow Frederick breaks in her grief and begins to feed the lake with her Western possessions, and there is also a structurally important and mysteriously intense recurrent image of the view out into the lake. The function of this image needs a subtler interpretation than it has yet received and, in fact, the poem as a whole needs to be read less as an expression of the difficulties of mixing cultures and more as the human tragedy it is.

The details of the poem are specific to their time, place, and culture, but these contribute to the narrative texture that roots the emotion. "A Scene at Lake Manitou" has as much in common with "By a Child's Bed" and "The Closed Door" as with any of the other Indian poems. Scott wrote "A Scene at Lake Manitou" in 1933, long after the death of his daughter in 1907, but that loss stayed green in him for the rest of his life. It adds a touch of poignancy to Scott's grandfatherly welcome of other people's children, like E. K. Brown's Deaver. The uncanny thing is that he also "foresaw" his loss. "By a Child's Bed" is haunting enough before one discovers that it was written in 1902:

> These fairy kisses,
> This archness innocent,
> Sting me with sorrow and disturbed content:
> I think of what my portion might have been,
> A dearth of blisses,
> A famine of delights,
> If I had never had what now I value most;
> Till all I have seems something I have lost;
> A desert underneath the garden shows,
> And in a mound of cinders roots the rose. (*Poems* 188)

This poem shows that Scott carried a parent's fears with him into the North. Retrospectively his treaty-making summers must have seemed a criminal sacrifice of time with his daughter.

To suggest that only parents may identify with other parents whose children are taken from them would be to underestimate the othering power of imagination and love. Still, shared situations multiply the intensity of the identification. Scott was travelling through a land in which infant mortality was extremely high, owing especially to the tuberculosis that is probably the death of Matanack and his father in "A Scene at Lake Manitou." In fact, two of the journals of July 27, 1906, record a death at Brunswick House on Lake Missinabie that probably influenced the poem. Samuel Stewart is silent on the subject. Edgar is brief and inadvertently ironic: "Very hot day — Bishop leaves early. Doctor Meindl concludes his work & Indian dies in evening." If Edmund Morris hadn't been a member of the party at this point, there would have been no indication that the Indian who died was a boy.

Stewart says that on July 27 Morris was "busily engaged in completing sketches made by him of several of the Indians," but Morris wasn't too busy to notice what was going on around him:

> Dr. Meindl examined the Indians in the little church. Many of them have the cough which so often leads to consumption, and — far away from the others — all alone like a wounded animal there was a young boy dying of consumption. The tent was covered by boughs of trees. He died this evg. and the chief read the service in the native tongue. He had no near relations and appeared frightened. (Q/EM)

This seems likely to be what Morris wrote, though what I translate as "frightened" might actually be "neglected." To read his diary is to understand well why Scott begins "Lines in Memory of Edmund Morris" with a joke about his friend's handwriting. Morris seems to go on from where the above passage leaves off to describe a long and monotonous dance held to honour the deceased boy.[1] The sketch in Morris's diary (see figure 11) seems likely to be his drawing of the scene he described verbally, though it appears with other sketches after his last journal entry. He probably flipped forward a few pages when he wanted to sketch something.

Figure 11

Some detail from this death scene recalls the poem ("boughs of trees" could be the "cedar screen," for example), but the death of a young boy with "no near relations" is clearly not the death of Matanack. It is interesting, though, that in his "Old Lords of the Soil," a Toronto newspaper article dated May 9, 1907, Morris recalls seeing "a squaw when her boy was dying offering up sacrifices to appease the Evil Spirit." This is to illustrate the general question that "How deep a hold the Christian religion has on these people it is difficult to say." Circumstantial evidence suggests that the young boy's death and the woman's sacrifice, even if separate occurrences (even if the latter were only recounted to Scott by Morris, who stayed in the North longer than the treaty party did), probably fed into "A Scene at Lake Manitou."

Suggestions have been made that Scott had a particular Lake Manitou in mind, either in Saskatchewan (Slonim) or on Manitoulin Island (Simpson). There is a perhaps likelier candidate just west of Lake Temagami — not on but near the treaty party's route. However, it seems just as likely to me that Scott picked or rather named his setting in the same spirit in which he rolled together a medley of actual experiences to create a single narrative. Manitou is a powerful word, after all, and one that most non-Native people would be likely to understand at least superficially. "A Scene at Lake Missinabie" would be as effective a title as "Night Hymns on Lake Nipigon," or "Spring on Mattagami," but it would be lacking in spiritual resonance.

Substituting Lake Missinabie for Lake Manitou doesn't pinpoint the poem's origin, because both the Widow Frederick and her "hand-sewing-machine" derive from Abitibi Post on the first leg of the 1906 journey. Gerald Lynch mentions the sewing machine (see figure 12), although he doesn't describe it quite accurately (51n). This is the photograph labelled "Indian Family, Abitibi 1906." The next photograph in the sequence (see figure 13) is of "The Widow Frederick." In Pelham Edgar's "Twelve Hundred Miles by Canoe" she is the "poor soul" of 70, "childless and a widow [who] craved medicine for loneliness." Edgar doesn't identify the woman by name, but his article is illustrated with the photograph mentioned above, captioned "The squaw who craved medicine for loneliness."

Figure 12, PA-59520

Figure 13, PA-59523

What about the phonograph that the Widow Frederick actually throws into the lake? None is mentioned as the possession of a Native, but Stewart says that "At [Long Lake Post], as at almost all the others we visited, a gramophone was kept going most of the day for the amusement of the Indians, who appeared to be highly delighted with the performance" (102). This would perhaps be the "Edison cylinder type of gramophone" mentioned by S. A. Taylor, in "Reminiscences of Lac Seul," as being ordered by post manager J. D. Mackenzie sometime after 1906. That was when Taylor was "transferred to the Lac Seul Post as book-keeper and assistant" (46). Scott says in an undated letter to Florence Leslie Jones "that all my poems dealing with Indians are true to aboriginal conditions; I dislike the words 'founded on fact,' but in truth there is fact in all these poems." He then goes on to say of "A Scene at Lake Manitou" that the poem "is very close to actuality" (NA/DCS). Both of these statements are somewhat equivocal, but the second hints at a single source for the poem. Would this have been witnessed or heard about? Might "actuality" have been composite? I can't say for sure. At any rate, the second last item in Scott's 1900–1910 notebook (though the date "15 Novr 14" appears just before it) is a list of subjects bearing, most of them, on "A Scene at Lake Manitou." These notes for the poem appear to be Scott's first exploration toward what it might focus on:

The boy going to hospital
Death of lad [?] with consumption
Starting [?] baby
Attempt of HB Co to get girl
The woman who tore everything to pieces
Wounded boy; throwing the household goods into water

Since Edmund Morris says that many people wanted "medicine for loneliness," one wonders how Dr. Meindl responded to the request. The request may sound naive as well as sad, but why would so many make it unless they had some expectation of getting satisfaction? Dr. Meindl seems to have been a regular doctor — nothing in his official report or in other accounts of his activities suggests otherwise — so he would have felt responsible for mending the body and practising preventative medicine to the best of his abilities. Indeed a non-Native doctor of the time would have felt that western medical science had outstripped Native healing in administering to the body (the irony being that white medicine was needed to combat imported white diseases — smallpox, measles, tuberculosis). Dr. Meindl would have been a remarkable medical man indeed had he felt, in 1906, any inkling of a need to address himself to the spirit, or even the mind, to use the term most westerners still conceive of as arranged in a binary relationship with body.

Loneliness is depression. There is a clue to what might have been needed for loneliness in Thomas King's *Medicine River*: "'A hot shower' said Harlen, turning on the dome light and looking at the map, 'is great for depressions. In the old days, we used to have regular sweats just for that reason. The old people were pretty smart, you know'" (106). A "sweat" is a session in a sweat lodge, a sort of sauna for the spirit practised by Ojibway as well as the Prairie Blackfoot of King's novel.

But the question of who heals Natives better, the white doctor or the shaman, is beside the point, isn't it? Yes and no. Healing is what the Widow Frederick is seeking for her son in the poem. Interestingly, no healer, white or Native, is mentioned in the poem as having been sought for Matanack, at least none other than Father Pacifique. The Holy Water came from him; Matanack "had worn his Scapular / always." Father Pacifique is an earthly representative of Jesus, a well-known healer whose healing is magic, though miracle is the name it goes under. Jesus defies physical mortality by simply recalling to its body the departed spirit of Lazarus. His story has understandably raised the Widow Frederick's hopes. Faith in holy water and scapular might seem either sense or superstition, depending on one's religion. But perhaps the active absence is that of the shaman. Would an expert shaman, administering to Matanack's spirit and body in concert, paying attention to the relationship between human spirit and the spirits at large, be able to cure the white disease, the "foe" that slays him? Here again there would be different answers, depending on one's conception of the body: matter, spirit, both?

To entertain such speculations is to treat Matanack as an actual patient, not as a verbal construct; it is to address the poem not as a poem but as a jumping-off point for extra-literary inquiry. Scott's Indian poems almost always stimulate such thinking, and there would be nothing wrong with it if it didn't masquerade as literary criticism. Is "A Scene at Lake Manitou" a document relevant to the question of assimilation, for example, to "the pain and frustration resulting from the clash of two cultures" (Lynch 51)? Does the Widow Frederick represent "the possibility of a creative reconciliation of the two cultures" (Simpson 75)? A qualified yes to both questions. But is the poem *about* these matters? Yes again, as far as I'm concerned, though I think we are talking now about secondary or even tertiary themes, subordinate to the tragic theme of inevitable death. To say so is to invert the usual priority in criticism of Scott's Indian poems, the assumption that the function of the poem is to make a statement, rather than to dramatize something. Yes, the shaman's absence is significant; no, it isn't central to the poem as a poem.

The Widow Frederick's name has attracted comment. Gerald Lynch assumes that the deceased husband was a white man. Janice Simpson recognizes this as an assumption, but builds on it, anyway: "perhaps the death of the white man was a prefiguration of Scott's fear, implied in the poem's final image, that attempts to combine the two cultures creatively are doomed to failure" (72). The word "implied" doesn't qualify this questionable generalization enough. In the matter of names Simpson makes an assumption of her own, the perfectly understandable one that Matanack is an Indian name (723). After all, it doesn't sound European. Scott may well have assumed that his readers would take it that way. There *is* a small chance that he remembered and would have expected his most persistent readers to discover that he had said something else on the subject in the first paragraph of his story "Spirit River":

> These things happened in the country of the Ojibway, where English and French begin to be merged with that soft language, and where all sounds are corrupted by a sort of savage slurring, particularly proper names, — Frederick becomes Matenack, Thomas becomes Toma, Pays Plat is Peepla and Teresa, Trasey. (*Elspie* 63)

There is a Trasey in "Spirit River," but no Peepla, Toma, or Matenack. There is a Toma in "Labrie's Wife," another (with Pierrish and Arcange) in "Roses on the Portage," and yet another in "The Mission of the Trees," where Matenack is the name of an Indian boy who dies of hunger.[3]

In "Spirit River," Frederick and Matenack are versions of the same word, the same name. I doubt that it makes sense to identify the two names in "A Scene at Lake Manitou" (Frederick Frederick is no name to give a character whose death you want taken seriously), but it does seem necessary to introduce the evidence that Matanack (or Matenack) is no Indian name, but a hybrid produced by the pull of one language on another. "Corrupted" and "savage slurring" are uncomplimentary, suggesting degeneration and not the vitality of a language in flux. Scott could not have been expected to regard the relaxation of English pronunciation and spelling as progress. His own language may have shifted, in certain plain-speaking poems (like "A Scene at Lake Manitou," in fact), away from inherited poetic conventions, but it would not have occurred to him that anything positive might come of hybridizing standard English. Well, Scott was no William Faulkner, thinking of his work from one end to the other as a single body made of organic parts. Most likely we aren't supposed to know (maybe he himself had forgotten) what he made of Matanack elsewhere, and the fact that it means Frederick should slide into the background.

What about the other name issue? Frederick *is* a European name, anyway, but that doesn't mean that the husband was white. Most members of the various Treaty 9 crews had European and Indian names both, just as many of the lakes and rivers have both — or sometimes more than two: English, French, and Native. Some of the signatories of the treaties, officially all

Indians, had English names; some had Indian names, whether or not they could write them. The Widow Frederick has an Indian name, Stormy Sky, given only in English translation; likely her husband had one, too. Since he died 12 years ago, it isn't necessary to introduce him by name. Part of the complication here is that Widow Frederick is less a name than a marker of relationship in patriarchy, a suppression of female identity. Scott has not fully restored the woman's Ojibway name (and he does use untranslated Native names in some poems and stories), but he at least has indicated something of her original identity.

Is Stormy Sky a symbolic name, then? Janice Simpson finds it a key to the Widow Frederick's character. A storm of sorts does erupt in the poem ("something broke in her heart") when the death vigil becomes insupportable and Stormy Sky explodes into action, throwing her "treasured possessions" into the lake in desperate barter for her son. But this is uncharacteristic. In the aftermath of her grief throes, resignation resurfaces ("She knew it was all in vain"), followed shortly by her old resolution. Retrospectively the outburst seems to have been (less for Matanack than for herself) a release from the tension of hopeless hoping. There is nothing stormy in her calm view of the future:

> She was alone now and knew
> What she would do:
> The Trader would debit her winter goods,
> She would go into the woods
> And gather the fur,
> Live alone with the stir
> Alone with the silence;
> Revisit the Post,
> Return to hunt in September;
> So had she done as long as she could remember. (*Cloister* 12)

What this phlegmatic woman will do now is what she has always done. Native names are not necessarily keys to character, and perhaps Scott is acting on that knowledge. Given what we know of the controlled Widow Frederick, anyway, the name is ironic. Pacifique would actually fit her better.

Reflecting on Matanack, on the Widow Frederick/Stormy Sky, makes a mere beginning on the subject of names in "A Scene at Lake Manitou." Along with the other proper nouns, so many that they stand out and alert the reader to examine the notational system they represent, names are doorways into this poem. To the general respectfulness lent the capitalized names just mentioned, including that of Father Pacifique, additional reverence is due to Jesus and Mary. Lake Manitou is capitalized as a place, but Manitou and Nanabojou are names parallel to those of Jesus and Mary.

Indian is capitalized, as would be expected; so is Christian. But with Holy Water and Scapular we seem to be in a discretionary area. Scott is elevating the objects represented by these words, and balancing them on the Native or natural side with Powers, Earth, Air, Water.

These last pairings of capitalized words are, in fact, an index of the cultural balance of the Widow Frederick's mind. They also create a frame of sorts for the central episode in which she breaks down. Just before this her mind is rambling: "Fitfully visions rose in her tired brain, / Faded away, and came again and again"; "Nanabojou / And the powerful Manitou / that lived in the lake" are "Mingled with thoughts of Jesus / who raised a man from the dead" (50). Once she calms down, after her outburst, this balance of Ojibway and Christian elements reasserts itself. The Widow Frederick decides that Matanack has "gone to his father / To hunt in the Spirit Land / And to be with Jesus and Mary" (52). This mixture of cultures may seem ironic to either Native or non-Native readers, but it appears natural to the Widow Frederick. At least the absence of authorial comment suggests that she normally feels no strain of reconciliation. What wrenches this mingling, this unity of diversities, out of simultaneity and into sequence is the strain of her grief. Then the capitalized Christian words are superseded by the capitalized Indian ones. It's not insignificant that the new religion gives way to the old, of course (suggesting, depending on one's perspective, either a regression or a return to roots), but that the two reassemble and cohabit again as part of the Widow Frederick's resignation is also significant. It means that this woman is not, like the "Half-breed Girl," tortured by mongrelism. She is more like Charles Wabinoo, in Scott's account: "the Indian at the best point of a transitional state, still wild as a lynx, with all the lore and instinct of his race undimmed, and possessed wholly by the simplest rule of the Christian life" (*Circle* 122).

I made something in chapter 3 of the fact that Scott patronizes Charles Wabinoo. Perhaps his speaker is patronizing the Widow Frederick. After all, Jesus and Nanabojou may be parallel figures, dying and reviving gods in their respective mythologies, but there is a huge difference between the faultless teacher/saviour and the trickster who is powerful and foolish at once. There is a huge difference between monotheistic and polytheistic cosmology. When he refers to Powers in the plural, and to "*the* Manitou in the lake" (my emphasis), Scott shows an understanding that spirit in Ojibway cosmology has not been drawn out of nature to dwell solely in the central figures. The Widow Frederick's ecumenism is simplistic, but there is no need to think of her as passively ignoring these differences because she is an Indian. She may be no Nistonaqueb, no intellect, but her simple-mindedness is readable as simply human. Scott may have *thought* that the Widow Frederick was merging an inferior with a superior system; he may have expected his readers to feel that sort of irony. But he didn't direct the reader to it, which means that there is no basis for reading racism into that aspect of the poem. The sentence in which the men "slouched away to their loafing" might sound like the notorious editorializing word "slunk" in "The Forsaken," but on a hot and humid August day, lying around seems sensible to me. I don't see reproaching these men for letting the girls get in "the last of the hay," since that is a game, not work. I don't think race is much of a factor in the poem, though Scott certainly hasn't skirted the damaging stereotype of the lazy Indian.

There are three other capitalized words: Post, Trader, and West. Added to the rest, especially since Scott is not usually given to uppercase proliferation, these suggest a stressing of the convention. With Scapular and Holy Water they help swing the voice of the narrator away from Duncan Campbell Scott and toward a persona that seems partly composed of the innocence of the Widow Frederick. After all, Trader is capitalized only in a section in which the third person of the narrator is clearly near the thoughts of the Widow Frederick. In the first line of the poem we read "fur trader's house," and then "trader" appears at the beginning of section 8. The trader is unnamed, so his position is what is being elevated in "Trader." This Hudson's Bay Company functionary has virtual control of the Widow Frederick's life. Like the other Indians, she is tethered to the "Post" by the "winter goods" advance, or "debit," she depends on the trader to give her against the furs she will bring him in the spring. English business, French religion: between them the "founding races" own her, body and soul.

Why is West capitalized? All of the other words are easier to figure than this one. If I were one of those critical dinosaurs, a devotee of Practical Criticism, I'd be obliged to make sure that no speck or smidgen of the poem were left unattached to an armature of unitary interpretation. What a relief those days are over. Why is West capitalized? I'll circle around to a possible answer.

D. M. R. Bentley has noticed that the "scene" in the title refers both to the dramatic scene that is recounted and to scene as in scenery ("Drawers of Water" 40). Some critics have felt that the scenery, particularly the view of the lake, comments on the scene. Any reader of the poem is going to feel the importance of these descriptions, which (not quite symmetrically) frame the narrative action, but there's a tendency to overinterpret, to paraphrase what they do so as to make them almost explicitly explain the action. Here they are:

> The lake was all shimmer and tremble
> To the bronze-green islands of cedars and pines;
> In the channel between the water shone
> Like an inset of polished stone;
> Beyond them a shadowy trace
> Of the shore by the lake
> Was lost in the veil of haze (lines 11–17).

Worn out with watching,
She gazed at the far-off islands
That seemed in a mirage to float
Moored in the sultry air (lines 30–33).

The islands had lost
their mirage-mooring in air
And lay dark on the burnished water
Against the sunset flare —
Standing ruins of blackened spires
Charred by the fury of fires
That had passed that way,
That were smouldering and dying out in the West
At the end of the day (lines 145–152).

Gerald Lynch observes that the landscape, at the end, has become "a waste-landscape." "The Widow Frederick may be 'resolute as of old,'" he goes on,

> but we are left to wonder how she is to traverse such a landscape without a son to live for and with a religion that is a mixed bag of Christian and Indian — spiritless Christianity, weak medicine. Although she achieved a questionable consolation with the thought that Matanack "had gone to his father / To hunt in the Spirit Land / And to be with Jesus and Mary," what value can such a religion retain in the shadow of the burnt-out image of the pines as "ruins of blackened *spires*. . . ." In this sense, the landscape with which the Indian is left to contend is both exterior and interior. That the poem is generally concerned with the Indians' future is suggested in the image of the fire that has passed, now "dying out in the West"; east-to-west is not only the physical direction taken by this fire that is "smouldering and dying away in ashes"; it is also the direction in which civilization moved, subsuming Indian culture. (53)

Janice Simpson takes this further:

> The wasteland world with which "A Scene at Lake Manitou" concludes is obviously not a breeding ground for a creative cultural synthesis, and the poem thus leaves the reader with the uncomfortable feeling that the woman, like her husband and her son, is doomed to be destroyed. (69)

I don't think the complex final image of the poem should be considered in isolation from the earlier versions of it (in the poem, in the day). What is *in* the three-part image we are looking at, what it's doing in the poem, is mysterious enough to compel interest. I think it's wise to honour that mystery, rather than stretching connectives or inventing context to lower it into the merely intelligible. What happens as the image changes throughout the day?

Possibly the "veil of haze" that obscures the distance is a morning mist, but the poem opens in what feels like the full heat of an August day. Probably what we see is heat haze. Now all of the first five sections (section 6 begins "suddenly something broke") should be seen as taking place in pretty much the same moment. Those early sections set the scene and introduce the antecedent context; there is no narrative advance. They feel quite full, of course, because we are offered a lot in them — not only the view of the lake, but the activity of the hay-makers, the image of the death watch, the history of the watcher and her son, her thoughts. But nothing happens until section 6. What then happens, with its aftermath, takes until sundown. It's astonishing, when you think of it, how foreshortened this action is. The Widow Frederick reaches her crisis, recovers from it, and plans out her future in a matter of hours. No one has commented on the speed of this recovery, perhaps because it doesn't feel unnaturally rapid. After all, the poem has very economically filled in those 12 years of the life of Matanack and his mother.

I think Janice Simpson feels the great distance from "bronze-green islands" to "standing ruins of blackened spires," because she suggests that the "rising mist uncovers images of destruction" (69) on the far shore of the lake, presumably, of which only "shadowy traces" may be seen at the poem's opening. But clearly they are the same green islands, changed utterly, at the end of the poem. I don't take literally the image of the forest fire that follows the dash. After all, as dramatic as the day has been, there was no forest fire on the islands in the lake. The islands now *look* as though they have been burnt up, but the sunset does that. The visual effect is reminiscent of this stanza in "The Piper of Arll":

> There were three pines above the comb
> That, when the sun flared and went down,
> Grew like three warriors reaving home
> The plunder of a burning town. (*Poems* 35)

But there is a nearer analogue of sorts. The forest fire is uncannily reminiscent of this sentence in "The Last of the Indian Treaties": "The Indian nature now seems like a fire that is waning, that is smouldering and dying away in ashes . . ." (110). Perhaps some unacknowledged pressure from this statement leads Simpson and Lynch to their anticipation of a bleak future, either for the Widow Frederick or her race. I don't see that kind of bleakness in the poem. The only time the Widow Frederick is definitely looking out at the lake is in section 2. Even then, there is no necessary attachment of the view to her consciousness. I don't want to be inflexible about this, just precise. What is sad about the end of the poem is not simply a lament for the waning of the race, but a reframing of an earlier image that appears at the end of section 4:

> He was just sixteen years old
> A hunter crafty and bold;
> But there he lay,
> And his life with its useless cunning
> Was ebbing out with the day.

Perhaps it seems perverse to possess quantities of cultural context (religious conflict or harmony, the decline of the red race) and not to press it all into service, but the function of context is never to bend a poem out of its natural shape. The sun as it sets at the end of "A Scene at Lake Manitou" temporarily blackens the trees outlined against it, creating a frightening *effect* of waste and destruction (distanced from a real forest fire by a mere dash) infused with deep emotion born of its gathering into itself the tragic waste of Matanack's youth.

Having said that, having dealt with the ending of the poem in the poem's own terms — that is, placing the emphasis on the emotional impact of the dénouement as a fulfilment of the emotional disturbance in the Widow Frederick and its echo in the reader — I want to acknowledge that a capitalized "West" does feel like more than a direction. The West (seen as the Occident) is capable of subsuming the English business and the French religion I spoke of. Keeping this possibility in mind, there are two potential takes on the preposition "in": when read as "dying away *in* the West" — in that direction, into — the phrase indicates absorption and assimilation — *if* one identifies "the fury of fires" with the Widow Frederick and the Widow Frederick with her race. The West may also carry something of the traditional association with a Christian Heaven, or divine source, as in "Good Friday, Riding Westward," or "Ode: Intimations of Immortality." This interpretation would multiply the irony. It seems important, however, to preserve the iffiness of all this; any attempt to assemble the haze of contingencies and assert that "A Scene at Lake Manitou" is about assimilation might well dissolve. It's not mere hairsplitting that brings me around to qualified agreement with Gerald Lynch: death by absorption is in the poem, yes, but in a resonance, a nuance. It's a question of proportion, or to use a photographic metaphor, of depth of field. Each reader/lens will adjust to it, will adjust it, somewhat differently.

Is it possible that "A Scene at Lake Manitou" is neglected because Scott's reputation has rested mainly with academics and academics aren't exercised by relatively simple poems? Simplicity often seems to require little analysis.

Perhaps that's not it; "The Forsaken," a much more famous poem, is also straightforward. Perhaps there is something else: in the attempt to gauge how Indian the so-called Indian poems are, shaving off points of authenticity for distance from the "real thing," it's possible to forget to feel the emotion these poems generate. In the absence of "compensating" complexity, the critical reputation of "A Scene at Lake Manitou" may have suffered from that tangential approach. I would like to see its Indianness muted and its lovely humanness praised.

NOTES

1. Somebody, either myself or Jean S. McGill, is inventing a path through the passage just quoted. In *Edmund Morris: Frontier Artist,* McGill deciphers thus: "a young Indian was dying of consumption and we visited him. It was a picture of loneliness. His wigwam was placed by the lake, far removed from the others. Boughs of trees had been placed over it to keep off the scorching sun but they had become dried up. Day after day like a wounded animal he awaited the end. It came quickly that night. A bull strayed into his tent and the boy died of fright, doubtless thinking in the dusk that it was an evil spirit. He had no near kin. The Indians were afraid to enter the wigwam but the Chief knelt by his side and read a sermon from their syllable bible or prayer book" (64).
2. See David Young, et al., *Cry of the Eagle: Encounters with a Cree Healer,* "an account of what a Cree medicine man [Russell Willer] was able to express to outsiders about the way he perceives the world and how he attempts to transform his vision into action" (vii).
3. "The Mission of the Trees" was written in November 1899, perhaps as a result of Scott's first Indian Affairs visit to Northern Ontario. The dying boy with almost the same name (Matenack/Matanack) suggests a comparison of the two poems, but they aren't much alike. "The Mission of the Trees" is a sentimental ballad metrically reminiscent of "Hiawatha"; "A Scene" is in free verse. There is something of the same pagan/Christian tension in both poems, but handled very differently. The "bad guys" in "The Mission" are pagans who turn on "Mizigun, the mighty hunter, / And his dear son Matenack":

   "These two Christians," — cried the pagans,
       "Breed our hunger and our woe,
   Let us kill them and their spirits,
       They are turning Wendigo" (*Poems* 309)

   Christian faith wins out in the poem, even over death; "A Scene" places the two religions side by side, with no overt valorizing of either.

9

"The Half-breed Girl"/ "At Gull Lake: August 1810"

I have a friend who is a painter, Tom Forrestall, and one day I asked him what he'd been doing that afternoon, and he said, "looking at windfalls." He'd spent the whole afternoon simply sitting and watching the changing pattern of sunlight on apples. Now the president of the Canadian Chamber of Commerce would probably consider that a useless act. But who knows? Maybe there is a God like the god described in the Old Testament and he saw Tom Forrestall looking at the windfalls that day and decided that on second thought he wouldn't destroy the world. Maybe the whole show will fall apart if there ever comes a time when there's nobody left to look at the windfalls.

Alden Nowlan, "Interview with John Metcalf"

NO CASE NEEDS TO BE MADE for anthologizing "At Gull Lake: August 1810." A magnificent poem, it is recognized as such. It has been much discussed, but far from exhaustively. One of the reasons for the considerable attention it has received, again, is the vortex of the assimilation debate that has flattened out the variety of the "Indian" poems. Dropping that context not only frees up Keejigo, the core character of the poem, to be herself, it also clears the way for a different understanding of the poem as cultural critique.

"At Gull Lake" can be traced to the Treaty 9 trips only very indirectly through "The Half-breed Girl," a poem that was actually written in the North. It's possible that "The Half-breed Girl" was in some ways a rehearsal for "At Gull Lake." Both poems have to do with a woman of mixed heritage and turbulent emotions. But "Watkwenies" and "The Onondaga Madonna," two sonnets from 1898, show that Scott was embodying cultural betweenness in Native women long before the Treaty 9 negotiations were even conceived of. It may help to sort out the kinds of intermediacy embodied in Scott's

Indian poems if I move to "At Gull Lake" by way of the sonnets and "The Half-breed Girl."

"Watkwenies" and "The Onondaga Madonna" foreground the figure of an Indian woman stranded as a remnant of the Indian "nation" — the word Scott uses in both sonnets as an equivalent of "race," though "race" occurs in "The Onondaga Madonna," too. This feeling of racial obsolescence, the decline of a "weird and waning race," is what Scott catches in both sonnets. History has placed these poems in a context of bitter irony, of course; "waning" euphemizes an excruciating and not exactly natural process of decline. But despite this undercutting, both sonnets dramatize transition quite eloquently. They illustrate the "then" and "now" of "The Last of the Indian Treaties." Both are structured similarly, with the sestet representing a later stage in the decline of the protagonists and their race.

Except for the word "once," in the first line, the octave of "Watkwenies" is set in the past, when vengeance was a way of life. The octave may depict the scene in which Watkwenies ("the woman who conquers") won her name — knifing a sentry as prelude to an Iroquois attack on "the dreaming hamlet on the hill" (a little reminiscent of the beleaguered "little town" in Lampman's "At the Long Sault"). The word "hamlet" makes it clear that the settlement being attacked is European. In this eight-line scene from a larger narrative of incursion and resistance, it is clear that the old way is thriving. Scott takes a step outside the European value system when he naturalizes vengeance and reduces the white presence in the poem to the generalized populace of a "dreaming hamlet." Lampman's Iroquois are "not men, but devils, panting for prey," which goes to show that a wonderful poem may be built on cultural obtuseness. The rude awakening in "Watkwenies" is only implicitly the concern of the speaker, who watches objectively from a mental place somewhere near this woman with the bloodthirsty knife.

So there is more than a temporal leap between octave and sestet. A large shift — a complete reversal, actually — is added to the normal lapse of time between youth and age (as in "The Forsaken," for example) in Watkwenies and her Iroquois people. Her day has "perished." Whatever the Indian agent is paying her ("interest money" has caused some confusion[1]), it's quite clear that the era of reserves, the paternalistic system of white control, has now prevailed over Native independence and freedom. When Watkwenies "weighs the interest-money in her palm," there is much more than money on her mind. The image conveys an instinctive and helpless shrewdness about the difference between then and now.

There has been no commentary on the game of snow-snake mentioned in the last line. Watkwenies hears the shouts of the "lads" playing as diminished echoes of the "war-whoops of her perished day." The main effect of the simile is ironic: the sounds that once meant battle now mean something close to what white people would call, in an athletic context, "rooting." The boys are throwing their snow-snakes, or wooden javelins, into a raised launching pad made of ice. The snakes, carved in pairs from the same sapling, have been cured, weighted at the front, polished, and then waxed for the day's weather conditions. They might slide as much as a mile, depending on the terrain, through a groove dragged in the snow by a log. The cheering encourages the snakes of one's own team and retards those of another. In "Watkwenies," the game represents what survives of an entire way of life; but in a more mundane sense, it contributes to the realistic texture of the poem. It lends the speaker authority, even if the reader has no idea what snow-snake is. Incidentally, whatever standing the pastime had in the Six Nations in Scott's time, it now survives as a serious and demanding adult winter field sport, the recreational counterpart of useful Native inventions, such as the snowshoe and the toboggan. In a small way, the survival of snow-snake is part of the aforementioned historical irony: not central to the poem, but not irrelevant, either.

E. K. Brown says that "The Onondaga Madonna" is about "the tragic confusion of the *métis,*" and he universalizes the story (as he does "The Forsaken," with comparisons to *King Lear* and *Père Goriot*) by calling it "not the specific tragedy of a European-Indian mixture, but the general tragedy of all blood-mixture" (*On Canadian Poetry* 131). This might seem a reasonable paraphrase of the poem (picking up on "weird and waning race," "tragic savage," and "nation's doom," not to mention "paler than she") until one asks what it is about blood-mixture that creates confusion. There might be confusion in the mind of Maria Campbell (*Halfbreed*) or in the narrator of Beatrice Culleton's *In Search of April Raintree* and — though much less so — in Thomas King's *Medicine River*, but what does blood have to do with it? Blood means race, and race is a myth that as recently as Brown's time seemed a valid way of explaining difference. Brown is not endorsing any theory of racial purity, but neither is he specifying whether the tragedy he refers to originates inside (in a conflicted nature) or outside (as when the "purebred" scorns the "mongrel"). The tragedy of the Métis — who are often even less advantaged than the so-called status Indians — has a social and political explanation. But I think "The Onondaga Madonna" is really about the tragedy of assimilation, and is one of the few Scott poems of which this can be unequivocally said.

I'm not sure that the Onondaga Madonna is Métis. It's true that "Her blood is mingled with her ancient foes" — a sentence needing the words "that of" between "mingled with" and "her" — but how do we know the "foes" are white? "The stains of feuds and forays and her father's woes" that dabble her "rebel lips" (an odd image) also suggest some mixture, but not decisively. If the woman is of mixed blood, the "savage," the "pagan," all that energy of "war and wildness," presumably of the Indian in a natural state, certainly predominates. What is a "tragic savage"? A member of an obsolete culture? What A. M. Klein says of the poet in "Portrait of the Poet as Landscape" may help:

> We are sure only that from our real society
> he has disappeared; he simply does not count,
> except in the pullulation of vital statistics. . . . (50)

The tragedy, then, shifts to the Madonna's child — no saviour, no promise of life everlasting, but, ironically, of doom. "Paler than she" recalls some words from Francis Bond Head that Scott quotes in "Indian Affairs, 1840–1867": ". . . as regards their Women, it is impossible for any accurate Observer to refrain from remarking that Civilization, in spite of the pure, honest, and unremitting Zeal of our Missionaries, by some accursed Process has blanched their Babies' Faces" (338). Head can't have been completely in the dark about the Process. Whether or not the Onondaga Madonna is herself a full-blooded Indian, as they came to be called, intermarriage has altered her son's pigmentation. Even in him, of course, the "pagan passion" of his mother seems little diminished, with "the primal warrior gleaming from his eyes." Well might he feel impatient, gloomy, sulky (endowed with uninfantlike prescience), because presumably there will be about as much work for a warrior when he grows up as there was for Charcoal. He *is* Iroquois, though, and no "pale-face," likely because his context is Iroquois. He's as Iroquois as the dramatist Drew Hayden Taylor is Ojibway. If appearances were conclusive, Taylor would *be* white. But he has no desire to claim whiteness, he doesn't feel mixed up, and according to "Pretty Like a White Boy: The Adventures of a Blue-Eyed Ojibway" he finds it only mildly annoying when he has to correct mistaken assumptions about his identity. So much for the waning of the race.

ASSIMILATION IS A CONCEPT heavy with white guilt, and it carries an intensity that has compelled Scott's critics to look for it everywhere in the Indian poems, as if there were no other theme to discuss. If it weren't for "The Onondaga Madonna," and perhaps "Indian Place Names" (leaving aside the nonfiction prose), there would be little foundation for stressing the theme of assimilation in most of the Indian poems. Assimilation, to Scott, meant the disappearance of the race, and that is certainly the thrust of the cameo in "The Onondaga Madonna." But dwelling on assimilation reduces the interest and significance of most of Scott's characters of Indian or mixed descent to regard them merely or even mainly as representing racial types or combinations. The half-breed girl in the poem of that title, and Keejigo

Figure 14, PA-59559

in "At Gull Lake: August 1810," are both particular people, individuals, and they are quite different from each other. We need to look beyond the question of assimilation to understand them fully — along with the poems they are in. But the theme should be screened out only temporarily, for it's not as though these poems have nothing to say about dominated and dominating cultures.

"THE HALF-BREED GIRL" was written on July 26, at Brunswick House (so the poem is dated in Scott's notebook, but drafts of some stanzas appear about a week earlier). It's just possible that he has in mind the oldest girl in a group of three, whose photographs he took there. One (see figure 14) shows them looking sideways, with the eldest girl's face almost hidden by her shawl. This makes her eye in profile very eloquent — shy, almost haunted. It's almost impossible to identify the subjects of Scott's poems, as I've said, because his raw material gets manipulated in the interests of story or poem or both. But if this photograph of the group of young girls and the also haunting photograph of a young mother and child (see figure 15) so interest a viewer like myself, surely the living people must have interested Scott.

Let's say that the tallest of those three girls, resting slightly on the canoe behind her, is the one Scott had in mind while he was writing "The Half-breed Girl." What adjustments would he have had to make? Unless he knew something that the picture does not show — perhaps she could not be admitted to the treaty, not being Native enough — he might have had to give her a Scottish father, somebody like James Miller of Mattagami. Of course, the suggestion of a Scottish connection appears in the photograph anyway, in the contrast between her moccasins and the plaid of her skirt (or dress) and shawl. The women at Brunswick House seem to have been wearing a lot of plaid when the treaty party came through. Plaid seems less prevalent elsewhere, judging by other photographs, so perhaps the incongruity of Native women in Scots plaid gave way to a deeper image — of *congruity* between primitive heritages, Scots and Ojibway. Scott says nothing in the poem about the dress of the half-breed girl, but if he were reading something in the dress of that tall girl in the photograph, it might have been

> The reek of rock-built cities,
>   Where her fathers dwelt of yore,
> The gleam of loch and shealing,
>   The mist on the moor,
>
> Frail traces of kindred kindness,
>   Of feud by hill and strand,
> The heritage of an age-long life
>   In a legendary land. (Poems 55–56)

Figure 15, PA-59563

This is what the half-breed girl might see and understand if the contents of her mind were not obscured by shadows and turbulent mental weather, constantly changing without clarifying.

The whole poem involves a sort of haunting by this "something behind her savage life / [that] shines like a fragile veil." That something, "what she knows and knows not," is her Scottish heritage. It torments her because she senses it without being able to identify what it is, and because that heritage, with its "wells of ancient tears," is neither bland nor neutral. She is often haunted during the working day, throughout the year ("the morns of winter," "the summer mornings"), but the worst time is when "she is at rest," with nothing but her thoughts for company. The opening of the poem might be a little more clearly set at such a moment, but that must be what is meant by her freedom from trap and paddle, portage and trail, because stanzas 3 and 4 show her still following the Native way, trapping and fishing — though it's the smell of the summer net that makes her yearn. Why? Is the net Scottish in origin? In the chapter of *Great Leader of the Ojibway*, entitled "How We Used to Live in the Old Days," James Redsky tells of gill nets made of rope from toughened milkweed (119); in life outside the poem, the net could have been indigenous. Perhaps the smell of the net just happens to be what triggers the yearning in this unstable girl. It *is* more interesting to think of the net's odour as touching an atavistic memory of some distant Scottish port, but the evidence doesn't quite permit that.

Since she's a girl, rather than a woman, one possible explanation for the turbulence of her mind — mixed heritage aside — might be the turmoil of adolescence. Much of the intensity of her emotions will sound familiar to anyone who has passed through that torment. "She fears [stanza 8] for something or nothing / With the heart of a frightened child." And the last stanza is a very plausible picture of an adolescent, stranded between childhood and adulthood:

> She covers her face with her blanket,
>   Her fierce soul hates her breath,
> As it cries with a sudden passion
>   For life or death. (56)

The adolescence analogy only goes so far, though, since she is unable to accept that invitation from the rapids, "Deep, careless and free," in the second last stanza. The implication is that she could respond, were she Native only, and not possessed by uninterpretable foreign urges. The suggestion is that until she dies she will never be able to let go of a whiteness that separates her from the land. At least that is one way to read the calling voice:

> A voice that is larger than her life
>   Or than her death shall be.

Since "life *or* death" is what she cries for in the last stanza, the poem ends by conveying the uncomfortable feeling that the voice of the rapids is a dangerous siren song to one as emotionally unsettled as the half-breed girl. Suicide might be a tempting way to resolve tormenting contradictions.

"The Half-breed Girl," like "The Onondaga Madonna," is a lyric playing variations on the theme of paralysis. It's unlike "Watkwenies," which is a severely curtailed narrative. That is part of the latter poem's power. The sonnet form condenses — especially in the temporal leap from octave to sestet — a great deal of change. Fourteen lines dramatically condense the period from European contact to conquest. I don't believe this tight, imported form is less appropriate to the wild subject matter than the looser, more improvisational form of the later narratives and meditative poems. It's true that the invention of forms in and for this country represented a further stage of adaptation to it, but that doesn't rule out success in older forms. If a poem works, it works. "The Onondaga Madonna" seems to me a little unfocused (What is "full throated"? Does it make sense for lips literally to be stained with a bloody past?), but not because of the sonnet form. The sestet perhaps burdens the Onondaga child with a weight of consciousness that strains credibility, but otherwise it's clean and affecting — disturbing in fact. The quatrains of "The Half-breed Girl," the rhyme and the anapestic trimeter, the alternating feminine and masculine endings, also seem to me consonant with the material of the poem. Quatrain follows quatrain, enlarging the terms of the girl's frustration without offering any release — unless perhaps in suicide. The poem obeys the psychology it employs to the unresolved end, and it conveys that oppressive, pent-up feeling very effectively.

"The Half-breed Girl" portrays a divided soul. It stays very close to that tormented consciousness, and correspondingly away from ethnographic content. The only image that may need annotation from that perspective is the "eyes of dead souls" that the girl sees through the smoke hole at the top of the wigwam when she wakes at night. This is the only reference to anything inherently Native beyond the external details of setting, and it suggests the life beyond death of ancestors. Divided souls so interested Scott that he seems to have produced a series of oblique self-portraits, though he was so fascinated by other experiences, images, seasons at the moment of transition, of becoming something else.

"Bells," a minor Scott poem written in October 1918, has a middle section that stands out to the reader of "The Half-breed Girl." The speaker of this poem is the lyric "I," perhaps one step nearer to the author than the "she" of "The Half-breed Girl," who is moved by the sound of bells tolling at dawn, moved almost, but not quite, to recover something from his memory; not happy memories, but "tremors in the quickened pool of tears / Within the windless deeps of memory." A bit too much metaphor there.

Here is the stanza reminiscent of "The Half-breed Girl":

> Echoes are in my soul, —
> Consonances and broken melodies, —
> Survivals frayed and remembrances
> Vanished and irretrievable. (*Poems* 250)

This melancholy nostalgia, frequent enough in Scott's poetry, is a reminder that the half-breed girl's affliction, leaving aside the details of her particular life, is not uncommon. Her life is not so different from what Scott's was at times; not so different from mine. All poems are self-portraits more or less displaced; all are masks of the poet. "A man sets himself the task of portraying the world," says Jorge Luis Borges. "Through the years he peoples a space with images of provinces, kingdoms, mountains, bays, ships, islands, fishes, rooms, instruments, stars, horses, and people. Shortly before his death, he discovers that this patient labyrinth of lines traces the image of his face." (*Dreamtigers* 93). Scott's effort to step over into the life of another draws him into a middle place — the poem — where the reader meets him, recognizable or not.

IN THE LETTER to Florence Leslie Jones already mentioned, Scott says that "At Gull Lake: August 1810" "is founded on an incident narrated by Alexr. Henry Jr in his journal of 1810." Leon Slonim has chased down the source passage and published it with notes. From that useful spadework we know that Henry supplied the names of Tabashaw and Oshawan, though not Keejigo and Launay. We know that Alexander Henry was pestered against his will by a wife of Tabashaw, who wanted liquor and possibly even sex. Henry doesn't sound quite as brutal as Scott's trader Nairne, but his disentanglement from the woman earned her a firebrand in the face. The whole historical episode, at least with regard to the role of the woman in it, could hardly have been more different than the poetic one. Scott transforms a sordid-sounding episode, apparently caused by a loose woman, into the tragedy of a woman's innocence and devotion brutally spurned and brutally punished. There is tragedy between Henry's lines, in the woman's craving for alcohol, but nothing of Keejigo appears in Henry's external portrait. Keejigo is wholly Scott's creation — her fabulously colourful appearance and careful dress for love, the tumble of the contents of her mind, and the astonishing lyric she composes for Nairne. She is totally focused on the object of her affections. Her tragedy is that only the reader can afford to fall in love with her.

Something else of importance doesn't come from Henry's journal. The prairie setting is convincingly established in a few textural details that ground and authenticate the narrative: the poplar trees, the sedges and grasses at the edge of the shallow lake, the massive storm, so impressive in the huge prairie sky, and the intense rainbow that follows it. The few details of setting, the few strokes of layered characterization in what is, after all, not a lengthy narrative, create an effect of great concentration, great verbal energy. Scott may have invented Keejigo, but he could not have invented the prairie — "the plains that we have loved," he calls it in "Lines in Memory of Edmund Morris." He had to have been where Henry was — on the prairie, in a general sense — to root his poem in such particulars. Of course, he changed the locale from the Red River in southern Manitoba to Gull Lake, but this is not necessarily the Gull Lake in Alberta that Slonim (143n) says it is. In answer to a query from A. S. Bourinot, Saskatchewan archivist Allan R. Turner wrote that "The Gull Lake of the poem may be Gull Lake, Saskatchewan. Certainly the topography is similar. We have little information about traders in the period — 1810 — which Scott selects. Just this summer an archaeological party, digging at Gull Lake, produced in a level of material relating to the early 19th century, a buffalo scapula with a bullet hole in it" (ASB August 25, 1960). Turner need only have been aware of Henry's journal to know that Scott was using his historical sources freely. The Gull Lake Turner writes about is near the Saskatchewan town of that name, and also near the Great Sand Hills of Cree legend. Whether Scott was thinking of an Alberta or a Saskatchewan Gull Lake, I suspect that he had a particular topography stored in his mind from one of his tours of inspection and used it to anchor his narrative. "It is my contention — my superstition, if you like —" says Robert Louis Stevenson, "that who is faithful to his map, and consults it, and draws from it his inspiration, daily and hourly, gains positive support, and not mere negative immunity from accident. The tale has a root there; it grows in that soil; it has a spine of its own behind the words" (*Essays* 131).

Setting is more than background, as Lyle Weis has noticed ("Order" 102). The poem's descriptive opening riddlingly introduces the components of the narrative and the images that will be reconfigured (some of them much expanded) several more times until they're soaked with association. The second time over it, the peaceful opening can be understood as a verbal bud about to open.

The poem opens in the present, a century after the events of the narrative have taken place. Nothing has changed in the interim. The fixed elements of the landscape — the "reeds on the shore," the "sedges and grasses," the lake itself, "the rolling prairie" — of the setting are subject, as before, to the mutable elements — the heat of summer, winter freezing, the moon, the morning star, passing storms — all but the sporadic storms being recurrent, predictable, cyclical phenomena. Each scene-setting element is put into place and then into motion. They are not only the fixed elements of the landscape as it lies while all "proceeds in the flow of time / As a hundred years ago"; they are the structural armature of the poem, set to gather story and emotion.

Setting aside the narrative content, for the moment, let's follow the musical development of the setting through the poem. The first elaborations of a prairie motif are folded into the description of Keejigo. Along with the tantalizing hints of her leaping consciousness, there are fragments of prairie images:

> Flutterings of colour
> Along the flow of the prairies,
> Spangles of flower tints
> Caught in the wonder of dawn. . . .

The word "flow," a sort of fusion of "the flow of Time" and the "rolling" of the prairie, is eloquent in this passage, but the whole phrase, "the flow of the prairie," is really a new image of time and space combined; the prairie itself takes on movement. This is how the whole poem works: images are introduced, changed, changed again, always remaining fundamentally the same. So the poem "proceeds" (in that other process word from the beginning of the poem) incrementally and cyclically.

These images of fluttering and spangle are fragments of a larger fragment, the entire unit from "Keejigo daughter of Launay" down to "vague as shadows cast by a shadow" being an incomplete sentence made of many parts that float without a focusing verb. The view of the prairie in this long fragment impinges on the consciousness of Keejigo, who is barely aware of it, who imbues everything that enters her mind with a tinge of her passionate devotion to Nairne. The "star of the morning," the storm, the moon, introduced at the beginning of the poem, appear again, too, but lightly annotated. Keejigo is associated with the morning star, "Star she was named for," and the storm, merely a word in the opening, now has a voice of "windrush and lightning," and a sinister association with "the beauty of terror." The moon of the opening is now compared to a "prairie lily," to "pure snow," to "the beauty of peace."

It's possible to follow various aspects of this dynamic setting through the poem — the storm, for example. Here again the slide of words into new context quietly knits parts of the poem while it identifies Keejigo with the storm. It's not in Keejigo's mind that the storm first appears; she has painted on her face not only the moon of peace, but the storm of terror in the "light ochre streaks" that "scored" her cheeks. But this is only clear retrospectively, as the storm approaches, "scored with livid ropes of hail," and when, nearer yet, the "lightning scored with double flashes / The dark lake-mirror . . ."

This far into the poem (about two dozen lines), the setting has not only accumulated several emotional associations, but the poem has also established a pivot into its future, the storm climax. That is to say, the setting that is described as external at the beginning next moves into Keejigo's mind, all tinged with hope and innocent "premonitions of love and of beauty," and is then turned outward again, as the mental turmoil is enacted in the macrocosm. Keejigo's "premonitions" are prophetic without being fulfilling because of the dual nature of beauty (terror and peace). Love will be denied her because of the impossibility of her situation and the brutality of the two men she is stranded between. In fact, her impractical courtship of Nairne releases a storm of physical violence that ends in her disfigurement and death. During the hush before the storm, in "Breathless the air under their shadows," those prairie poplars make another appearance. When Keejigo is driven from her supplication before Nairne's tent, she goes "down a path by the lake," past the reeds and sedges, now "grey as ashes / Against the death-black water." The reeds and sedges are then "smashed" and the poplars are stripped of leaves as the storm blazes by.

Following these details of place through the poem shows how insistently Scott returns to them, attaching to them all the eruptions of one eventful August day when a drama of frustrated love blows up into the drama of a furious prairie storm. The setting is structural; it supports the theme-with-variations composition of the poem. Also, the prairie becomes almost interchangeable with Keejigo. All that happens externally on this August day, all that endures from day to day, year to year, is implicit in her loving mind.

Keejigo's physical description, dressed in her colourful best, reflects the flutter of her mind as she sits before Nairne's tent. Whatever she is doing there is delayed suspensefully until her state of mind has been introduced. Then we are told that Keejigo

> had found her hero,
> And offered her body and spirit
> With abject unreasoning passion,
> As Earth abandons herself
> To the sun and the thrust of the lightning.

Is it because she is both French and Saulteaux that her mind is whirling so, like that of the half-breed girl? Keejigo is "troubled by fugitive visions / In the smoke of the camp-fires, / In the close dark of the teepee. . . ." All that Keejigo "thinks" is in the present tense, but how can she be sitting before Nairne's tent and also be by the campfires and in the teepee? Different times and places are layered in her mind. This explains how both morning and night, storm and calm, there and here, past, present, and future can flit through her mind without anything predominating or fixing. The "fugitive visions" motif is expanded in images of layers or degrees of inaccessibility: "Dreams of sounds unheard — / the echoes of echo," premonitions "vague as shadows cast by a shadow." The absence of a controlling verb is what permits all this mental flow.

Is there a mixed-blood tragedy in all of this ardent instability? Keejigo is totally different from the half-breed girl in knowing absolutely what she wants. She is focused in "abject, unreasoning passion," open to Nairne as elementally as Earth to the thrust of the lightning (Earth being the only word other than "Time," and perhaps "Chief," that is capitalized in a discretionary way). "At Gull Lake" isn't centrally about a casualty of assimilation, then; it's a rather straightforward love tragedy. The vagaries of love itself are enough to explain Keejigo's turbulent consciousness. What sets her apart from the general run of lovers is a discipline of love so powerful that she scarcely registers the dangers of her position. The poem she speaks to her heart is like a mantra. She keeps speaking it after she has been driven away from Nairne's tent; perhaps it helps her to accept the firebrand: "She held her face to the fury / And made no sound." Her passionate innocence is apparently indestructible by anything external, even this terrible physical cruelty. There is no such serenity anywhere in "The Half-breed Girl." The two poems only superficially resemble each other.

Keejigo's mind is not only made up and determined in undivided devotion — emotional turmoil being to her no impediment to action — but she also expresses herself as an artist. I use the word "artist," rather than the more specific "poet," so as to include her self-decoration. She sits before Nairne's tent as a self-made visual icon, dressed in antelope skins decorated by the coloured quillwork that predates Native beadwork. The antelope and the porcupine are with her (totemically?), as are the moon and the storm on her cheeks. By the end of the poem, some of these decorations have come to seem like visual intimations of her fate. Like everything else, then, Keejigo's appearance is not neutral; it's part of the relational fabric of her life into which all things are interwoven. Antelope and porcupine are relatives of crane, wolverine, the wind, and the flower of Keejigo's lyric in which she identifies herself with each of these aspects of nature. She offers herself to Nairne as a metaphorical amalgam of natural things. The lyric is extremely lovely and sophisticated. The core of offering, "I am here my beloved," is repeated in each stanza, the "I" never explicitly attached to the figurative metamorphoses of Keejigo's imagination. The last stanza then contains the other two stanzas in the gentle imperatives ("Take the flower in your hand" and so on) that now bring the lover into the poem.

Nairne's return is "Drive this bitch to her master." The gross mismatch of feeling is shockingly ironic. Nairne is a trader; perhaps Keejigo's passion is alienating his customers. Not even a lover likes to be shot for love, of course, and though his command is brutal, Nairne can't be blamed for not returning Keejigo's love. He is apparently unmoved by her dress, and nothing of her music, spoken "to her heart," gets through to him. Is Keejigo stranded between two cultures or between two men? The latter, I believe.

The question most asked by critics of "At Gull Lake" is what might be meant by the ambiguous beauty in it — of peace, of terror — and I will end my discussion by attempting to answer them. But there is one other "problem" worth worrying a little. This is the image of the rainbow that marks the transition between the fury of the storm and the peace of its aftermath:

> The setting sun struck the retreating cloud
> With a rainbow, not an arc but a column
> Built with the glory of seven metals. . . .

Something other than the rainbow of nature is being described here: it's not curved, and it's made of metals. Of the two characteristics of this unusual rainbow, the metals are easier to make something literal of. Prairie rainbows are at times so intense as to seem translucent, bordering on the opaque. The seven metals might be an intensified metaphorical register of that fact. This is worth suggesting, but remains ultimately unsatisfying because no rainbow made of light is ever as solid as metal. Rainbows seldom take the shape of a column, either, but Fred Wah (or else his father, whom he addresses in this passage) seems to have seen one: a "rainbow over your youth vertical like that on the prairies that rainbow stood straight up into the sky on the horizon you'd think in the winter sun ice crystals could form unbelievable . . . " (*Waiting for Saskatchewan* 79). Perhaps both poets are thinking of the partial rainbow created when the sun shines on water vapour collected in a cloud.

D. M. R. Bentley takes a grand tour through hermetic texts and Scott's other poetry in search of evidence to support his idea that the rainbow image indicates "the presence in a small but important part of Scott's work of various images and ideas which are evocative of hermeticism . . ." (22). Thus, "According to the Alchemists, the seven visible planets correspond to the seven principal metals" (3), and so on. Bentley organizes a great deal of interesting information that doesn't connect with the rest of "At Gull Lake." His findings are tangential to Scott's work as a whole, in fact. Unlike Elise, Scott hasn't an arcane bone in his poetic body. His poetry acknowledges reality beyond reason, but I don't feel a source in any particular mystical system. Bentley is rightly tentative about his explorations. Is there anything of context for the image of that iconic rainbow elsewhere in the poem? Not really. Keejigo herself is a kind of rainbow — not only in the colourful quillwork, but in the vermilion "in the roots of her hair," the powder blue halo of moons on her cheeks, and the ochre marks on her cheeks. But all that, if artistic, is natural enough. There is also a certain solid physicality to the "livid ropes of hail," the "nervous vines of the lightning" of the approaching storm. Those "quivering vines of the lightning" are still flashing against "the purple deeps of the vortex" as the storm departs. One notices how not only solid but static the rainbow image is, and then perhaps thinks how active and passionate are all the colours in the poem, even the "flutterings of colour," "spangles of flower tints," earlier on. Whether peaceful or turbulent, the colours are part of the poem's "flow," the flux of experience, and part of its elusiveness. Might the rainbow be a momentarily solid and static iconization of all that is multiple and moving? The "*glory* of seven metals" is hardly a negative image," so there is no simple binary opposition between the multiple rainbow spectrum and the final solitary "snow-pure" light of the moon, "free of all blemish of colour" in "the heaven of midnight."

Still, in the second last verse paragraph, two complex images contrast vividly The first is not the rainbow alone, but all that colour stark against the lightning-scored purple storm cloud; the second is the moon, pure white against the "midnight" black background of the sky. To each of these visual images a sentence is devoted, and the third sentence (or phrase, rather) of the verse paragraph, "After the beauty of terror the beauty of peace," expresses the two images in different words, tells us what we have been looking at.

None of what I've said explains the artifice of the rainbow column, but it does show that it functions in the poem as part of the symbolic manifestation of "the beauty of terror." Attempts to rationalize the image should not obscure its enduring unexpectedness. The eye of reason can't transfix it, and yet nobody argues that it's out of place, like some metaphysical conceit in a realistic poem. I think readers have always sensed the rightness of the image, surreal rather than metaphysical. Can "the beauty of terror" be described? No, but a glorious, seven-coloured column, superimposed on a great pulsating bruise is both vivid and enigmatic enough not to diminish the concept.

Actually, the beauty of terror doesn't strike me as a difficult concept. Whoever asked the Scott experts what it meant, at the 1979 Scott Conference, got no answer. Maybe I can atone now for my silence then. I've already suggested elsewhere (*Bees* 82) that the beauty of terror makes sense as a version of the double hook of *mysterium tremendum* in Dennis Lee's vocabulary:

> Canadian literature has long included an experience which the theologians call *mysterium tremendum* — the encounter with holy otherness, most commonly approached here through encounter with the land — to which an appropriate response is awe and terror. It is a very different thing from alienation. ("Rejoinder" 33)

Exhilaration and fear is a common enough response to the otherness of wilderness, and it intensifies before manifestations of nature's power in storms — and earthquakes, volcanic eruptions, and floods, of course, but storms are Scott's favourite expressions of that power. The end of "Night Hymns on Lake Nipigon" is one good example.

But there's another useful gloss on the beauty and terror of storm in the Brontë section of Scott's travel essay, "Wayfarers." "One is prone to think of Haworth," he says, "as always in shadow and mist, the very centre of storm" (*Circle* 96). "Here was the nest of [Emily Brontë's] imagination and just beyond the wall was the source of its power and the solace of a troubled heart, — the moors" (99). "Here she discovered the beauty and terror of *Wuthering Heights* and brought to life the Shakespearean Heathcliff" (100). "The beauty *of* terror" condenses this "beauty *and* terror," but surely one better understands what Scott means in "At Gull Lake" by thinking of the dionysiac energies of Heathcliff and Catherine in *Wuthering Heights.* There is a "beauty of peace" in that book, too, but it pales against the passion of storm, the irrational, obsessional, even demonic power of a love that can never die. In *Wuthering Heights,* too, appears the same "primitive" interdependence of human and natural life that animates "At Gull Lake: August 1810."

IT'S INTERESTING that Scott should approach Haworth via a comparison with "the clarity of Canadian skies and the rolling, unconfined fields of North Saskatchewan where the wheat is ripening" (*Circle* 95). On the way to Haworth the sun "falls on a landscape which takes its interest from associations that crowd out any thought of a country innocent of events greater than sowing and reaping" (95). This is the version of Western Canadian history — a blank — that outraged Rudy Wiebe when he discovered the suppressed heroic stories of the Cree, who had occupied the land before him (see "On the Trail of Big Bear"). Ironically, "At Gull Lake" itself acknowledges the drama of a Canadian history that is not blank, merely because it isn't the drama of white people.

It's also ironic that the event in Canadian history embroidered into the poem issues from a perspective sympathetic to the Native others that Scott was, in his official role, doing his best to suppress. This is a conundrum of contradiction beside which the bright mysteries of the poem might well pale. Who cares about the meaning of the rainbow in a poem written by a man responsible for genocide? Sorting and resorting my own priorities, I'm often brought up short by this sort of question. If the answer is nobody, no person of conscience, then (living in words and off the proceeds of words) I've been wasting my life.

But it's not a good question that sorts words and action, literature and life, into completely different compartments. Outside of the care of committed and loving and disinterested custodians, orphan words go bad and they kill. All our care cannot prevent them from sometimes doing so anyway; then imagine a world, of words, without us. Hard questions make us try harder, though. This one takes me back to Nairne. His appearance in the poem is as brief as it is brutal, but it lasts long enough to establish him as a standard European. He cuts a figure disturbingly like the Scott of the nonfiction. This Scott is not brutal (no successful bureaucrat is), but he is like Nairne in being *outside.* He is alienated from the people he administers. The failed contact between Nairne and Keejigo indicates a new way of expressing the old Scott/Indian conundrum. Keejigo's world, that lovely, integral microcosm, was created by a Scott who went *inside* it, and thus is not like Nairne.

"Labrie's Wife" shows Archibald Muir's cultural blindness ironically, from a point of view near him; "At Gull Lake" goes inside Keejigo to flip-flop the irony by turning the trader into the Other. Keejigo is fully rounded and Nairne is flat, and that puts the cultural shoe on the other foot. It's like seeing the Treaty 9 party through the eyes of Nistonaqueb. The exchange is so thoroughly realized that *of course* we wonder why it couldn't have carried over into Scott's life and work. But the poem is a story, not a platform, and stories have a way of telling themselves. Separating ideology from story is as easy as getting the yoke without breaking the egg. But an omelette can be nourishing. Telling so movingly of a cultural impasse as to unite reader and underdog, "At Gull Lake" encodes liberating knowledge.

NOTES

1. If "interest money" is treaty money, why not use the understood term? Melvin Dagg assumes an equivalency of the terms. Watkwenies "knows what is owed her, 'she weighs it,' it is only 'the interest money,' and as head of Indian Affairs Scott also knew what was owing — the principal. Treaty money is merely interest, tokenism" (Dragland, *Book of Criticism* 186).

10

Captured on the Wing: "Lines in Memory of Edmund Morris"

Dear Scott

You have joined our club as a lay member have you not? The private view is on the 9th May. The Proctor & Ernest Lawson come from New York. The other Lawson from London. Make an effort & slip off. Meet all the patrons. It would do you no small bit of good.

Yours Sincerely
Edmund Morris

IS THIS THE FAMOUS DOCUMENT referred to in the opening of "Lines in Memory of Edmund Morris," the unanswered letter from Edmund Morris?[1] Only the legendary bad handwriting and the reference to Phimister Proctor tie this letter to the poem. And the reader *can* actually decipher the specimen after perhaps half a dozen passes at it. The problem of decipherment here is not quite equivalent to going cold at "Cuneiform or Chaldaic," though sometimes it is with Morris. Some of his correspondents might have preferred cuneiform; cuneiform is legible once you have the key. The 1906 diary is a struggle, as must have been the western diaries written between 1907 and 1910. We owe the publication of those fascinating journals to Mary FitzGibbon's efforts. If Scott had literally been "poring over" Morris's "script," trying to figure out how to answer it, we would expect to find in it, in Morris's "famous scribble," words capable of sustaining the alternative readings Scott supplies in the second verse paragraph of his poem:

I gather from the writing,
The coin that you had flipt,
Turned tails; and so you compel me
To meet you at Touchwood Hills:

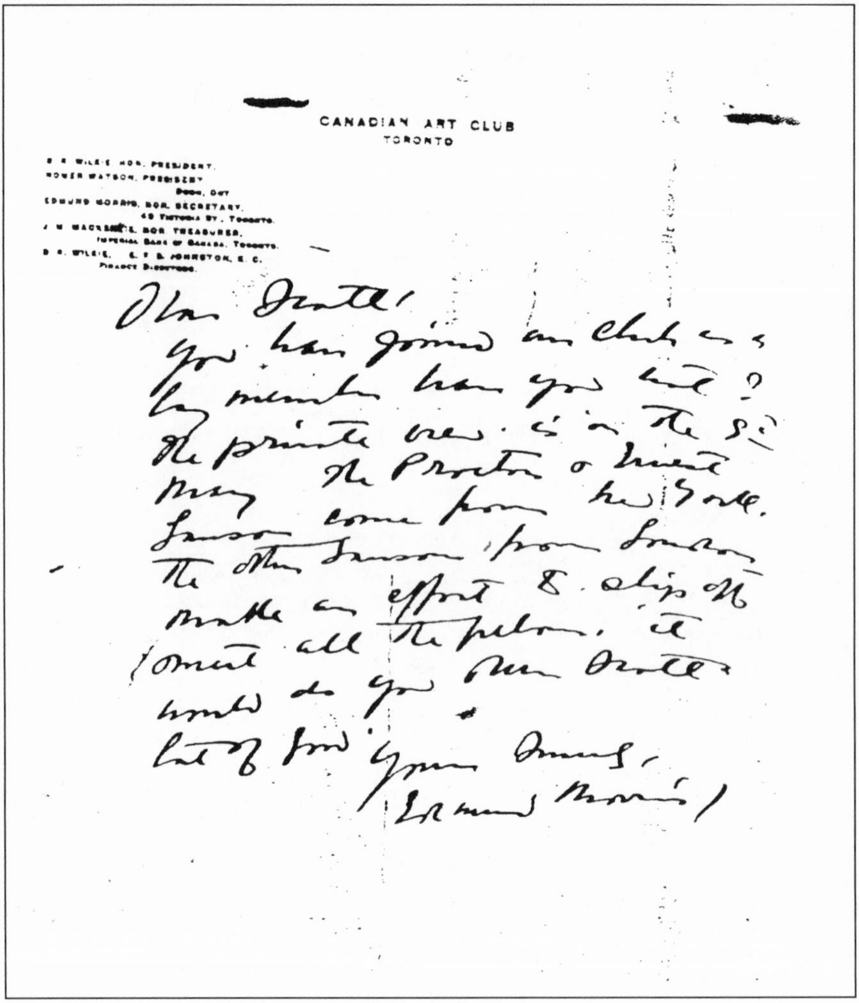
CANADIAN ART CLUB
TORONTO

Figure 16, letter to Duncan Campbell Scott from Edmund Morris

> Or, mayhap, you are trying to tell me
> The sum of a painter's ills:
> Is that Phimister Proctor
> Or something about a doctor?

Perhaps we should be looking for another letter written some time before Morris died, by drowning, on August 26, 1913. Perhaps not; the epistle — in this case an undeliverable letter to a friend — is a genre that contributes an armature to the elegy, and Scott may also have been fictionalizing Morris's letter, or combining more than one of them. "Nobody knows."

Morris was travelling with the Treaty 9 party in 1906 on commission from the Ontario government "to portray the Indian leaders involved in the transactions. His success in this assignment," says Mary FitzGibbon, "gained him another commission from the Ontario government in the following year, to portray major figures in the tribes living father west" (*Diaries* 3). The treaty trip was thus for Morris what it was for Scott: the start of something artistically important, and it's appropriate that Scott's elegy, set in the West, where Morris spent much more of his time among the Indians, quietly folds their 1906 experience into it.

The issue of sources for "Lines in Memory of Edmund Morris" is as important and interesting as for any of the other poems I've been writing about. Following them up is a way of sketching in some of the features of the man Scott was remembering. And, as before, remarking on the sources from which they derive (slightly effacing the boundary between life and poem) conveys a sense that the poem was constructed of choices and shapings of the original rich experiences it gathers together. As before, a survey of the backgrounds reveals Scott manipulating fact to serve the truth of the poem. And since the sources are geographically and otherwise more various than those of the other poems, annotating them contributes proportionally more to its interpretation. I read Leon Slonim's notes to "Edmund Morris" with interest and gratitude, but I want to induce those backgrounds and sources into a dance with the meaning of the poem.

Why Touchwood Hills, for example? Perhaps something resembling the words did appear in Morris's original letter, if there *was* a single original, but more important than its mere reference value is this first introduction into the poem of the prairie, which is the setting for most of its stories. "Touchwood Hills" is, as Slonim says, "a group of hills in central Saskatchewan" (south-central Saskatchewan, actually), but they are also in the vicinity of a group of Cree reserves not far from Fort Qu'Appelle, a place that figures later in the poem. Even Phimister Proctor has something of a western connection. He was, as Slonim notes, a member of the Canadian Art Club to which Morris devoted a lot of time and energy; specifically, he was a sculptor whose work Morris actively promoted when he was out West in 1909. While discussing with the premiers of Saskatchewan and Alberta the matter of commissions for Indian portraits of his own, Morris suggested commissions for Proctor — "to make statues of buffalo for either side of the entrance of the [Saskatchewan] parliament Bldgs. & for the prison," and "an equestrian group of wild animals of Alberta for the grounds of the [parliament] Bldgs" (*Diaries* 88). The buffalo actually showed up, according to Mary FitzGibbon, standing on "either side of the stairway in the entrance of the Manitoba legislature" (128n). A photograph of Proctor's sculpture "Indian Warrior of the Plains" illustrates Scott's essay "Indian Affairs 1867–1912" (617).

So Proctor is something more than a fascinating name. He is another artist — like Morris, Scott, and Sakimay — concerned with recording a vanishing way of life. Sakimay was probably one of those aboriginal artists Morris encouraged to record his exploits on buffalo robes. That is to say, it's quite possible that Sakimay's "painted robe / Where in primitive pigments / He had drawn his feats and forays" had originally been supplied by Morris himself. One of his steadfast purposes in the West was to preserve what he could of a vanishing aboriginal past. To that end, he took photographs, painted portraits of Indian "types" (*Diaries* 67), encouraged governments to commemorate Indian heroes, collected Indian artifacts, history, and legends, and supplied Indian artists with the robes for recording their past. Legends interpreting some of these pictorial histories may be found in *Diaries*, and some of the robes are now in the Morris collection at the Royal Ontario Museum.

There is no written evidence that Scott and Morris ever sat together in Sakimay's tent, with the kinnikinnick[2] and the stories, but *Western Diaries* shows that they at least met in the vicinity. Around July 25, 1910 (he is not punctilious with dates), Morris mentions meeting in Regina, "D. C. Scott the poet & his wife. He has been to the coast & is on a tour of inspection of the reserves, now going to Duck Lake & File Hills" (154). Then, at Lebret on August 9, he was "surprised to find D. C. Scott, Wm. M. Graham & their wives" (155). On August 10 he writes, "Go with Scott & Graham to the Sioux Reserve — Standing Buffalo's" (155). The only other reference to Scott in the journal is interesting in view of the official position on Indian ceremonies. On July 21, Morris writes that he has agreed to "speak to Graham & Scott to see if . . . all the Indians might have a dance on their respective reserves but would make no promises" (140).

On his travels, Morris often heard complaints about the government, and he thought many of them justified. "The present Government seems determined to break the reserves" (120), he says in October of 1909. If he didn't always identify Scott with the government, as his continued warmth toward the poet suggests, perhaps that was owing to his ability to distinguish between the man and the civil servant. Perhaps there *was* a real difference.

At any rate, when Morris died it was not only Scott who lost a friend; the Indians did, too. Possessing private means, Morris had no authority beyond himself to answer to, no need to drive himself the way he did. But he pursued his career in art and took up causes. Canadian art was one, the recording of Native culture was another, and the interests were combined in his portraits. He was given various names by the Indians he met, but the one that has stuck was bestowed by Blackfoot chief Running Rabbit: "Kyaiyii, sometimes Bear Robe, after a great Blackfoot chief he had heard of as a boy" (*Diaries* 18). Morris was no detached observer of Indians. He was capable of joining their dances (this never seems to have happened in the summers of 1905 and 1906), and he caused a sensation by singing an Ojibway song at a Stoney camp in Morley, Alberta (*Diaries* 52). We don't know whether or not others in the treaty party were paying that kind of attention to Native culture in 1905 and 1906, so it may be wrong to single Morris out from the company, but I can imagine him listening to Jimmy Swain's fiddle with different ears than Scott's. The example of Morris's "inconsequent rhymes" that Scott records in his poem, after all, is from an American folksong whose first line appears in "Tom Dooley," but whose rhythm is likely that of the sprightlier "Get along Home, Liza." "[K]eep on singing, Morris, you son-of-a-gun, singing all the time or you're lost and Canada can't do without *your* stuff" (McGill, *Edmund Morris* 152), wrote another friend. Apparently Morris was something of a vocalist. To pick up an Ojibway song he must also have been a man with open ears.

"Lines in Memory of Edmund Morris" is set on the prairie. It makes artistic sense, preserves the poem's geographical integrity, that those parts of the poem likely inspired by the 1906 Northern Ontario journey should not be tagged as such. But the only time Scott definitely travelled with Edmund Morris was in 1906. The section of the poem beginning with "How often have we risen without daylight" probably derives from 1906, if the "we" includes Edmund Morris. It seems to, at first, but soon begins to shift and broaden to include artists in general — those who wish to render the sliding passage of experience from one state to another. The "we" in the poem is encumbered with nothing of the welter of a travelling treaty party. There is, as with certain of the other poems of northern lineage, a plucking of the central personages out of the social context in a sort of closeup or filtering effect. Scott may have gathered his predawn ("without daylight") experience mainly in 1905, when some force, possibly T. C. Rae, was driving the treaty party to rise much earlier than it felt obliged to do in 1906 — and also to travel on Sundays.

Was Scott present in 1910 when Morris painted Nepahpenais (Ne-pah-pee-ness, Scott spells it in the poem), the Saulteaux chief whose name means Night Bird? Morris's diary doesn't say. It may be that Scott is conflating what he found out about Morris's activities in the West with those of 1906, when Scott certainly observed Morris painting. Scott's photograph of the sitting of Chief Cheesequinini (figure 17) proves that. Morris actually painted Nepahpenais "at least five times" (Simmins and Parke Taylor 54). On the occasion in 1910 when the chief was one of several sitters on the same day, Morris's diary records a good deal of what Nepahpenais told him about his battle experiences and his guiding for the HBC. Scott is not mentioned, and it sounds as if Morris must have been listening, rather than singing. Again, on July 17, 1908, Morris makes no mention of Scott as being present at the Crooked Lake agency where "The Indians are assembled for the

Figure 17, PA-59587

Treaty payment" (67). But this day was particularly interesting because Morris painted not only Nepahpenais but also Acoose, son of the Acoose (or Akoose) of Scott's poem. Morris also met the father and recorded his story:

> I paint Acoose, Man Standing Above Ground. He is 61 years — his father still lives, kept by the priests, though he is 103 years. His mind is quite clear & I talked with him in French. He is blind & his skin looks like parchment. His name was known far & wide in his time. Acoose was the fleetest of the Saulteaux. He used to compete with the whites in races & always outrun them. He went to hunt moose once & fell in with 9 elk. His bullets had slipped through his pocket so he ran them down the first day then drove them 60 miles to his own camp at Goose Lake & killed them. This brought him renown in his tribe. (67)

Scott may have had the story of Acoose either verbally from Morris or from Amelia Paget's book, *People of the Plains,* which Morris had also read. Morris received a copy of the book in July of 1908, just after having marked Poundmaker's grave — a coincidence, since his portrait of Poundmaker, from a photograph, appears in the book, as does his 1906 pastel of the Ojibway Cheesequinini. Morris corrects Mrs. Paget about the elk in a marginal note: "Mrs. Padgett [*sic*] is wrong in referring to them as deer" (67). He must have later changed his mind about the deer, or else come to see the interchangeability of such detail in the oral tradition, because he calls them deer himself in the catalogue to his 1909 exhibition. Scott, however, makes them antelope.

Poundmaker[3] had died while visiting Crowfoot in 1886. Morris's guide to his grave was John Drunken Chief, who

> asks me to write on a slab to mark the last camp of his uncle Crowfoot. The circle of stones with the small circle for the fireplace is still there. It was in a beautiful spot on the prairie above the cut bank of the Bow overlooking the valley & the Blackfoot Crossing. The Indians always encamp in beautiful places. (92)

Morris painted an inscription on a stone for Crowfoot a few days after visiting the Sioux reserve with Scott and Graham, but there is no evidence that Scott saw him do it. Maybe that's why he misrepresents Morris's act of remembrance — painting a marker, not marking "the site of his tepee / With a circle of stones." Those stones had still been there, luckily, and they can be seen in a photograph Morris took and used to illustrate "An Ancient Indian Fort," his article on a site he discovered in the same area ("this valley of the Bow is of great historical significance" [257]) of the Blackfoot Crossing that so fascinated him.[4] Scott's poem is true to Morris's genuine feeling for Crowfoot, but the word "pastime" — pulled into place by the need for a rhyme with "last time" — suggests neither that Morris was asked to mark that sacred circle nor that he came to revere Crowfoot. Respectful references to the great chief abound in the *Western Diaries*.

Melvin Dagg sees the reference to Napi ("Napiw," in Scott's spelling, but the rhyme is with teepee) applauding Morris's memorializing as evidence of the "depth of Scott's understanding and sensitivity to the Indian" (185), but the sensitivity may actually be Dagg's. To be sure, Scott must have understood that Napi (Old Man) is the Blackfoot trickster/creator. He could have learned that much from talking to Morris, or reading Amelia Paget or other sources. He may have known some version of the creation story Dagg quotes from George Bird Grinnell's *Blackfoot Lodge Tales* (a source for both Morris and Paget, as well), and a reader does need to identify Napi in order to understand the compliment being paid to Morris. But, after all, Scott has done nothing but use the name. How much he knows beyond that is impossible to tell. Napi's unglossed appearance is important, however, because it opens the poem up to a reader's active participation. The word, the name, is therefore made to seem like one the reader ought to know. Napi's importance is palpable before the reader understands why.[5] This is a brilliant move technically; if it sends a reader out to the source, so much the better. Today, sorting out how much Scott knew about Napi seems less important than asking who Scott was to speak for him.

There is a curious juxtaposition in the section of the poem that begins with Crowfoot's grave. Crowfoot was the chief of the great Blackfoot Confederacy, and he's odd company for Sakimay and the Saulteaux. As the story of "the man without a name / The hated Blackfoot" suggests, the interval of the "evening at Qu'Apelle, / In the wigwam with old Sakimay" (of the Crooked Lake reserve where Akoose was painted) is a transition between stories about ancient enemies. That interval is, in fact, a sort of time machine, whose mechanism (besides the kinnikinick) is the robe on which Sakimay has painted "his feats and forays." Perhaps the legend of the Nightmare Blackfoot appears on the robe; the word "foray" in the account may suggest this, but not necessarily. The legend, presented without any commentary, conducts the reader to a time when the "supernatural" was real. "Legend" it may be that Sakimay recounts, but he tells this nightmare as an eyewitness. A weird evening indeed for a couple of white men, and perhaps it's all the more impressive if Scott invented it, because once again the circumstantial detail makes the account feel convincing. It might be considered a failure to discriminate, this shaking of Saulteaux and Blackfoot into the same container, but it's worth observing that what connects the representatives of these two tribes in the poem is Edmund Morris. Also, the slide from tribe to tribe is easily accomplished by the memory whose operations are very much on display in the poem. Remembrance is near the core of what the poem is about.

What of the two place-names, Nantucket and the Isle of Orléans, that appear in lines 5 and 6? They speak of divergences in the lives of busy men; that is their main function in the poem. The specifics also help to root the account in North American geography. Such effects stand out in a body of poetic work little marked by geographic detail, but Scott was not merely being realistic. He had been visiting New England in 1913 (his in-laws lived there), and Morris was visiting Horatio Walker at the Isle d'Orléans when he was drowned. Walker was a member of the Canadian Art Club, and Scott also had occasion to visit him. A darkness settles over the Isle of Orleans when it's understood that Morris drowned there, in the St. Lawrence River, perhaps having fallen from the railway bridge near Ste-Anne-de-Beaupré, perhaps a suicide.

Rupert Brooke broke the news to Scott. Morris was one of the many Canadian contacts to whom Scott had introduced Brooke during the Georgian poet's North American visit. "I've just seen —" Brooke wrote Scott on September 12, 1913,

> with that sick catch in the throat one gets when one's skimming the paper, and lights on bad news — that Edmund Morris was drowned lately. It must be a fortnight ago. But I've only now learnt of it by the chance of picking up an old Toronto paper. He was very good to me when I was in Toronto, and we made half plans for some great excursion North the next time I could get away to Canada for a summer. (TF)

Brooke wrote again in October to apologize for having "so abruptly" communicated the bad news.

All that I have learned about Edmund Morris, from his diaries, his articles, his paintings and photographs, from Jean S. McGill's book — all of it explains why Scott would have felt the loss of the man deeply enough to address an elegy to him. Not that this context is crucial. One needs to know nothing more about Morris than the poem offers to be convinced of the man's value as a friend of Scott and others, like Crowfoot.

Morris's death and the exercise of memory that it sets off is the poem's point of departure. Morris himself and the experience he and Scott shared (fictionalized or not) are the core of this philosophical meditation on the power of memory, and the nature of art and its relationship with being, this threshing of life to its kernel. This poem inspired by a death ends by affirming life. Morris is the occasion; deep emotion about his loss sends Scott deep into the genre of elegy, deep into life.

"Lines in Memory of Edmund Morris" is similar to "The Height of Land," in that it issues directly from Scott's experience. Both are autobiographical, meditative poems, in which Scott attempted to distil his thought. They are poems of lyrical thinking, something that Scott's friend E. W. Thomson (who had never heard of Morris) noticed about the former. Writing to Scott on July 29, 1915, Thomson observed that "The Form throughout has the exceeding merit of seeming made by the Thinking. Nothing superfluous, nothing forced; some elusiveness of meaning enchants to close attention, and completes the charm" (PA/DCS).

Was "Thinking" what Scott meant when he said that "poetry must have brain at the bottom of it or it is nothing" (*Some Letters* viii)? He uses exactly the same words in a 1920 letter to Pelham Edgar, going on to say about Yeats that "too often his [poetry] is as you say mere Irish moonshine" (ASB). Is brain incompatible with myth and music? Maybe Scott wanted to distance himself from the Canadian artistic standard as represented by Douglas Bush in 1926: "Our writers think that tourist enthusiasms before mountain or rivulet make cultivation superfluous; indeed they seem to fear that some fundamental brain-work would take the bloom off their spontaneous emotions" (217). Gordon Johnston feels that Scott's emphasis on brain is "giving away his belief that a rational perception of the world is primary" (13), and it is probably true that too much reason and too little inspiration explains the production of indifferent poems. But Scott may have believed that "intuition is the measure of knowledge"; "The Height of Land" ends by asking if that is so. "Lines" and "The Height of Land" show that brain and art may be quite compatible. "Lines" is more intricately constructed than has yet been pointed out, and its (lyrical) thinking is conducted in layers of metaphor that stack up much more thickly than a reader notices at first. If the measure of a poem's thought is the difficulty of constructing an interpretation capable of doing justice to its intricacy and nuance, then the seemingly accessible "Lines" turns out to be tougher than it looks.

I don't share Thomson's opinion of "Lines" as "perfect art." Some of the rhyme is forced. The word "pastime" only stands out when it's (unfairly) compared to the actual experience it isn't meant to represent directly, but "glow-peaks," coined to rhyme with "snow-peaks," hardly makes sense on its own. "Inditing," to rhyme with "writing," is heavy, too. One might object to "fist" as a rhyme for "mist," except that Scott actually used the former term as a synecdoche for his own handwriting in his letters. There are a few of Scott's personal clichés of archaism or poeticism: "clomb," "tenebrous," "even" (for evening), "pellucid," "snood," and "shell-tint." When Scott asked Edgar for comments on the poem, he suggested substituting "passionate" for "passional," but Scott wrote back "I think I will let this stand. It means quite the same as 'passionate' and has a better sound (*More Letters* 50). More poetical, he meant; he sometimes let sound effects run away with him:

> How shall we transmit in tendril-like images,
> The tenuous tremor in the tissues of ether. . . .

"Duncan was of course very avid of verbal delights," wrote R. H. Coats to E. K. Brown in 1950. "I think he was a little too fond of strange words if they happened to be musical" (PA/EKB), he went on, and that's a fact. However, the musical excess is alliterative in the passage just quoted.

The weakest section of the poem follows the folksong Morris sings to himself. Scott "turns the charming nonsense song," says Gordon Johnston, "into a coherent, rational, and unfortunately, dull narrative of profound but unclear significance" (260). I don't think the story's significance is unclear — I'll return to it — but there *is* something off about this little narrative of Eliza and her lover. Partly, I think this is because of the forced transformation of the American folksong into a symbolic narrative set in some vague and remote European mountains. The thirty-line elaboration of the song is one of Scott's dream poems (like "Amanda" and "A Reverie"), embedded in a poem of quite a different sort. I'm not fond of it as poetry, but I am interested in its contribution to a formal metamorphosis more extreme (variable rhyme schemes forming couplets, tercets, quatrains, and blank verse in short or longer lines), and a structure more metonymic (sections abutting without transition) than that of any other Scott poem. Content aside, the whole poem is a conversation between elements regular and irregular.

THE AKOOSE SECTION of "Lines" is often picked out for anthologizing, which suggests that the piece is both self-contained and detachable — also that it's superior to the rest of the poem. I don't think so. There are problems with the poem, but it represents a formal stretch for Scott that is interesting even when it isn't working perfectly. Gordon Johnston goes on from the passage quoted above to say that the narrative based on the folksong "is one of the failures of the poem, but it reveals the structure of the whole. The poem moves from the presentation of a casual or minor event as remembered to an expansion of it, and then to a reflection on it. The second section expands on the first; the seventh expands on the climactic sixth . . ." (120). E. K. Brown feels that the sixth (Akoose) section illustrates the fifth, and that the seventh relates "The death of Akoose to the death of Edmund Morris" (*On Canadian Poetry* 136). Perhaps because neither critic finds the poem an unqualified success both are selective and casual, hinting at the nature but not the complexity of the poem's structure. I think "Lines" is much more sophisticated, structurally and otherwise, than anyone has yet suggested, but then only Sister Catherine Kelly has concentrated on the whole poem in itself, rather than as one of a group of poems.

Actually, it's a challenge just to describe the poem's movement — charting both the many connections between the seven parts, so divided by Scott's asterisks, and the differences between them. Except for the first part, each of the others, slightly reworked, could almost stand on its own. But it turns out that all are carefully and sometimes minutely interrelated. The most obvious binding device is that armature of epistle.

"Dear Morris — here is your letter" opens the poem, which begins again with the same address 17 lines later: "Dear Morris, (now I'm inditing / And poring over your script)," and again at the end of this section, "Yes, Morris, I am inditing — / Answering at last it seems. . . ." Part 1 is a sort of extended "address" to the letter, a moving into the poem proper. With its gentle humour, its natural mixture of rhyme and colloquial rhythms, it may seem little more than that, but some of the images introduced here turn out to hold, kernel-like, the substance of themes addressed much more extensively (and more explicitly) later in the poem. Part 1 *is* the whole poem. That is more or less true of the other parts, as well. After the first part, the refrain-like address fades out as Morris is invited to "look over my shoulder" in the opening to the next section. The writer of this letter can't shake his knowledge that the power of answering has literally been denied him, but he goes ahead anyway, defying death, that apparent barrier to communication. The address to a dead man would be a rhetorical strategy, nothing more, except that the poem later affirms the belief that "beyond the end" — personal and universal — something survives. And the poem goes on to make another (Rilkean) assertion: the love at the heart of what human beings, by living well, insert into the passing scene includes "the peerless love / Of things not seen." Part 1 keeps turning up in other parts of the poem, translated into figures less plain and simple.

The epistle address obviously patterns part 1, then, and it continues less explicitly remodelling the elegy form throughout the rest of the poem. In part 2, it's apparent in the "we"; in parts 3 and 4, in the address to "you." In part 6 Morris is addressed again: "Here, Morris, on the plains that we have loved. . . ." And when "we" returns in part 7, even if the pronoun now refers to humanity at large, it feels like a return to this friendship, as well. Very few such moves are needed to join the sections of the poem in the epistle genre. Beyond this sort of recurrence the lines of relation are more subtle.

The last section of part 2 is a pair of quatrains in ballad metre. They may seem like afterthoughts, because without them the other three sections of part 2 are structured quite tightly. What the quatrains do is begin a narrative in which the "new moon" (rising out of the evening of the previous stanza) is personified as a young heroine, "all shy on venturing / Into the vast night," lost but with a "silver star" given by the gods for companion. The story is not developed, scarcely needs to be, because its ballad-form fairy-tale opening locates us in a genre whose plot is relatively predictable. But a sort of development of the story, a variant of the initiation of the innocent, takes place in part 4, where the story of Eliza, born in Morris's nonsense verse and changed "into something wistful and strange," feels like a sidelong continuation of the story of the young moon. What happens to Eliza? A symbolic romance doesn't give you details, but it's clear that some sort of fall — such as might be experienced by a young woman venturing into the unknown in her "snood of virgin light" — takes place:

> Her lips with a wound were acquiver,
> His heart with a sword was sundered,
> For life was changed forever
> When he gave her the horn to blow. . . .

This not only continues the moon narrative; it also illustrates the "ache" of knowledge that replaces the plenitude of the "preconscious moment when love has fluttered in the bosom . . ." This movement, this fall, is not only important to the whole of "Lines," but is central to Scott's poetry as a whole, and I will return to it. For the moment it might be said that underlying the poem is an archetypal loss-of-innocence story that it would be too crude to name as that of Adam and Eve. The poem is quite secular, after all; the last section echoes the biblical apocalypse only in that the world as we know it comes to an end. The teleological metaphor, which continues into a rebirth, is organic: a tree bears fruit which blooms, rots, and splits to release its successor-seed. To this cycle, also, there is much more which will have to be discussed in its place.

Without the ballad stanzas, we have in part 2 a beautifully symmetrical, balanced three-part meditation on the North, "a land that man has not sullied with his intrusion. . . ." This passage supports the view of the North offered by "The Height of Land." The terms for North and the meditations about it are different, but there is the same sense of the land as uncrowded and magnificent — nature with no smudge of civilization or technology upon it. In this part of "Lines" a full day is rounded, framed by the opening half-way between a question and an exclamation — "How often have we risen without daylight" — and the beginning of the last section: "How often have we seen the even." Both of these stages of the day are seen as "passages" (combining movement with a sense of quotation, as of a work of literature or music, though what is actually evoked — Titian — is painting), or preludes to the day and the night. They are beginnings composed of change. There are "crystal forms" in the evening to match the "crystal dawn." The feeling is at once of hush and change, of a miracle of light, of colour, like another miracle, the formation of a bud. The mood is predominantly positive throughout, with just that hint of "ache" that follows the rise to climax of becoming. This hint is picked up in "the ashes of roses" in the second last line. The concentration on the stages of becoming throws the emphasis off ache and ashes and onto beginnings. In fact, we're in the presence of an imagistic version of part 7, where the rotten plant produces a seed "to kindle otherwhere." "Vanish and revive" is the phrase in part 2 that looks ahead to part 7, where the image of ashes also appears as a prelude to rebirth.

There is a very complex business going on in the mornings and evenings of part 2, especially in the mornings, whose purity in process is recorded in a variation on the image of the shrine (blending purity and passion), which appears in "At Gull Lake: August 1810" and "The Water Lily." And while the prelusive moments are being described, a three-part interrogation is being conducted, perhaps having to do with language, and certainly with art. Two of the questions are addressed to the apostrophized dawn: "How shall we distil your virginal freshness," and

> How shall we simulate the thrill of announcement
> When lake after lake lingering in the starlight
> Turn their faces towards you,
> And are caressed with the salutation of colour?

The third question is more general, but still full of awe for its subject and awestruck by the challenge of capturing and making intelligible a miracle:

> How shall we transmit in tendril-like images
> The tenuous tremor in the tissues of ether,
> Before the round of colour buds like the dome of a shrine,
> The preconscious moment when love has fluttered in the bosom,
> Before it begins to ache?

These questions are not answered before "how shall" melts back into the "how often" of the opening — except by what the words actually do. They do distil, simulate, transmit, even while the speaker calls into question the possibility of doing so, though the result is no worded version of what nature does. Something of how the dawn and sunset look and feel is combined with an insertion of "man" into the scenes — man for whom mere perception is not sufficient, who is always vulnerable to the fall into consciousness, words, art. My paraphrase lacks the subtlety of the poem, which may not be so rich in colour as a sunrise or sunset, but whose layers of metaphor hold a richness of their own: the sunrise is a plant growing a flower, which is the dome of a shrine whose opening is the dawn of fallen love. The critic has a challenge of transmission, too, caught up like the poet in that old romantic curse: the transcendent vision or miraculous experience dimmed by inadequate receptors in the poet, and then further dulled in words.

Lest the reader think I'm discovering too much self-reflexivity in part 2, let me flash briefly backward and then forward for a moment — first to the fourth section of part 1, when Scott first announces the theme of writing, of trying "to render / The tissues of fugitive splendour / That fled down the wind of living," and then to the opening of part 5, whose pessimistic take on life is rejected in these words: "But nay! That is a thought of the old poets, / Who sullied life with the passional bitterness / Of their world-weary hearts." Retroactively, the word "sullied" joins life and prehuman land, "man," and "the old poets." Words, too, can be intruders, invaders.

I have already said a little about part 3, about the bridge it creates between the old enemies, Saulteaux and Blackfoot, and about the "time machine" of Sakimay's painted robe. This parallels the poem Scott is writing. "Well I remember," he says. That is what he is doing, writing lines in *memory* of his friend that recall not only the friend but also some of those others, with their experiences, that fascinated him. Memory is one of the main themes introduced in part 1. "I would have you look over my shoulder," says the speaker,

> Ere the long dark year is colder,
> And mark that as memory grows older,
> The brighter it pulses and gleams.

Here is another revival that rebukes the passage of time. This one doesn't fade as the year does (the metaphorical life-year that in the word "colder" looks ahead to the apocalyptic time-year which fetches up in part 7 with forms of the "old world," "cold upon her marble heart . . ." but "pulses" like a heart and shines. The consolation of the elegy, understated in the single word "joy," gathers strength from the consolation of optimism that has been planted in each section of the poem.

Part 3 recalls Scott and Morris on the prairie — Morris performing a memorial rite for Crowfoot parallel to Scott's for him — in the presence of a man recalling his own "savage" past in art and legend. Part 4 follows part 3 quite naturally; the "I remember" of its opening harkens back to "I recall" in part 3, and then moves to the only passage that depicts Morris as an artist in his own right, as another who renders what flees down the wind of living, another of those who retard the flight. "Art grows and time lingers" under Morris's skillful fingers. But Morris does not linger. This section of the poem, the one generally considered least effective, is arguably of first importance, being the only one to refer, if obliquely, to Morris's death.

The narrative/song of Eliza and her beau (lover?) "has a change"; it's a tune called by death, played in a minor key. The narrative actually describes a sort of circle, though, beginning with the first two lines of Morris's song, containing the theme to be varied, and ending in a variation on it. The symbolic sounding of the horn turns out to have been a huge mistake of the sort that unforeseeably changes life for the worse. It releases the shadow to quench the colour of the mountains and obscure the chalet and all the beauty of the setting which recalls the wilder natural beauties of part 2. The stars are eventually "victorious" even so, as "a light rediscovered the chalet." The movement of this section is, then, like that of several of the others — into the darkness and out the other side. Not quite into joy, but light has the last word here.

Something else is restored at the end of this narrative: the mystery that was captured by Eliza's horn, a mystery meant to be free. One way of expressing the centrality of this part of the poem is to show that it highlights a question of the catching and freeing of "meaning" that is raised in other parts. It first appears in part 1, that slant introducer of important themes and motifs, in the joke about Morris's handwriting. His "famous scribble," that "cryptic fist," conceals "Meanings held in a mist." The humour almost disguises the resonance in the last line of other approaches to the question of meaning elsewhere in the poem. Meanings in a mist would be close to chaos; meanings *held* in a mist sounds more like order. The meaning that Scott seeks is not some sort of static paraphrase of the essence of life; he's looking for words to capture the uncapturable: "the preconscious moment" that Kristevans would now call the semiotic — preconscious pulsions and drives that survive in language as disruptions or distensions of its laws (Kristeva 40). In "Lines," something of the semiotic is alive in Scott's long sentences, his double meanings, his complex metaphorical conceptions. This thinking takes us back to Morris himself, to a friendship that avoided the frequent contact in which tensions are wont to surface:

> So memory has nothing to smother,
> But only a few things captured
> On the wing, as it were, and enraptured.

"Captured" echoes "held" ("meanings held in a mist"), and both are picked up in "caught," which refers to the cadence Eliza blows on the horn, "the meaning of life in one phrase caught." The catching of meaning is overreaching. It ruins the lives of the two collaborators; it releases the ambiguous shadow of death ("desolate, slow and tender" — and note the framing use of the word "tender" in part 2) that obscured the beautiful clarity of the mountain peaks. And the aftermath is a dark variation on "meanings held in a mist":

> The scene that was veiled had a meaning,
> So deep that none might know. . . .

The Eliza narrative holds the most negative aspect of the poem's inquiry into the vagaries of capturing meaning: catch it and you'll be sorry. Nobody does literally catch the "essence of this world" (the difficulty of the quest is a principal theme of part 2), but the imagined achievement can be dramatized in a symbolic narrative.

What is it the "old poets" say? How do they sully life with their world-weariness? They presume to catch the meaning of life in "one phrase" — or one sentence, at least: "Tears are the crushed essence of this life." Having entered it into the record, Scott rejects that verdict, the closure as much as the pessimism. The version he endorses is not only optimistic but in flux:

> We of the sunrise,
> Joined in the breast of God, feel deep the power
> That urges all things onward, not to an end,
> But in an endless flow, mounting and mounting. . . .

This is the spiral of progress that powers the ecstatic ending of "The Height of Land," rendered in a long flowing sentence very like the one that closes that poem.

"We of the sunrise." What shall we of the (1990s) sunset make of that phrase? Sunrise in itself suggests life, warmth, beginning, but in part 5 the word recalls the complex sunrise in part 2, where the loveliest moments are those *before* the literal and metaphorical rise of the sun, where the mystery of returning dawn is seen as both precious and fragile. Here is the rest of the context for that sunrise in part 5. "We of the sunrise" claim

> not overmuch for human life,
> Sharing with our brothers of nerve and leaf
> The urgence of the one creative breath, —
> All in the dim twilight — say of morning,
> Where the florescence of the light and dew

> Haloes and hallows with a crown adorning
> The brows of life with love, herein the clue,
> The love of life — yea, and the peerless love
> Of things not seen, that leads the least of things
> To cherish the green sprout, the hardening seed;
> Here leans all nature with vast Mother-love,
> Above the cradled future with a smile.

Tears of lament, "failure and weakness," are swept aside in a burst of rapture composed of two impulses, one instinctive and one willed. The instinctive "urgence of the one creative breath" is Scott's version of Dylan Thomas's "[life] force that through the green fuse drives the flower." The will-driven urge is the almost anticlimactic, duty-bound business that ends part 5:

> Persistence is the master of this life;
> The master of these little lives of ours;
> To the end — effort — even beyond the end.

These lines acknowledge that raptures of love and creativity aren't everything. Besides those few things effortlessly "captured / On the wing" (the terms are from part 1), life includes "the constant grinding of one mind on another." The wonderful given world is yet full of pitfalls, traps, obstacles to consciousness. It never fully opens to the mind, and yet the mind won't be denied approach. "Our brothers of nerve and leaf" are spared the "divine discontent and longing" (Grahame 1) of humans. We are driven to embrace life, despite the danger of sullying it with our worship. This happens symbolically in Scott's "Prairie Wind," in which the personified wind (a mask of the poet, though addressed as "you")

> paused on the fern-green margin [of a mountain tarn]
>   And saw on the surface stilly
> The face of a star in the water
>   That looked like a water-lily;
>
> Then you rushed on the frail enchantment
>   As if 'twere a passionate duty
> To carry to far away deserts
>   The charm of the virginal beauty;
>
> But the closer you pressed and regarded;
>   Ripples rippled over in fretwork
> And the vision was twisted and vanished,
>   Confused and astray in the network;

You hovered above the surface,
  For the waters to cease their tremble,
For the star to be liquid lily,
  For the colour to reassemble;

But the vision you found in the twilight
  You could never again recapture,
It was lost in one careless impulse
  In the first wild rush of the rapture. . . . (*Poems* 270–271)

Is the wind, troubler of waters, richer or poorer for having glimpsed what it can never study? The word "disconsolate" in the last stanza suggests the latter, but in Scott's poetry at large the question remains open.

It's quite clear from part 7 of "Lines" that a passive response to the riches of the world is not being endorsed, notwithstanding the hazards of active human response. The two elements, effort and love (Labor and the Angel?), are conceived of as having their combined effect, having *had* their effect, on the world. The "something" that escapes from the old world, finally run down and stopped, is what was there from the beginning, responding through time to the "urgence" of the "creative breath." This is "soul or essence, — / The sum of life": Meaning with a capital M. To this, something has been added by human habitation:

So the old world, hanging long in the sun,
And deep enriched with effort and with love,
Shall, in the motions of maturity,
Wither and part, and the kernel of it all
Escape, a lovely wraith of spirit, to latitudes
Where the appearance, throated like a bird,
Winged with fire and bodied all with passion,
Shall flame with presage, not of tears, but joy.

This vision of phoenix-like renewal out of the cold ashes of the world's dead self shows what is meant by "even beyond the end" in part 5. The intensity of effort and love is a Rilkean husbanding of the planet whose effects are real but can't be measured. Belief that progress is being made is an act of faith in "things not seen":

Where is the rule
To measure the distance we have circled and clomb?
Catch up the sands of the sea and count and count
The failures hidden in our sum of conquest.

One reason why Scott's optimism feels earned is that he sets progress into this immeasurable backdrop of time, against which "these little lives of ours" are played out. The spatial equivalent is the single line of cosmic context tossed into the description of the evening with Sakimay in "Lines":

> As the kinnikinick was burning;
> The planets outside were turning,
> And the little splints of poplar
> Flared with a thin, gold flame.

It's a pity Scott didn't apply the rigour of this thinking about time and change to his charges, the Indians, whose way of life he expected to see exchanged for a foreign one in his lifetime.

The story of Akoose, in part 6, is a tale of the survival of youth in an ancient body, of the spirit that made Akoose a legendary runner. His old age recalls the old world in the final section. He is "withered and spent," just as the old world is "shrivelled with ripeness." He, too, experiences a (temporary) return of youth:

> Once when sharp autumn
> Made membranes of thin ice upon the sloughs,
> He caught a pony on a quick return
> Of prowess and, all his instincts cleared and quickened,
> He mounted, sensed the north and bore away
> To the Last Mountain Lake where in his youth
> He shot the sand-hill-cranes with his flint arrows.

This second youth is brief, but it's surely effort "to the end." And survival beyond the end, seeing that Akoose does not die, but rather lies down with family ("the populace of leaves / In the lithe poplars whispered together and trembled"), "Gathered at last with the Algonquin chieftains," to sleep "forever amid the poplars, / Swathed by the wind from the far-off Red Deer / Where dinosaurs sleep, clamped in their rocky tombs."

The end of part 6, like most of the other sections, draws in much of the rest of the poem — especially in the last five lines:

> Who shall count the time that lies between
> The sleep of Akoose and the dinosaurs?
> Innumerable time, that is yet like the breath
> Of the long wind that creeps upon the prairie
> And dies away with the shadows at sundown.

Sleep is not death; from a sleep one may awaken. In this possibility, Akoose and the dinosaurs are contemporaneous, even though, paradoxically, "innumerable" time separates them — the same unmeasurable distance of time mentioned in part 5. Where do they meet? What is the eternal essence they share? There is no precise answer. But that breath of the prairie, introduced with the "yet," as though time were nothing to *it*, recalls "the [part 5] urgence of the one creative breath." This might feel like the breath of God the father, of Genesis, except that the anagogic figure in the poem seems androgynous.

Recall the innocuous-looking figure of the "aboriginal shy dwellers in the broad solitudes" in part 2, who

> Are asleep in their innumerable dens and night haunts
> Amid the dry ferns, in the tender nests
> Pressed into shape by the breasts of the Mother birds[.]

Look at the comma after "ferns." It carries the sense of "and," but the absence of conjunction permits the feeling that all of those "shy dwellers" will fit into the nests of the birds. Then look at the capitalized "Mother." The next time that word appears it's again capitalized and generalized into "all nature with vast Mother-love." So the figure that links the female containing figure with that of the male ("joined in the breast of God") turns out to be "pressed into shape by the breasts of the Mother birds." Or perhaps I should merely say, so as not to overstate these subtleties of interrelatedness, that the line in part 2 sends forth a tendril to touch both masculine and feminine images in part 5.

WRITING ABOUT THIS POEM has been an eye-opener for me. The act of putting the technique of the poem into my own words has helped me see much more clearly what I was only sensing before I began to write: the simultaneity of the parts of the poem, their tendency to nest one within the other. The meanings of the poem are not contained in any central kernel, because each layer is the same, and yet a variation significant enough not to be subsumed within any other. Should the narrative of Akoose serve only as illustration of the ideas and images that frame it in parts 5 and 7, or vice versa? Has the comic introduction of important themes any less gravity in the long run than their more seriously presented analogues? The poem's sections are discrete; their arrangement in sequence does lend greater emphasis to the later stages of the poem, but the absence of transition reduces the element of linearization among the sections.

It's interesting how little this elegy concentrates on its central subject. The poem is "to" Morris much more than it's about him. Morris and Scott and Akoose and the "brothers of nerve and leaf" make up a community. The poem cleaves to the heart of it, to the kernel of that entire community —

tiny in the context of time and space — and the source of rejoicing found in that is a consolation offered *to* Morris as much as it's derived, for survivors, from his memory. After all, a little of the "we" introduced in section 2 carries forward through "we of the sunrise," to

> What we may think, who brood upon the theme,
> Is, when the old world, tired of spinning, has fallen
> Asleep, and all the forms, that carried the fire
> Of life, are cold upon her marble heart —
> Like ashes on the altar — just as she stops,
> That something will escape of soul or essence, —
> The sum of life, to kindle otherwhere. . . .

The letter has faded, but not the sense of Edmund Morris looking over the poet's shoulder. What is said often feels as if it is said for both of them. The tears of grieving are dried in acts of loving memory. Morris is not dead; he's there between Scott's lines.

WHAT I HAVE JUST SAID is deeply felt. If I anticlimactically press on a little further, it's not to take any of that back. But it would be ironic if a poem about memory so impressed a critic as to render him amnesiac. Not having forgotten what this book is about, I want to revisit briefly the "land that man has not sullied with his intrusion." It might seem picky to point out that the line lacks an essential modifier ("man" should be "the white man"), but the usage that empties the North of inhabitants other than non-humans — ironically called "aboriginal" — inscribes an unfortunate habit of mind that still persists. In *Literary Images of Ontario,* W. J. Keith calls the North illustrated by Scott's story "Vengeance is Mine," "a rugged land that stifles human language as easily as it obliterates human distinctions" (119). The word "human" in this otherwise acceptable assertion is being asked to cover more than it can. For Archibald Muir of "Labrie's Wife," Indian laughter has at best "an unmeaning sound" (*Elspie* 149), but he is a character of 1806, in a story published in 1923. I doubt that Keith really wishes to reinscribe this old blindness. His chapter on "Ambivalent Indians" ends this way: "Perhaps the final image of the Indian in early Ontario was one that was romantic, aesthetically powerful, emotionally gripping, excitingly different — but, alas, not accepted as fully human"(49). Amen to that "alas."

NOTES

1. R.L. McDougall thinks not. He says in "D. C. Scott: A trace of Documents and a Touch of Life" that Scott, working on "Lines" by October 1913 "had before him Morris's last letter, probably written in the early weeks of July and left unanswered by Scott. It is not amongst the Scott-Aylen papers. But the invitation of the preceding spring is there, the only Morris holograph preserved in the file, and this note has its own connection with the 'Lines'" (137). I wonder. If we allow Scott some scope for invention, the preserved note is probably close enough. McDougall's decipherment of the note differs slightly from mine, which is entirely appropriate.
2. A smoking mixture that varies, but is typically made up of bearberry or sumac leaves, the inner bark of red osier dogwood, and (often) tobacco.
3. There is a story in Jean S. McGill's *Edmund Morris: Frontier Artist* that places D. C. Scott, bizarrely, at the burial of Poundmaker. McGill's source is a letter to Morris from the painter William Brymner, who claimed to have been present at Poundmaker's funeral himself. At the age of 26 Scott was neither the Dr. Scott McGill refers to nor the superintendent of Indian Affairs. It would be difficult to imagine *that* Scott digging Poundmaker's grave. The scene is so surreal as to be strangely compelling, even if impossible. If Scott had been in the West so early in his career, he would not have written to Pelham Edgar on May 22, 1901, about a proposed western holiday/inspection tour, that "it would make my work much more interesting to have some experience of western conditions." At any rate, Brymner's letter of September 19, 1909 (fascinating for its eyewitness account of a Thirst Dance), shows that the man referred to is another Scott, a farm instructor.
4. Scott may have been perpetuating an error first made by C. H. Gooderham, who remarks in the memoir quoted by Leon Slonim (15, 526) that "on one of [Scott's] visits to the Blackfoot Reserve I took him to see land marks which Morris had made when he was doing portraits of Indians in 1909. The Indians had shown him the spot where Chief Crowfoot had died and he had marked it with a ring of large stones."
5. This poem is no place for Scott to introduce the raunchy side of Old Man that Robert Kroetsch has such fun with in *The Stone Hammer Poems*. Kroetsch anticipates the cultural appropriation debate by acknowledging that he has stolen the stories, but invokes the trickster spirit of Old Man as his justification.
6. For an account of one of his swift descendants, see "Song for Mooshum: Paul Acoose," in Brenda Zeman's *To Run With Longboat*. "So tragic, that Mr. Scott," says the narrator after quoting part of the ending of "Lines," then she goes on: "The man I've heard about in the stories was anything but. He must have been close to sixty when he asked Mooshum Paul and his brother King and their cousin Felix Penipekeesick to run with him. Somehow, old Acoose not only kept up to them; he outran them. Old Penipekeesick saw what happened and he told old Acoose, 'I don't know why you're always showing off.' Old Acoose never lost his haughtiness. 'Hah!' he said, 'You're so slow. Just like an old woman!' He would have laughed to read about himself in Mr. Scott's poem" (218).

11

Gathering of Waters: "The Height of Land"

Something really does happen to most people who go into the north — they become at least aware of the creative opportunity which the physical fact of the country represents, and, quite often I think, come to measure their own work and life against that rather staggering creative possibility — they become, in effect, philosophers.

Glenn Gould, "The Idea of North"

We meditate with our whole lives: with our passions and mind and flesh and our past and our deepest hungers.

Dennis Lee, "Polyphony: Enacting a Meditation"

"HE MOUNTED, SENSED THE NORTH, and bore away . . ." He sensed the North. When the aged Akoose's instincts clear and quicken one last time, a mental compass points him to his heart's desire. His youth and the North are as one, though death is part of that equation too, because north is the direction of Akoose's last resting place. "Sensed the north and bore away" — why is that line so much more thrilling than, rationally, it ought to be. Why does "The Height of Land" so excite me? Are these variations on the same question? Apparently my mental compass points north, too, up toward and beyond the height of land.

My reaction to "The Height of Land" is a little more complicated than this, but North — the spirit of the North — is probably near the core of it. The pull of North is so strong that it could wreck this chapter, but I'll try just to sketch in what needs thorough exploration — a little of what I feel places "The Height of Land" near the core of the Canadian imagination. I'm not alone, sensing North, not alone in feeling a trace of permafrost in the country's southern margin. In even so urban a poem as "Civil Elegies," Dennis Lee finds the Henry Moore statue in Toronto's Nathan Phillips Square "flexed by / blind aeonic throes / that bred and met in slow enormous impact" (39), a chunk of the North in the centre of the south. The Moore is a symbol, of course, and our nordicity may be simpler to see in Clark Blaise's version of minds moulded by a country that really has no South:

> Winnipeg should not exist, except as an urban planner's act of defiance, an experiment on the heartless Russian model. Yet it does exist, like Edmonton exists, like Montreal exists, and the effects of that anomaly — the intense communalism, the isolation, the pride, the shame and absurdity of carrying on normal life at forty below — create a population of stubborn, sceptical survivalists, hungry for recognition and certification, a people born with the ache of anonymity and the conviction that they'll always have something to prove. (*Resident Alien* 179)

Overstatement cuts the other way in Stephen Leacock's essay, "I'll Stay in Canada":

> It's the spaces that appeal. To all of us here, the vast unknown country of the North, reaching away to the polar seas, supplies a peculiar mental background. I like to think that in a few short hours in a train or car I can be in the primeval wilderness of the North; that if I like, from my summer home, an hour or two of flight will take me over the divide and down to the mournful shores of the James Bay, untenanted till yesterday, now haunted with its flock of airplanes hunting gold in the wilderness. I never have gone to the wilderness; I never go to it; I never shall. But somehow I'd feel lonely without it. (*Funny Pieces* 291)

Where did that image of the "mournful shores," so reminiscent of Scott's "loneliness and desolation" (*Circle* 120), come from? Something Leacock read or was told, perhaps. If he had been to James Bay he would have known not to situate gold hunters there. Leacock's is an ethnocentrically "untenanted" and generic North, not a real one, but his embrace of the North from a distance is quite common in the writings of Canadians on the subject. Most of us, living in a settled strip along the southern margin of the country, don't let our distance from the North prevent us from claiming it as our own, sometimes to the dismay of those, white as well as Native, who do live there. E. K. Brown shows how we do this in his essay "Now, Take Ontario."

Hyperbole must be allowed for in this vivaciously-written 1947 *Maclean's* piece, in which Brown shows himself willing to speak about the importance of the North to most Ontarians, even though, like Leacock, he confesses to having no personal experience of it and also to desiring none. "The central and northern parts of Toronto are where I am most at home" (*Responses* 99), he says, and goes on: "Nothing could entice me into one of [those primitive northern cottages Canadians are so fond of occupying for the summer] now or forevermore!" And yet, he generalizes,

> In the best book written on Canada, André Siegfried said that the crucial factor in a country's history is the particular dream that haunts the imagination of its people. The Ontario dream is of the north, the land of mines and lakes and forests, the margins of civilization, the approaches to the unknown. (101)

What feeds this dream in a man who never goes north? "I nourish my northern dream," Brown says, "on painting and poetry" (102). I don't introduce as authorities on the North men who have never been there. Brown, at least, is not literally wrong about it, but he knows about the North as he knows about Native peoples — at second hand. Still, Leacock and Brown *are* catching something basic to Canadian identity — a myth of the North inspired, at times, by rumours of geography and by artistic renderings of actual experience there. It would be silly to dismiss the power of this myth to shape us simply because it's a myth. It's a myth compatible with fact, unlike the Northwest Passage myth that George Bowering deconstructs in his novel *Burning Water*: sometimes myth *is* lie. Vancouver is on roughly the same parallel as Estevan, Saskatchewan, and Cochrane, Ontario; whatever we say about nordicity is going to ring rather differently on the balmy West Coast than in the interior, but even there people are able to appreciate the literal foundation of Gilles Vigneault's "mon pays, ce n'est pas un pays, c'est l'hiver."

Leacock and Brown are Ontarians, and so is W. L. Morton, who generalizes for the whole country a pattern implicit in the words of the other two: "The line which marks off the frontier from the farmstead, the wilderness from the baseland, the hinterland from the metropolis, runs through every Canadian psyche" (*The Canadian Identity* 93). North, or nordicity as some prefer to call it, is certainly a factor in the experience of every southern province of the country — Edmonton, Alberta, for example, calls itself "the gateway to the north" — but many parts of Canada's cottage country extend quite far south, and some modified wilderness experience is accessible to anyone. Anyone can get to the Algonquin Park that nourished Tom Thomson's painting. It's never deserted, of course, seldom a source of extreme solitude. Otherwise, it hasn't changed much since Thomson's time.

That Edmonton motto is picked up by Robert Kroetsch in his essay on "The Canadian Writer and the American Literary Tradition," in *The Lovely Treachery of Words*. Kroetsch is one Albertan who sees in that gateway metaphor something more than a Chamber of Commerce slogan. Like his friend and colleague Rudy Wiebe, he is drawn to the North. "The Canadian writer, in my experience," he says, "is a person caught between *north* and *south*" (53). South is America, technocracy; North is silence:

> This silence — this impulse towards the natural, the *uncreated,* if you will — is summed up by the north. The north is not a typical uncreated frontier, a natural world to be conquered and exploited. Rather, in spite of inroads, it remains a true wilderness, a continuing presence. We don't want to conquer it. Sometimes we want it to conquer us. And we don't have to go there literally in order to draw sustenance from it, any more than the American had to go literally to the west. It presses southward into the Canadian consciousness. (*Treachery* 54)

There again is that insistence that the North feeds us — us being mainly writers, in this instance — from a distance. This from a man whose northern experience on the Mackenzie River inspired his first published novel, *But We Are Exiles.* Such assertions can be made only by one in whom the North has lodged, visually or verbally, for whom North radiates association. Real news of the real place has got to come out. Even the silence reaches us in words, names: igloo, John Hornby, the Klondike, Dan McGrew, Albert Johnston, Sir John Franklin (Erebus, Terror), *le pays d'en haut, les voyageurs,* Nuliyuk, the Northwest Passage. The news is a study in itself. It takes form in Al Purdy's *North of Summer,* in the wonderful documentary novels of Elizabeth Hay, and on and on, in a multiplicity which recalls the familiar figure of the Inuit's many words for the forms of snow. Rudy Wiebe's *Playing Dead: A Meditation Concerning the Arctic* is a whole anthology of northernness in itself, incorporating into his essays the northern journals, poems, stories, songs, autobiographies and scholarship of others, both white and Native. Looking *up* south from the arctic (the frontispiece of his anti-Eurocentric book is an inverted map of Canada entitled "Inuit View to the South"), he wonders

> why Canadians have so little comprehension of our own *nordicity,* that we are a northern nation and that, until we grasp imaginatively and realize imaginatively in word, song, image and consciousness that North is both the true nature of our world and also our graspable destiny we will always be wishing ourselves something we aren't, always stand staring south across that mockingly invisible border longing for the leeks and onions of our ancient Egyptian nemesis, the United States. Is climate, is *weather* to be all that determines what we think ourselves to be? (111)

"The Height of Land" had already answered no, but of course a poem needs listeners.

When Duncan Campbell Scott was writing, the north-south split could sometimes be expressed in terms of east and west. "Spring on Mattagami" is a very different poem from "The Height of Land," but Scott stands on a mental height in that poem, too, seeing two ways, and contributing something to the myth of the North:

> There [Italy] is the land of fraud and fame and fashion,
> Joy is but a gaud and withers in an hour,
> Here is the land of quintessential passion,
> Where in a wild throb Spring wells up with power. (*Poems* 43)

The "crowded southern land" of "The Height of Land" will not superimpose on and dissolve into this decadent European East, yet the West is the North, as filtered though the heart of a forlorn lover. The North is more soberly described, or invoked, by other Scott personae or narrators, though seldom without this sense of the elementally passionate lurking as potential. It often pushes his characters into extreme acts. Because he went into the North with his eyes and heart open, Scott made his northerly-inspired writing a powerful tributary to the northern myth that draws us, and, some say, sustains us. The myth needs periodic grounding for literary minds who don't find romance deflated by fact, and that may be particularly true of Canadians, those lovers of documentary.

Actual residents of the Ontario North, feeling their region undervalued and its identity misunderstood, may find all this talk of myth by southern Canadians ironic. The boom and bust rhythm plagues the North much more than it does the South, as one-industry towns are established only to founder when the industry disappears. And such incursions caused the original residents of Northern Ontario, the Cree and Ojibway, to request the treaty in the first place. To them, the North is hardly a fabrication of white writers and painters. They certainly have their myths, which are not the invention of individuals, but an expression of their collectivity — human, animal, plant, and physical universe. Scott's generalized "region spirit" perhaps hints at something pluralistic in Ojibway thought. "Each valley or any other earth form — a meadow, a bay, a grove, a hill," according to Basil Johnston, "possesses a mood which reflects the state of being of that place" (*Ojibway Heritage* 33–34). He expands on this theme in *Ojibway Ceremonies*: "Where that presence [of Kitche Manitou] was greatest — at the top of a mountain, in a whirlpool, in a cave, on a small island, or in a cavern in rocks at the water's edge — the Anishnabeg would offer tobacco to the mysteries who abided there" (33). Samuel Stewart records such an offering being made by the Treaty 9 crew at "Granny Rock" (Iroquois Falls). Is it a stretch to imagine a power parallel to that of the Great Spirit speaking obliquely through the region spirit in Scott's poem? Not as great as one might expect, given the animism of the setting and the mysteries ("the spell, golden and inappellable," the "ancient disturber of solitude") that are associated with the murmurings of the region spirit. I'll return to this theme after I discuss the poem, but first there are sources to introduce.

I HAVE BEEN DEMONSTRATING that the other poems deriving from the 1905–06 treaty trips are not mere versified journal or autobiography. Scott almost always takes the lived experience and rearranges it. Experience provides a pool of images from which, like any artist, he can draw to create something newly authentic. This happens again with "The Height of Land," even though the Pic River and August 1906 can be pinpointed as the particular place and time to which the poem refers.

Of course, the seed of the poem may have been sewn much earlier than 1905. Before they formed a title, the words "The Height of Land" appear in Scott's 1900–1910 notebook between drafts of "Peace," dated November 15, 1902, and a poem dictated to Scott by Elizabeth, dated May 10, 1903. Scott's first official trek across the height of land was probably in 1899. Then he and his party crossed it on the way to Fort Albany in 1905, and recrossed it on their southward journey that same summer. They crisscrossed the divide during the more southerly 1906 trip. Some of the poem's images might have been drawn from any one of several experiences in either summer. In both 1905 and 1906 it was common for the tents to be pitched over "a revel / of roses," common to pass "wide blueberry plain[s]." It was usual to spend some time in front of a campfire before turning in, though Scott would seldom, if ever, have been alone to meditate, with guides "dead asleep," and I doubt that he ever meditated all night, as his speaker does in "The Height of Land."

Chees-que-ne-ne (his name at least) was appropriated for the poem from the more southerly Chapleau, and transformed into one of the "Indian guides," as we know from the several views of him. There is Morris's portrait of the man, a Scott photograph of Morris sketching him, and a couple of photographs taken of the sitting (figure 18). Who was "Potàn the wise" (the name also appears, without the epithet, in "Spring on Mattagami")? I haven't found an original for him, though the name appears in the dedication of Norval Morrisseau's *Legends of My People The Great Ojibway*: "To My Grandfather Moses (Potan) Nanakonogos."

As usual, then, Scott chose details for his poem from here and there on his northern trips. More importantly, the height of land is a symbol that focuses all of his northern experience, what it showed him of his southern life, and what the contrast between North and South helped him to draw together of his entire experience and thought. Obviously, much more than even those two whole summers coalesced in the poem.

Still, it's exciting to find that the poem is rooted in the actual geography of the last phase of the 1906 trip — the journey up the Pic River from Heron Bay, over the height of land, to Long Lake Post. The upward trip began at

Figure 18, PA-59599

5:50 p.m. on August 1 and ended at the post on August 8 at 11:30 a.m. The party reached the height of land portage at 3:15 on the 7th, according to Samuel Stewart. His journal, as usual, supplies the most detail about the ascent, though Pelham Edgar and Edmund Morris were also keeping track of it. The return journey, the one given in a sort of shorthand (numbers and names of rapids and portages) by Pelham Edgar, quoted in chapter 2, began on August 10, "shortly after noon," and ended back at Heron Bay at 7:25 p.m. on August 14.

The ascent of the Pic was arduous, because the rapids and falls were numerous and close together. The water of certain streams was muddy; sunken logs punched holes in canoes, which then had to be repaired. All of this is distilled, in the first section of the poem, to a progress "up through the spreading lakes / From level to level," though there was actually more stream and less lake than at many other points of the journey. Two images from later sections, corresponding between poem and journals, confirm that the Pic River is the one Scott has in mind. These (the "last weird lakelet" and the "bush fire") are jammed together in the poem to create a dark reminder of the power of "the ancient disturber of solitude," though they were not experienced in such close proximity. The fire, in fact, was found on the descent. Here is the "weird lakelet," "where the paddle stirred unutterable stenches," in the prosaic words of Samuel Stewart:

> Soon in another marshy stream. The water in this stream we also found to have an extremely unpleasant smell, owing to its being thick with decomposed vegetable matter. The water or mud is so thick in Mud Lake, which we now crossed, that it required all the strength of the men to push or paddle the canoes through it. (118)

Edgar's journal has two names for the lake: "Water Lily (Mud) Lake." "Muddy smelling stream" is his only olfactory note. This small complex of stream and lake was negotiated after lunch on August 7, shortly before reaching the height of land.

Now here is Stewart's version of the fire that had greatly altered the height of land on the way back:

> The only special incident that marked our return journey was a big bush fire that almost barred our way at the big height of land portage. This fire had evidently started soon after we passed through here [?] on our way north, and must have burned fiercely for a time, as was shown by the number of trees that had fallen across our path. (125)[1]

This fire and the bad-smelling stream or lake are properly joined for dramatic effect in the poem, which again is quite different from the journey that produced it. Stewart's diary, containing the bare facts, reads something like a novel, with suitable detail and a cast of characters — the party of Grand Trunk Pacific men, one of whom, having gone ahead of his party without supplies, sustained an injury and spent "six days without having received any attention, and unable to do anything for himself" (114); the "ten Indians in five canoes who were engaged by the Revillon Frères, or as they are generally called the French Company, or the Opposition" (121); and, of course, the post, the treaty signing, the speeches and all the rest. Scott is not seeking that detail for his poem, rich as much of it is. He simplifies the external context and lets the essence of his entire northern experience stand free.

The narrative of the poem is simply summarized: A man with two Indian guides, having paddled a northern river-and-lake system against the current up to the height of land, finds that the peace of the evening campfire teases his mind in and out of thought throughout a whole meditative night. The poem ends as the dawn "Tolls out from the dark belfries of the spruces." The poem's dynamic structure enacts the night-long vigil, with all the shifting activity of the meditating mind, and that will need to be traced in detail later.

I MENTIONED THAT Scott's productivity during the treaty trips must have been owing to the clearing from his mind of the hordes of details that any city dweller with job, spouse, child, friends, and all — never mind literary aspirations — must process. The "peace" in "The Height of Land," like the "rest" that so interests Scott in other poems, is much desired but hard to reach. Music can sometimes inspire it, whirling us

> with one transfiguring touch
> Out of the sordid and inconsequent world
> Into an ageless realm, and there unfurl[ing]
> All that the Masters know of the strange maze
> That we call Life. (*Poems* 272)

So can poetry, as in the hands of someone like Keats, who, Scott says,

> schooled his heart with passionate control
> To compass knowledge, to unravel the dense
> Web of this tangled life. . . . (*Poems* 152)

Such signs (maze and web) of what Scott calls, in "The Height of Land," "all the welter of the lives of men," naturally make frequent enough appearances in his work. He lived his life in the maze, after all; it was what he needed release from — not merely a holiday, during which the pace of his life might slow. Because he was a poet he required a corresponding intensification of his receptors, a sharpening of mental focus, and (the reason for real excitement) a heightened preparedness for the calling out of something inside him by something outside. This, in the North, is the "spell"

> Golden and inappellable
> That gives the inarticulate part
> Of our strange being one moment of release. . . .

I'll circle back to this release and its significance, but there is another context for it that should be introduced first: the direct echoes that appear in *Untitled Novel.* The most obvious analogue is Robin Garrabrant's retreat from "the wrangle within those stone walls" (297) of Ottawa politics to the shore of Lake Achigan, but certain verbal echoes in the novel make it quite clear that the wilderness is only one such creative withdrawal. Aime Godchere, wise father of the calculating Adrienne, offers to Barbara Applegarth his "odd theory that every one who wishes to lead the spiritual life must have a temple of his own in which to worship, where no one else may come" (276). "The rooms in which we live are burdened with associations," he goes on, "They have existences of their own, which are but thin shadows cast by the lives that have been spent in them; the images and recollections which they call forth burden the spirit, there can be no concentrating in the midst of such a multitude" (276). Spurned by the husband through whom she had hoped to find fulfilment, and alienated from her son, what Barbara needs is an entrée not so much to the spiritual life as to her own identity. That is exactly Robin's problem, and his "temple" is the North.

Scott is not simple-minded about this. Robin brings "his own world" into the northern solitude: "the wilderness was peopled with his loves and loathings. It was at times a dream to him but the rest, the quiet, the balm of silence was having its way with his spirit. Natures such as his obtain self-knowledge in flashes" (298). Correspondingly, Barbara's Achigan is the room in the mansion that she remodels and reserves for her own use:

> Barbara, without expectation, without hope, knelt in the small core of silence. As her personality fell away from her she was conscious of nothing, all the accumulation of experience and memory that was the sum of her individual life was held aloft. She was before God in essence as he had cast her into the world. Long she knelt but she gained no knowledge of herself. In these supreme and rare moments strength is given one, knowledge comes by flashes and from action. (307)

Robin and Barbara clearly represent two aspects of the question of self-knowledge in the novel, and the echoes I have highlighted are evidence that the novel is not without design, but a reader of "The Height of Land" also thinks of "here there is peace in the lofty air, / And Something comes by flashes / Deeper than peace." The novel and the poem are not probing precisely the same realm of intuition. What the two characters in the novel learn, by flashes, is more limited and less mysterious. They learn about themselves, in variations on the standard epiphany of fiction. These epiphanies read a little like studies, sketches in preparation for the deeper insights of "The Height of Land."

WHAT SCOTT IS TRYING to embody in the poem, and to probe, is the distillation of a lifetime's thought. He tried to do this one other time (not counting certain poetic and fictional echoes of "The Height of Land"), in a letter to Elise — tried and failed, his prose style having let him down. But the attempt is fascinating, not least because it shows, by contrast, that the thinking in "The Height of Land" is impressive.

I spoke in chapter 3 of the importance of Scott's letters to Elise Aylen as a key to nuancing his character. It's a shame that the epistolary conversation we now read is one-sided. It would be helpful to know what Elise said to provoke Scott into setting his philosophy of life onto paper. Between the lines of Scott's March 16, 1929, letter I read that she is depressed, apparently wondering what life is about. Perhaps she was already feeling the need for religious or philosophical sanctuary that took her to an ashram in India after Scott died. At any rate, Scott sends an enclosure with his letter, introducing it as "The pencilled page I did a few days ago. It seems feeble & ineffective & as misty as can be but I think I'll send it. I'm not a philosopher you know but only someone who, so intensely, would like to help you to [?] be very cheerful till your companion returns. . . ." What Scott writes is the foundation of his faith (the reason he calls himself a man "of the sunrise"): his foundation in flow, in mystery, which produces joy. I quote the whole statement:

> The pressure of the mystery of life & the universal is intense. It may become torment but it may become a solace. If the mystery were solved for an individual *that* life would have lost all flavour, if the solution became a possession of the race mankind would cease to exist[.] But without *knowing* the secret of being, what joy to *feel* oneself in the flow & very essence of the mystery, content to have this unsolvable secret between oneself and the Master of Life. This quiescence [?] will result in greater receptivity and the soul will gather [?] messages, hints, intuitions from the great centre of all feeling that will surpass any knowledge that it could gain by searching for *positive knowledge.* Then why suffer Elise? I ask a question I cannot answer — For a mind and heart like yours there should be an equipoise and an agreement but the lack of physical strength comes between them. (PA/S-A)

Here Scott breaks off ("I feel foolish in writing this as I am not bringing help with full hands") and bursts into one of the most poignant cries to be found anywhere in his writing: about how little he has accomplished in "a life of drift."

The whole statement, with its giving and its taking away, requires tactful interpretation. For Scott and Elise, very close but not yet betrothed (at least the undated love letter follows the offer of encouragement in the Scott-Aylen papers), Scott's statement might have been, though deeply felt, a sort of position paper. He might have been reassurable. He might not always have been down on himself. And no doubt for both of them the act of offering the statement far transcended its content. For Scott there was the possibility of trustingly speaking his heart as only a lover can; for Elise there was the profound compliment of being offered the deepest confidence a man like Scott can give — the secret of his vulnerability. I hope, anyway, that she was able to see it that way. I hope she didn't want Scott on a pedestal, even though it looks like that's where he put her.

Scott's "philosophy" is secular here. As elsewhere (if not everywhere), he slides away from God to the Master of Life. Some of what he believes sounds very like Keats's "negative capability," although the business about "flow" does not. The curious turn in the piece is on that word "quiescent," because the state of mind in which mystery is accepted and the receptors of the soul laid open to "messages, hints, intuitions from the great centre of all feeling," this passive openness, is problematical in the social sphere, where action is necessary.

It tightens Scott's piece considerably to consider the philosophy and its undercutting frame (including the introduction in the letter) as two halves of one whole. Scott is clearly saying what he believes and then losing faith in his own faith because he can't respect what he has done with his own life. He starts out to communicate a source of joy and ends in depression. "Thought and deed," to invoke the relevant terms of "The Height of Land," do not align. Of course the word "torment" appears twice in the first part of the statement. A fine line seems to separate joy and torment in the soul questing for the meaning of life. And then, even for the one who finds joy in relaxing to life, opening himself up, there is the occupational hazard of unfitting oneself for action ("I have never fought against anything . . ."). As I say, putting it thus draws the contradictory parts of the statement together, artificially creating a paradoxical figure like the one in "By a Child's Bed": "all my spirit's sphere, / Grows one half brightness and the other dead . . ." The "halves" of the prose statement don't balance so nicely, and they should not be reduced to a balance Scott never gave them. Had he meditated a little more deeply, perhaps he might have incorporated that blot or shadow on his life into his philosophy, but he didn't — not writing to Elise, anyway. Is it something of this shadow that creeps into "The Height of Land" in the forms of primeval stream and terrifying bush fire? Here, again, there is no balance. "The Height of Land" reverses the order of the elements of Scott's statement to Elise, so that the sunrise wins out. To put it another way,

> Thus we have seen in the retreating tempest
> The victor-sunlight merge with the ruined rain,
> And from the rain and sunlight spring the rainbow.

Scott is no Berryman, no Robert Lowell, to harrow up his personal soul in public. What he felt of personal darkness went into the storms and nightmares in his work, into certain disturbances of an "ancient disturber of solitude" — into symbols. At times, as in "Powassan's Drum," in the savage cruelties of "At Gull Lake" and some of the stories, and in the "last weird lakelet" section of "The Height of Land," he made the darkness unforgettable. If he hadn't, he might have sent Elise a copy of "The Height of Land" to cheer her up and spare himself the penning of a misty, inadequate expression of his view of life.

It's important to remember Scott's caveat ("I'm not a philosopher"), his obvious reluctance to write out a prose version of his philosophy, and his clear dissatisfaction with what he wrote. It should be accorded the same provisional status Scott himself gave it. Whether its being unguarded and not for publication confers more or less significance on the statement depends on the view of it one takes. I tend to take it very seriously, as much for the stylistic raggedness as because it is heartfelt, but I resist making too much of what may well have been written in a sour mood. We shouldn't assume that we have the real Scott in these words because they stand out from almost everything else he wrote. I insert them into the flow created by all of his writing, and the tributary of the words others have written about him. The reader may ponder them further as an analogue to "The Height of Land" (or to "The Fragment of a Letter," "Meditation at Perugia," and "Poetry and Progress"), saying only one thing more: the context of Scott's statement is like the context of the ascent of the Pic River: relevant to the interpretation of the poem, to which I now turn, but leaving the challenge of interpretation intact.

WHAT SCOTT STATES to Elise becomes a question at the end of "The Height of Land." It's one thing to remark on the insoluble mystery of life; it's quite another to give it a body. This is what "The Height of Land" does: it enacts its thought quite clearly to the casual reader, yet offers mysteries to the reader who attempts to map precisely its complex forms of thinking and feeling. It's not the complexity of the poem that keeps me interested; it's the simplicity of that complexity. The poem speaks about and to the heart and soul, often in the language of the senses. No paraphrase can capture it.

It has been truly said that "The Height of Land" is a philosophic or meditative poem. More than that, it's a poem *about* thinking, about conditions in which thinking thrives, and some of the results it produces. But we ought not to privilege thinking as method and theme of the poem when the poem itself does no such thing. Such privileging is, of course, natural to readers looking for paraphrasable meaning. These will be predisposed to miss the fact that most of "The Height of Land" is sensuously concrete and never devoid of thought, because every concrete image is given a spin into sentience and enigma. Scott establishes the sights and sounds, even the smells, that pervade the speaker's night-long northern vigil. In fact, variations in what can or cannot be seen or heard mark the differences in atmosphere from section to section. So the vigil is anything but statically described, in terms of what the senses are offered to respond to. None of these appeals to the senses is neutral; the imagery thickens up the experience while it dissolves the border between subject and object, perceiver and perception, and creates local mystery, minute interactions between the external world (land, sky, water) and the soul (both reason and intuition).

To put this another way, the descriptions — of the campfire scene that opens the poem, the climb to the height of land, the disgusting lake and terrifying bush fire, even of the sunrise — all vibrate with meaning in excess of the objects or scenes they present. They are each invested with deep emotion. Thus it's impossible to read past them in a linear progress, each detail vanishing as the next is reached. "Answers" to the meaning of life are not found exclusively in the last section, which is after all mostly composed of questions, but in each of the sections. And what each "means" in itself is modified by what each "means" in relation to the other. Later I'll be more precise about this, by examining the easily-overlooked short section reflecting on the stars. But first I want to follow the sound of the wind and the other sounds and sights as they fluctuate through the poem, and use that basis to establish the temporal progress of the poem.

First,

> The wind sounds in the wood, wearier
> Than the long Ojibwa cadence
> In which Potàn the Wise
> Declares the ills of life
> And Chees-que-ne-ne makes a mournful sound
> Of acquiescence.

This is the end of the day around the campfire, when the sound of the personified wind (heard rather than felt, owing to the ring of protective spruces around the clearing), is likened to those of the desultory complaints of the guides. Energy is low at the end of an arduous day. The tiredness is shared by the wind, the guides, the embers of the fire. And soon all sounds die.

"Here" is the word that opens the poem; "now" opens the second and third sections. These are successive moments that differ according to the fluctuations of the wind, among other things. The peace of the first section is intensified by the silence of the second, and both peace and silence are preparations for a deeper apprehension of "Something" that passes understanding, that is both provoked by and transcends the senses.

The second section is a flashback. The wind doesn't appear in it, being a factor only around the campfire. This section relates the physical approach to the height of land, up to "here," where peace and that Something are again introduced, and the latter is expanded on. This is the key to the poem's structure: an irregular, incremental repetition created by motions of the speaker's mind toward and away from a mystery he senses, but for which there are no words — a tough, untieable knot of intuitive knowledge that draws the speaker to worry at it again and again. Physically tired at the end of the day (the beginning of the poem), he is in a state of mental excitement by the end of the night. He greets the dawn of a sleepless night that has been anything but *nuit blanche*: the last lines pulse with energy. The *sound* of those lines answers the questions they ask. But I'm getting ahead of myself.

The third section returns us to the wind in the trees, now linked with other sounds and, in fact, scarcely recognizable as wind:

> Now are there sounds walking in the wood,
> And all the spruces shiver and tremble,
> And the stars move a little in their courses.

Once again, "quiet ensues and pure starlight and dark," and with it "thought reawakens." The rest of part 3 is a record of that thought. Part 4 flashes back to the day's journey, but is very different in content and tone from the last flashback, being composed of episodes of pure fear. In the fifth section, the speaker reacts to the stars that periodically draw his eyes upward. That is the pattern I want to deal with next.

The final temporal change in the poem begins as "dawn / Tolls out." It's signalled by the sound of a lemming stirring the fern, and by other "eft-minded things" that "feel the air change" and begin their day. All of the thought and feeling in this last section concerns the dawn and cycles of its diurnal return. The returning dawn is, naturally, a return of light in a brilliant sunrise, a treat for the eyes, but the ear is not forgotten. Something of the quickening wind of being is present as the speaker hears

> The thrill of life beat up the planet's margin
> And break in the clear susurrus of deep joy
> That echoes and reëchoes in my being[.]

In fact, the alternating rhythm of the physical and mental motions of the poem is there in the third last line, a recapitulation not only of theme but of structure, when the speaker feels "the long light flow, the long wind pause."

So much for what is heard. The visual faculty gets its biggest feast in the last section, in the excitement of the dawn, but there have been delights for it earlier. Another rhythm of alternations, a visual one, is caused by points of light in the darkness — particularly after the fire has died — which draw the eyes skyward. "The stars are up, and far away," is the line with which a vertical dimension cuts the horizontality ("the watershed on either hand") of the poem's spatial orientation. Periodically, the eyes are drawn upward and the stars reflected upon. Like other aspects of the physical environment, the sky swims in and out of focus, as the mobile mind of the meditator focuses now on what he sees or hears or smells, now on what those sensuous experiences make him think about. The stars, "up and far away," are introduced in terms of their distance and remoteness from the earth-bound speaker, but the second star image is a nocturnal mirror of the earth:

> The spruces have retired a little space
> And left a field of sky in violet shadow
> With stars like marigolds in a water-meadow.

The night is not forgotten in section 2, even though it consists of a flashback to the day, but the stars don't figure in it, only

> . . . the enormous targe of Hudson Bay,
> Glimmering all night
> In the cold arctic light. . . .

The movement of the stars "in their courses" in section 3 is probably (like the retreat of the spruces) illusory, the result of one of those periodic turbulences in the trees, and it catches the eye only briefly. The longest meditation on the stars then follows the terrifying section 4, and is relief from the nightmare memories of the trip to this point. Perhaps it's this nightmare context that changes the stars again. (Literally, these stars will have "done" the same thing all night; what animates them is the metamorphosing thoughts of the speaker.) Now, for the first time, the stars attract this travelling mind as symbols having something, in their remoteness from us, to say about what it means to be human:

> How strange the stars have grown;
> The presage of extinction glows on their crests
> And they are beautied with impermanence;
> They shall be after the race of men
> And mourn for them who snared their fiery pinions,
> Entangled in the meshes of bright words.

To comment on this passage is to move into interpretation of what the mind *makes* of what it sees and hears, beyond laying out the poem's concrete sensory details. So it might be well first to observe how very present all that physical information is, how important to the dynamism of the setting, especially in time. "No two moments land with the same sideswipe," says Dennis Lee (*Civil Elegies* 41), and in that spirit a reader is conducted in a flow from phase to temporal phase of the night, marked by a return to observations of the northern surrounding. Of course that environment is never felt as emotionally neutral; it is always resonating with the mind that perceives it. And at times the speaker goes beyond "mere" ecstatic being in this northern night with his sensory pores wide open. At times he takes where he is and what he sees as stimuli to reflection about the nature of life elsewhere and anywhere. To that horizontal/vertical physical grid that orients a reader spatially, a temporal grid is added, and the passage just quoted, about the stars, is part of it.

Put another way, the poem encompasses a single night, with flashbacks to the preceding day — perhaps twenty-four hours all told. From "now," though, and from "here," the speaker's mind ranges back to the time of cave-dwellers, forward again into "the Christ-time" that we inhabit, and thence into the future. The questions asked in the last section are all about the future. The poem ends in the present, once again, in an ecstasy of wonder at the possibility that in the here and now the speaker has come as near the core of life as anyone ever has or will. *If* "intuition is the measure of knowledge," he may well stand "at the zenith of our wisdom," now. But the stars of the brief section 5 are part of that future, too, and they represent a less ecstatic version of it. The tone, in fact, is slightly elegiac.

Certain ambiguities make section 5 difficult to paraphrase,[2] but I'll try to unpack the lines fairly simply, for a start. The mutability that characterizes the twenty-four hour period the speaker has put in (and which Scott's words embody) is generally felt as a good, being the opposite of stasis. In section five it becomes an ill. "Beautied with impermanence" is the paradoxical expression of what the stars represent — a future end to the "race of men," who must love what they have to leave. The beauty is, presumably, a projection of the mind capable of thinking apocalypse. The stars are personified as mourners by this mind, perhaps because it cannot bear to think of the universe totally bereft of sentience. "Extinction," at any rate, seems reserved for the "race of men" whom the stars will survive. Possibly the most interesting thing about the passage is the way it torques, in its last two lines, into a covert version of the myth of Icarus or some similar winged overreacher. The most interesting thing of all is that the transgression (leading to the demise of life?) takes the form of logos — the reaching in verbal flight for "bright words," becoming "Entangled in the meshes" of them. The passage is brief and suggestive, rather than definitive, but it is not inserted merely to be dropped. The metaphor of poet's "flight" is picked up again in the last section.

Gently, almost surreptitiously, the poem opens a window on itself, on its writer. The "I" appears once in section 4, and then courses through the very personal ending of section 6, but for the most part, "The Height of Land" deflects attention from the speaker onto what his senses record, and onto what he thinks about "we" or "us," the human race. This is especially true of sections 2 and 3. When the "I" appears in the final section, it marks a departure from the human in general. The climax in affirmation, then, is a series of questions asked by a man who is speaking only for himself. The speaker moves by fluctuant stages of the poem to that final ecstatic motion of his mind; the ecstasy in it is palpable and not to be dismissed by stressing the contingency in which it is set, but the ecstasy is composed of elements, transfigured, that felt very different in previous stages of the poem. The ending recalls these earlier stages, and sends the reader back to them: to the vegetable peace, the mind-stretching insights, the visceral fears, the melancholy vision of a post-human era in the section about beautied stars.

One future that is envisioned, then, is a time after humanity. The brief section 5 is not apocalyptic, but serves as a speculation rather than a warning, because it feels as far into the future as the stars are distant. However, it constitutes one limit of the poem's temporal parenthesis, the other being the time of the primitive "cave-dweller." And the cave-dweller, with his pictographic articulation, is introduced principally for purposes of analogy. The questions asked about the future in section 5 take as their starting point the results of thinking. Not everything in the poem involves either perceiving or thinking, however; there is a response of the soul or heart, rather than the mind, that seems to involve neither — or may be an augmentation of both. "Thought reawakens" after the passage about the "spell" and the "gathering of the waters." I will return to the latter; first, the results of the thinking.

Thought "is linked" "with all the welter of the lives of men" that has already been identified with "the crowded southern land," but the *thinking* is removed from all that. Like the upland air, thinking is clear. It's "here, where we can think," that the tempest of life ("welter," in metaphorical guise)

> parts, and it appears
> As simple as to the shepherd seems his flock:
> A Something to be guided by ideals. . . .

The image of idealistic interpenetration of thought and deed that ensues is quite exaggeratedly utopian. As Tracy Ware has pointed out, "the key word is 'appears'" (19), and it's supplemented by "seems." Here is a rainbow harmony that — at a vantage point so remote from the complexities of human conflict that erase such visions — might well seem attainable. It is a beautiful vision that one might summon in the peace of a remote northern campfire, as if to say, why can't life be like that? It's handy to remember the illusions of the speaker of "Spring on Mattagami." All his romantic problems would disappear, according to him, if he could persuade his love out of the welter of Venice and into the wilderness, where "the pulse of love beats all one way." But he isn't objective, being in the grip of a love-lorn obsession that he projects onto the country itself. The speaker of "The Height of Land" doesn't make that mistake.

Having introduced the pastoral ideal of harmonious life just barely undercut in section 3, the speaker is free to wonder in section 6 whether the progress of human thought may be rendered as a Viconian ascending spiral.

> How often in the autumn of the world
> Shall the crystal shrine of dawning be rebuilt
> With deeper meaning!

The annual and diurnal cycles are both present here — the first near its end, the second at its beginning. Meaning is the issue. Does it progress? Does it progress in cycles of thought, returning each to a version of the solution represented by the simplicity of the shepherd (indeed the version in section 6 is a reprise of the utopian vision in section 3), but penetrating deeper? Might we reach a stage of thinking some time in the future whose whole basis is further advanced — "Love" no longer being the foundation — compared to which

> the vision
> Of noble deed and noble thought immingled [might]
> Seem as uncouth . . . as the pictograph
> Scratched on the cave side by the cave-dweller
> To us of the Christ-time[.]

In the future, will everything be solved? The full scope of the mental territory in question is repeated in images of twin mysteries, the skies (above) and the seas (below). Will "the deep [be] fathomed," "the firmament charted"? We know what answer Scott gives to that question from within a self-cancelling discourse — his letter to Elise — that doesn't participate with the mystery. At the end of "The Height of Land," where one might expect the definitive alternative ("the sunrise as I see it"), thought seems to be suspended again in favour of, first, the evidence of the senses and, second, information whose source is beneath or beyond the senses. Now it's necessary to go back into the poem to examine its most fascinating and difficult images — the golden spell, the peace "deeper than peace," "the ancient disturber of solitude" — to show how they work locally and to make good the claim that all of this and more is present in the climax of the poem, making it definitive and anti-definitive at one and the same time.

One aspect of the incremental repetition of the poem is its approach to, retreat from, and return — not only but especially — to the few central images in which the poem's meaning seems most to inhere. I hope to have made a case for the meaning of the "background" by now, but it would be perverse to claim for it an importance equal to, say, the "spell, golden and inappellable."

The spell doesn't appear until part 2, in apposition to "that Something [that] comes by flashes / Deeper than peace," which had appeared, without elaboration, in section 1. What can we make of it immediately? One way to deal with the layers of meaning that accrue to the "Something" is to annotate them as they are laid down. First, "Something" is capitalized, and thus dignified above the level of question-carrying pronoun. But what is deeper than peace? Peace is a restful state of mind and body; Something more profound than that must be more inner yet. It must go nearer what we sometimes think of as the core of the mind — the mind's mind (the kernel of life, perhaps, that appears in "Lines in Memory of Edmund Morris"). Is deeper than peace an increment of peacefulness to something approaching nirvana? It might be safe enough to attribute a restful transcendence to the image on its first rather matter-of-fact appearance, and even its next. But I think this depth is what the last part of the poem is written out of, and it's not peaceful; it is full of agitation, to the point of ecstasy. But nothing of that is felt in section 1.

Section two adds this:

> — a spell
> Golden and inappellable
> That gives the inarticulate part
> Of our strange being one moment of release
> That seems more native than the touch of time,
> And we must answer in chime;
> Though yet no man may tell
> The secret of that spell
> Golden and inappellable.

At such time as the deep is fathomed, the firmament charted (those mysteries of life conceived on a vast scale), presumably the secret of the spell (the mystery as concentrated essence) will be known. Not yet, is what we hear; the poem ends in a question: never? The Something is a spell in which three possible dictionary meanings might be involved. One is a verbal formula possessing magic power. There is no "Master of Life" (caster of spells) in the poem, so no such source and ultimate appeal is localized, and the spell may vibrate through a slightly wider range of meanings, one of which is a brief attack of indisposition or, more likely here, of enlightenment. The other relevant meaning is a brief but indeterminate period of time (after all, the duration of the spell, or the effect of it, is as brief as its importance is great). "Golden" adds both a warmth of colour and an association of value to the spell, and "inappellable" is similarly ambiguous. K. P. Stich has observed that inappellable carries the sense of unnameable, and says also that "the spell is inappellable and evokes fate or an ultimate prison . . ." (7). Correcting Stich, Tracy Ware points out that the *OED* definition sanctions only the second meaning: "that cannot be appealed against; from which there is no appeal" (17). But surely unnameable is also present, if only as a French source legible in the English word. That meaning is not incompatible with the other, though inappellable in the legal sense suggests something more absolute and final than does inappellable in the naming sense. I don't think there is any justification for projecting this as far as Stich does, into an evocation of "fate or an ultimate prison from which the poet's words cannot release him" (7), because the Something and the spell are always associated in the poem with things positive.

In fact, the spell, far from imprisoning, "gives the inarticulate part of our strange being one moment of release. . . ." What does this mean? I think it presupposes a view of the "native" (natural, a birthright) in human "being," that stresses what words can't reach. The place of "native" in the sentence makes it a near-opposite to "strange," or foreign. Is flashing into a state "deeper than peace" a return to origins, to a preverbal (or "semiotic") state outside of time as natural as civilization is artificial? If so, the release would be a homecoming, a momentary return to origins. This crudely phrases an experience that doesn't seem to form in words. The "inarticulate part" answers a call, not in words, but in a sort of tuning fork "chime" or vibration. There is no choice but to respond ("we must answer") when the deepest instincts have been touched.

The word "chime" has an equivalent in the third section, in "echoes," but we need to return to the beginning of section 2, to consider an image that is folded into the image of the shell, permutating the complexity of both in section 3. The height of land is not only a watershed; it's a place of origins. The waters flow north and south from here, but here is also where they originate. It's that conception Scott animates when he introduces the possibility of a sound beneath sound, a sound that isn't physical:

> There is no sound unless the soul can hear
> The gathering of the waters in their sources.

The image is that of a spring, or springs, but if their sounds are audible only to the soul, the sources must be spiritual, or at least mental. "Unless" is not definitive, and neither is "seems." When the image is repeated with slight variation in section 3, the suggestion is planted that an individual soul has escaped "the touch of time" in a return to origins.

It's interesting that the second time the "soul" feels near the source(s), it's not silence, but sound, that appears to locate it there, as another repeated image, "the disturber of solitude," is layered on or in.

> The ancient disturber of solitude
> Breathes a pervasive sigh,
> And the soul seems to hear
> The gathering of the waters at their sources;
> Then quiet ensues and pure starlight and dark;
> The region-spirit murmurs in meditation,
> The heart replies in exaltation
> And echoes faintly like an inland shell
> Ghost tremors of the spell. . . .

Can we identify the "disturber of solitude?" What is the disturber's relationship to the "region spirit?" As with other images, full speculation about this disturber requires factoring in its further disturbances in section 4 of the poem; but those will be put on hold for the moment.

The word "ancient" establishes a primitive anteriority to this disturbing presence — another image that lays bare the primitive roots of the present. These images certainly pile up. "Disturber" introduces a slightly disquieting undertone into the primary note of solitude and peace. The experience being recorded in this phase of the poem is still mainly pleasant, but it will darken in the next section, when "The ancient disturber of solitude / Stirs his ancestral potion in the gloom." The disturber seems, Janus-like, to have two faces: one beautiful, one terrible.

The "pervasive sigh" of the disturber and the "murmur" of the region-spirit draw them together. The latter seems a particularized spirit of place and the former a presence one might meet anywhere. But it's difficult to separate them neatly because the region, or vicinity, of the height of land contains those terrifying images of bush fire and weird lakelet connected with the ancient disturber — become, in increment, a sort of magician or shaman-figure a little reminiscent of Powassan, capable of transforming the peaceful upland into a scene of utter terror. Technically, section 4 is a memory, or flashback, but at first it feels as though those terrifying experiences are happening now. Once again, as the soul "hears" the gathering of the waters, the "spirit loathes" the primeval lakelet. Insofar as the disturber of solitude is associated with the sources, and then with the region-spirit, and also the "exaltation" with which the heart responds to its murmur, it's a positive force; when it stirs up nightmarish memories, it's anything but. The two forces, or faces, need to be joined. The result is extremely ambiguous. Perhaps the source itself is ambiguous.

Whether or not the region-spirit is identifiable with the ancient disturber of solitude, it does seem a source of the spell, because "the heart replies in exaltation" is parallel to "we must answer in chime." Then, as usual, the incremental technique goes a little further, adding a romantic image of the distance of the heart from the source, reminiscent of Wordsworth's "Ode: Intimations of Immortality" ("Though inland far we be, / Our Souls have sight of that immortal sea / Which brought us hither".) What "comes by flashes" is faint echo, "ghost tremor" — evidence of source, perhaps, but certainly evidence that the secret of life takes hold of an individual without his/her consent and reminds him/her what more there is than meets the eye to being human.

Now let's return to the end of the poem, having prepared some context for the sort of hearing going on there, and the sort of seeing. The sunrise comes in astonishing oceanic-synaesthetic images — "shoals," "deluge-light," "whelms," "inundant." There is a drowning in sensation, accompanied by a sound that appeals, once again, to the inner ear, the ear of soul or spirit:

> now I hear
> The thrill of life beat up the planet's margin
> And break in the clear susurrus of deep joy
> That echoes and reëchoes in my being[.]

This is a question capable of being framed as a statement, since the speaker is not questioning what he hears, only whether anyone else will hear it. In "susurrus" there is that murmur of inner wind heard earlier. The answer that became an exaltation is now firing again and again in the "deep joy" of the sunrise. All of this is the response of the senses, of the spirit to the evidence of the senses, and it may be as good as it gets: this feeling may be "the zenith of our wisdom."

At the end of the poem, "knowledge" and "wisdom" are immediate and palpable. Feeling may be primary, in fact, if we need to establish a priority. Thought and feeling seem reconciled in the "deep influx of spirit" that is identified here with the flow of "the long light," the pause of "the long wind." What are those duration words doing here, attached to images that appeared in the first section of the poem? What comes by flashes is outside the touch of time, which is felt to be stretching out in this ecstacy. All that liquid sunrise flows into the speaker, but this is an "influx of spirit."

The mystery is intact at the end of the poem. Solving it was never Scott's purpose. What he has managed is to grasp and put a reader in touch with something of what it feels like to be full of knowledge and feeling, perched on the brilliant edge of an epiphany.

"THE HEIGHT OF LAND" belongs in a book about the Treaty 9 trips, having clearly been inspired by the ascent and descent of the Pic River in 1906, but it is not one of Scott's "Indian" poems.

Wait a minute.

If "The Height of Land" is not an "Indian" poem it is not so in some fascinating respects that take us back into the poem. The "Indian guides are dead asleep" in the first line of the second section, so that would seem to be it for Native content. "Dead asleep" is actually rather ominous, a way of sweeping the Indians off the stage of the poem, a way that resonates uncomfortably with the cultural pattern of, in Leslie Monkman's phrase, "Death of the Indian." Perhaps I overstate a mere resonance, but it does seem necessary to take note of that strong word, "dead."

A strong word, meant to draw the reader's attention? The thought would die if not for the fact that the names Scott chooses for his guides are anything but neutral. Potàn means "the blower or windmaker," according to Basil Johnston, and Chees-que-ne-ne means "The Tent Shaker."[3] These names are too powerful to show up in the poem by accident. Let me put this another way: even if Scott had no conscious knowledge of the meaning of the names, even if he chose them merely for their sound and for the note of authenticity they would lend a poem set in the North, still they bring *knowledge* into the poem. Suddenly "The Height of Land" is yielding a problem typical of Scott's Indian poems: it houses this knowledge, this information, with which it is tempting to credit Scott, but there is no certainty that he possessed it consciously, no external evidence that he knew the meanings of those names. If he did know, would he have intended the irony that a shaman (possibly two) reduced to the role of guide is servant to a representative of the dominant culture? That is a heavily-freighted subject to introduce only to drop it as the poem goes on to explore the speaker's relationship with his own civilization. Perhaps it comes down to this: if Scott knew what he was doing with those names, he can't have faced up to all the implications of their use. Some of them don't do him credit, either as man or artist.

My hunch is that Scott knows without knowing, that an instinct for power in words drew those names into the poem, where they have lain inert, as mere local colour, until now. Knowing their meaning, knowing also that to an Ojibway (Basil Johnston), the "mournful sound" Chees-que-ne-ne makes refers not to "acquiescence," but to communication with Manitou, one feels the bearers' presence animating the fluctuating wind, touching "region-spirit," "disturber of solitude," and "Something" with a tinge of the indigenous. Potàn and Chees-que-ne-ne are and are not absent after part 1. The poem is not (quite) their dream.

NOTES

1. Did the treaty party unwittingly cause this fire? Stewart suspects a crew of Grand Trunk Pacific Railway surveyors. He says that his own party had been very careful with fires. They would have had to be more careful than the 1905 pre-Albany crew, then. Stewart was not very impressed with their alacrity in putting out a blaze that had spread from the campfire to a nearby tree. In "Twelve Hundred Miles," Edgar makes quite a lot of the waste of timber caused by fires the party saw or heard about in the summer of 1906, and makes a plea for improvement in the forest ranger system.
2. To which pronoun, "they" or "them," does "their" refer, in "they shall be after the race of men / And mourn for them who snared their fiery pinions, / Entangled in the meshes of bright words"? It's possible that the stars are the winged adventurers, and that men snare them.
3. Communicated through Arni Brownstone, Johnston's colleague in Ethnology at the Royal Ontario Museum, in a letter to me.

12

Third Eye

> *You look into the moving, dark, strange Mackenzie River and you will see nothing but yourself; though you will not appear the same as you always imagine yourself.*
> *Rudy Wiebe,* Playing Dead: A Meditation Concerning the Arctic

"[N]OT THE PROBLEM SOLVED," says "The Fragment of a Letter," "but just / The hope of solving opened out and thrust / A little further into the spirit air" (*Poems* 123). Very well, but some problems don't seem to circulate in air, whether of spirit or some more ordinary, but light and optimistic, ether. Some problems are hidden and hiding depths, mysteries fecund and stinking, "slimy viscid things the spirit loathes" (49).

Scott's writing aligns not only "horizontally" on a mental height of land dividing North and South, but also vertically above and below:

> Soft with the silver drip of the regular paddles
> Falling in rhythm, timed with the liquid, plangent
> Sounds from the blades where the whirlpools break and are carried
> Down into darkness;
> Each long cadence, flying like a dove from her shelter
> Deep in the shadow, wheels for a throbbing moment,
> Poises in utterance, returning in circles of silver
> To nest in the silence. (*Poems* 24)

Two spirals: one whirls down; one wheels up, then circles and subsides. In the local context of "Night Hymns on Lake Nipigon," these are falterings of human sound uttered in "wild nature," foreshadowings of whelming in the "splendid hollows of booming thunder," of the fabulous storm that outruns the canoe at the end of the poem. But along the vertical axis of Scott's work as a whole, downward is innerness, the darkness of an obscurity that no one sees except through a veil or mask. Often enough, that innerness is associated with water. It would be silly to ignore the upward movement of spirit in Scott's poetry and thought. It's a true movement of his mind, and he gives it wings at the end of "The Height of Land." But the reader of Scott, worrier at the Scott "problem," has equally to go down into darkness.[1] This might be the case even supposing that Scott was carrying no guilt and fear from his relationship with Native peoples, so it makes no sense to pile up the evidence in "the beauty of terror" or "the little evil thoughts that trouble beauty" ("The Water Lily" 198), and so on, and attribute the lot to Scott's guilt. It *will* be helpful to revisit "Powassan's Drum," where I feel answers to the problem posed at the beginning of this book forming in nightmare. But first I need to resist the temptation to end this book in Scott's house, in his beloved music room, where his whole life was arguably contained.

WHY THE TEMPTATION? Scott's music room has all the marks of an integrative symbol, a gathering of the live terms of, say, a high modernist novel to vibrate in satisfyingly loose but firm association. The figure of Scott's music room offers itself so naturally that it would be perverse not to say what it has to show. In fact, I'm far from the first to arrive at 108 Lisgar for the purpose of reading the music room as a system of signs. E. K. Brown ended up there in his "Memoir," setting Scott's "exquisite maturity" in "the huge high-ceilinged room at the back of his rambling house" (xli); so did Arthur Bourinot, following Brown, in "Some Personal Recollections of Duncan Campbell Scott" (*More Letters* 7). R. L. McDougall arrives there, too, but with a touch of irony, realizing how considerate it was of Scott to have summed himself up in the possessions that he assembled over his fifty-odd years in the same dwelling: "Perhaps all of us enjoy the nice reciprocation between the authorized viewpoint and the authorized endings of many of Scott's poems, where resolution, stasis and a certain sense of elevation bring all tensions to a perfect close" (130). And here I am in my turn, lugging my respect and my irony in the same pack, tempted also to read in this domestic symbol the fossilized deposits of Scott's whole life and art.

The house at 108 Lisgar Street in Ottawa has disappeared, but some of the rooms in it are preserved in words. The kitchen is gone, so is the dining room, the whole top floor — all but one room — much of the house that Belle, and then Elise, would have presided over. What remains in the words of friends and interpreters is the poet's house, not that of his first and second wives. 108 Lisgar must at one time have borne Belle's stamp. Her imperious personality would have insisted on a say in decoration. Her loss as much as Duncan's was sadly remembered by a few of Elizabeth's toys that were always kept on the music room hearth. But what would the shy Elise have brought to this place that was almost an icon before she moved in?

Scott loved her dearly, but would he have understood how rootless one might feel in a house full of mementoes and associations she has had no part in gathering?

Mrs. Wilfrid Eggleston is the only one who takes us upstairs to a room of Elise's that she is clearing out in preparation for her move to India. It is shortly after Scott has died, and Mrs. Eggleston is shocked to find Elise "a school-girl let out on holiday, bubbling with excitement, barely able to contain herself, her face alive and glowing, looking forward to her trip to India, something she had always wanted to do; if all went well, she planned to live there. On and on she went" (*Literary Friends* 118). What does this say of Elise's life with Scott? She must have lived in his shadow, as he may have lived in Belle's. But she might have loved him as deeply as he loved her (see his quartet of sonnets, "Twelfth Anniversary") and still felt a new world opening up to her when he was gone. R. L. McDougall's "The Story of Elise Aylen" has the effect of supporting this impression, since it really begins when she leaves Ottawa. One glance upstairs, at a house in the chaos of packing.

Which room was it that Arthur Bourinot speaks of as containing Scott's Indian artifacts? "One of the rooms in the Scott house always held a peculiar fascination: the walls were hung with Indian relics & trophies & habiliments: buckskin belts covered with bright beads; tomahawks, and even paintings of braves in full regalia. What boy would not have been intrigued by such a display?" (TF Notes for an article on D. C. Scott). Bourinot is speaking of a childhood fascination; Scott must have added to his collection over the years. He came by some Kwagiulth paraphernalia under dubious circumstances in 1922. If this "Indian" room was the music room or the library, wouldn't Bourinot have said so? He makes it sound like a small private museum. A later observer (Alfred Sykes) does say that "About the polished oak furniture [of the music room] were Indian things, glinting silver and pieces of leather and woven geometric designs" (Eggleston 115). "Along the walls," says E. K. Brown, "were low bookcases filled, for the most part, with first editions and the collected works of modern poets; on top of them were varied mementoes of his relations with the Indians . . ." (xli). Maybe the music room *was* that small Indian museum. Perhaps the music room doubled as the library on whose rug Rupert Brooke tumbled with Scott's cat Skookum in 1913. Perhaps he kept his own books here, those he would occasionally present to visitors in his "golden" age, joking that he had no other way of getting rid of them.

Anyway, it was Scott's beloved music room that attracted most searchers for a natural setting in which to place him. This is the room that looks most like a self-portrait. It was a mask, as favourite rooms always are, and a display of the self Scott had prepared for others to see. Others were obligingly reverent of it. It was where he and Belle, he and Elise, entertained; it was where musical guests played. "Lubka Kolessa has played here, Murray and Frances Adaskin, on one occasion the Hart House String Quartet" (McDougall, "Trace" 128–29). The walls were crowded with pictures by Emily Carr, Lawren Harris, Walter J. Phillips, Clarence Gagnon, Horatio Walker, and others. "Over the mantel one by Pegi Nichol McLeod," says Sykes (*Friends* 115). Emily Carr wrote on July 2, 1941, "Mr. [Ira] Dilworth told me he had been to your house & how lovely your big room, all Canadian was. I was proud to think my pictures had found a home in it" (NA/DCS). There were photographs, one of Keats above Scott's reading chair, and one of John Masefield, about which Scott wrote to the laureate on August 24, 1946, saying that he had treasured it since 1912. "It is now in my Music room side by side with the snapshot of yourself and Leonard W. Brockington a copy of which he gave me with your signatures" (TF). There was the grand piano with Karsh's photo of Scott at the piano standing on it. There were his collections of records and musical scores. "I remember when the recordings of Sibelius's 7th Symphony first came out," says an unidentified friend in the typescript of a New York Philharmonic radio broadcast on March 12, 1944,

> ([Scott] was probably the first man in Canada to have them.) We were sitting in the beautiful music room of his house in Ottawa, as he was preparing to start the machine. Just as a little joke I said, 'you haven't got the score of it have you, Duncan?' You must remember that the music was new, having just been published in Finland, and Ottawa was the last place in the world I would have expected to find a score at that moment. But with a twinkle in his eye, he said 'Yes I have' — and handed me the full orchestral score. (ASB)

The favourite chair had a reading light and a pile of books always on the table beside it. It must have been this room Lawren Harris was thinking of when he wrote Scott on May 21, 1944, to say that "It was a delight to see you and visit you in your own home — what a lovely aura your home has . . ." (PA/DCS). From the window, Scott could look out on the corner of his garden that A. S. Bourinot says, "was devoted to Canadian wildflowers": "clumps of Trilliums and Wood Daffodils" (TF).

E. K. Brown found this the ideal setting for Scott in his "perfectly tolerable, perfectly beautiful old age" (xli), because it contains so much of the life of this cultured man. "I am a bit vain in the belief that I have appreciated the Arts and have cultivated my tastes" (*Poet and Critic* 80), he wrote in a rare boast to Brown. Being a life of culture in a still-colonial nation (Ottawa: the last place in the world), Scott's was a marginal Canadian life, and it grew more so in his old age. Some of the newspaper reports of his various anniversaries have the air of reminding the reading public of a cultural treasure hidden in Ottawa. He was never forgotten during his lifetime, but neither was he the grand old man of letters, a title to which he had some claim.

Most descriptions of Scott's music room are like most early accounts of his life, whether at home, at work, or in public: eulogistic. Most observers examine this portrait, this collection, this composition of the local and the foreign, the domestic and the exotic, the "civilized" and the "savage," with pure pleasure. Nobody dwells on the ragged dispersal of the Scotts' effects when Elise finally sold the house. Only Robert McDougall mentions this, and even he takes off his critical hat (as he confesses) to describe the music room with the memorious old poet in it. It's such a lovely picture that I feel like a spoilsport asking the necessary awkward question so many have wished they could put directly to the collector: where did you come by your Indian artifacts, Dr. Scott?

A guided tour of the music room would likely produce many unexceptionable answers: some were likely purchased on trips or given as gifts on personal or official occasions. Of course, all such items are metonyms for various First Nations cultures, exotic relics of "a" race thought to be dying:

> Their past is sold in a shop: the beaded shoes,
> the sweetgrass basket, the curio Indian,
> burnt wood and gaudy cloth and inch-canoes —
> trophies and scalpings for a traveller's den.
> (A. M. Klein, "Indian Reservation: Caughnawaga," *Rocking Chair* 11)

To each item clings the ambiguity of museums, those preservers of often appropriated Native artifacts, and of the exhibitions they mount, increasingly controversial exhibitions like "The Spirit Sings," at the Glenbow Museum in Calgary, or "Out of Africa," at the Royal Ontario Museum in Toronto. After Six Nations objections, a false face mask was, in fact, removed from the former, a response to one of many requests by First Nations peoples for the return of tokens of their past. So the mere existence of a minor museum of Native artifacts in Scott's house raises questions that nothing else there does: questions formed by the whole renegotiation between Native and white cultures that is happening all over the continent. And the hope of high modernist containment in Scott's music room begins to fray. The Scott "problem" rears its head again. And, of course, my question addressed to Dr. Scott was disingenuous.

Potlatch! A Strict Law Bids Us Dance is a film that concentrates on the 1922 government prosecution and conviction of the Kwagiulth for potlatching, the imprisonment of some of the celebrants at Dan Cranmer's 1921 Potlatch, and the outrageous confiscation of coppers, dance masks, and other ceremonial paraphernalia. The film shows that the Potlatch involves much more than the "pagan" ceremony, much more than the flouting of the European economic system, that Scott thought it was. The Potlatch is about relationship — between humans and spirits, humans and animals, humans and humans. It is the locus of all contracts, records of births, naming, marriages, and deaths, transfers of property, and much else. It is central to a whole way of life. To mutilate that way of life is easy: ban the central ritual. This is the dismal story of the residential and industrial schools, the racist story of forced assimilation, all over again. It's also a small cross section of "the major wave of potlatch arrests, charges, prosecutions, convictions, and jailings in British Columbia" (Tennant 101), the "campaign against the potlatch" (Cole and Chaikin 109) that took place after Scott became deputy superintendent and introduced amendments to the Indian Act intended to simplify these procedures.

What happened to the Potlatch paraphernalia? According to the film, some of it went to museums, some to private collectors, some to Duncan Campbell Scott.[2] It's shocking enough to watch this savaging of a culture that should be envied for having such cohesion, without seeing its holy symbols dispersed as artifacts and souvenirs.

Was it one of the masks obtained in the aftermath of the Potlatch prosecutions that Scott sent to John Masefield? "I shall be delighted to see and to own a Red Indian dancing mask," Masefield wrote on December 13, 1928. "Some years ago a young American, who happened to be in Oxford, danced some Red Indian dances for us and I thought them most moving and thrilling." Perhaps, he speculated, the mask would be useful in a production of *Doctor Faustus* that he was soon to be involved with. A play full of devils.

And again, we wind up in a web of contradictory facts. Scott's music room seems to serve well enough as a containing symbol — all the parts of Scott's life rounded up and held together — until we get to the Indian display. Then there is a jumble, not only of the dark side of appropriation. It also comes from other facts that clash and don't connect. Marius Barbeau (along with Edward Sapir, John Swanton, Diamond Jenness, Franz Boas, and others) defended the Potlatch as having religious and social importance; Marius Barbeau was one of those with whom Scott collaborated on a 1928 publication, *Three Songs of the West Coast: Recorded From Singers of Nass River Tribes, Canada.* Barbeau was the folklorist who recorded the songs. Ernest (later Sir Ernest) MacMillan set them to music and introduced them, saying that "the difficult task of providing comprehensible and singable English versions in the spirit of the original has been most ably fulfilled by Dr. Duncan Campbell Scott, to whom I wish to acknowledge my indebtedness" ("Introductory Note"). Barbeau and Scott are on opposite sides of the Potlatch question, and still they hang out with each other in this way?

And Scott seems to have known on some level that masks and other Native paraphernalia had power. In his one act play, *Joy! Joy! Joy!*, one character frightens another to death with an Indian dancing mask ("gorgeous and barbaric," "a hideous demon-mask" PA/DCS) from Alert Bay — where Dan Cranmer's Potlatch was held. This somewhat unlikely *deus ex machina* reminds me of Scott's response to a Walter J. Phillips wood engraving in the 1947 monograph on his artist friend. The whole book says at least as much about Scott as it does about Phillips. One thing it reveals is Scott's lack of qualification for writing it, not that this would be so patent if he didn't keep bringing it up. One of the most revealing passages in this whole idiosyncratic book is the impressionistic overreading of "Kingcome Inlet" (1933):

> I would draw attention to the weird power in this print; it seems to me to depict a native of that region with only a veneer of what we call civilization facing a vestige of aboriginal culture. Kingcome Inlet is on the coast of British Columbia near Alert Bay. The Indian is warned from the coast by a threatening figure, the import of which he may not fully realize, but his boat is of native design. He could not improve on that for his life purposes and he clings to it; but the fetish that faces him bears no message. The villagers that erected it have disappeared and with it the feeling that made the uncouth figure alive with awesome pride. The gulls swooping around are careless of both, and obey an instinct that has not altered for years beyond number. The moment is treated by the artist as drama. In the foreground the sea with lines of disturbance in the water that will relapse into calm and in the background the silent mountains with their slow-moving glaciers and as the sole conscious actor this fisherman who has neither full possession of what we call "our civilization" nor of his racial traditions, afloat, lost and speechless between both. (*Walter J. Phillips* 38)

I don't see all this in the print. The encounter is certainly dramatic, but it looks to me as if the man in the boat and the totem figure face each other in a moment of communication. The totem does look somewhat ominous, but I wouldn't call it "threatening." I see no way of concluding anything about the man, not even that he is Native, let alone stranded between traditions. Scott seems to be looking *through* the engraving at a mythos he once made up and wrote out in stories and poems and now remembers dimly. The interpretation of Phillips's print reads like self-parody. There is a consciousness of power here, but thrown away, diluted, cheapened. Once, when his own powers were at their height, Scott *could* haul in an image like this on his own. I don't make much of Scott's "Kingcome Inlet," weak reprise of his own early work that it is, except as one more sign that little of his early apprehension of the Native situation had changed by the last year of his life.

If I were writing a novel about the 1905 and 1906 treaty-making, I would have to finesse the fact that the climax happens at Lac Seul in the very first encounter with the people Scott was sent to visit, as he confronts the representative of an alien culture who is perhaps his equal in debate. Scott tells us nothing beyond stereotype ("cunning old devil") about Nistonaqueb, because Scott was not learning much, not at least with his reason. Or else he would not have been able to ask, in "The Last of the Indian Treaties,"

> What could they grasp of the pronouncement on the Indian tenure which had been delivered by the law lords of the Crown, what of the elaborate negotiations between a dominion and a province which had made the treaty possible, what of the sense of traditional policy which brooded over the whole? Nothing. (*Circle* 115)

Nothing. Nistonaqueb's discourse is emptied of meaning, as he and the other shamans and elders are unselved into pronoun. There would have been not so much as a word to round out into a world of suppressed meaning had other members of the expedition not written about Nistonaqueb. Into the blank of Scott's nothing now flows the traditional ways that brooded over Nistonaqueb's words.

Time has broken the bubble of "civilization," of "progress," that was Scott's world; it has ironized his career in Indian Affairs. Now we can see him practising a version of Orientalism on the Indians (they cannot represent themselves, they must be represented), and we can see his public discourse serving the conveniently unselfconscious spread of European culture that Mary Louise Pratt analyzes in her essay quoted in chapter 2.

Various documents of the Lac Seul episode undercut "The Last of the Indian Treaties," not to mention Scott's other prose on Indians and Indian Affairs, but surely nothing could be more eloquent on the limitation of his conscious, official statements than "Powassan's Drum," his own poem of white incomprehension. It speaks against him. The drum across Lac Seul in 1905 had a voice that he still could not comprehend when he wrote the poem in 1925. The drum then and now is the gift of the Creator, an agent of prayer. But Scott's comprehension stopped well short of Marlow's in *Heart of Darkness*, the novel of imperialism (with its roots in an account of "Leopold McClintock's successful search for relics of the [Franklin] expedition" [Warkentin 337]) that would inevitably haunt any novel I might write about Scott and Treaty 9. "Whether [the drum] meant war, peace or prayer," says Marlow, "we could not tell." "War, peace or prayer" is at least a list of alternatives.

Naively, I looked a long time at Scott and Treaty 9 from inside the white bubble before seeing that a researcher, lacking some means of bouncing himself away from his material, contributes to the nonconspiracy of silencing voiceless peoples. That was when I began to find out all I could about the peoples with whom Scott was making treaty. What I have found so far in written sources is a drop in the bucket, but just the looking has shifted everything. One shift of the many gives me new eyes for looking at that photograph of Scott at the Root River portage; it turns my attention to the lower half of the image where Scott and Stewart seem to be disappearing in the Root River. The North itself hadn't such power to dissolve Scott's personal and cultural assurance. The expedition into it was too controlled, too insulated. I sense that Nistonaqueb and Powassan, those nesting nightmares that Scott called up when he wrote "Powassan's Drum," almost possessed such power.

"I know now that I have never fought against anything nor worked for anything but just accepted & drifted from point to point — I have dimly felt that if I worked & protested & resisted I should be wrecked — So maybe you will understand why with some gifts I have done so little." Perhaps it's the temptation of fiction that draws Scott's confession of "a life of drift" into a force-field with "Powassan's Drum." Maybe so, but I've been careful for long enough, despite having known from the beginning that the only sure approach to Scott is through the imagination. It's too easy to contextualize "Powassan's Drum" with Scott's confession, but something needs to be done with the fact that the poem floats free of the company of the other "Indian" poems. The best of those are enlightened in contemporary terms and various in their handling of Native ethnicity. I feel that "Powassan's Drum" issued from some part of Scott that was inhabited by a darkness capable of refuting him. A darkness of his own imagining, impotent to dislodge his conscious, public self, but fully capable of shadowing it. Brain is not at the bottom of "Powassan's Drum"; *nightmare* is, "Moulded out of deep sleep," the sleep of reason.

Writing about Wacousta, the "giant dream figure" (3) that he finds haunting, James Reaney says

> there seems to be something about the Industrial Revolution that breeds these Gothic this/that stories: all the rationality of progress only expells Orc, desire, fancy, love to have it come back one foot higher and ravening for your bank account guts. Frankenstein's monster, Wacousta, Hitler, Roderick, Madeline, Jack the Ripper, Captain Nemo, Psycho's motel-owner are kin and illustrative. ("Topless Nightmares" 7)

Also illustrative is this, from Dennis Lee's "The Death of Harold Ladoo":

> For a civilization cannot sustain
> lobotomy, meaning the loss of awe,
> the numbing of *tremendum* — and its holy of holies
> goes dead, even the

> nearest things on earth
> shrink down and lose their savour —
> it cannot dispel the numinous, as we have done for
> centuries without those exiled gods and demons rushing back
> in subterranean concourse,
> altered, mocking, bent on genocide.
> For the gods are not dead; they stalk among us, grown murderous.
> Gone from the kingdom of reason they surface
> in hellish politics, in towering minds
> entranced by pure technique, and in an art refined by
> carnage and impotence, where only form is real.
> And thus we re-enact
> the fierce irrational presencing we denied them — only warped
> grown monstrous in our lives. (53)

They surface in icons of hatred.

Scott's imagination ventured north. Prophetically, it pointed in the cardinal direction of the Canadian compass. His imagination also drowned. When sinking into drowning is also going in behind the mask — as in "Powassan's Drum" — it's also the shark fin showing above the aestheticized "drowned poet"[3] of "The Piper of Arll." White guilt, yes. Also the European nightmare of nihilism, the horror of meaninglessness dissolving the dream of "civilization." Or, the obverse of this, a nightmarish clarity, a seeing with the third eye, as Margaret Atwood re-visions it, showing

> only the worst scenery: gassed and scorched corpses at the cave-mouth, the gutted babies, the spoor left by generals, and, closer to home, the hearts gone bubonic with jealousy and greed, glinting through the vests and sweaters of anyone at all. Torment, they say and see. The third eye can be merciless, especially when wounded.
>
> But someone has to see these things. They exist. Try not to resist the third eye: it knows what it's doing. Leave it alone and it will show you that this truth is not the only truth. (61–62)

Atwood's "Instructions for the Third Eye" ends confident of vision. At the end of *Murder in the Dark,* the Atwood mask is "of the sunrise." But I don't end there.

As this book written to explore it draws to a close, a mystery still lies somewhere between this mild private man with the social conscience that made him a reluctant public man, the tireless worker for various causes — many if not all involved with shaping Canadian identity — and his role as the administrator of Indian Affairs. To most of Scott's white contemporaries, there was no gap. Listening to those people who were suppressed by "his" policies opens the gap wide. What complicates things is that third term, his "Indian" writing. It lies between the private citizen and the administrator, wholly of neither. Valuable writing tainted by an origin in systemic racism, it divides one's allegiance between the poetry and the Indians. And so divided it will remain; the problem will not be solved. That much I think I know. Sometimes I exult to know it. Sometimes I think that what has taken me all these pages to lay out is a nonproblem, that there is nothing unnatural about severe contradiction in the same life. Why then labour to build bridges of motivation over the chasms of mystery? Why not stop reading Scott like an old-fashioned novel. "The loved is what stays / in the mind," says Robert Bringhurst,

> that is, it has meaning,
> and meaning keeps going. This
> is the definition of meaning. (*Pieces of Map* 68)

What resists loving but must be embraced anyway — *that* keeps going, too. Therefore I do not conclude.

❦

ARTHUR BOURINOT SAYS that Scott's Indian name was Da-ha-wen-non-tye. This is a Mohawk word, properly spelled Tahawennontye. According to David Maracle, of the Centre for Research and Teaching of Canadian Native Languages at the University of Western Ontario, it would probably have been the ceremonial gift of Six Nations Mohawks. Bourinot records the translation of this name as "Flying or floating voice, us-wards." The translation is no name a man would ever want to use. Flying Voice, by itself, would be attractive. There is a hint of speed and of "wingèd words" in it. Floating Voice, on its own, is a few degrees less appealing. Levitation going nowhere. If the full name were to work in English, there would have to be a way of folding in the "us-wards," which gives the direction of the flight or the floating. A one-way flight. A talking rather than a listening? Is this really "Disembodied Voice," the man we never see whose words control our lives? The man for whom one truth is enough. David Maracle doesn't discount the possibility of an ambiguity in this gift-name. *De*hawennontye, he says, would be "words flying in both directions," a Mohawk metaphor for an untrustworthy person.

*

"LITERATURE WRITTEN in Australia and Canada on native subjects by non-native, Eurocentric writers," says J. J. Healy, "is likely to hold little interest for the Aboriginal or Indian reader. Such literature, irrespective of its imaginative power, is likely to have the smell of conquest. It is likely to have a narrative arrogance, one which subjugates Amerindian or Aboriginal space to the master narrative — social, political, ideological — of the dominant culture"

(69). I wonder about that first "likely." I wonder if George Bowering doesn't have a truer, less essentializing, take on this matter albeit in a novel. "Whenever they could," the narrator says of the first and second Indians in *Caprice*, "they tried to satisfy their curiosity about the white men." The elder tells the younger that "The people of my grandfather's grandfather's time paid the price for not watching everything the newcomers were doing. In our time the wise man will know everything that goes on in this valley" (129). These men watch everything that goes on in the novel. They see less than a hawk sees, but they process information beautifully. They're terrific readers. If they had been willing to offer anything of their meta-sensibility, or even some hard information, to the white people whose story they are so perceptively observing, they would be a figure for what I want and need: the double of this book, the one that begins in Cree or Ojibway culture and writes its way toward Scott.

*

IN THE SUMMER OF 1994, Michael Bucknor is about to give a graduate seminar on the William Wordsworth of *The Lyrical Ballads*. Michael has never seen a daffodil, and he's quietly gleeful about that. The twinkle in his eye is attitude. It isn't often that what you don't know can be made to work for you, but Michael has prepared a postcolonial reading of poems like "I Wandered Lonely as a Cloud," the first Wordsworth he ever encountered. In his approach, the daffodil is not a flower universally known and admired; to Jamaicans like himself the daffodil is a question. A month earlier, I could have shown Michael a few daffodils in my backyard and soiled the purity of his valuable ignorance. Or maybe only "a crowd, / A host of golden daffodils" could have done that. I've never seen enough daffodils in one place to set my own heart dancing. Maybe Wordsworth's daffodils should be a problem to native-born Canadians as well.

Michael Bucknor is in his second year in southwestern Ontario, having shivered good-humouredly through two of our cold winters while accommodating himself to our distant ways. We have accepted large numbers of tropical people into our northern country. Our South is plenty northern to them, as the North Scott was canoeing in 1905 and 1906 is a long way south of the arctic. What is true North? What is North at all to these Canadians of tropical origin: Rienzi Crusz, the Sri Lankan-Canadian writer of "Sun Man" poems, or Olive Senior, Jamaican-Canadian author of *Gardening in the Tropics*, published by "the Canadian publishers," McClelland and Stewart?

To that question, there are many answers. One of them is George Blake, now of Oshawa via the Caribbean. Among other things, George is a storyteller; he tells Jataka tales (of the Buddha) and Caribbean folktales. He also loves to canoe in the Ontario Near North and feels no incongruity in that. Doing so, a first-generation Canadian who grew up in the tropics, is he less or more adapted to the land than the second-generation Scott was in 1905 and 1906? The land accepts those who accept it, after all, regardless of race. Nothing will measure such differences, and I don't really want an answer. What I want is a way to avoid looking north with only my own native eyes. Because the racially stable white Canada dreamed by Scott and his contemporaries never came true, it's wonderfully possible to estrange my own vision in diverse ways. I have worked at this by putting myself through stories (and The Story) of First Nations peoples. Much of the alienation I found there has its parallels in the stories of other Canadians unable to claim one of the white ethnicities heraldically displayed in English Canada's unofficial anthem:

> The thistle, shamrock, rose entwine
> The Maple Leaf forever.

The fleur de lys of Quebec is significantly not twining nicely with the others — neither in the song nor, in 1994, the nation.

Because of a chance encounter with Michael Bucknor, I'm reconsidering daffodils and diverting my northern thoughts through a tropical filter. I once considered adopting Gwendolyn MacEwen's wonderful poem "Dark Pines Under Water" as the last of these elliptical passages, but I think I have sufficiently elaborated the intertwining of North, water, change, and loss of identity. Now, in the words of Michael Ondaatje's "Spider Blues," I use my "ending / to swivel to new regions / where the raw of feelings exist" (*Rat Jelly* 63–64).

NOTES

1. For a useful mapping of the symbolic ups and downs in Scott's poems, see Kathy Mezei's "From Lifeless Pools to the Circle of Affection: The significance of Space in the Poetry of D. C. Scott."
2. Scott certainly hounded the Potlatches, as he resisted the settlement of British Columbia land claims, and perhaps he came to *be* the Department of Indian Affairs for the Kwagiulth and others. Douglas Cole's *Captured Heritage: The Scramble for Northwest Coast Artifacts* confirms the allegation of *Potlatch* (a film he and Ira Chaikin call "excellent" [1] in their later *The Iron Hand Upon the People: The Law Against the Potlatch on the Northwest Coast*). About the part of the Potlatch material that went East, he says: "The bulk of the collection was kept by the National Museum in Ottawa with a portion, about one hundred pieces, donated to the Royal Ontario Museum in Toronto. Eleven items were retained by Indian Affairs and displayed in Scott's office; all but two of these were sent to the National Museum in 1932" (253–54).
3. See Milton Wilson in "Klein's Drowned Poet: Variations on an Old Theme." This is a wonderful article that valorizes the closed economy of "The Piper of Arll" because in it Scott "escapes from the peevish nostalgia and spasmodic violence which are the personal sediment in his work as a whole" (Dragland, *Duncan Campbell Scott* 136). "Sediment" is an apt word, but the violence at least is more than personal, and perhaps it's Wilson who is the escapee.

Works Cited

Archival Materials

Canadian Broadcasting Corporation, Toronto

CBC 2d2s. National School Broadcasts. September 16, 1967. 2515 470916–2 on 860714–14(3): Duncan Campbell Scott reading "A Song" [*Circle of Affection* 54]

Hudson's Bay Company Archives, Winnipeg

HBCa E. B. Borron, "Report on Indians in Southern Department," 1890 D76/15/Fac 1–55

HBCb Daily Occurrences Journal, Osnaburgh Post (1901–1906) B 3/a/205

HBCc Albany Post Journals (March 20, 1904–November 18, 1906) B/155/a/95

National Library, Ottawa

ASB A. S. Bourinot Papers

Public Archives of Canada, Ottawa

PA/EKB E. K. Brown Papers MG 30 D 61

PA/DCS Duncan Campbell Scott Papers MG 30 D 100

PA/S-A D. C. Scott — E. Aylen Papers MG 30 D 276

Department of Indian Affairs Archives

RG10a RG10 Vol. 725: William Scott, Oka Indian Report

RG10b RG10 Vol. 1028: D. C. Scott Journal (June 30–September 6, 1905); Pelham Edgar Diary (May 22–August 16, 1906)

RG10c RG10 Vol. 3105, 309–350–3: James Bay Agency Survey of Treaty No. 9: W. Galbraith Journal (1910); James S. Dobie Survey (1912)

RG10d RG10 Vol. 3033, 235, 225: Treaty No. 9 The James Bay Treaty-Reports, Correspondence, Drafts, Memoranda, Order in Council

RG10e RG10 Vol. 11, 399: Samuel Stewart Journal (June 30–September 9, 1905; May 22–August 15, 1906; June 15–July 1, 1908)

RG10f RG10 Vol. 6810, 473–12: Hearings testimony, 1921–22

National Photography Collection, Ottawa

Acc. 1971–205, Box 3266 F1: Treaty No. 9 Photographs

Queen's University Archives, Kingston

Q/RK Raymond Knister Papers

Q/LP Lorne Pierce Papers
Q/DCS Duncan Campbell Scott Papers
Q/EM Edmund Morris Papers
Thomas Fisher Rare Book Library, University of Toronto, Toronto
TF Duncan Campbell Scott Papers
Victoria University Library, Toronto
V/EKB E. K. Brown Papers
V/PE Pelham Edgar Papers

Government Documents

Canada. Commission on Conservation. *National Conference on Conservation of Game, Fur-Bearing Animals and Other Wild Life.* Ottawa: King's Printer, 1919.

Canada. *The James Bay Treaty, Treaty No. 9 (Made in 1905 and 1906 and Adhesions Made in 1929 and 1930).* Ottawa: Queen's Printer, 1964.

Canada. Sessional Papers. Department of Indian Affairs. *Annual Reports.*

Ontario. Presentations to the Royal Commission on the Northern Environment, 1977 to 1983.

Cat Lake Band, Chief Jasper Keesickquayash. Osnaburgh, December 6, 1977.

Lac Seul Band, Chief R. Ningewance. Sioux Lookout, November 7, 1977.

Locke, James. Moosonee, February 1, 1978.

Moose Factory Band Council. Chief Munroe Linklater, February 2, 1978.

Wesley, James. Moose Factory, February 2, 1978.

Works by D. C. Scott
(In chronological order)

"Coiniac Street." *The Globe* November 23, 1889.

The Magic House and Other Poems. London: Methuen, 1893; Ottawa: Durie, 1893; Boston: Copeland and Day, 1895.

[Silas Reading, pseud.] "Open Letter to a Member of Parliament." Ottawa, *The Evening Journal.* Tuesday, February 21, 1893.

"Canadian Feeling Toward the United States." *The Bookman* (June 1896), 333–36.

Labor and the Angel. Boston: Copeland and Day, 1898.

"A Decade of Canadian Poetry." *Canadian Magazine* 17 (1901) 153–58; Lorraine McMullen, ed. *Twentieth Century Essays on Canadian Literature.* Ottawa: Tecumseh, 1976.

"Lord Strathcona." *Ainslee's Magazine* 8 (1901–1902), 552–60.

New World Lyrics and Ballads. Toronto: Morang, 1905.

John Graves Simcoe. Makers of Canada Series. Ed. D. C. Scott and Pelham Edgar. Toronto: Morang, 1905; Toronto: Oxford University P, 1926.

Via Borealis. Decorations by A. H. Howard. Toronto: Tyrell, 1906.

"The Last of the Indian Treaties." *Scribner's* XL (1906), 573–83.

"George Meredith, The Dean of English Novelists." *Munsey's Magazine* 38, 6 (March 1908), 798–802.

"Introduction." Amelia Paget. *People of the Plains.* Ottawa: Department of Indian Affairs, 1909.

"Introduction." *Traditional History of the Confederacy of the Six Nations.* Prepared by a Committee of the Chiefs. Ottawa: Royal Society of Canada, 1912.

"Notes on the Meeting Place of the First Parliament of Upper Canada and the Early Buildings of Niagara." *Royal Society of Canada Proceedings and Transactions.* Third Series, 7 (1913–1914), 175–91.

"Indian Affairs, 1763–1841." *Canada and Its Provinces* (Vol. 4, Section 2, Part 2, *British Dominion*). Eds. Adam Shortt and Arthur G. Doughty. Toronto: Glasgow, Brook and Co., 1914.

"Indian Affairs, 1840–1867." *Canada and Its Provinces* (Vol.. 5, Section 3, *United Canada*). Toronto: Glasgow, Brook and Co., 1914.

"Indian Affairs, 1867–1912." *Canada and Its Provinces* (Vol.. 7, Section 4, *The Dominion*). Toronto: Glasgow, Brook and Co., 1914.

Lundy's Lane and Other Poems. New York: Doran, 1916; Toronto: McClelland and Stewart, 1916.

"Relation of Indians to Wild Life Conservation." *National Conference on Conservation of Game, Fur-Bearing animals and Other Wild Life.* Ottawa: King's Printer, 1919.

"The Red Indian." *The Times* (London), Tuesday, May 25, 1920.

Beauty and Life. Toronto: McClelland and Stewart, 1921.

"Poetry and Progress." Presidential Address delivered before the Royal Society of Canada, May 17, 1922. *Royal Society of Canada Proceedings and Transactions,* 3rd Series, 16 (1922), xlvii–lxvii; *Canadian Magazine* 60 (1923), 187–95; Dragland, ed. *Duncan Campbell Scott: A Book of Criticism,* 7–27.

The Witching of Elspie. Toronto: McClelland and Stewart, 1923. Rpt. New York: Books for Libraries, 1972.

"The Aboriginal Races." W. P. M. Kennedy, ed. *Social and Economic Conditions in the Dominion of Canada.* Philadelphia: American Academy of Political and Social Sciences, 1923.

The Poems of Duncan Campbell Scott. Toronto: McClelland and Stewart, 1926; Introd. John Masefield. London: Dent, 1927.

Three Songs of the West Coast, by Marius Barbeau. English version by Duncan Campbell Scott. Transcribed and Arranged by Ernest MacMillan. London: The Frederick Harris Co., 1928.

"Archibald Lampman." *Addresses Delivered at the Dedication of the Archibald Lampman Memorial Cairn at Morpeth, Ontario.* London: The Western Ontario Branch of the Canadian Author's Association, 1930.

"Foreword," *Roses of Shadow,* by Elise Aylen. Toronto: Macmillan, 1930.

"The Administration of Indian Affairs in Canada." Ottawa: Canadian Institute of International Affairs, 1931.

"Foreword." Percy F. Godenrath, Comp. *Catalogue of the Manoir Richelieu Collection of North American Indians.* Montreal: Canada Steamship Lines, 1932.

The Green Cloister: Later Poems. Toronto: McClelland and Stewart, 1935.

"Clarence Gagnon: Recollection and Record." *Maritime Art* 3, 1 (October–November 1942), 5–8.

The Circle of Affection and Other Pieces in Prose and Verse. Drawings by Thoreau MacDonald. Toronto: McClelland and Stewart, 1947.

Walter J. Phillips. Toronto: Ryerson, 1947.

Selected Poems of Duncan Campbell Scott. Ed. E. K. Brown, with a Memoir. Toronto: Ryerson, 1951.

Selected Stories of Duncan Campbell Scott. Ed. and Introd. Glenn Clever. Ottawa: University of Ottawa P, 1972.

In the Village of Viger and Other Stories. Ed. and Introd. Stan Dragland. Toronto: McClelland and Stewart, 1974.

Untitled Novel, ca. 1905. Ed. John Flood, with an Afterword. Moonbeam, ON: Penumbra, 1979.

Powassan's Drum. Ed. Raymond Souster and Douglas Lochhead. Ottawa: Tecumseh, 1985.

Secondary Sources

Anon. "Bard of Silent Northland Stirs Hearers with Poems." Toronto, *The Globe,* Thursday, April 23, 1925.

[Anderson, David]. The Bishop of Rupert's Land. *The Net in the Bay; or, Journal of a Visit to Moose and Albany.* London: Thos. Hatchard, 1854.

Appiah, Antony. "The Uncompleted Argument: Du Bois and the Illusion of Race." *Critical Inquiry* 12 (Autumn 1985), 21–37.

Arnold, Matthew. *Poetical Works.* Ed. C. B. Tinker and H. F. Lowry. London: Oxford University P, 1966.

Ashcroft, Bill, Gareth Griffiths, and Helen Tiffin. *The Empire Writes Back: Theory and Practice in Post-colonial Literature.* London and New York: Routledge, 1989.

Atwood, Margaret. *The Journals of Susanna Moodie.* Toronto: Oxford, 1970.

———. *Survival: a Thematic Guide to Canadian Literature.* Toronto: Anansi, 1972.

———. *Murder in the Dark.* Toronto: Coach House, 1983.

Baker, Marie Annharte. "Borrowing Enemy Language: A First Nation Woman Use of English." *West Coast Line* 10.27/1 (Spring 1993), 59–68.

Bentley, D. M. R. "Drawers of Water: The Significance and Scenery of Fresh Water in Canadian Poetry." (Parts 2 & 3). *Contemporary Verse II* 7.1 (November 1982), 25–50.

———. "Alchemical Transmutation in Duncan Campbell Scott's 'At Gull Lake: August 1810,' Some Contingent Speculations." *Studies in Canadian Literature* 10, 1–2 (1985), 1–23.

Bird, John, and Diane Engelstad, eds. *Nation to Nation: Aboriginal Sovereignty and the Future of Canada.* Toronto: Anansi, 1992.

Birney, Earle. *The Collected Poems of Earle Birney.* Vol. 1. Toronto: McClelland and Stewart, 1975.

Blaise, Clark. *Resident Alien.* Harmondsworth: Penguin, 1986.

Boas, Franz. *The Ethnography of Franz Boas: Letters and Diaries of Franz Boas Written on the Northwest Coast from 1886 to 1931*. Ed. and Comp. Ronda P. Rohner. Trans. Hedy Parker. Chicago: University of Chicago P, 1969.

Borges, Jorge Luis. *Labyrinths: Selected Stories and Other Writings*. Ed. Donald A. Yates and James E. Irby. Pref. Andre Maurois. New York: New Directions, 1964.

———. *Dreamtigers*. Trans. Mildred Bayer. Pref. Victor Lange. Introd. Miguel Enguidanos. New York: Dutton, 1970.

Borland, John. *An Appeal to the Montreal Conference and Methodist Church generally, from a charge by Rev. William Scott*. Montreal: "Witness" Print House, 1883.

Bourinot, A. S., ed. *At the Mermaid Inn: Wilfred Campbell, Archibald Lampman, Duncan Campbell Scott in "The Globe" 1892–1893*. Ottawa: A. S. Bourinot, 1958.

———. *Some Letters of Duncan Campbell Scott, Archibald Lampman and Others*. Ottawa: A. S. Bourinot, 1959.

———. *More Letters of Duncan Campbell Scott* (2nd Series). Ottawa: A. S. Bourinot, 1960.

Bowering, George. *Burning Water*. Toronto: Musson, 1980.

———. *Caprice*. Markham, ON: Penguin, 1987.

Bringhurst, Robert. *Pieces of Map, Pieces of Music*. Toronto: McClelland and Stewart, 1986.

———. "This Also Is You: Some Classics of Native Canadian Literature." W. H. New, ed. *Native Writers and Canadian Writing*. Vancouver: University of British Columbia P, 1990.

———. *The Elements of Typographic Style*. Vancouver: Harley and Marks, 1992.

Brooke, Rupert. *Letters From America*. With a Preface by Henry James. London: Sidgwick & Jackson, 1916.

Brockington, Leonard. "Duncan Campbell Scott's Eightieth Birthday." *Saturday Night* (August 1942), 25.

Bromige, David. *Threads*. Los Angeles: Black Sparrow, 1971.

Bronte, Emily. *Wuthering Heights*. London: Oxford University P, 1976.

Brown, E. K. "Duncan Campbell Scott: An Individual Poet." *Manitoba Arts Review* II (1941), 51–54.

———. *On Canadian Poetry*. Toronto: Ryerson, 1943; Ottawa: Tecumseh, 1977.

———. "Now Take Ontario." *Maclean's*, June 1947. 12: 30–32; *Responses and Evaluations: Essays on Canada*. Ed. and Introd. David Staines. Toronto: McClelland and Stewart, 1977.

———. "Memoir." *Selected Poems of Duncan Campbell Scott*. Toronto: Ryerson, 1951.

Brown, Jennifer S. H., and Robert Brightman, eds. *"The Orders of the Dreamed": George Nelson on Cree and Northern Ojibway Religion and Myth, 1823*. Winnipeg: University of Manitoba P, 1988.

Bryce, P. H. *The Story of a National Crime: Being an Appeal for Justice to the Indians of Canada*. Ottawa: James Hope, 1922.

Bush, Douglas. "Making Literature Hum." Douglas M. Daymond and Leslie G. Monkman, eds. *Towards a Canadian Literature: Essays, Editorials & Manifestoes*. Vol. 1. 1752–1940. Ottawa: Tecumseh, 1984.

Byatt, A. S. "Interview" with Jeffrey Canton. *What!* 28 & 29 (December 1991), 5–8.
Cameron, Anne. "The Operative Principle is Trust." Libby Sheier, Sarah Sheard, and Eleanor Wachtel, eds. *Language in Her Eye.* Toronto: Coach House, 1990.
Campbell, Maria. *Halfbreed.* Toronto: McClelland and Stewart, 1973.
———, and Linda Griffiths. *The Book of Jessica: a Theatrical Transformation.* Toronto: Coach House, 1989.
Carey, Peter. *Oscar and Lucinda.* London: Faber and Faber, 1988.
Carroll, Lewis. *Complete Works.* Introd. Alexander Woolcott. Illust. John Tenniel. New York: Vintage, 1976.
Chamberlin, J. E. *The Harrowing of Eden: White Attitudes Toward Native Americans.* New York: Seabury P, 1975.
Clark, Joan. *The Victory of Josephine Gull.* Toronto: McClelland and Stewart, 1989.
Cogswell, Fred. "No Heavenly Harmony: A Reading of Powassan's Drum." *Studies in Canadian Literature* 1 (Summer 1976), 233–37.
Cohen, Leonard. *Beautiful Losers.* Toronto: McClelland and Stewart, 1966.
Cole, Douglas. *Captured Heritage: The Scramble for Northwest Coast Artifacts.* Seattle: University of Washington P, 1985.
———, and Ira Chaikin. *An Iron Hand Upon the People: The Law Against the Potlatch on the Northwest Coast.* Vancouver/Toronto: Douglas & McIntyre; Seattle: University of Washington P, 1990.
Conrad, Joseph. *Heart of Darkness: An Authoritative Text, Backgrounds and Sources, Essays in Criticism.* Ed. Robert Kimbough. New York: Norton, 1963.
Culleton, Beatrice. *In Search of April Raintree.* Winnipeg: Pemmican, 1983.
Dagg, Melvin H. "Scott and the Indians." *The Humanities Association Review* XXIII (1972), 3–11; S. L. Dragland, ed. *Duncan Campbell Scott: A Book of Criticism.* Ottawa: Tecumseh, 1974.
Davies, Barry, ed. *At the Mermaid Inn: Wilfred Campbell, Archibald Lampman, Duncan Campbell Scott in The Globe, 1892–93.* Toronto: University of Toronto P, 1979.
Dempsey, Hugh. *Charcoal's World.* Saskatoon: Western Producer, 1978.
Denny, Peter. Note to the author, 1993.
Derrida, Jacques. *Of Grammatology.* Trans. and Introd. Gayatri Chakravorty Spivak. Baltimore and London: Johns Hopkins UP, 1976.
Dewdney, Christopher. *Predators of the Adoration: Selected Poems 1972–82.* Toronto: McClelland and Stewart, 1983.
Dewdney, Selwyn and Kenneth Kidd. *Indian Rock Paintings of the Great Lakes.* Toronto: Quetico Fdn./University of Toronto P, 1962.
———. *The Sacred Scrolls of the Southern Ojibway.* Toronto: University of Toronto P for The Glenbow Institute, 1975.
Dickason, Olive Patricia. *Canada's First Nations: A History of Founding Peoples From Earliest Times.* Toronto: McClelland and Stewart, 1992.
Dickens, Charles. *Great Expectations.* Ed. R. D. McMaster. Toronto: Macmillan, 1965.
Dragland, Stan, ed. *Duncan Campbell Scott: A Book of Criticism.* Ottawa: Tecumseh, 1974.

Driben, Paul and Robert S. Trudeau. *When Freedom is Lost: the Dark Side of the Relationship between Government and the Fort Hope Band.* Toronto: University of Toronto P, 1983.

"Drums." Typescript. Ojibway–Cree Cultural Centre, Timmins, ON.

"Duncan Campbell Scott." *The Toronto Daily Star,* Thursday April 23, 1925.

Edgar, Pelham. "Twelve Hundred Miles By Canoe: Among the Indians in Northern Waters." *Canada* IV (November 24, 1906), 255; "Second Letter" (December 22, 1906) 436; "Ottawa to Abitibi" (January 5, 1907), 515–16; "Latchford to Matachewan" (January 19, 1907), 61–62; "Biscotasing to Fort Matagami" (February 2, 1907), 156–57; "Fort Matagami" (February 16, 1907), 245–46; "The Homeward Journey" (March 16, 1907), 412–13.

———. "Duncan Campbell Scott." *The Dalhousie Review* VII, i (April 1927), 38–46.

———. "Travelling with a Poet." *Across My Path.* Ed. Northrop Frye. Toronto: Ryerson, 1952.

Eggleston, Wilfrid. *Literary Friends.* Ottawa: Borealis, 1980.

Eliot, T. S. *Collected Poems 1909–1962.* London: Faber, 1963.

Fee, Margery. "Why C. K. Stead didn't like Keri Hulme's *the bone people*: Who Can Write As Other?" *Australian and New Zealand Studies in Canada* 1 (Spring 1989), 11–32.

Fiddler, Chief Thomas. *Legends from the Forest.* James R. Stevens, ed. and Trans. Edtrip Fiddler. Moonbeam, ON: Penumbra, 1985.

———, and James Stevens. *Killing the Shamen.* Moonbeam, ON: Penumbra, 1985.

Flood, John. "The Duplicity of D. C. Scott and the James Bay Treaty." *Black Moss* 2nd Series, 2 (Fall 1976), 50–63.

———. *The Land They Occupied.* Erin, ON: Porcupine's Quill, 1976.

———. "Native People in Scott's Short Fiction." K. P. Stich, ed. *The Duncan Campbell Scott Symposium.* Ottawa: University of Ottawa P, 1979.

Frye, Northrop. *The Bush Garden.* Toronto: Anansi, 1971.

———. *The Secular Scripture: A Study of the Structure of Romance.* Cambridge, MA: Harvard University P, 1976.

Gates, Henry Louis. "Editor's Introduction: Writing 'Race' and the Difference it Makes." *Critical Inquiry* 12 (Autumn 1985), 1–20.

Geddes, Gary. "Piper of Many Tunes: Duncan Campbell Scott." *Duncan Campbell Scott: A Book of Criticism.* Ed. S. L. Dragland. Ottawa: Tecumseh, 1974.

Gerson, Carole. "The Piper's Forgotten Tune: Notes on the Stories of D. C. Scott and a Bibliography." *Journal of Canadian Fiction* 16 (1976), 138–43.

Goldie, Terry. *Fear and Temptation: The Image of the Indigene in Canadian, Australian, and New Zealand Literatures.* Kingston, Montreal, London: McGill-Queens UP, 1989.

———, and Daniel David Moses, eds. *An Anthology of Canadian Native Literature in English.* Toronto: Oxford UP, 1992.

Gould, Glenn. "The Idea of North." Brochure in *Glenn Gould's Solitude Trilogy.* PSCD 2003–3. Toronto: CBC, 1992.

Grahame, Kenneth. *The Wind in the Willows.* Illust. G. H. Shepard. New York: Scribner's, 1908.

Grant, George. *Technology and Empire.* Toronto: Anansi, 1969.

Grant, S. D. "Indian Affairs Under Duncan Campbell Scott: The Plains Cree of Saskatchewan 1913–1931." *Journal of Canadian Studies* 18,3 (Fall 1983), 21–39.

Grinnell, George Bird. *Blackfoot Lodge Tales.* New York: Scribner's, 1892.

Healy, J. J. "Literature, Power and the Refusals of Big Bear: Reflections on the Treatment of the Indian and of the Aborigine." Russell McDougall and Gillian Whitlock, eds. *Australian/Canadian Literatures in English: Comparative Perspectives.* Melbourne, Adelaide, Brisbane, Perth: Methuen Australia, 1987.

Highway, Tomson. *Dry Lips Oughta Move to Kapuskasing.* Saskatoon: Fifth House, 1989.

Hirano, Keiichi. "The Aborigine in Canadian Literature." *Canadian Literature* XIV (1962), 44–47.

Hughes, Ted. *Crow.* London: Faber, 1971.

Hurston, Zora Neale. *Mules and Men.* Preface by Franz Boas. New Foreword by Arnold Rampersad. Illustrations by Miguel Covarrubia. New York: Harper and Row, 1990.

Hutcheon, Linda. "Incredulity Toward Meta-narrative: Negotiating Postmodernism and Feminisms." *Tessera* 7 (Fall/Automne 1989), 39–44.

Innis, H. A. *The Fur Trade in Canada: An Introduction to Canadian Economic History.* Prepared by S. D. Clark and W. T. Easterbrook. Foreword by Robin W. Winks. University of Toronto P, 1962.

Itwaru, Arnold Harrichand. *The Invention of Canada: Literary Text and the Immigrant Imagination.* Toronto: TSAR, 1990.

JanMohamed, Abdul R. "The Economy of Manichean Allegory: The Function of Racial Difference in Colonialist Literature." *Critical Inquiry* 12 (Autumn 1985), 59–87.

Johnson, A. W. "The Role of the Deputy Minister." W. D. K. Kernaghan and A. M. Williams, eds. *Public Adminstration in Canada: Selected Readings.* Toronto: Methuen, 1971.

Johnston, Basil. *Ojibway Heritage.* Toronto: McClelland and Stewart, 1976.

———. *Ojibway Ceremonies.* Illustrations by David Beyer. Toronto: McClelland and Stewart, 1982.

———. *Indian School Days.* Toronto: Key Porter, 1988.

———. "One Generation From Extinction." *Native Writers and Canadian Writing.* Ed. W. H. New. Vancouver: University of British Columbia P, 1990.

Johnston, Gordon. "Duncan Campbell Scott." Robert Lecker, Jack David, Ellen Quigley, eds. *Canadian Writers and Their Works* Poetry Series Vol. 2. Toronto: ECW, 1983.

Jones, D.G. *Butterfly on Rock.* Toronto: University of Toronto P, 1970.

Keith, W. J. *Literary Images of Ontario.* Ontario Historical Studies Series. Government of Ontario. Toronto: University of Toronto P, 1992.

Kelly, John. "We Are All in the Ojibway Circle: My Genocide is Your Genocide." Submission to the RCNE, November 3, 1977; Michael Ondaatje, ed. *From Ink Lake.* Toronto: Lester and Orpen Dennys, 1991.

King, Thomas, ed. *All My Relations: an anthology of contemporary Canadian native fiction.* Toronto: McClelland and Stewart, 1990.
———. *Medicine River.* Markham, ON: Viking, 1990.
———. *Coyote Columbus Story.* Toronto/Vancouver: Groundwood, Douglas & McIntyre, 1992.
———. *One Good Story, That One.* Toronto: HarperCollins, 1993.
———. *Green Grass, Running Water.* Toronto: HarperCollins, 1993.
Kinsella, W. P. *Shoeless Joe.* New York: Houghton Mifflin, 1982.
Klein, A. M. *The Rocking Chair and Other Poems.* Toronto: Ryerson, 1948.
Kogawa, Joy. *Obasan.* Markham, ON: Penguin, 1981.
Kreiner, Philip. *People Like Us in a Place Like This.* Ottawa: Oberon, 1983.
———. *Contact Prints.* Toronto: Doubleday, 1987.
Kristeva, Julia. *Revolution in Poetic Language.* Introduction by Leon S. Roudiez. New York: Columbia University P, 1984.
Kroetsch, Robert. *But We Are Exiles.* Toronto: Macmillan, 1965.
———. *The Stone Hammer Poems, 1960–1975.* Nanaimo, B.C.: Oolichan, 1975.
———. *The Lovely Treachery of Words.* Toronto: Oxford University P, 1989.
Lampman, Archibald. *The Poems of Archibald Lampman.* Ed. with memoir, Duncan Campbell Scott. Toronto: Morang, 1900.
LaViolette, Forrest E. *The Struggle for Survival: Indian Cultures and the Protestant Ethic in British Columbia.* Vancouver: University of British Columbia P, 1961.
Leacock, Stephen. "I'll Stay in Canada." *Funny Pieces: A Book of Random Sketches.* New York: Dodd, Mead, 1936.
Lee, Dennis. *Civil Elegies and Other Poems.* Toronto: Anansi, 1972.
———, and Robin Mathews. "Rejoinder." *Saturday Night* 87 (September 1972), 31–33.
———. *Savage Fields.* Toronto: Anansi, 1977.
———. *The Gods.* Toronto: McClelland and Stewart, 1979.
———. "Polyphony: Enacting a Meditation." *Tasks of Passion: Dennis Lee at Mid-Career.* Toronto: Descant, 1982.
Lessing, Doris. *Prisons We Choose To Live Inside.* CBC Massey Lectures Series. Montreal: CBC Enterprises, 1986; Toronto: Anansi, 1992.
Lilburn, Tim. "Thoughts Towards a Christian Poetics." *Brick* 29 (Winter 1987), 34–36.
Long, John. *Treaty No. 9: The Half-Breed Question, 1902–1910.* Cobalt, ON: Highway Bookshop, 1978.
———. *Treaty No. 9: The Indian Petitions, 1889–1927.* Cobalt, ON: Highway Bookshop, 1978.
———. *Treaty No. 9: The Negotiations, 1901–1928.* Cobalt, ON: Highway Bookshop, 1978.
Lynch, Gerald. "An Endless Flow: D. C. Scott's Indian Poems." *Studies in Canadian Literature* 7, 1 (1982), 27–54.
Macbeth, Madge. *Over My Shoulder.* Toronto: Ryerson, n.d.

MacEwen, Gwendolyn. *The Shadow-Maker.* Toronto: Macmillan, 1969.

Marshall, Tom. *Harsh and Lonely Land: The Major Poets and the Making of a Canadian Tradition.* Vancouver: University of British Columbia P, 1979.

Matthews, John. "'Redeem the Time': Imaginative Synthesis in the Poetry of Duncan Campbell Scott and Christopher Brennan." *The Duncan Campbell Scott Symposium.* K. P. Stich, ed. Ottawa: U of Ottawa P, 1979.

Masefield, John. *In the Mill.* New York: Macmillan, 1941.

McDougall, Robert L. "D. C. Scott: A Trace of Documents and a Touch of Life." K. P. Stich, ed. *The Duncan Campbell Scott Symposium.* Ottawa: University of Ottawa P, 1979.

———, ed. *The Poet and the Critic: A Literary Correspondence Between D. C. Scott and E. K. Brown.* Ottawa: Carleton University P, 1983.

———. "The Story of Elise Aylen." Om P. Juneja and Chandra Mohan, eds. *Ambivalence: Studies in Canadian Literature.* Foreword by Margaret Atwood. New Delhi: Allied, 1990. Rpt. in *Totems: Essays in the Cultural History of Canada.* Ottawa: Tecumseh, 1990.

McGill, Jean S. *Edmund Morris: Frontier Artist.* Toronto and Charlottetown: Dundurn, 1984.

———. "Edmund Morris Among the Saskatchewan Indians and the Fort Qu'Apelle Monument." *Saskatchewan History* (Autumn 1982), 101–107.

———. "The Indian Portraits of Edmund Morris." *The Beaver* (Summer 1979), 34–41.

McInnes, T. R. L. "History of Indian Administration in Canada." *The Canadian Journal of Economic and Political Science* XII (February–November 1946), 387–94.

McKay, Don. "Local Wilderness." *The Fiddlehead* 169 (Autumn 1991), 5–6.

McLuhan, Marshall and Quentin Fiore. *War and Peace in the Global Village.* Coordinated by Jerome Agel. New York: Bantam, 1968.

Mellen, Peter. *The Group of Seven.* Toronto: McClelland and Stewart, 1970.

Metcalf, John. *What is a Canadian Literature?* Guelph, ON: Red Kite Press, 1988.

Mezei, Kathy. "From Lifeless Pools to the Circle of Affection: The Significance of Space in the Poetry of D. C. Scott." *The Duncan Campbell Scott Symposium.* Ed. K. P. Stich. Ottawa: U of Ottawa P, 1979.

Minh-ha, Trinh T. *Woman, Native, Other: writing postcoloniality and feminism.* Bloomington, IN: Indiana U P, 1989.

Monkman, Leslie. *A Native Heritage: Images of the Indian in English-Canadian Literature.* Toronto: University of Toronto P, 1981.

Morris, Edmund. "Old Lords of the Soil." Toronto, *The News,* Thursday May 9, 1907.

———. "An Ancient Indian Fort." *The Canadian Magazine* 36 (1911), 256–59.

———. *The Diaries of Edmund Montague Morris: Western Journeys 1907–1910.* Transcribed by Mary Fitz-Gibbon. Toronto: Royal Ontario Museum, 1985.

Morrisseau, Norval. *Legends of My People The Great Ojibway.* Ed. Selwyn Dewdney. Toronto: McGraw-Hill Ryerson, 1965.

Morrison, James. *Treaty Research Report: Treaty Nine (1905–06): The James Bay Treaty.* Ottawa: Treaties and Historical Research Centre, Indian and Northern Affairs Canada, 1986.

———. "The Poet and the Indians: Duncan Campbell Scott Woos the Muse and Negotiates Treaty Number Nine." *The Beaver* (August/September 1988) 5–16.

Morse, Eric W. *Fur Trade Canoe Routes of Canada, Then and Now.* Toronto: University of Toronto P, 1969.

Moses, Daniel David. "Native People Should Tell Native Stories." *Notes From the Underground: Newsletter of the Toronto Small Press Book Fair 1990,* 7.

———, and Terry Goldie, eds. *An Anthology of Canadian Native Literature in English.* Toronto: Oxford UP, 1992.

Morton, W. L. *The Canadian Identity.* Madison: U of Wisconsin P, 1961.

New, W. H. *Dreams of Speech and Violence: The Art of the Short Story in Canada and New Zealand.* Toronto: U of Toronto P, 1987.

Nishnawbe-Aski Nation: A History of the Cree and Ojibway of Northern Ontario. Timmins, ON: Ojibway-Cree Cultural Centre, 1986.

Nowlan, Alden. "Interview with John Metcalf." *Canadian Literature* 63 (Winter 1975), 8–17.

Noyes, Alfred. *Two Worlds for Memory.* London and New York: Sheed and Ward, 1953.

Olson, Charles. *Selected Writings.* Ed. with introduction by Robert Creely. New York: New Directions, 1951.

Ondaatje, Michael. *The Collected Works of Billy the Kid.* Toronto: Anansi, 1970.

———. *Rat Jelly.* Toronto: Coach House, 1973.

———. *In the Skin of a Lion.* Toronto: McClelland and Stewart, 1987.

———, ed. *From Ink Lake: Canadian Stories.* Toronto: Lester and Orpen Dennys, 1990.

O'Hagan, Howard. "A Mountain Journey." *Queen's Quarterly* 324–33.

———. *Tay John.* New York: C. N. Potter, 1960.

Orwell, George. *Nineteen Eighty-Four.* London: Secker and Warburg, 1949.

Paget, Amelia M. *People of the Plains.* Introduction by Duncan Campbell Scott. Toronto: William Briggs, 1909.

Patterson, E. Palmer. "Poet and the Indian: Indian Themes in the Poetry of Duncan Campbell Scott and John Collier." *Ontario History* 59 (1967), 69–78.

Potlatch!: A Strict Law Bids Us Dance. U'Mista Cultural Society, 1975. 16 mm, 53 min.

Pratt, Mary Louise. "Scratches in the Face of the Country; or, What Mr. Barron Saw in the Land of the Bushman." *Critical Inquiry* 12 (Autumn 1985), 119–43.

Reaney, James. *Poems.* Germaine Warkentin, ed. Toronto: new press, 1972.

———. "Topless Nightmares, Being a Dialogue With Himself by James Reaney." *Halloween.* London, ON: James Reaney, 1976.

Redsky, James. *Great Leader of the Ojibway: Mis-quona-Queb.* Ed. James R. Stevens. Toronto: McClelland and Stewart, 1972.

Renison, Robert John. *For Such a Time As This.* Toronto: McClelland and Stewart, 1947.

Richardson, Boyce, ed. *Drumbeat: Anger and Renewal in Indian Country.* Toronto: Summerhill/The Assembly of First Nations, 1989.

Ross, Malcolm, ed. *Poets of the Confederation.* Toronto: McClelland and Stewart, 1960.
Ross, Sinclair. *As For Me and My House.* New York: Reynal and Hitchcock, 1941.
Rushdie, Salman. *Imaginary Homelands.* London: Granta, 1991.
Said, Edward W. *Orientalism.* New York: Pantheon, 1978.
———. *Culture and Imperialism.* New York: Knopf, 1993.
Salusinszky, Imre, ed. *Criticism in Society: Interviews with Jacques Derrida, Northrop Frye, Harold Bloom, Geoffry Hartman, Frank Kermode, Edward Said, Barbara Johnson, Frank Lentricchia, and J. Hillis Miller.* New York and London: Methuen, 1987.
Scott, William. *The Teetotaller's Handbook,* in four parts, being a compilation of valuable information for the use of all classes, with an introduction and appendix. Toronto: Alfred Dredge, 1860.
———. *Report relating to the affairs of the Oka Indians, made to the Superintendent General of Indian Affairs.* With an appendix. Ottawa: McLean, Roger, 1883.
Simpson, Janice. "Healing the Wound: Cultural Compromise in D. C. Scott's 'A Scene at Lake Manitou.'" *Canadian Poetry* 18 (Spring/Summer 1986), 66–76.
Slonim, Leon. *The Critical Edition of the Poems of Duncan Campbell Scott.* Ph.D. Diss. U of Toronto P, 1978.
———. "A Source of Duncan Campbell Scott's 'Charcoal.'" *Studies in Canadian Literature* 4 (Winter 1979), 162–66.
———. "D. C. Scott's 'At Gull Lake: August 1810'" *Canadian Literature* 81 (Summer 1979), 142–43.
Spivak, Gayatri Chakravorty. *In Other Worlds: Essays in Cultural Poetics.* New York and London: Routledge, 1988.
Stevenson, Robert Louis. *Essays in the Art of Writing.* London: Chatto and Windus, 1905.
Stich, K. P. "North of Blue Ontario's Shore: Spells of Emerson and Whitman in D. C. Scott's Poetry." *Canadian Poetry* 12 (Spring/Summer 1983), 1–12.
Stow, Glenys. "The Wound Under the Feathers: Scott's Discontinuities." George Woodcock, ed. *Colony and Confederation: Early Canadian Poets and Their Background.* Introd. Roy Daniells. Vancouver: U of British Columbia P, 1974.
Sykes, W. J. "The Poetry of Duncan Campbell Scott." *Queen's Quarterly* XXXVI (1934), 51–64.
Taylor, Drew Hayden. "Pretty Like a White Boy: The Adventures of a Blue-Eyed Ojibway." *This Magazine* (August 1991), 29–30.
Taylor, S.A. "Reminiscences of Lac Seul." *Moccasin Telegraph* (Fall 1962), 46.
Tennant, Paul. *Aboriginal Peoples and Politics: The Indian Land Question in British Columbia, 1849–1989.* Vancouver: U of British Columbia P, 1990.
Thornton, Mildred Valley. *Indian Lives and Legends.* Vancouver: Mitchell, 1966.
Titley, E. Brian. *A Narrow Vision: Duncan Campbell Scott and the Administration of Indian Affairs in Canada.* Vancouver: U of British Columbia P, 1986.
Tostevin, Lola Lemire. *Frog Moon.* Dunvegan, ON: Cormorant, 1994.
Vanasse, Joseph L. "The White Dog Feast." *Canadian Magazine* 30 (November 1907), 62–64.

Wah, Fred. *Waiting for Saskatchewan.* Winnipeg: Turnstone, 1985.

Ware, Tracy. "D. C. Scott's 'The Height of Land' and the Greater Romantic Lyric." *Canadian Literature* 111 (Winter 1896), 10–25.

Warkentin, Germaine, ed. *Canadian Exploration Literature: an Anthology.* Toronto: Oxford UP, 1993.

Waterston, Elizabeth. "A Small Mercy." Rev. of *Selected Stories of Duncan Campbell Scott,* Ed. Glenn Clever. *Canadian Literature* 61 (Summer 1974), 111–13.

———. "The Missing Face: Five Short Stories by Duncan Campbell Scott." *Studies in Canadian Literature* (Summer 1976), 223–29.

Weis, Lyle. "D. C. Scott and the Desire for a Sense of Order" Ph.D. Diss. University of Alberta, 1983.

———. "D. C. Scott's View of History & the Indians." *Canadian Literature* (Winter 1986), 27–40.

"Whose Voice Is It Anyway?: A Symposium on Who Should Be Speaking For Whom." *Books in Canada.* 20.1 (January-February 1991), 11–17.

Wiebe, Rudy. *The Temptations of Big Bear.* Toronto: McClelland and Stewart, 1973.

———. "The Death and Life of Albert Johnson: Collected notes on a possible legend." Diane Bessai and David Jackel, eds. *Figures in a Ground: Canadian Essays on Modern Literature Collected in Honour of Sheila Watson.* Saskatoon: Western Producer, 1978.

———. "On the Trail of Big Bear." *A Voice in the Land: Essays by and About Rudy Wiebe.* Edmonton: NeWest, 1981.

———. "Proud Cree Nation Deserves Much More Than 'Funny' Stories." Toronto: *Globe and Mail,* February 18, 1990.

———. *Playing Dead: a Contemplation Concerning the Arctic.* Edmonton: NeWest, 1989.

Wigston, Nancy. "Nanabush in the City." *Books in Canada* (March 1989) 7–9.

Wilson, Milton. "Klein's Drowned Poet: Variations on an Old Theme." *Canadian Literature* VI (1060), 5–17. Rpt. (section on "The Piper of Arll") S. L. Dragland, ed. *Duncan Campbell Scott: A Book of Criticism.*

Woolf, Virginia. *A Room of One's Own.* London: Hogarth, 1929; London: Grafton, 1977.

Wright, Ronald. *Stolen Continents: The "New World" Through Indian Eyes Since 1492.* New York: Houghton Mifflin, 1992.

Yeats, John Butler. *Early Memories: Some Chapters of Autobiography.* Churchtown, Dundrum: The Cuala Press, 1923.

Young, David, Grant Ingram, Lise Swartz. *Cry of the Eagle: Encounters with a Cree Healer.* Toronto: U of Toronto P, 1989.

Zeman, Brenda. *To Run With Longboat: Twelve Stories of Indian Athletes in Canada.* Ed. David Williams. Edmonton: GMS Ventures, 1988.

Index

G

H

I

J

K

L